In Search Of Eldorado

Ciarán de Baróid

Ogham Press Belfast

By the same author

Ballymurphy and the Irish War. A history of the North of Ireland's low-intensity war of 1969 to 1997, as seen through the eyes of a working-class community in West Belfast.
'One of the most remarkable books to emerge from the Northern conflict. I can't recall any other book which gives the reader the same accessibility to the streets of Belfast.' - **John Kavanagh, Irish Post**.

Down North: reflections of Ballymurphy and the early Troubles. An account of living in Belfast's Ballymurphy, a republican stronghold, during the early years of the North of Ireland's 'Troubles'.
'This book illustrates - with poignancy and humour - how individuals and communities resisted a period of intense military occupation.' - **Gerry Adams**.

A Little Madness: travels on the hippie trail. Travel as it was in the counter culture days of the early 1970s
'A cross between Boswell and Johnson's Tour of the Western Isles and Che Guevara's Motor Cycle Diaries.' - **Southern Star**.

Published 2020 by Ogham Press
5-7 Conway Street
Belfast BT13 2DE

ISBN: 978-0-9566166-4-7

Typeset from USB Stick by Leslie Stannage Design,
430 Upper Newtownards Road, Belfast BT4 3GY.
Artwork by Leslie Stannage Design.

Printed by W&G Baird, Greystone Press,
Caulside Drive, Antrim BT41 2RS.

Cover Photo: The Gathering of the Highland
Clans, Papua New Guinea, September 1978.

Back Cover: Cora, Avenue of the Dead,
Teotihuacán, Mexico, March 1979.

Contents

CHAPTER   PAGE

'Gaily bedight
A gallant knight
In sunshine and in shadow
Had journeyed long
Singing a song
In search of Eldorado...'

Edgar Allan Poe (1809-1849)

Notes

El Dorado, originally *El Hombre Dorado* (The Golden Man) was the term used by the Spanish Empire to describe a mythical chief of the Muisca people of the Altiplano Cundiboyacense of Colombia. This man was said to ritualistically cover himself with gold dust and immerse himself in Lake Guatavita, high in the Colombian Andes. Over time *El Dorado* changed from being a man, to a city, to a kingdom.

A second rumoured location of *El Dorado* inspired several expeditions in the late 16th century. In this case, *El Dorado* was said to be a city called Manõa on the shores of legendary Lake Parime. By the late 19th century, however, most people had dismissed the existence of both the city and lake as a myth.

The title of this book owes nothing to the legend. Nor does it owe anything to the fact that Cora and I spent some nights in a campsite called *El Dorado* in San Blas, Mexico. It is simply the fact that Edgar Allan Poe wrote a jingling poem that in its simplicity captured a mood...

This book describes a journey undertaken at the end of the hippie era, before the onset of international tourism, before guide books, before sense. Keep that in mind.

As with all journeys, the people with whom you travel, and those you meet along the way are the essence of the story. First and foremost in that long list is Cora whose wit and wisdom saved many a day and whose companionship made each day what it was. Then in no particular order come all the others who appear in these pages. At the risk of leaving anyone out, I won't name them here.

The exceptions are Alan Dodds and Glenys Sharma (née Kitchingman) who shared with me their notes of the journeys we undertook together, allowing a more rounded account of the times described. Other than that, the story is based on the diaries I maintained during the times described and the details gleaned from the photographs we took.

In a small number of cases, names have been changed to protect the guilty and the innocent. To avoid the confusion of switching between imperial and metric as the story unfolds, I have kept all measurements in imperial except when an individual has made a statement in metric, if that makes sense.

Finally, a special thanks to Marie Cavanagh, my first reader, who provided helpful comments and suggestions in a time of the Great Coronavirus Lockdown.

Ciarán de Baróid, October 2020.

To Aibhlinn and Ciara

INDIA TO THAILAND

PAKISTAN

TIBET

NEPAL

BHUTAN

BANGLADESH

BURMA

LAOS

THAILAND

INDIA

Bay of Bengal

Gulf of Thailand

Delhi

Kanpur

Allahabad

Varanasi

Gorakhpur

Kathmandu

Pokhara

Mandalay

Rangoon

Thaton

Chiang Rai

Chiang Mai

Chiang Sen

Bangkok

Hat Yai

CHAPTER 1

The Magic Bus

To the tourist, travel is a means to an end;
to the traveller, it's an end in itself.

Marty Rubin (1930-1994)

There and then it could well have been over.

A lad who had swapped the idea of growing old for the alternative had cut across us on a 50cc motorbike. A young boy straddled the tank. A side-saddled woman, presumably the mother, sat behind. She was cradling an infant, her sari inches from the spinning chain. We slammed on the brakes and the tuk tuk swerved sideways, straight into the path of an oncoming bus. If we hadn't braked, we would have hit the family and they would have hit the bus. But we were now filling that frame.

'Son of a bitch!' our driver yelled.

The woman smiled. The motorbike lad zig-zagged off towards reincarnation. And we had the first of many lucky days. The bus banked hard and missed us. All we suffered was a dose of the flutters and a shrill rebuke of bus horn.

'Lick monkey ass!' our driver bellowed and gave the bus the fingers. He then looked back at us and smiled: wasn't this the greatest show in town? 'Now,' he said, still smiling, 'we take a short cut.'

I hate short cuts. Sometimes they work but mostly they don't. They especially don't work in a back street full of hawkers' stalls, rickshaws, bicycles, horse-drawn tongas, pushcarts, goats, pigs, pedestrians and sacred cows. Which is exactly where the tuk tuk landed. As we laboured through, one of several monkeys dropped from a tangle of overhead wires, snatched an apple from a pavement market and was chased by a woman with a broom. Further on, a pauper community stirred to life in the underbelly of a bridge, the waft of their matinal excretions thickening the air while black vultures circled in a white sky. And just as it seemed that we had reached some kind of pinnacle, an elephant came marching down the street.

Welcome to Delhi, the elephant said. *Glad you could make it...*

Short cut now not doing so well, we wriggled back to a main artery so we could jump any lights that might have the audacity to show themselves.

'He *seriously* needs to bloody-well slow *down,*' Cora growled, supposedly to herself but loud enough to be heard up front.

'You have fright?' the driver retorted. He had picked us up in Connaught Place. A big Sikh with blazing eyes and a grey beard that fled from his cheeks to the folds of a black turban. 'Do not worry,' he consoled. 'I will bring you to a very good, very cheap hotel. *Old* Delhi is where you will find this hotel.'

We broke a red light. We swung right. We swung left. Traffic shot out from all sides. We circled a roundabout against the flow and careered down a one-way street. *He probably drives like this all the time,* I told myself over and over. *Why should he die today?* It seemed to work - until the cry came from up front.

'Wrong way!'

We slowed down. We veered into a wide arc. We faced the oncoming traffic. Horn blaring, our flimsy contraption charged. *Into the Valley of Death...*

'Oh Jesus, Mary and Saint Joseph,' Cora said. 'He's a shaggin' maniac.'

We wheeled into another back street and smacked an oncoming tuk-tuk. Swearing like a standup, our man jumped from the cab, ran to the other tuk-tuk and swung a badly aimed fist at the face of the driver who was apparently 'the son of a piece of shit'. When he missed the face he lashed out with his boot against the tuk-tuk.

'Crazy bastard,' he said when he got back in.

We finally reached the heart of Old Delhi where the 'very good, very cheap hotel' - a tin-roofed shack in an alley - was full. We no longer cared. We grabbed our rucksacks and jumped. No more tuk tuk. We would walk back to Connaught Place and look for lodgings to match our budget.

It wasn't that we didn't have money. We just didn't have all that much given what lay ahead: a few months in India and an overland journey to Australia that included a crossing of the Timor Sea from Bali. Even with a fair wind to our backs, we figured on being pretty broke by the time we reached the Timor Sea. But we needed that fair wind to get that far which meant economizing all the way. The final part of the plan - not based on any really deep research - was to find a working passage on some rich guy's yacht going from Bali to Darwin. We would then work in Australia to fund the second leg of the trip.

Now that we were on foot, the psychopathic heat that had met us at 6.00 a.m. at Palam Airport was becoming a bit of an issue. Also, I was becoming a bit annoyed that India seemed nonplussed.

Women, with pierced noses and arms sheathed in bangles, floated by in saris and shalwar-kameezes, many carrying on their heads earthenware pots, copper trays, or great bundles wrapped in cloth. At times, these were piled so high and carried with such ease that they seemed glued to their heads. Men smiled and chatted. Children found space to play. Rats scurried from open sewers. But for us there was no escape. Not even in the shade.

'The cool of April in India,' Cora said. 'Who was it who told me about that...?'

'April is springtime in Ireland,' I had assured Cora back in Belfast. 'So April must also be springtime in northern India.'

Logical enough but not exactly correct. April is *summer* in northern India; and summer in northern India is a stinking-hot and humid hell. The later in April, the worse it gets. This was April 22nd.

'Between ourselves,' Cora said, 'you don't have a great handle on the weather.'

With sweat dripping from our noses and elbows, and shirts stuck to our bodies, we arrived back at Connaught Place and found ourselves a cheap room in one of the back streets that fanned out from that most iconic of Delhi's landmarks. A musty, second-floor, cell-like hovel with peeling green walls, and ceilings streaked in black fungus, was ours for a modest sum. Lit by a 25-watt bulb, it had a small window that overlooked an enclosed yard and a rattling overhead fan that sighed to a depressing halt every time the electricity died. Window bars kept the city's monkeys at bay.

The owner of the hotel, a small, fat, bald man in a grey vest and lungi, told us that the grubbiness of the room was all due to the weather.

'Today everything is damp.'

'What about tomorrow?' I asked.

'Tomorrow, my friend? Only the gods will know... But today you can pay for your sleep.' He told us to give him a shout if we needed anything. 'My name is Chandresh,' he said. 'It means Lord of the Moon.'

'Well there you go,' Cora chirped happily when he was gone (although 'happily' could be a false memory). 'We're in the house of the Lord of the Moon. I always knew I'd end up here one day. Things are looking up.'

'Here at last,' was my own small contribution. 'Even if we *did* have to fly.'

This was my third attempt at India, both of the others being overland. The first had died in Kabul in 1970 due to amoebic dysentery and funds reduced to £15. The second, with Cora in 1971, had died on the fires of the Bangladesh War which had forced us to turn back from Pakistan. But now we had finally made it, albeit by a mode of transport that I had hitherto deemed to be the antithesis of true travel.

'But,' I had to concede, 'I suppose it did save us several weeks of overland slog. And, short of the plane dropping from the sky, it guaranteed that we got here.'

'And what a grand place to be,' Cora said. 'Let's see. We have a single rope bed with no mattress. We have ants and cockroaches running around the floor. And look! Lucky us. What's that I see on the ceiling?'

A translucent green gecko lay in ambush above the light. This little bug-eater would become the hallmark of cheap accommodation all the way to Australia.

Exhausted from the overnight flight from London, we spread a sleeping bag on the bed, buried ourselves in the shadows and tried to get some sleep while the scalding sky poured in through the window.

Outside, stupid squirrels and mynah birds hopped about the trees.

When the sun went down, we joined several hundred Indians and scores of bats in the drifting spray of a large fountain that sat in nearby Central Park. At midnight, however, the fountain was turned off along with all of Delhi's water supply to combat a seasonal drought. We slunk back to our room where the ants, cockroaches - and several geckos now - had been joined by squadrons of mosquitoes, while the fan blew the same dead, fetid air through its cracked and rattling blades. If it sounds like a downer, take no notice. Strange as it may seem, people like us - lovers of the basics - find a gravitational pull in the likes of this. Although Cora occasionally comes out with bad words.

'No chance of a shower I suppose,' she said on this occasion, sinking back on the bed. 'The sweat is stinging my eyes.'

'We could ask Lord of the Moon,' I suggested. 'I saw him moving about.'

'I am sorry,' Lord of the Moon said when located. 'I cannot intervene in this matter.'

Two sleepless hours later, Cora sprang upright.

'Answer me this,' she said. 'Where would there be water?'

Delirious, I thought as she crept from the room. But, practical as ever, she unearthed our partial salvation. In the outdoor kitchen she found a metal bucket half full of stagnant water and mosquito larvae. By dabbing a wet towel to our bodies and lying motionless under the fan, we were finally able to cool ourselves to a point that was almost tolerable. Around half four in the morning, we drifted into unconsciousness.

That was why we found ourselves on the magic bus.[1] On the second day of our journey around the world.

* * *

It was afternoon when we came across the 28-year-old Bedford: a hippie bus all the way from England and parked in Connaught Place. Painted sky-blue, it had a joint-smoking Jimi Hendrix lying the full length of one side, and clouds of hash-smoke emanating from its open windows. Taped beside the door, which smelled bitterly and ominously of rusting metal, was a hand-written note:

Delhi to Kathmandu. Twenty dollars. Leaving 2.30 p.m.
April 23rd. Stopping at Agra, Benares and Pokhara.

'There must be a god after all,' Cora said.

'What about India?' I groaned, albeit half-heartedly. 'After all the effort to get here.'

'India can wait,' Cora said. 'But we need to be on this bus.'

Fry in India or flee to the cool Himalayas was a no-brainer. It would also prove a pivotal move. Cutting India and its costs from the trip at that stage probably saved the whole venture.

A skinny woman who was out in the street, washing pots in her T-shirt and knickers, called to us. She was in her early twenties and had half her face hidden behind straw-coloured tresses; but the hair failed to hide the iodine that daubed that half of her face and much of her right arm.

'Hi there,' she said in a strong Cockney accent. 'I'm Glynis. If you'd like to join us, you need to be back 'ere for two o'clock.'

---

1.   The original Magic Bus operated from a cockroach-infested office in Amsterdam's Dam Square, filling seats on an assortment of decrepit vehicles that ferried droves of trail-blazing hippies along the Hippie Trail to India. In time, the term became generic.

'Would we be able to pick up visas for Nepal along the way?' I asked. 'We don't have any.'

'No problem. You can get them at the border.'

'Chalk us in then,' I said and rummaged in our passport pouch for the forty dollars. 'Have you been long on the road?'

'A year now,' Glynis said with a bit of a grimace. 'But we've run out of money and make a livin' ferryin' freaks[2] between Kabul and Kathmandu. Used to be twelve of us when we left London, but the others all dropped out. There's just me and Charlie and Bob now. Which means we don't have a permanent driver. We were lucky to 'ave found Steve, our present driver, in Kabul.'

Charlie, pale and emaciated with long, lank brown hair, was Glynis's boyfriend. He waved from inside the bus where he and Bob, a tall half Indian with a beard and long, thinning black hair, were stoking a chillum of hash.

'Did you have to buy the others out?' I asked.

'Naw,' Glynis said. 'When they dropped out, they left their shares be'ind.'

'Did you hurt your face?' Cora asked, no longer able to ignore the iodine.

'Yeah,' Glynis said. 'Me and Charlie were crossin' the road yesterday when two guys came along on a motorbike an' ripped off my shoulder-bag. I tried to 'ang on an' they dragged me along the bleethin' street.'

Peering inside the bus I noted that those on board included a handful of less hippie-looking hippies, but were mostly those lads and lassies who'd find it hard to get that job in the bank.

Within half an hour we had brought the complement of the magic bus to sixteen.

* * *

At four o'clock in the afternoon, to a ceremonial blast of chillums and incantations to the Hindu god, Shiva, we left Connaught Place in heat so potent that it shimmered from the ground in waves. A few minutes later the bus sputtered its way around a sharp corner and broke down. *Not a great start,* said I to myself. However, a push to a nearby garage,

---

2.   The term used by young hippie-leaning travellers of the time to describe themselves.

a piece of wire and the ingenuity of an old Indian mechanic, and we were back on track again.

The next challenge was how not to run over the people determined to throw themselves under our wheels.

'See that Charlie!' Glynis shouted. 'They're tryin' to collect on the bleethin' insurance.'

Finally, we were free of Delhi and out on the open road where the air blowing through the open windows inspired a wave of camaraderie. Life stories were swapped, cigarettes were shared and chillums did the rounds. We were heading east on the Grand Trunk Road that ran right across the Ganges Plain to what was then known as Calcutta. Peacocks ran through the scrub. Green parrots flashed from the trees. Busy villages floated by. Buffaloes wallowed in water holes. But any drift towards relaxation or the astral plane was short-lived.

A drive along the Grand Trunk Road of 1970 was not for the faint-hearted. The nub of the problem was the Grand Trunk Road itself: two dirt shoulders and a single ragged tarmac lane wide enough for one large vehicle. This encouraged attitude. Everyone wanted to be the one. Buses, oil tankers and massively overloaded trucks - some with drivers who were drunk or 'protected' by holy icons - charged one another, horns blaring, in a game of chicken. When nobody blinked, the mangled remains would litter the Grand Trunk Road.

'They think they own the bleethin' road,' Charlie seethed at Steve as we were repeatedly pushed onto the dirt. 'Call their bleethin' bluff.' That, on the Grand Trunk Road, was poor advice.

Nevertheless, the normally becalmed Steve, a clean-cut Englishman with short blond hair, morphed into Spartacus. Grabbing a Bowie knife, he began to wave it out the window at approaching vehicles.

Bucking the trend, the next close encounter caused us and an oncoming truck to pass one another at a crawl. None the less, the two Sikhs in the truck thought it would be very funny to force us further onto the dirt. What a shock when Steve leaned over and stabbed their cab three times. Who's the funny guy now, eh?

'Boom Shiva Shankar!' said the crowd on the bus as celebratory chillums belched out another round of delirium.

An hour out of Delhi we stopped at a village for a drink. Bullock-carts, sacred cows and camel-trains came to a standstill as we were surrounded by a sea of staring faces. When Glynis went to the toilet the crowd followed. When the swarthy Canadian we called Daniel from

Quebec[3] went, the crowd followed again.

'In fairness,' Cora said, 'if I was in Cork and us lot turned up, I'd be staring too.'

At the next stop, Daniel from Quebec, stoked up on amphetamines, was prepared.

'FUCK IT!' he roared and leapt from the bus in among the multitudes.

Back on board again, people mingled in a gettimg-to-know-the-neighbours manner. Cora sat next to Eleanor, a dark-haired, Liverpudlian with high cheeks, brown eyes and a fiercely independent spirit. Eleanor was probably close to thirty, making her the senior of the company. Smoking Indian *bidis* non-stop, she talked of having spent six years in India and Nepal. Over this time, she had, by her own account, perfected every ruse needed to bypass the legal, medical and bureaucratic requirements of both countries.

'I'm a part-time writer and part-time smuggler,' she confided when asked how she funded her travels. Exactly what Eleanor ever managed to write or smuggle remains a mystery as she was much stoned. Of the staring crowds of India, she had this to say: 'For a place billed as the Nirvana of the Hippie Trail and the home of peace and love, it reduces an awful lot of freaks to standing in the middle of crowds, screaming at the top of their lungs: "Will ya just fuck away off and leave me ALONE!"'

I sat next to the fourth Englishman on board - tall, lean Max who sported a mop of brown curls and a two-month beard that made him look top-heavy. Consummately shy, Max generally avoided eye contact and spoke sparingly. You'd say, 'Good morning Max, hot day again,' and instantly feel that an inner verbal dam had ruptured. Max would later team up with myself and Cora. And all three of us would team up with George from California.

Staid, bearded, with a thick head of curly hair and round glasses, George planned to leave the bus in Pokhara to meet a fellow Californian.

'We shared the road from Istanbul to Kabul,' he said. 'And he's hanging out there, waiting for me to catch up. Then, we'll head on together to Kathmandu.'

It was a meeting that would prove tragic in the end.

As the day wore on everyone grew lethargic and silent: stoned, hot, and tired from sleepless Delhi. An hour after dusk, we were stopped by the cops on a quiet stretch of road.

3. To distinguish him from a second Daniel - Daniel from France.

'Hide the dope!' Charlie yelled as the bus rumbled to a halt.

Two cops climbed on board, both dressed in military-style uniforms and sporting old Lee Enfield .303s. The older of the two, a tall, distinguished-looking man of about forty with a clipped moustache, spoke to the company through a fog of ganja smoke which he duly ignored.

'Dacoits,' he warned. 'Many dacoits in this area. Very dangerous bandits. We will send two policemen with you if you like.' The younger man nodded eagerly.

One of the largest concentrations of dacoits in India centred on the badlands of the Chambal Valley, a virtually unmapped network of ravines that covered thousands of square miles and came to within forty miles of Agra. The area offered refuge to large numbers of bandits who often achieved Robin Hood status within their own communities as they engaged in killings, robberies and kidnappings during forays out of the ravines. Pursuing struggles of caste and clan, they fought running wars with the Indian cops, and were often summarily executed when caught. Occasionally, they came in from the ravines for choreographed surrenders at huge public ceremonies attended by state governors and ministers, whereupon a short spell in prison was followed by widespread public adulation. They also sometimes tied ropes to trees across the main road to Agra on nights like this to stop and rob the likes of us.

But the offer of an armed escort was declined by the bus crew and the two cops left, shrugging their shoulders. We continued on to Agra, the bus levitating in a genial cloud of hash.

'Bastards probably wanted baksheesh,'[4] Charlie said, standing at the front of the bus, thin, ragged, and pop-eyed, with hair strapped in a headband, like some buccaneer captain from the Spanish Main.

* * *

We arrived late to a city asleep. However, we managed to rouse the moon-faced owner of the misnamed Relax Restaurant, a frequent haunt of the bus crew just up the street from the Taj Mahal.

'Welcome my friends! Welcome!' he gushed as we funneled in through the door. 'I missed you *so-o-o* much.'

---

4.   A small amount of money given as a tip or bribe.

He proceeded to cook us a mountain of a meal while Eleanor lit up a *bidi* and went off to check the accommodation. She came back from the courtyard none too pleased.

'Looks kinda rough out there,' she said. 'Bare rope beds in a couple of rooms, more beds outside with the mozzies, and the rest of us in here on the floor. Not exactly luxurious. I want to sleep on the bus.'

And thus did Eleanor ignite a war. Just a bitty little war for now, but time was on its side.

'Nobody sleeps on the bus,' Charlie said.

'Why not?'

'Because I say so.'

'A freak acting like a pig,' Eleanor said to the rest of the company. 'Who does he think he is?'

'The owner of the bus,' Charlie said. A tense silence settled over the Relax Restaurant as people silently took sides in the coming war.

Morning saw grim faces at breakfast. Those who had slept on the restaurant floor and out in the courtyard, lying semi-naked in the suffocating heat, had been devoured by mosquitoes. Those in the rooms had been caught between the mosquitoes and what we assumed were bedbugs. I woke up from the few hours' sleep to find a belt of red spots around my midriff. I had no idea what did it. Cora's face, arms and ankles were a mass of lumps. Her right eyelid was virtually sealed. A reaction to mosquito bites.

'All Charlie's fault,' Eleanor said. 'He's probably immune. Blood's nothing but poison.'

'You say somethin'?' Charlie asked.

'You hear ziss, man?' Daniel from Quebec said to crack the tension. 'In South America, zere is ziss fly, ze botfly. It bites you and it lays ze eggs. Zen zey hatch as maggots and eat your flesh.'

'I was really enjoying this omelette,' Cora said. But Daniel's tactic worked for now, unleashing a torrent of personal horror stories, humorous in hindsight, that were to travellers what ghost stories were to children.

To get the day into gear, Daniel then popped his morning amphetamines. 'Good for ze salt loss,' he said.

* * *

In the early light the Taj Mahal glowed a soft pearly pink, its domes and minarets rising to the sky like living things. Built by Moghul emperor, Shah Jahan, as a mausoleum for his wife of eighteen years who died in childbirth, it has been described by Bengali poet, Rabindranath Tagore, as a 'tear [that] would hang on the cheek of time'. Barely five years after its completion[5] in 1653, Shah Jahan's son, Aurangzeb, staged a violent coup, overthrowing his father and imprisoning him in Agra Fort. The deposed emperor was to spend the rest of his days under house arrest, looking across the Yamuna River at the mausoleum of his dead wife.

We got in shortly after sunrise, before any crowds appeared; but it was a relatively quick visit. An hour after going through the front gates, we were on the bus again. Next stop on the itinerary: Varanasi (Benares). With a possible overnight in Kanpur.

* * *

It was mid-afternoon and stinking hot. We were bouncing along the heavily rutted Grand Trunk Road when Steve yelled from the front. In the middle of the road, directly ahead, stood an enormous bull elephant. On its neck sat a mahout in yellow dhoti, white shirt and white turban. Thin and in his late thirties, he was accompanied by a younger, long-haired companion in a black loincloth, whose face and bare chest were streaked in ashes. Both carried tridents. Steve pulled up and we all piled out. The mahout waved encouragement as we checked his mount. The younger man viewed us with nervous fascination. But the relevance of the elephant's position only became clear when we decided to move off again and were met by a single, shockingly blunt word.

'Rupees,' the mahout said.

We had on our hands an elephant toll-gate.

'Everyone back on the bus,' Bob, the half-Indian crew-member, ordered. 'This could get out of 'and.'

'Rupees!' the mahout shouted as Steve started the engine. 'No pay, no go.' He turned the elephant to face the bus.

'We'll shift yer bleethin' elephant,' Charlie promised.

Golden rule, Charlie, I said to myself. *Whatever you do, don't annoy that elephant.*

India was twenty-nine years independent. Democracy had been overthrown ten months ago when an 'Emergency' was declared and Indira Gandhi adopted dictatorial powers. Her son, Sanjay, was touring the country with his family-planning programme of forced

---

5.   It took 20,000 workers 21 years to complete the Taj Mahal.

sterilisation. And we were on the Kanpur road, about to lock horns with a bull elephant and a mahout's mate who was stabbing at our back tyres with a trident.

'Push 'im off the road!' Charlie barked.

'He's big,' Steve said.

'Oi there!' Charlie shouted from the open door. 'You better get that bleethin' elephant off this bleethin' road. You 'ear me? 'ho the bleethin' 'ell do you think you are?' Turning to Steve, he added, 'Call his bluff.'

'*Sacre bleu!*' Daniel from Quebec shouted. 'I think ziss is a big mistake.'

'How will anyone explain it to my mother?' Cora wanted to know.

Steve inched forward to call the mahout's bluff. The elephant lowered its head until head and ears filled the windscreen. Steve nudged forward again, and the elephant heaved. A gentle effortless heave that pushed us firmly backwards.

''ho the bloody 'ell does 'e think 'e is?' Charlie roared. ''e can't do this!'

The elephant, ever so calmly, heaved again.

I could see the headlines, the kind of thing you've probably read yourself: 'Drug-crazed hippies killed by mad elephant.'

But Steve was hero of the hour. Screeching into reverse, he swung in among the trees and skirted around the elephant in an eclipse of dust. And onward, ever onward, went the magic bus.

* * *

It was dark. Steve was wrecked from dodging livestock and people who were bedding down on the road. Still well to the west of Kanpur, we stopped in a large village to ask about accommodation. The next hotel, we were told, was fifty miles away.

'No way can I go on,' Steve said. 'Too dangerous.' Just then an old man in a white lungi and long white hair stepped forward.

'Please, you stay here,' he said. 'You are welcome. Nobody is driving in the night.'

'How much?' Steve asked. 'Rupees?'

'No rupees,' the old man said. 'You sleep free.'

'Where?' Steve asked. 'I don't see any sign of any accommodation.'

'No problem,' the old man said. 'You will see.'

Without further ado, he spoke to the owner of the village's one open food stall - a box in which the man cooked, ate and slept; and in no time at all we were seated to steaming plates of rice and dahl. Then, bit by bit, the accommodation mystery was solved. Villagers came out of their own homes with rope beds until sixteen of them lined the main street. But the appearance of beds along the main street wasn't a universal hit.

'No way am I going to sleep out here' Eleanor said. 'On the main road? In full view of the *natives*? I want to sleep on the bus.'

'Nobody,' Charlie said, 'but nobody sleeps on the bus.'

'I hope a tiger gets you.' Eleanor snarled.

'Ellie,' Bob said. 'It's only one night.'

'How can *only* apply to this?' Eleanor asked.

'Well, it's sleep in the street,' Charlie said, 'or don't sleep at all.'

Across the company, silent sides were taken again.

After we'd eaten, three musicians melted in among us, one with a set of tablas, one with a flute and the third with a harmonium. Over the coming hours we sat under a diamond-speckled sky, sharing cigarettes and smiles with the villagers, basking in the mingled fragrance of incense, sweating jasmine and burning hash, and listening to the most perfect music in the world. Eleanor got so whacked that her eyes crossed and she conked out and didn't give a shit any more about the natives.

Eventually, in cut-off jeans on a rope bed in the main street of an Indian village, I began to drift off to the strains of a north Indian raga. The hum of crickets mingled with the subdued voices of Indians, Australians, Americans, Europeans and a Malaysian Indian called Jaswinda. A bat swooped low on leathery wings. Mosquitoes homed in on their targets - mostly Cora it seemed.

And soon it was dawn again, with a rising sun slanting across the black tarmac of the pot-holed road to Kathmandu.

* * *

'Stop the bus!' Bob called as we left the village. 'It's Baba Fiji.'

We had almost missed him, an old man with a mane of grey hair, a goatee and a small bundle under his arm. He was standing at the side of the road in a white turban and the saffron lungi of a sadhu. Sixty-two years old, he had come from Fiji twenty-six years before, and had since been wandering the roads of India and Nepal. He had met Bob in Delhi and had recognised the bus on his way through the village shortly before sunrise. A search of the sixteen beds had confirmed the presence of Bob and the possibility of a lift to Nepal. So, with a modest belief in providence, Baba Fiji, sadhu and sage, had simply waited.

'It is karma,' he intoned as he climbed aboard. 'You will maybe take me to Kathmandu, and maybe we will share the food.' He sat in next to Bob, tightened the turban around his straggly hair, and smiled benevolently. 'Very good friend I make with them,' he said through betel-stained teeth. 'Very good friend.'

He sat cross-legged with his eyes closed and fingertips together in a posture of pious concentration, and prayed for us all in a low moan.

'Baba Fiji is a very holy man,' Bob said. 'He's heading for a great reincarnation.'

Chillums were lit and arms raised in a heartfelt incantation to Shiva. *Boom Shiva Shankar...* and *Bam bam bholonath...* Or something to that effect.

Cops with heavy, five-foot, bamboo *lathis* cleared our path through the streets of central Allahabad in the middle of the day by gratuitously thrashing the locals. East of the city, we ran into wide, tree-dotted expanses of glaring white sand where plodding camels slowed the pace and the road became two lines of planks. The drifting sand stayed with us to the banks of the Ganges where a single-laned pontoon bridge led to the far side. Here, there were further chillums, and more incantations to Shiva from Baba Fiji and the half of the company who had converted to Hinduism since arriving in India. The sacred, glistening Ganges commanded exceptional reverence.

'The most sacred river in whole of India,' Baba Fiji said. 'You drink the water, you have the good life.'

'Or maybe no life?' I smiled. The holy man glanced sideways.

'Baba,' he advised, settling himself into a pose of cross-legged, luminous beatitude, 'you must smoke more charas [hashish]. Then you will know the River *Ganga*.'[6]

We pulled up behind a truck and a crowded local bus that had passengers occupying the entire roof. Vultures circled in the thickening afternoon heat as we waited behind a metal boom. Once the oncoming vehicles had crossed, it was our slot. Passengers, however, had to walk. Flopping out of our airless bubble, we joined the crowd from the local bus for the trudge to the tea shops on the far side. Under a roof of thatch, held aloft by six bamboo poles, Cora and I sat at a metal table with Baba Fiji. Baba Fiji hummed a tune.

'Something's gone wrong,' Cora said. 'Nothing's moving on the bridge.'

'Ah yes,' Baba Fiji said. 'There is leaving somebody with a can. One truck, I think, it runs dry - no benzin.'

---

6.   The Indian name for the river.

'Half way across the bloody river?' I croaked.
'Yes baba. Only half way. We must wait now. Long time.'
'India,' Eleanor said, coming from behind. 'Love it, or leave it.'

* * *

My travel diary, written late into the night of April 25th 1976, tells me:
'Varanasi [Benares] is one of the oldest living cities in the world. Siddhartha Gautama, the Buddha, walked its streets in the 6th Century BC, and it was an old city then. A place of mystics and intrigue, with a maze of narrow back streets crowded with temples and bazaars, it provides an energy-charged location for a night stroll. Every nook and cranny is alive with the extraordinary spectacle of the perennial religious gathering that is the city's essence. Marigolds spatter the alleys. Incense and candles burn at temple entrances. Cavern-shops provide food, clothing, religious artefacts, flowers, incense, beads, camphor, and the charas much loved by the sadhus who gather here in huge numbers.

'Weaving through the labyrinth of shrines and temples, shaven-headed pilgrims, and those cremating the dead, form steady streams, all ultimately bound for the river. Dead bodies are carried on stretchers, carts and pairs of bicycles. With faces and arms streaked in ashes, men, women and children, half-naked priests and stoned sadhus, jog past to the pounding of drums, the clang of cymbals, the tinkling of bells and the blaring of trumpets. In alcoves just big enough for a single cross-legged man and his work, the hammers of industry pound on as they have for centuries. This is where Hindus who can afford it come to cremate their dead. This is where millions of pilgrims come to bathe at the sacred ghats. [The steps that separate the Ganges from the temples that line its banks.] To die here is to achieve moksha, a final release from the cycle of reincarnation...'

The bus crew knew a 'great hotel' - the Central - down by the river. It turned out to be a jaded chipped building with faded yellow walls. One look at the damp, oven-like crypts that were the cheaper rooms resurrected all the horrors of Delhi.

'Couldn't do it,' Cora said. 'It's bringing back all the trauma.'

We opted for the comparative luxury of a one-roomed shack on the roof where our neighbours were the rhesus monkeys that colonised the upper reaches of the city. They would spend the next two days inventing ingenious ways of trying to separate us from our food and equipment.

Exhausted by the heat and travel, we locked the shack door and went to sleep. When we opened our eyes again it was dark. Down in the restaurant we found Max and long-haired, biker-mustachioed Mike from Washington hunched over banana lassis.

'How's the craic?' I asked.

'The crack?' Mike asked. 'What crack?'

'Not that crack,' I said. 'The other craic.'

This led to an unintended conversation about that Irish term that can mean news, gossip, fun, entertainment or the craic itself and can occasionally lead to confusion. An example would be the time my elderly mother picked up a couple of young American women who were hitchhiking in West Cork. When the conversation drifted to social problems, one of the Americans asked if there was any crack [cocaine] in Cork. 'Oh there is,' my mother gushed to the consternation of the two hitchhikers. 'There's *great* craic in Cork.'

'Maybe you'd like to join us?' Mike said once the craic had been sorted. 'We're going for a stroll down to the ghats. It might be a bit cooler by the river.'

Dodging the cowshit and human crap that lay everywhere, and trying not to waken the rickshaw-wallahs, or get bitten by mad rats or mad dogs, or gored by cantankerous bulls, we left the Central and wound our way down through a maze of alleys to land at Dashashwamedh Ghat, the main ghat of Varanasi, and probably the most spectacular due to the nature of its temples. At this late hour the terraces above the river were virtually deserted except for huddles of pilgrims gathered like ghosts in the glow of small fires. Their subdued voices mingling with the lapping of water against the hulls of tethered boats added further to an ethereal tableau. In puddles of light cast by naked bulbs and oil lanterns, large bats swooped on bugs that had escaped from the nightmares of seriously disturbed children.

'What in the name of Jaysus is that!' broke the riverside spell. A beetle the size of the palm of your hand had crash-landed on Cora's shoulder.

'The soul of the ancestors,' Mike droned.

'You like a night visit to the burning ghats?' A shadowy figure in a turban with a low, rasping voice appeared out of the ether. 'Good body burning. We go in my boat.'

'No thanks,' Max said.

'Then what do you do here at the ghats?' the boatman asked.

'Walking,' I said as we hurried away. 'We go walking.'

'Careful,' the man advised. 'Many scorpions by the river at night.'

'Shouldn't have had that last joint,' Mike said as we beat a retreat back to the Central Hotel. As Hemingway put it, *Courage is grace under pressure.*

'In Benares you do two things,' Bob said over more banana lassis and a charas top-up. 'You get as close as you can to the inside of the Golden Temple[7], and you take a boat ride to the burning ghats. It's a positive thing to be cremated in Benares, sending people on to the next incarnation with a big 'alo around their 'eads.'

'What if it's a frog next time?' Mike asked. Bob let the smoke in his lungs rip forth in a hopeless fit of coughing.

'Don't let old Baba Fiji 'ear that,' he choked. 'He'll 'ave a fucking seizure.'

* * *

On the morning of April 26th, in searing heat, Cora, Max and I made our way back to the river along with Jim and Denis, the two Aussies on the magic bus. Jim, who had lived in Thailand with six women for several months, now lived with visions of syphilis. Denis was on his way from Bombay (Mumbai) where he had left his surf board. Both were among the less hippie-like of the bus passengers.

Dashashwamedh Ghat was teeming with pilgrims, food stalls, flower sellers and boatmen. The steps that had been empty last night were shaded in large parasols around which scores of the faithful streamed on their way to the river.

'Look,' Cora pointed. 'Just like Baba Fiji said, people are drinking the water.'

'That explains all the cremations,' Denis said. 'You come here. You drink the water. You die. You get cremated.'

As our purpose was to visit Manikarnika Ghat, one of Varanasi's two 'burning ghats', we looked for our rasping friend of the night before but he wasn't to be found. Finally, we agreed a price with a younger boatman and, pushing off with the help of many hands, we wobbled into the middle of the river and headed north. Behind us the morning light glowed across the moored boats, parasols, towers and temples that stretched away to the south. A gentle breeze generated by the

---

7. Kashi Vishwanath Temple (The Golden Temple) is one of the most significant places of pilgrimage in India. Destroyed and rebuilt many times over the centuries, the present temple dates from 1780 and was built to replace the previous temple, destroyed in 1669 by Shah Jahan's son, the Mughal emperor, Aurangzeb, who had then built a mosque in its place.

boat's momentum cooled our faces.

'Boy coming,' the boatman said, pointing to a splash at the riverbank. Some guy had dived into the water. Swimming out to our boat, he dragged himself on board.

'*Namaste,*' he beamed. 'My name is Sudhish. I am your guide.'

'And we're overcrowded,' Cora said. 'And didn't order a guide.'

While we adjusted to this turn of events, Sudhish began to name the various shrines and temples on the riverbank.

'Body-burning place very good,' he assured us. 'You like very much...'

He was in mid-sentence when three small dolphins with long snouts broke around the boat.

'Ah,' Sudhish said. 'These animals, they eat bodies of medical students and people with smallpox.'

'What?' I said, flabbergasted, and digesting the fact that there existed such a thing as a river dolphin.

'Yes my friend. They eat these bodies.'

'Why medical students?' I asked.

'Because only whole people cremated. Bodies not whole, we throw in river. That is the Hindu custom.'

'But how does that relate to medical students?'

'Because medical students give pieces of body to hospital for study. When they die, not too much left. So body put in river.'

'Amazing,' I said. 'A terrible end for a medical student.'

'Yes my friend. Most very terrible.'

Several pyres were ablaze on a muddy riverbank when we made landfall at Manikarnika Ghat. With barely enough room for our boat, we squeezed in between two barges full of wood and the boatman hopped ashore. As we struggled to disembark, a shaven-headed man lit a brushwood torch from the ghat's eternal flame, said to have been burning from the dawn of time, and set fire to another pyre.

Beyond the pyres, three other bodies, swaddled in saffron shrouds, lay on rough stretchers. Yet another was being dipped in the river in preparation for cremation. On both sides of the steps, pilgrims gathered at the temples. Further up the incline, the crowded buildings of the old city looked set to topple over. Once ashore, we were enveloped by smoke that smelled terribly like burning chicken while a wild dog ran off with a half-incinerated, smoking arm.

'You will see here,' Sudhish said, 'no single medical student.'

As our little party briefly peered into this corner of Hinduism, and Sudhish tried to haul us off to his 'brother's carpet shop', Bob went mad back at Dashashwamedh Ghat. He drank the river. When we met himself and Baba Fiji outside the Golden Temple a couple of hours later, he was hopelessly transformed. Glassy-eyed from a bhang (cannabis) lassi and wearing an extra turban of Baba Fiji's, his face was streaked in ashes like the old sadhu's. A garland of marigolds hung around his neck. He could now enter the temple as a 'Hindu'.

'Shiva gave me the word,' he said. 'The *Ganga* water would be safe.'

He and Baba Fiji then gave us two opposing sets of directions to the Central Hotel before turning for the temple where, amid chanting and praying and the ringing of bells, it was announced to Shiva that two more pilgrims, albeit slightly disreputable fellows, had arrived. One of them, perhaps hard of hearing, had just now misheard the word of Shiva.

Further up the alley we were stopped by a Brahmin priest who tried to sell us hash; and what's more, according to Jim who tried it, bad hash.

* * *

Varanasi slipped behind as we turned north into the hazy plains of Uttar Pradesh. In among the trees, the mud huts gave way to small isolated villages of bamboo, wicker and thatch. There were palms, tobacco plants, bananas and rice-paddies. And fewer people, although a stop anywhere would still guarantee the miraculous appearance of a crowd.

All fine but for the fact that the bus was giving trouble again and Bob was verifying the folly of delusion. Yesterday's gulp of the sacred Ganges had him by the guts. Since morning he had looked sick; but by mid-afternoon he looked like he might soon be dead. He lay on the floor at the back of the bus, wracked in fever, crumpled in spasms of pain and chewing little balls of opium while Baba Fiji prayed over him.

'The Ganges water yesterday,' Glynis' said. (A reasonable conclusion.)

'The water was fine,' Bob groaned. (A dubious conclusion.)

'It could be typhoid or cholera,' Jim whispered.

'Hope it's not contagious,' Max said.

As Bob refused to contemplate hospital, there was nothing we could do but motor on. Further up the bus the chillums were in rotation and tired, bad-tempered people were tossing in salt to counter the headaches of heat exhaustion.

We stopped at Gorakhpur, where trishaws provided the bulk of the city's transport, and all but the writhing Bob went to eat. Our choice was the railway station. From the outside, it looked modest enough:

a yellow building with a clock-tower and three arched entrances. But inside, we discovered one of India's largest rail junctions, with crowded platforms, steam trains, and carriage roofs packed with those passengers who were short of cash.

And windows into the other India. A woman begging for herself and her child. A man without legs scuttling around on a trolley. A sheaf of skin and bones dragging himself along the ground in a shredded shirt. A man with leprosy, missing his upper lip and nose.

Sometimes it was hard not to simply look away. Not to mention how it felt to be heading for the station restaurant.

Inside, shielded from both worlds, we sat at a long table under one of the fans and looked at a menu that must have offered a hundred dishes. Immediately, a nifty young waiter with slicked-back hair and a waxed moustache rushed to the table to fastidiously jot down our orders. But when the food came, none of the meals, planted down with considerable randomness, bore any resemblance to anything that had been ordered.

There were complaints on a large scale.

'So very sorry,' the waiter said. He ran around the table, picked up the plates and re-arranged them in similar random fashion.

'Just eat,' Eleanor suggested, 'before he takes the lot away and gives them to some other tables. Or better still, gives them to some of the people out on those platforms.' It couldn't have been better said.

In a corner of the restaurant a man had attracted a gathering: he was reading to them from a newspaper.

South of the Nepalese border, the bus pulled off the road. Parking under a mango tree, we lit a fire and made tea for Bob, immediately conjuring up a crowd who emerged like genies from a seemingly empty landscape. In rich afternoon light, a couple of chillums were stoked while domestic matters were sorted.

First of all, Baba Fiji and Jaswinda, who was Malaysian Indian, were without passports. Jaswinda's had been stolen, along with his money, in Delhi. In his early twenties, long-haired Jaswinda had to date been pretty sanguine about the loss.

'I will deal with the issue of not having a passport,' he said, 'when there is such an issue.'

For Baba Fiji there was no problem: sadhus could cross the border freely. Jaswinda had the right face but the wrong clothes, so we dressed him up in Baba Fiji's spare lungi and Bob's turban. A few smears of clay and the miracle was complete - Jaswinda the Punjabi holy man. To avoid suspicion, the two 'sadhus' would cross the frontier on foot.

'Right,' Charlie said once Jaswinda had been sorted, 'from here on, no dope on the bus. Anyone carrying anything is to give it to Baba Fiji to carry across.'

'Nobody tells me what to do with my stash,' Eleanor snapped. 'Especially not you!'

'Too much ze orders,' Daniel from Quebec said, tossing in a few more amphetamines to stop himself from conking out from too much hash.

The wars were brewing again when Bob appeared at the door of the bus.

'It's like this,' he said. 'Anyone who wants to carry their own gear across can drive as well, 'cos me an' Steve will be walkin'.

Bob collapsed back into the interior, leaving the issue settled. But bad blood was festering under the mango tree. (Cora and I were with Charlie on this one.)

As the last of the daylight was scattered by a twilight of awnings, glowing lanterns and sweating jasmine, we reached the Indian border post. It was closed. But, with Indian indifference to time, which for once worked in our favour, the officials let us through.

And as we snagged on the barbed wire of Indian bureaucracy and form-filling, Baba Fiji and Jaswinda sauntered past as if they had never seen any of us in their lives.

* * *

With a crumbling vehicle and no permanent driver, the bus crew had decided, unbeknown to the rest of us, that they should sell the old Bedford in Kathmandu. This required them to smuggle it into Nepal. As a bus is a large item to be smuggling anywhere, Charlie figured on slipping it in unannounced.

'Carnet de passage please.' the customs man at the Nepalese frontier said, and the plot unfolded.

'We don't need any carnet for Nepal.' Charlie said.

The customs official, a grey-haired man in his late forties, was polite at first. 'I must have the carnet,' he said. 'It is necessary for Nepal.'

'No, it's not,' Charlie countered. 'I was told in London that we don't need it.'

'Yes, it is,' the customs man said, bristling slightly.

'No,' Charlie persisted. 'No carnet is needed for Nepal.'

You had to hand it to Charlie: he wasn't a quitter. Neither, unfortunately, was the customs man.

'I will fix you,' he snapped and off he stormed.

Although none of the passengers had seen this coming, the altercation piqued four of them disproportionately.

'They're carryin',' Glynis said to Steve.

'Charlie,' I said, feeling that things were slipping away, 'remember that Cora and I need to pick up visas at this border. Now that we're here, we don't need anyone annoying anyone else.'

'Tiger country tomorrow, man' Eleanor said in support. 'In tiger country nobody should have to put up with shit like this.'

'It'll be sorted,' Charlie said.

A few minutes passed before the customs man came back with a very surly, mustachioed cop in tow. Looking like he'd just been woken up, the cop squinted from under the peak of his hat.

'LONDON!' he bellowed into Charlie's face. 'What is London? This is Nepal! This is a free country! No England here. No London too. Tomorrow morning, nine o'clock, all of you go back to India.'

Good one Charlie, I thought, wanting to strangle him.

But who pays the piper calls the tune. A full mutiny and talk of refunds forced Charlie to relent: the carnet was produced and the banishment order repealed. Nevertheless, it took an awful lot of mettle for myself and Cora to follow the retreating cop back to his hut to explain that, perchance, there was a slight matter that had been overlooked...

CHAPTER 2

Jet It Or Forget It

In the morning there was uproar in the border town of Bhairahwa. Cora and I had returned with our visas from the Immigration office to find Baba Fiji and Jaswinda on the perimeter of a large crowd. They were looking despondently towards the bus which was swarming with cops. The tensions that had simmered since Agra had finally come to a head. Baba Fiji rolled his eyes and Jaswinda explained.

'After walking to Bhairahwa last night, we slept in the street. It was very cold and we were awake early in the morning. One hour ago, we found the bus here. Then, when we were giving everyone back the charas from last night, Charlie noticed that four people were not collecting any. [The four who had been spotted by Glynis.] Charlie ordered them from the bus, and a big fight broke out. Then Charlie called the police.'

'Charlie make many troubles,' Baba Fiji said with a shrug of his shoulders. 'Charlie very foolish boy.' In fairness to Charlie, he was always going to be holding the short straw. Herding cats was never going to be an easy job.

Surprisingly, Eleanor, who had protested so loudly under the mango tree, was not among the evicted.

* * *

'Get a load of this!' Steve shouted. 'It's the Himalayas!'

A moment of silence while tired eyes picked out the enormous grey wall seeping east to west through the morning haze, then a tsunami of euphoria unlike anything ever seen across the known world. People hooted and howled. They shouted *Oh shit I don't believe it!* and *What a sight for sore eyes!* and *Where the fuck did that chillum go?*

Twenty minutes later we were in the foothills of the Annapurna Range. Bye-bye to the heat and humidity of the plains. As the air cleared, the grey wall became individual mountains, from which grew forests, valleys, rivers and waterfalls. Elation rippled through the bus.

The past was forgotten.

Spotting a roadside waterfall, Steve pulled over and we all spilled out. Clothes littered the roadside and we were in the water, being nibbled by fearless little fish, within seconds. The relief of cold, clean water, surging in effervescence in a deep pool below the fall, was ecstasy. People stayed under for so long that other people wondered if they were ever coming up. But as ecstasy briefly prevailed, a new issue was pushing to the fore. The mountains were visiting hell on the bus. The old engine was issuing groans and snorts that sounded frightfully human.

'Sounds like it's 'aunted,' Glynis said.

Cora wasn't wild impressed when we slipped out of gear and briefly rolled backwards on the next bend.

'Jesus, Mary and St. Joseph,' she said. 'This is worse than one of Crowley's crocks.' Crowley had been one of her childhood neighbours. He owned or sold the said crocks.

Although traffic was greatly reduced in the mountains, the road itself was an unnerving obstacle course of potholes, boulders, cattle, buffaloes, and the driving style of locals who mistook hairpin bends for the Monaco Grand Prix. Reminders of how that could end were to be found at the bottom of ravines or, in some cases, jammed against trees that had brought a tumble to a halt.

There were also those bits of road that had disappeared, washed away by the rains of the encroaching monsoon, leaving a band of mud barely wide enough to take the bus.

At one of those sections, we found a bunch of workmen tossing basketfuls of soil over the edge to rebuild the foundation that had once supported the bitumen. The sound of tumbling water rising from a gorge far below made the endeavor look like a skit from a Chaplin movie.

'Road finish,' one of the workmen said. Steve and Charlie went to take a look.

'Road is anything but "finish",' Steve announced on his return. 'But we might be lucky. It might take us across. We'll see how it goes.'

'That seems a bit vague on the question,' Jim from Australia said. 'Does that mean that we might also *not* be lucky?'

Being a person myself who likes heights if I can fall safely in every direction, I had a premonition that I should now be on foot. Cora said she'd be sick any minute. However, like all the other fools on board, we stayed put as the bus lurched out onto the mud and the workmen cleared off to give us an unimpeded run.

Hugging the cliff while pitching and sinking, we jerked forward. We then slammed to a halt with a communal shriek as the bus tilted towards the drop. Although there was no point, Cora and I grabbed one another. Jim who had lived so dashingly with his women in Bangkok, threw himself from his aisle seat to the floor. Fellow countryman, Denis, landed on top of him. Seven or eight voices hissed 'Jesus!' in rapid re-conversions from Hinduism. Even Baba Fiji lost his composure, concluding that perchance his luck wasn't so hot any more. Bob on the floor, asleep or unconscious, was the only calm note on board.

Seeing life in suspension, I peered out my window and there was nothing between me and the gorge. With one door jammed against a cliff and the other opening into space, there was no escape. Besides, we were afraid to move lest we tilt ourselves into termination. One of the workmen looked underneath the bus to assess our chances. When he reappeared, he gestured that we should pray.

However, in a series of shrieks and shudders, and tingling pauses each time we keeled towards the dip, we somehow made it across. As soon as we did, Baba Fiji rolled out the door and kissed the ground. The rest of us tumbled after him in a kind of jocular hysteria.

'Steve,' the normally silent Max said, 'you are the best bloody driver in the world.'

'Or the worst,' Jim said. 'For trying... Take a look at the wheel tracks. The outer dual at the back of the bus was spinning in air.'

'It really is true what they say about Nepal,' Eleanor said. 'Jet it or forget it.'

* * *

There was now a hole in the radiator and the bus was constantly slipping out of gear. Few on board believed that it had any hope of reaching Kathmandu. We were having similar doubts about Bob, stretched out in the back and burning with fever. Nevertheless, we trundled on.

On another level, Cora was a mess from Bhairahwa's mosquitoes. Despite having had the only net in the five-bed room, her face was a corrugation of bumps, her eyes were half-closed, and her ankles were so badly swollen that she was limping.

'Very bad mosquito you have,' Baba Fiji declared. 'Soon we fix.'

'Is there a pharmacy somewhere?' Cora asked.

'Shoo-o-o,' Baba Fiji said, like a homeopath whose nose had been rubbed in codeine.

In the next village, a tiny hamlet of ochre and thatch, he called aside four older men who were slaughtering a buffalo. They checked Cora's face and nodded. One man left and came back with a bottle half-filled with a clouded brown liquid.

'Special oil,' Baba Fiji said. 'From special tree. You must put everywhere.' An hour later the swelling and limping were gone and the bites were reduced to red dots.

We were now filling the radiator every twenty minutes and Charlie and Glynis, beaten by their border failure with the carnet, were bemoaning the fact that they hadn't sold the bus in India.

'If you'd sold the bus in India,' Steve reminded them, 'you'd have no more means of making a living.'

'Who cares?' Glynis shrugged. Her face said, *I'm done with the Hippie Trail.*

On a broad horseshoe bend, we passed the next engine-cooling time by dangling our legs in a stream and watching freshwater crabs scuttle off into stony crevices.

On the far side of the bend, half hidden in undergrowth, seven women in tunics and bright *fariyas* (a type of sarong) were slashing leaves from the trees. One stuck a billhook into her waistband and shinnied up one of the trunks. As we basked in the sunshine, the women began to sing, their voices carrying across the valley and rolling back from the mountains in harmonizing echoes. The fantasy was crowned by clouds of butterflies and a heat-shimmer that left the women and the trees in ethereal suspension.

'Tolkein based *Lord of the Rings* on Nepal,' George from California said but it wasn't true.

We stopped for tea at the next village, a dozen stone and thatch huts that clung precariously to the side of a mountain. Having located the tea hut, we were ushered inside by two older women with faces shriven by wind and sun. Dressed in red tunics and black *fariyas*, they wore long plaits, rows of earrings and magnificent chunky necklaces of turquoise and red Himalayan coral. In the semi darkness they settled us down on cushions and rough benches and laughed delightedly at the state of derangement into which some of our company had sunk.

'Chirasmi,' one of them called to a third woman who was bent over the hut's cooking fire, tending a hanging kettle.

'*Sacre bleu!*' Daniel from Quebec exclaimed when the woman turned. 'I am in love.'

'A-a-a-ah,' the oldest of the women laughed. 'You like daughter?'

The woman at the fire stood to her full height and smiled. Almond eyes. High cheekbones. Hair that cascaded from a red headband. A midriff glistening between a lime-green tunic and the waistband of her *fariya*.

'She seventeen year,' the mother said. 'You like? Daughter make good wife. No more need Nepal visa.'

'Very beautiful,' Daniel agreed. 'I come back in Nepal and maybe I marry. But first I must go to Kathmandu to ze temples. I must go to India again when it is not so hot...'

'A-a-a-ah,' the mother laughed, seeing that she was losing her prospective son-in-law. 'Maybe other time. Maybe now, you like buy stones?'

She reached up into the tree-trunks that supported the roof and pulled down a carefully folded rag. Inside was a collection of rubies, sapphires, tigers' eyes and moonstones!

* * *

Under a large and luminous afternoon sky, we chugged into Tansen. The little hill town west of the main road was reached by way of a dirt track. Perched high in the Mahabarat Range above a deep valley, this hideaway of steep cobbled streets, pavement markets, wooden balconies and tiny shops, was once the centre of the Kingdom of Palpa, founded in the 16th century by Tharu warriors from the Terai Plain. In the late light the surrounding hills, converted to rice terraces on the lower slopes, glowed red.

'We can't go any further today,' Steve announced. 'The bus has had it.'

Amid renewed mumblings of discontent, we parked in the cobbled square. The local mechanics - two masters of improvisation whose zeal was matched only by their lack of tools and equipment - were summoned. 'Tomorrow' was the verdict. Across the square we had our first meal of the day in an open-fronted restaurant run by an excitable little man who swung a heavy, razor-sharp kukri in wild arcs as he explained through Baba Fiji's interpretations that he had most certainly not gotten our orders wrong.

That evening a storm lit up the mountains around Tansen. Distant blue pulses become massive displays of forked lightning followed by the crack of exploding thunder and a downpour that turned streams into rivers. Breaking from the others to escape the growing cabin fever that we were all probably feeling, Cora and I sat on the rim of the valley and watched enthralled as the lightning bounced off the hills around us. In those day I believed that lightning hit other people.

Back in town, we all bedded down free on the floor above the kukri-man's restaurant, accompanied by the owner, his family, and seven Nepalese wayfarers.

In the early morning one of the women of our company snuck out and crapped on the flat roof of the restaurant but was spotted by the kukri man who made her clean it all up.

'You have to shit *somewhere*,' she later proclaimed. No truer words were ever spoken.

After a quick breakfast we left Tansen with the mountains washed in post-rain clarity and cloud hanging in the valley. Climbing on towards Pokhara, we topped a rise to find ourselves staring north at the gold-tinted snowfields of the Annapurna Range and the tenth highest mountain in the world. Bob got up to look. His fever had finally broken. Though shaken and wretched-looking, he was on the mend.

'Tomorrow morning,' Eleanor said, 'we'll be looking up at Machapuchhare and that's one hell of a way to eat breakfast.'

* * *

Prior to the Chinese invasion of Tibet, Pokhara had been an important trading post on the arduous route between India and Tibet. However, the town had remained a hidden gem to the wider world until 1970 when the road on which we had just travelled was built. Cocooned in its mountain basin beside Phewa Tal, Nepal's second-largest lake, it offered dramatic vistas of the 22,943-foot spike of Machapuchhare ('Fishhtail'), along with Dhaulagari, Annapurna and Manaslu all rising to more than 26,000 feet.

Backed by the sub-tropical rainforest that ringed the valley, the lakeshore was where battered spirits could be rekindled. Comfortably hot during the day and deliciously cool at night, it had a pace of life that bordered sleep.

'One look,' Cora said as we dropped into the valley, 'and I just know we're getting off this bus.'

'Me too,' Max said.

And me,' George from California said. 'This is where I meet my friend.'

In fact, half the passengers got off. After fond goodbyes, Cora and I wandered down to the Trekkers' Retreat, one of a handful of cheap lodges on the lakeshore. Two huts of stone and corrugated tin, divided into rooms, provided the accommodation. A thatched open restaurant with outdoor tables and chairs provided the food. Surrounded by trees, flowering shrubs and bamboo, it was run by 23-year-old Shyam, a slim, mild-mannered Nepali who came from a village in the mountains.

'I have many persons stay here,' Shyam said, unlocking the door to our room. 'From Australia, Canada, Germany. But you the first from Ireland.'

Just then we heard familiar voices: Max and George from California had moved in next door.

The accommodation was basic: plank beds with thin, faded mattresses and just enough room for a tiny table. The door had an inside bolt and an outside padlock, and the windows were shuttered, back and front. Along with the now familiar quota of ants, cockroaches, mosquitoes and geckos, we were host to several noisy crickets and three enormous brown spiders.

Once we had settled, Max, George, Cora and I adjourned to the restaurant where we joined two lads who were in the grip of the roaring munchies: a thick-set, bearded Aussie named Dick and a small New Zealander named Tony who reminded me of Buffalo Bill.

'Gidday mate,' Dick said. 'And welcome to one of the great munchie houses of Asia. We have pancakes with bananas and honey, apple pie with custard, and mugs of steaming hot chocolate.'

'Apple pie and custard,' I called.

'Me too,' Cora said.

'Cook,' Shyam said as he shovelled the goodies onto the table, 'he very special. He cook long time at Chinese Embassy in Kathmandu. The people, they come from all over lake to eat cook's lemon meringue pie.'

'Any yetis about?' Max asked.

'Many, many,' Shyam said. 'In mountains.'

As we tucked into second helpings of apple pie with custard, dusk was shattered by an outrageous cacophony. Crickets and frogs burst into a great bellowing and the trees and bamboo thickets filled with fireflies.

A bong flamed in the middle of the table, courtesy of Buffalo Bill.

'What do they think of the life?' Shyam wondered aloud of his wayward guests.

Back at the huts all the wildlife not earlier in our rooms was making a gallant effort to make up for lost time.

* * *

In Pokhara, life was governed by the sun, the moon and impulse. The day would begin with dusty shafts of light peeking through cracks in the window-shutters. We'd rise to a ringing chorus of birds, and a pink fire sweeping the peak of Machhapuchhare. Shyam would have coffee on the go, and the smell of cooking would mingle with that of fire smoke. After breakfast, we'd go for a stroll, feel the fresh breeze, listen to the insects and watch the rising sun scatter the mist over the silent waters of Phewa Tal.

Once the sun was up, the women who lived behind the lodge would arrive, naked to the waist, to wash at the pump under the papaya trees at the bottom of Shyam's garden. Surrounded by butterflies, they would shout good morning while they poured water over one another and washed clothes. The children were then scrubbed and hung in cradles from the doorframes of the houses. Plastered in red ochre and roofed in dark thatch, the houses were set back among the trees like elf dwellings. After breakfast the women, with infants strapped to their backs, would leave for the fields or cross in dugouts to the far side of the lake to gather firewood.

Later, the Tibetan hawkers, refugees from across the northern borders, would arrive with religious trinkets, coral, turquoise, chillums, pipes, daggers, jewellery and tolas of black hash. If we wanted to buy, it was barter time; if not, they sat with us and shared cigarettes and asked about the world beyond.

While George spent the first few days trying to track down the fellow Californian he was to meet in Pokhara, Dick, Tony, Max, Cora and I replenished our physical and emotional resources by scoffing the cook's pies and sampling the competition in the half dozen minor eating houses along the twenty-minute walk to the lake temple that was the daily focus of Pokhara.

The little pagoda-temple, connected to the shore by 150 yards of causeway, was surrounded by rocky ledges from which sprouted trees and pockets of delicate alpines. Spread along the ledges, twenty or thirty young hippies could be found taking a mixture of sun and Nepalese hash. They included a couple of 'Orange People', disciples of the Hindu guru, Bhagwan Shree Rajneesh. Easily distinguished by their saffron dress, they had diverted to Pokhara while on their way to Rajneesh's ashram at Pune in India which was attracting an increasing number of Westerners.

Close to the causeway, a small group of sadhus who lived under a tree blasted away on an eternal chillum to Shiva, their tridents buried in the ground, tea-water on the fire and a garish picture of their favourite god nailed to the tree. Much drunkenness happened under the tree, and one of the sadhus, a rogue from Rajasthan, so incensed the locals that six young men stripped him naked one afternoon and tossed him into the lake.

Last time anyone saw the offending sadhu, he was dragging his sorry skin down the southbound road out of Pokhara.

At night we had frogs, crickets, fireflies and the clouds of moths that flocked to the oil lamps. And we had guitar music, thanks to the instrument that I had carried from Ireland. And each night, for the duration of our stay, Cora and I observed one ritual: we walked in the darkness down to the temple, past the fairy-tale houses of the village where the glow of lanterns added magic to the red mortar and thatch, past sudden patches of unseen flowers sweating powerful scents, past the sadhus muttering like ghosts over their cooking fire, past the sleeping water buffaloes that would start from the earth without warning.

Out at the end of the causeway, the temple would be in complete darkness except for the green arcs of the fireflies and the ocean of stars in the sky. On the lake, wavering lights would burn reflections into the black water - villagers fishing from dugouts, paddles muffled by the night, one man holding a burning torch, another a small triangular net. The fish would rise to the flickering flames... And all of it would be ours.

Sometimes we'd slide into the inky shock of cold water, happy, silent and free.

* * *

The wet season was rolling in, each passing day bringing more rain. Every morning, after a brief clearance, the high mountains would disappear in a diaphanous haze that slowly rose from the valley and promised an afternoon downpour.

'No trekking today,' Dick would say as he wrapped a rag around the mouthpiece of the day's first chillum. On the third such day, George arrived back to the Trekkers' Retreat looking worried.

'Did you find your friend?' Cora asked.

'Yeah, I found him,' George said. 'He's in the Mission Hospital in town, and he's got amoebic dysentery.'

'Bad?' I asked, being an amoebic dysentery veteran.

'Man,' he said, 'he sure don't look good. He's shitting blood and mucous and can't even hold water. One of the nurses says he's been getting worse ever since he was brought in five days ago. He thinks he's dying. He's asked me to ring his folks if he doesn't make it through.'

'No need for that, mate,' Dick said. 'That's too depressing. He'll be okay.'

Over the coming days the quiet, bearded Californian made the pilgrimage to his friend's bedside every morning, returning in the evening with news of further deterioration. Every morning, with growing apprehension, we watched his departure, and every evening his homecoming, but I doubt if any of us really appreciated how serious his friend was. Until one afternoon when George came home early. We were sitting by the lakeside not far from the Trekkers' Retreat when he came loping towards us from the direction of the town, his curly hair soaked from an earlier downpour. We knew from fifty yards away that it was bad. Long before we saw the red of his eyes.

'What happened, man?' I asked. (We all said 'man' in those days.)

'He's dead,' George said. 'I was holding him and he died in my arms just over an hour ago.' He sat down beside us and stared out at the lake. 'It was a horrible, lonely way to die. Thousands of miles from home, thousands of miles from his folks, begging for life and the people he loved. Just ten days ago man, he phoned his folks to say how well everything was going...'

George took a bus to Kathmandu the following day.

'I can't deal with this,' he said. 'I'm going home to California.'

We were all shattered. Out here, so far from the old familiar, one of our own had died. It was a strange feeling. Grief for someone none of us knew. And for a distant family that would now have to deal with getting him home.

'It just goes to show,' Cora said, 'how easily your luck can run out.'

* * *

On the morning George left, Dick, Tony, Max and I, still shaken by the death of George's friend, invested in thirty grams of Nepalese Black and got cook to stick it in a chocolate gelatine pie. I don't know if this was supposed to make us feel better or worse. (Remember, this was all a long time ago when such activity was the common denominator among young trailblazers.)

Cora, who in times of need can always muster enough sense for both of us, declined her portion of the gritty enterprise. More for us, we said.

We chopped up the fifth portion between the four lads to avoid the waste of a decent pie. We really didn't need to. The first portion was enough to knock a horse on its rear end. An hour later nothing would do me but to borrow a dugout from one of the fishermen and cajole

Cora - as it was bright and sunny - into joining me on an excursion to the far side of Phewa Tal.

'If you want my considered opinion,' Dick said, 'that's a bad idea. Lake's full of parasites and snakes. The parasites will devour you in seconds if they get in your mouth.'

No sooner had we left the shore than the dugout began to rock. I had to flop to the floor to avoid being dumped overboard among the surrounding tangles of venomous snakes.

'Weeds,' Cora said as she struck out with the paddle for the far shore.

On arrival, she changed to a blue bikini and lay in a sandy hollow in the sun. As she disappeared into the hollow, a thought struck me.

'Right,' I said. 'I'm away into the forest.'

'See you later,' Cora said from her prone position. No takers there.

In among the red trunks it was cool and damp. Barefoot, I pushed uphill for fifty yards through ferns, flowers and fungi. Deep in the forest a bird broke the silence, a single note that spiralled to impossible heights until it cut off dead, to be answered further up the slope by another. Then, to my horror, I heard the crashing sound of a charging yeti! As I turned to bolt, the real truth dawned: it was a leopard. Running for the boat, I shot past Cora in her hollow.

'Leopard!' I yelled, although I must confess that the leopard may not have meaningfully existed. 'Run for it!'

'Leopard my arse,' Cora said, leaning up on one elbow as I jumped into the boat.

Disconcertingly ignoring the crisis, she lay down again, hidden from the view of a perambulating Englishman who looked like Salvador Dali and was at that very moment rounding the next bend - just as my very eyes fell on two slobbery, bloated leeches gorging themselves between the toes of my right foot.

'A cigarette!' I roared at Cora. 'Quick! Hurry! I need a lighted cigarette. NOW!' (The plan was to burn them off.)

The Englishman stopped dead. He looked about. There was nobody else in sight. Visibly astonished, it was occurring to him that he had stumbled on a serious nicotine habit.

'Okay man,' he stammered, fumbling in his shoulder bag. 'Just you take it easy now... I'm coming man, fast as I can...'

'It's the leeches...' I began.

'Sure man,' he agreed, hands outstretched placatingly. 'You just calm down now and tell them bad leeches to go away...'

He lit a cigarette, stuffed it in my mouth and backed off down the lakeshore without ever seeing Cora.

A touch of the cigarette and the leeches came off in two spurts of blood, but the Englishman missed it.

'We've got to get out of here,' I said to Cora. 'It's all gone bonkers.'

'What's gone bonkers?' she asked.

'You won't believe it. This place is sort of *haunted*.'

'Yeah,' she said. 'Everywhere I go is sort of haunted. By *you*.'

By the time we got back to the Trekkers' Retreat another tremendous electrical storm had broken. In a growling wind, hail the size of ice-cubes rattled down on the tin roof of our hut and sent every living thing with any sense scooting for cover.

'Sometimes,' Shyam said, 'the hailstones, they kill the cow and the buffalo.'

I went to the room and hid under my sleeping bag. Max, next door, was hiding under his. We maintained communication.

* * *

Max, Cora and I travelled together to Kathmandu. Twenty years earlier, it was a capital to which visiting dignitaries were carried over mountain trails in palanquins. The King's cars were shouldered in from India by teams of porters. Now, ancient Kathmandu, with its cobbled lanes, temples and pagodas, some dating back to the 12th century, was the Shangri-La of the Hippie Trail. Amid a plethora of garish shrines to Shiva, Kali and Ganesh, history and mythology blended seamlessly at every leaning street corner and stone courtyard. In the bazaars where many of the tiny shops had sunk below street level, life went on as it had for centuries.

In 1976, before any real tourist industry had established itself in Nepal, the pioneering souls who made it that far were largely young hippies. The present landmark known as Freak Street is their indelible legacy. In *A Season in Heaven: True Tales From The Road To Kathmandu,* David Tomory would later describe how this infamous street '...*consisted of maybe ten lousy hotels with dismal tenement rooms in which the inmates dismally sat all day, spitting out the windows. You needed an umbrella to get down Freak Street.*'

This downbeat portrait was not how I remember it although I do sense the proximity of our next-door neighbour who is soon to feature in this story.

From the bus station, we walked to Durbar Square, the heart of the old city, and checked in at Freak Street's dilapidated Everest Lodge, which lay around the corner from the square's palaces and temples.

In a hub of blissful decadence, black marketeers and petty corruption where the smells of incense and hash mingled seamlessly, we spent the next week in virtual inertia. Excursions rarely stretched beyond the temples of the square, or a taxi ride to a religious festival in Patan on the far side of the Bagmati River, or a spell dodging the bicycles, rickshaws and braying donkeys in the alleys of the bazaar, or a visit to the Star Restaurant down the street, where on our first afternoon, we rediscovered Charlie, Glynis, the recovered Bob, Jaswinda and Baba Fiji.

'We're still stuck with the bleethin' bus,' Bob told us. 'We'll probably take it back as far as Kabul if we can find another driver among the 'ippies of Freak Street.'

'Then me and Charlie are goin' home,' Glynis said. Hippie Trail exhaustion had finally triumphed.

* * *

The Royal Kumari, the Living Goddess of Kathmandu, was, according to local belief, a reincarnation of the Hindu goddess Taleju, the wrathful form of the goddess Durga. She was to be found in a red-brick, three-storey palace that had, since 1757, stood on the southern side of Durbar Square, around the corner from Freak Street. On our first afternoon in Kathmandu, Max, Cora and I paid a visit.

The most striking thing about the visit was how casual and informal it was. When we arrived in Durbar Square it was deserted, most people having fled indoors to avoid the coming storm that was sweeping in over the city in banks of massing cloud. With nobody at the palace entrance - a heavy wooden door guarded by two stone lions - we simply went on through to a courtyard as deserted as the square, but for a single older man who instantly vanished. Surrounded by tiers of latticed windows covered in weather-rubbed carvings of peacocks, lions and multi-armed gods battling one another for supremacy, we looked for the goddess but she wasn't about. Nevertheless, there was a clue to her whereabouts: the courtyard centerpiece. On the third floor, opposite the entrance, a corbelled projection of three magnificently-carved windows seemed to have been dropped out from the roof on hinges. Its elegant decay spoke of antiquity, mythology and legend.

According to the manager of the Everest Lodge, it all began during the 16th-century reign of King Trailokya Malla of Bhaktapur. The king used to play dice with Taleju at night and she would advise him on matters of state. However, he gradually became so besotted by her beauty that he tried to seduce her. Taleju was outraged and told the king that he would never again see her in goddess form. Smitten with remorse, he pleaded for her return, so Taleju came to him in his dreams. She promised to reappear in the body of a virgin girl of the Newari Buddhist *Shakya* caste, and gave detailed instructions on the ways in which the girl would be recognized. These included thirty-two physical traits. Ever since, the Kumari had been selected as directed by Taleju, from Newari infant girls, taken from their families and shut away in a cloistered life until the goddess vacated their bodies at puberty or the first sign of blood loss or illness.

Cultures and religions have a lot to answer for.

'Anybody there?' Max called.

A woman appeared with a bucket of washing.

'Is the Kumari about?' Cora asked. The woman looked up towards the third-floor centerpiece and called out. Nothing happened. She called again and gave us a reassuring glance. A minute later, a shy young girl, made up with theatrical excess, appeared at the middle window of the centerpiece. Behind the make-up, it was impossible to tell her age. She looked down at us without expression.

'Wave and say hello,' Max suggested. We did. And as quickly as the Kumari had appeared, she was gone.

'All wrong I'm sure,' Cora said. 'Probably some kind of insult.'

After our brief audience with the Kumari, we decided to ignore the threat of rain and check out the alleys fanning out from Durbar Square. What we found was stunning: a living museum of ancient houses with beautifully carved doors, eaves, windows and balconies. A legacy of a time when the city was a Newari centre of culture and art before the Gurkhas conquered the Kathmandu Valley in 1769. The charm, however, was somewhat dented by the stench of shite and rotting garbage that prompted regulated breathing.

'Like a World War I gas attack,' Max intoned.

The sense of decay was further evidenced in the stone public baths. In a sludge of stagnant, scum-topped liquid that had once poured in as water, people washed themselves and their clothes, cleaned pots and scrubbed vegetables.

'The scourge of Kathmandu,' Max said of the vegetable-scrubbing. 'No wonder people get sick.'

This is why you don't eat salads, I reminded myself. But salads or not, I would find that it was hard to dodge the scourge of Kathmandu.

Three days later, Max, Cora and I were eating at the Star when it struck. Ripping stomach pains and a race to the loo.

'I think I'm coming down with something,' I said when I came back.
'You look grey,' Cora said. 'What does it feel like?'

'Amoebic dysentery,' I said. 'I'm passing blood. It feels like it did in Kabul.'

In the morning, at the Shanta Bhawan Mission Hospital, my diagnosis was confirmed.

'Cyst of entamoeba histolytica,' the young Sri Lankan doctor said. 'You have amoebic dysentery. But do not worry, it is in the early stages.'

How anyone could fit not worrying into the same sentence as the disease that had hospitalised me six years earlier and had killed George's Californian friend back in Pokhara, was beyond me. But the doctor was spot on: a course of antibiotics had me back on my feet in days. In the interim, a new threat to life sprang from the most unexpected quarter - straight through the French windows of our room at the Everest Lodge.

Cora and I were two floors up in a fairly nondescript box with a couple of creaking beds and walls of faded blue. The saving feature was the balcony that overlooked Freak Street and was shared with the adjoining room. On the second night of my illness, I was sitting on one of the beds, studying a map of South East Asia. Cora was reading on the other bed. The windows leading to the balcony were closed. Great then was our surprise when they burst open, and our next-door neighbor stumbled through. In Irish we would have called him a *fear fada* (a long man). In our street, when I was a boy, he would have been Lanks the Lighthouse. In English he was a string of undiluted misery: an emaciated Frenchman with hollow, sooty eyes and a ponytail that hadn't been washed in weeks. One look and you knew he was running on bad fuel. But more disturbing was the large knife in his right hand.

'My *passeport*,' he slurred. 'Or I kill you.' A dispiriting prospect under any circumstances.

'We know nothing about your passport,' I said, keeping an eye on the knife and looking around for a suitable loose and heavy object.

'My *passeport*,' he said again, voodoo in the sooty eyes, 'Give me or I kill you.'

At this the slightly-built Cora put down her book. 'You heard him,' she said with uncanny composure. 'We don't have your passport. Now get the hell out.'

The Frenchman stopped dead. He made guttural noises. He shook his head several times. Then, without a shot being fired, he shrivelled into a simian stoop and retreated out through the balcony window. Cora returned to her book as if nothing had happened. I closed the window, said that was one mad bastard, and went back to my map.

Memory is a funny thing: in the harvesting of the years, this entire incident - recorded in my travel notes as a significant event - has been entirely obliterated by Cora.

Two days later we were frantically retreating, along with Max, from the 2,000-year-old Buddhist temple of Swayambhunath, two miles west of the city. The source of bother on this occasion was not the aggressive temple macaques who stole people's cameras, but a shower of rocks, bottles and dog's abuse hurled by a woman who mistakenly thought we hadn't paid for our Coca-Cola.

'Like Dunkirk,' Max muttered as we fled down the 365 steps that led to safety.

On our way back to Durbar Square we met Ivor the Swede, one of those who had been evicted from the magic bus at the Nepalese border. Ivor, spindle-shanked, stoned out of his skull and dressed in a T-shirt and badly-hanging lungi, had been a nuisance on the bus, always late for every departure while the rest of us stewed in the heat.

'I know a short vay,' he said. Hours later, as night closed in, we were wandering lost among sodden paddy fields and Ivor still knew the 'vay'. The only saving grace was the firefly that attached itself firmly to the lapel of Max's jacket.

'It's a major breakthrough,' Max proclaimed, 'in the relationship between humankind and the humble firefly.' It was, I believe, his longest ever statement.

Finally, a night came when - time to move on again - Cora and I sat in our room with tickets for a plane that left for Rangoon in the morning. As there was no legal overland route between Nepal and Burma, or between Burma and Thailand, we had a double plane-hop ahead of us. In our Kathmandu finale, we swapped addresses with Max, and the three of us set off for the Star where we lay on cushions and drank rice beer amid the chillums. Over in the corner a Jesus Freak was playing the guitar. A sign above his head proclaimed: 'No drugs'.

Through the haze an old man with long grey hair and a goatee materialised. He was dressed in a saffron lungi and white turban, and he carried a small bag over one shoulder. He saw us and threw up his hands in a feigned euphoria of recognition. Besides us three, old Baba Fiji was now the last of the bus company still in Kathmandu.

'We're leaving for Rangoon tomorrow,' Cora told him after we had shared some food, 'We'll come back to India some other time when it isn't so hot.'

'Ah yes,' the old sadhu said. 'Maybe on that day too I go back to Fiji. You make good trip, eh? Some day you come back too. Maybe yes.

Maybe no. You ask many questions of the life. Maybe you find answers where you go.'

He then sucked on a passing chillum, bade the three of us farewell, and got up to go. He looked lonely and mournful, a man adrift on a river of remembrance, condemned to a perennial turnover of friends.

'That guy in the corner keeps staring at us,' Cora said. 'The guy with the beard.'

'Where you from?' the staring one asked when I looked his way.

'Ireland,' I said.

'I know that',' he said. 'So am I. But whereabouts?'

'Cork.'

'I'm from Dublin meself,' he said. 'I only ever knew two guys from Cork. I lived with one of them in a squat in London, a guy called Deckie Bennett. He had a mate called Niall.'

Cora and I gaped at one another. The Niall he was talking about had to be my younger brother. He and Deckie Bennett, an old friend, had gone to London together.

What were the chances? The first Irish person we ever met while travelling, and we were connected.

CHAPTER 3

A Week In Burma

According to Freak Street lore, two bottles of Johnnie Walker Red Label and two cartons of 555 cigarettes, purchased at the duty-free shop at Kathmandu airport and sold on the black market of Rangoon, would earn us enough cash to finance our stay in Burma. So we, and a dozen others of like mind, arrived at Rangoon airport on the weekly flight from Kathmandu with our mandatory onward air tickets and identical duty-free bags, and were stamped through by customs officers who knew damn well the purpose of the duty-free. But to give cover, we would need to legitimately change a few dollars into Burmese kyats and show the bank slip when leaving the country.

In 1976 the maximum stay in Burma was one week, as laid down by the regime of General Ne Win, the military dictator who had taken power in a coup d'état in 1962. Using the excuse of communist and tribal insurgencies that had been ongoing since independence in 1948, Ne Win's generals had attempted to create a one-party socialist state. Private enterprise had been nationalised and foreign businesses forced to leave; but the programme had resulted in chronic economic breakdown, isolating Burma from the rest of the world and creating massive shortages of luxury goods. (In the night markets, we were told, you could buy Burmese jade for toothpaste, but that may not have been true.) A rich and fertile agrarian state that was once the largest exporter of rice in the world had been reduced to ruin. And, despite their best efforts, the military were unable to curtail the communists or the separatists, operating from bases in the mountainous jungles of the interior.

Along with the other travellers from our flight, we made our way from the airport to Rangoon's YMCA hostel in Maha Bandoola Street, a large concrete building suffocating in pre-monsoon heat that was, however, eminently pleasant compared to Delhi. En route, we were struck by the lushness of the vegetation, the houses on stilts, the palms, the orange-red blossoms of the flame trees, the trishaws and pony carts, the sarongs worn by both genders, the thanaka[8] smeared on the faces of women, the friendliness of everyone we met and the decay of the city centre.

Our neighbours at the hostel were an Australian couple fresh from Japan where they had amassed a small fortune staging sex shows in some Tokyo night club ('If you have to work,' the guy said, 'you might as well do something you enjoy.'), and a couple of New Age Frenchmen who didn't believe in 'chemical medicines' (the 'ch' pronounced as it is in 'chase') until one of them got sick during the night and came banging on our door to see if we by any chance had any 'chemical medicines'.

After settling in, we went downstairs to the restaurant, open on one side to the elements. Hungry after a long morning, we ordered what the Burmese misleadingly called 'soup'. Unfortunately, we also ordered mains. During the meal, we noticed a rat of mongoose proportions running about the garden. Andrew Selth, an Australian diplomat posted to this city in 1974 would later describe how '... *there was a lively debate among the diplomatic corps as to the most rat-infested public buildings [in Rangoon]. Many named the YMCA where backpackers often stayed...*'

'We have many rats in Rangoon,' a voice said. 'This one is the greater bandicoot rat. It grows to eleven inches and then there is the tail.' The voice belonged to 19-year-old Boon-Mee, a curly-headed, 20-year-old student seated at the next table. 'We have another with the name of the *lesser* bandicoot rat. That is the most common in the city. Maybe you have seen some damaged buildings? This is from the burrowing of the lesser bandicoot rat. It weakens the foundations, and the walls and pavements fall down.'

Nothing to do with the generals.

In those times, travel guide-books were still in the future. Although Tony and Maureen Wheeler, founders of *Lonely Planet*, had published *Across Asia On The Cheap* in 1973, most people had never heard of the 94-page stapled booklet. Information was gleaned from people coming the other way or you stumbled on it yourself. You can therefore imagine the surprise of hitting the streets of Rangoon, looking up, and finding a 367-foot pagoda looking back from Singuttara Hill. Shaped like a bell and plated in gold, this, it transpired, was the most important

---

8.   A yellowish cosmetic paste made from ground bark.

Buddhist shrine in Burma and one of the oldest religious sites in the world. Legend had it that the original stupa was erected to house eight hairs of the Buddha, brought back to Rangoon by Burmese merchants in 500 BC.

Close up, the complex was massive, with the principal stupa surrounded by sixty-four smaller pagodas, seventy-two shrines and dozens of statues and icons. And tiles that burned our bare feet as we hopped about in the mad tropical heat to the amusement of the maroon-robed child-monks who seemed to be everywhere. Along with its coat of gold, estimated at twenty-seven metric tons, the top of the stupa, too high for the eye to discern, was decorated with 5,448 diamonds, 2,317 rubies, sapphires and other gems, and 1,065 golden bells. At one time it had also housed the world's biggest bell.

Back at the YMCA, our friend, Boon-Mee, enlightened us.

'King Dhammazedi, a Mon king of Lower Burma ordered a census to be done in the second half of the 15th century. When his ministers also took too much tax from the people - nearly 300 tonnes of copper - the king became very angry. To calm him down, the ministers suggested that he could use the copper to make the biggest bell in the world that could be given as a present to Schwedagon. The bell was to be twelve cubits high and eight cubits wide and would weigh 294 tonnes. It was made in 1484. [We had no idea what a cubit was.]

'The bell was in Schwedagon until 1608 when the Portuguese stole it to make cannon guns. They rolled it down Singuttara Hill to Pazundaung Creek. Then elephants pulled it on a raft to the Rangoon River where it was tied to a Portuguese warship. But, somewhere close to Monkey Point, the raft broke and the bell sank, and also the ship. Five years later, in 1613, the Burmese killed all of the Portuguese and executed Filipe de Brito, their leader, on a bamboo stake.'

The bell has never been found.

Just before dark, a peal of thunder cracked with that bomb-sound of the tropics and the rain came down in white sheets. Within seconds a silver cataract poured from the restaurant awning into the garden to the delight of three naked children who danced in glee as the water gushed over them. Outside, anything that wasn't firmly tied down slithered away in a brown torrent.

'You go now,' one of the hustlers who hung about the YMCA whispered in my ear. We were seated under a sign that said 'No black market here'. 'There is a man outside who will buy Johnnie Walker and the three fives.'

* * *

After two days of steamy Rangoon, we left for Mandalay on a morning train of riveted steel panels with wooden interiors hauled by a steam engine. We shared our carriage with a cross-section of Burma's rural and urban dwellers, two Buddhist monks, a mountain of bags and boxes, and chickens that escaped from a cage and ran about the floor. An old woman with a charming, toothless smile and eyes like a frog sat opposite us with her grandson in the knee-knocking intimacy of cane seats inhabited by the same bugs that had ambushed the backs of my legs, at shorts level, in the restaurant of the YMCA.

At regular intervals the old woman's face would show signs of hunger. She would reach down behind her tiny feet - the result of foot-binding in her youth - and produce yet another basket of cooked prawns to offer around, until Cora and I were immersed in a crunching, ankle-deep midden of shells. Other people showered us with biscuits and fruit purchased from station vendors who often travelled long distances with the train, to finally jump off at fantastic speeds, their legs spinning as they hit the ground.

'How,' I asked Cora, 'do you practice something like that?'

'I haven't a clue,' Cora said. 'I'm reading.'

In the afternoon it rained and the wooden shutters went up, blotting out most of the daylight. The roof leaked and the heat in the compartment raised a stench from the prawn-shells, eggshells, chicken crap and fruit skins that littered the floor. I left Cora - no longer reading, but dozing in the seat - and went to sit at an open door between carriages. Outside, rural Burma rolled by in grey rain as we droned on towards Mandalay.

Houses on stilts with tin roofs were wrapping up against the monsoon which was bringing churning rivers from the high jungles to join the Irriwaddy, one of the chief trade routes to Burma's mountainous north and east. In land already inundated, and in small lakes, people were fishing and paddling small boats. In the paddy fields along the western base of the Shan Plateau, men and women guided ox-drawn wooden ploughs through thick mud, the rain spilling off their conical cane hats. Children rode on black buffaloes, one with a shotgun across his lap. How, I wondered, could you leap from a speeding train, hit the ground and not cartwheel into oblivion?

* * *

We stayed three days in Mandalay, at a guesthouse run by a plump, jovial woman in her mid-fifties who smoked endless fat cheroots and went by the name of 'Auntie', not Auntie anyone in particular, just plain old 'Auntie'. Her face heavily made up and her hair tied back in a bun, she was an unusual member of the guesthouse-proprietor class.

'Before the revolution,' she told us through her interpreter Sai, quiet, thin, and possibly in his early thirties, 'I had two factories that made soap. The government took one; but before they could take the other, I destroyed it myself. Now, the guesthouse is my life. Not to make the money, but to make the people who come to Mandalay happy.'

Sai pointed to the free tea and mangoes as evidence of Auntie's bounty.

On our first morning in Mandalay, Auntie and Sai brought us to see the ruins of her second factory to show us how well she had wrecked it. With a mix of sadness and defiance, she showed us where each stage of production had taken place.

'You understand' Sai said, 'Auntie is a strong woman. She does not have fear.' He himself did have fear, having spent several years as a political prisoner of the regime.

Leaving the ruined factory behind, we drove to wooded Mandalay Hill and climbed 735 feet past demons and ogres to the Sutaungpyai Pagoda, built where the Buddha was said to have predicted the rise of a great religious city. Auntie, who had waited at the base of the hill, then went home with her driver, a gentle, slightly-built, bespectacled man of about sixty. Sai, Cora and I hit the nearest pub where we were each given an empty bottle and a coupon that entitled us to refills from a cask in the corner. If you preferred, you could have a macabre pink infusion with lumps of white matter floating on top. The pub called it tea.

While we rehydrated on beer, Sai who was of the Shan minority spoke bitterly of his people's struggle for separation from Burma.

'Shan resistance goes back to the 16th century when the Shan kingdoms came under attack from the Burmans. They fought back and did not allow themselves to be ruled by the Burmans. During British rule in the 19th century, the Shan area was controlled by the British 'Governor of India' as a separate state. But in 1921 the British made the Shan State a province of Burma.

'In February 1947, at the Panglong Conference, our Independence leader, Aung San, met with ethnic groups, and agreed that the Shan, Chin and Kachin people would have full autonomy. Aung San was assassinated in July of that year, six months before independence, and some fighting developed when the British left, but the agreement held until the coup of 1962. General Ne Win broke the agreement. Ethnic leaders were arrested and the Burmese army began to attack the people in the mountains. The Shan and the other groups have been fighting for justice and independence since then. At the moment the government in Rangoon controls only twelve percent of the country.'

Sai never mentioned why he himself had been imprisoned.

We left the bar and took a taxi to the ruins of Mandalay's old royal palace, destroyed during World War II by allied bombing. From there it was a short walk to the Royal Palace Monastery where, reunited with Auntie's driver - and an Englishman who went by the name of Grapes - we ran into the Nats.

The monastery was originally part of the royal palace in Amarapura. When the capital of the Burmese kingdom was moved to Mandalay in 1857, the building followed and became part of the new royal palace. When King Mindon died in 1878, his son moved the building to its current location outside the palace grounds and converted it into a monastery, which saved it from the bombing of World War II. Built entirely of exquisitely-carved teak, it contained depictions of mythical creatures, animals, dancers and flowers. In the main chamber an image of the Buddha was being worshipped by Nat spirits. Cora, being a woman, was not allowed into this part of the building. The Nats were clearly misogynists.

Buddhism is said to have arrived in Burma in the third century BC, but it didn't establish itself in earnest until the 11th century when the empire-builder, King Anawrahta, was converted by a Mon priest. But beneath the surface, old animist traditions of Nat worship bubbled away, gradually fusing themselves into Burmese Buddhism regardless of efforts to stamp them out.

Here are Nat facts later imparted to us by Boon-Mee at Rangoon's YMCA: Nats are spirits. They are everywhere - in trees, in rocks, in caves, on mountain peaks, on the bends of rivers. They can bring luck and prosperity to those who appease them and danger and misfortune to those who don't. There are male and female Nats, most of them malevolent. The worst and most powerful are those that have evolved from people who died horrible deaths. You have to bring the Nats food and water.

Nat homes, about a foot high and containing offerings of food, were to be found beside many Burmese homes. A bit like the leprechaun I housed in the back garden as a child. (The worst day ever was when the ungrateful little shit buggered off.)

As we made our way home from the monastery, the night stalls were filling the pavements. Food was cooking; carts, drawn by horses and bullocks, were arriving with vegetables; bats were swooping on the insect bonanzas of street lights; and 555 cigarettes were being sold *individually* at the top end of the market.

'See,' Sai said back at the guesthouse, 'Aunty has sprayed your room.' The floor was littered with the dead: mosquitoes, cockroaches, spiders, ants and a scorpion. 'Tomorrow,' Sai promised, 'you will go to Sagaing Hill where there are 600 pagodas with golden roofs and more than 6,000 monks and nuns. It is twelve miles from here. Aunty's driver will take you there.'

'I wish we had more time in Burma,' Cora said. 'There's so much to do and see.'

'It is possible,' Sai said. 'Do you have a pen?' He took a scrap of paper from his pocket, borrowed my biro and scribbled down a name: General Zhang Qifu. 'If you have time when you go to Thailand, you can maybe call to this man and he can take you back over the border. He is the commander of a Shan army fighting the government of Burma. If you go to the village of Ban Hin Taek the people will contact him for you.'

'Thank you very much,' I said. 'That would be great.'

'Is there something the matter with your head?' Cora asked.

Sometimes it can be hard to win.

When Sai left, we turned on the rickety fan, plugged some of the holes in the window's mosquito mesh and let on we were in The Ritz.

The following afternoon found us having tea and biscuits with a Buddhist monk - a friend of Aunty's driver - in a monastery that was part of the sprawling Buddhist complex of Sagaing Hill. The monk, a gentle, pious old man with large protruding ears and a poker face, sat like the Buddha himself, served us cake, bananas and mangoes, and said that we should visit all of Sagaing Hill's pagodas. As that would have taken longer than a Burmese visa, we chose the U Min Thone Ze Temple with its crescent of forty-five gleaming, golden-caped Buddhas, and the Soon U Ponya Shin Pagoda, reached by a covered staircase that ran 780 feet uphill to dizzy vistas of the Irrawaddy River and the plains beyond.

To the south the rains had come on with a vengeance. Houses had become islands with boats tied to their stilts. Animals were sheltering on atolls of high ground. Trees and bamboo thickets were rising from their own reflections. The railway track was a great serpent gliding above the submerged fields of the Irrawaddy Plain. It was the time of leeches, displaced snakes, wallowing buffaloes and jubilant amphibians.

Crossing this sodden landscape I raised the dent created in our finances by the flight into Burma and the onward flight to Bangkok. (No cheap flights in those times.)

'The hop from here to Bangkok will be decisive. Once we make that jump we won't have enough money to backtrack if for any reason we need to.'

'In for a penny, in for a pound.' Cora said.

Back in Rangoon they had no room at the YMCA but the friendly staff let us sleep on the stage of the hall where young men practised bando, a kind of kung fu. We laid our sleeping bags on the floor and climbed in, and a big fat rat galloped over Cora's chest.

Jesus, Mary and Saint Joseph!

CHAPTER 4

Domain Of The Opium King

*'The Thai Song Greet near Hualamphong station. Of course it's long
gone now, but kinda refreshing to imagine there being so few places in
Bangkok where you could reliably meet Western travellers back then.'*
Comment from just_bob on a *Lonely Planet* website in 2008,
describing Bangkok in the 1970s.

* * *

Along with this small, three-storey hotel, there was also the Malaysia.

In June 1976, in the so-called Land of Smiles, the Malaysia Hotel was
a drab, high-rise, concrete block of 120 rooms[9], overlooking breadfruit
trees, coconut palms and its own swimming pool. Since the end of the
Indo-China War, when the G.I. clientele was lost, prices had been cut
in half. Four U.S. dollars for a double.

A note pinned to the back of each door, warning chiefly against
possession of drugs, also contained the following under Section
E: *'Kindly be advise that hotel guests of the opposite SEX are not
authorised to visit Bachelor in your rooms - of this command to you
or take your guests to your room too - However, careful observance
of your - incur the RISK.'*

In other words, no stray women in the bedrooms. But in the
bedrooms they were, and hanging out the windows, and outside the
lobby and over at the pool.

The Malaysia had been built in 1967 as part of the hotel-building spree
aimed at the U.S. troop trade during the Indochina wars. It became a
haunt of the travellers in 1975 when the Americans fled Vietnam with

---

9.   After major redevelopment, it is today a much more salubrious establishment

their tails between their legs. Low prices now meant low maintenance as evidenced in the peeling paint, loose wires, broken cisterns and roaring air-conditioning. The loss of the U.S. troops had also left behind a population of underemployed sex workers, some attracted to the low-budget trade at the Malaysia despite the watchful eye of a leather-faced, pot-bellied old patriarch who sometimes guarded the lobby. After close on a decade of G.I. indulgence, the old man was the last champion of Section E of the bedroom notes, and would occasionally rise from his chair with a growl and charge forth in singlet, shorts and flip-flops to physically eject any dodgy-looking woman trying to sneak past. One misplaced effort during our stay involved the Thai wife of one of his foreign guests.

Bangkok in 1976 was a humid, noisy, violent city obscured by fumes and dust. Along with the rest of Thailand, homicides were on an epidemic scale in a country suffering the spillover from the Indochina wars, the crime surge linked to the country's heroin trade, in-fighting between gangsters, high levels of domestic murders and random street killings. (A row between a Coca-Cola vendor and a Pepsi vendor over who should trade at a particular corner culminated in one of them shooting the other dead.) Shop-fronts in the city were filled with gruesome photos of mutilated bodies and bloated corpses fished from the canals. You were advised to leave your passport in the hotel safe, carry only essential money and not wear jewellery in the streets. However, the most life-threatening gamble eventually turned out to be the act of venturing out into the city's traffic and surviving the buses. This we discovered in the company of 24-year-old Patricia, a German woman of calm disposition and very blonde hair who was an investigative journalist at home and a neighbour of ours at the Malaysia. 'That was very strange,' Patricia would say each time we braved the wonders of Bangkok.

The guiding maxim on the buses was that they were never full. When our conveyance wheeled up to the kerb at Rama IV Road, there was already attached to the outside a large part of the human race. We were to somehow stitch ourselves to its extremity.

Some kindly Thais who saw our alarm dropped from the knot. A cavity to the interior opened and Cora and the placid Patricia were sucked inside. To my horror, I was left to cling to the knot, my back arched to the slipstream. When a further layer attached itself to me I began to react with the desperation that drives drowning people to batter the crap out of other drowning people in the scramble for the lifeboats. Whosoever was going to be shaken loose, it bloody-well wasn't going to be me. Finally, like a piece of rubble in a glacier, I was pushed through the door. The problem now would be getting out again at the other end.

Our goal that Saturday morning was to visit the Grand Palace and the city's weekend market, said to be the biggest open-air market in the world. An unexpected outcome would be a journey into the wilds of northern Thailand.

In the extravaganza of tents, parasols, stalls, carts, baskets and animals that made up the market, Patricia spotted some diversions. In one corner two men had gathered a small crowd by teasing a pair of cobras, then chasing after them with a wooden box. In another, a fire-eater sprayed flames on the crowd. In a third, four children with shaved heads and costumes of red and black were dancing and singing to the rhythm of cymbals while their father tapped on a small drum.

'I think they are hill people from the north,' Patricia said. 'From an area close to Laos and Burma. The Golden Triangle. That is where all the heroin comes from. I think it is possible to walk there.'

'Before you say anything...' Cora advised. But it was too late.

By the day's end I was elaborating like an old hand on our new project with Patricia and two others who had joined us during an obligatory stroll through the night market of Patpong, the red-light district that had in its day done for many an American G.I. and would in the future host the rampant international sex safaris that would flood its streets along with those of Pattaya and Phuket.

'So, now you have a plan?' Patricia said as we all had dinner together.

'There's no plan,' Cora said. 'It just grows in any old way, and not always for the best.'

'That's a bit unfair,' I said even if it wasn't.

During a break in the plan, Jean-Marie from France told of how he once had a travelling companion taken by a Nile crocodile as they both forded a river in Ethiopia.

'He thought it was a rock and stood on it. The crocodile lashed him with its tail and then dragged him under the water. There was nothing I could do.'

Uget from Switzerland told how she'd been robbed in her hotel room that very morning.

'And I woke up with an eejit,' Cora said as I burbled on about the Golden Triangle.

Caught in my growing enthusiasm, Patricia decided to move in with Jean-Marie.

'*Oh o-ui,*' Jean-Marie mouthed when Patricia, ample of bosom, wasn't looking.

Cora was also inspired. By the time we were back at the Malaysia that night, she was a convert to the Golden Triangle.

* * *

Dominique had about him the refined features of an intellectual. Tall, angular, and square-jawed, with wire-rimmed glasses and a flop of fair hair that hung in waves to his shoulders, he was dressed in shorts, sandals and an open shirt that showed a frame stripped of all excess flesh. Sindi, a petite woman with long straw-coloured hair tied back in a bun, wore glasses and sandals similar to Dominique's, along with a loose black shirt and white Indian trousers.

Shortly after we had met on the overnight bus from Bangkok to Chiang Mai, Dominique and Sindi had become the other half of our new expedition.

'We also have another option,' I remembered. 'We have the name of a rebel general who lives in northern Thailand and might be able to sneak us into Burma for a look around.'

'Because we go home to France soon,' Sindi said, 'we can be reckless, but not that reckless.'

'He'll be alright in a minute,' Cora said. And that was the end of that.

Red-eyed from lack of sleep, we arrived in the morning by trishaw at *Je t'Aime Riverside*, one of the better cheapies of Chiang Mai. The collection of brick and tile bungalows sat in a garden of cashew trees, coconut palms and banana plants on the banks of the Ping River about a mile from the town. Each bungalow consisted of a spacious room, and a bathroom with a glassless window that beckoned to mosquitoes, spiders, geckos - and the black scorpion that was sleeping in our bed. We were met by the owner, a small, lean man with receding temples who was in his early thirties.

'Greetings,' he beamed as he led us to our bungalows. 'You have come to the most beautiful lodge in Chiang Mai. My name is Wanchardan. I am the owner. Also I am an artist. When you are free, maybe tomorrow, you can come to my gallery in the town.'

'Certainly,' I said. 'And maybe you can help us. We're planning to walk in the Golden Triangle and need some information.'

'That will not be a problem,' Wanchardan said. 'I have a map at the gallery. When you come to visit, I will give it to you.'

This was good news. Going into the jungle with a map was far better than going into the jungle without a map. Until we saw the map.

'It is here somewhere,' Wanchardan said. We were in the gallery and he was poking about in a drawer. 'Ah, 'I have it.' He handed me a small Manilla envelope on which somebody had drawn a squiggly line with dots denoting the villages of Banmai, Cienka, Noyai, Koumintang and Yappa. That was the map. Next to Cienka Wanchardan had written 'saw-pits'.

Over the coming days Dominique, Sindi, Cora and I walked the temples of Chiang Mai. In the evenings we constructed our Golden Triangle itinerary with the aid of Wanchardan's map.

'Not much better,' Cora said, 'than a copy of the *Beano*.'

In defence, we were novices. Jungles? So what...? If there were moments of doubt, they were linked to the 150 tons of heroin coming down annually from the Golden Triangle and the resultant levels of crime and police activity to be found in Chiang Mai. Most troubling, as evidenced by the story of a New Zealand couple, was that crime and cops were often one and the same thing.

The couple had been asleep in their room in the town when the cops came bursting in, one of them brandishing a submachine-gun.

'You've been smoking heroin,' the submachine-gun cop said.

'No, we haven't,' they said. Whereupon the cop took a phial from his pocket and sprinkled white powder over the bed.

'Now, you have,' he said. 'You pay fifty dollars.'

When the cops left, they fled to *Je t'Aime*.

'By the way,' the woman added, 'there's a French guy in the local clink. He got two years for a tiny trace of smack in one of his pockets. He needs people to visit him and bring him food.'

Dominique, Sindi, Cora and I went to the prison the next day. At the doom-laden gate, Dominique had a thought.

'What if they frame us like the couple from New Zealand?'

'He needs us,' Sindi said. 'He's French. We must go.'

'We're Irish,' Cora reminded me as we entered.

While waiting to be processed in a rough reception area that smelled of piss and dread, a cop stood beside us, took a Buddha stick[10] from his pocket, casually rolled it between fingers and thumb and looked us up and down. The other cops ran a three-monkeys show.

There were also normal bandits in Chiang Mai, partial to western denims and much given to stripping travellers on the way home to places like *Je t'Aime Riverside*. The dozen or so travellers at the lodge

---

10. Powerful Thai marijuana threaded around a five-inch sliver of bamboo.

therefore tended to cover the lonely mile from town in daylight, and pass away the evenings in the restaurant, swapping yarns and chilling out on Buddha grass and mugs of Milo. On our final such evening, a three-foot green snake swallowed a frog outside our door.

News came through shortly afterwards from Wanchardan that one of the restaurant staff had been busted in town trying to buy heroin for some foreigner. Paranoia draped a sinister veil over *Je t'Aime*.

'Bad signs,' Cora said. 'The night before we head up north.'

* * *

A four-hour bus ride took us from Chiang Mai to Fang. The road followed the Ping River through rice fields and villages before climbing into the Chiang Dao Valley where elephants hauled logs down dirt tracks to trucks that were carrying away Thailand's teak forests. We reached Fang in the middle of the day.

Nestling among the hills of the Shan Plateau, nothing of the town's compact appearance betrayed its reputation as a conduit for opium smugglers, a recruiting ground of warlords, and home to remnants of Chiang Kai Shek's Kuomintang army who had fled China after the Communist takeover of 1949. The only prominent feature was a smiling, stringy trishaw man in an undersized straw hat, white singlet and knee-length shorts, who was waiting at the bus station.

'You like stay my home?' he asked. 'Good food, good sleep.'

'Ah,' he said when we accepted. 'No more vorking today.'

With the four of us and our packs compressed into the two seats of the trishaw, we set off along a dirt track until we came to a bamboo and thatch hut rising on stilts from the middle of a field. A large tree sheltered the roof from the afternoon sun.

'This my vife,' our host said as a thin woman with hair tied back climbed down from the house to greet us. 'And this my chidderen,' he added, proudly pointing to a girl of fourteen and a boy of eight.

'Ve go up,' he said, lifting Sindi's pack and taking off up the ladder. But, we had barely set our packs down when the plan changed and the second of many sudden pronouncements came.

'Ve go take shower.' He led the way back down the steps and across through an area of swamp until we came to what could only be described as a raging flood.

'Ve svim here,' the madman declared, pointing at the passing tangle of broken trees, swirling brown water and dirty scuds of yellow foam. Before anyone could stop him he dived in, to be whipped fifty yards downstream in a blink.

'This man is dangerous,' was Sindi's view as he dragged himself with some difficulty clear of the torrent. Next on the agenda was a walk through tall, broad-bladed grass that nicked our legs with sharp edges.

'You vatch! You careful! You vatch!' our man shouted, pointing at our feet to illustrate some grave threat that lived in the grass and had us hopping and yelping at the slightest touch. Back at the hut we discovered the nature of the threat: leeches.

Our host was now emerging as a man with a deep sense of obligation towards his guests. He had few resources; but we would reap the benefit of them all.

'I haf Mrs. Bong,' he said, gingerly producing a home-made bamboo water-pipe from under an old towel. 'Maybe you haf Mr. Ganja?'

Dominique pulled out a Buddha stick and Mrs. Bong was on. We were then shown everything in the house that was moveable, including a flintlock rifle tucked away in the rafters.

'For scare bad man. Now ve eat.' He called to his wife who was cooking on a fire beneath the house.

We had no sooner started into our omelettes and rice, than the insects came. Hundreds of them. Flying out of an advanced dusk, flapping disproportionately large wings, they descended from the open windows and the space between the walls and the roof. Drawn by two naked oil lamps, they got in our hair, beat around our faces and dropped into our omelettes. As each was felled by the flames, the host snatched it up, ran it back over the nearest lamp for an even roast, and popped it into his mouth.

'Number one food in Thai-land,' he announced.

By the time we had eaten, the insects had all suicided over the oil lamps and it was pitch black outside. We were sitting with the door open and the bong in rotation, listening to the crickets and watching the fireflies when an uproarious bellowing rose from the swamp.

'Ah,' our man said. 'Ung-ang.[11] Number one food in Thai-land... Now, ve go my cousin's house.'

It was to be the coup de grace. Leading us through the night along a dark dirt path full of hopping and fluttering bugs, he steered us to a wooden house among the trees. 'No talk Mrs. Bong,' he urged as he

---

11.   We later read that this was the Asian Painted Frog.

ushered us inside. There, while the 'cousin' and his wife, a couple in their forties, brought tea, cake and lychees, and introduced their sons, and we all sat on the floor in the light of oil lanterns and did small talk for an hour, their young daughter watched coyly from a corner of the room. Then our man got up and went to a large framed photograph on the wall. The winner and runners-up in a Miss Universe competition. A tad out of place on the edge of the jungle.

He pointed to the young woman in second place. He then arced his finger across to the shy young woman tucked away in the corner.

'Same, same,' he said. 'She number two in universe.'

Early next morning we bade goodbye to our trishaw man at Fang bus station. It was now another hour along a rough track through hills and forests to the village of Tha Ton where the road, such as it was, terminated at the Kok River. The morning was sticky and overcast, but tempered by a cool breeze from the river. The rainforest was humming with insects.

Over bowls of noodles, we waited at the village wharf for the boat that would take us downriver to our trailhead at the tiny hamlet of Banmai, the first dot on Wanchardan's map. Gradually we were joined by villagers who had come upriver to trade and were now returning to the bush. There were halting efforts to communicate; but in the end, we simply provided the entertainment.

'This is it,' Sindi said.

'This is it,' Cora agreed. 'Are we right in the head?'

'Maybe we should check the map,' Dominique said, 'to see where we are.' He wasn't serious. And there was no point anyway. Wanchardan hadn't written us in.

From here on our real map would have to be the hill people living in one of the most lawless places on Earth.

* * *

We left Tha Ton at noon on a long skiff, powered by an outboard motor with an extended screw that trailed behind to give excellent manoeuvrability. Eight passengers in all and a good deal of baggage. The boatman, a lean, middle-aged man in a navy tunic and baggy grey trousers, stood at the back and pushed us off with a pole before whipping the engine to life. An hour would take us to Banmai. Half way there, the skies blackened for a ten-minute downpour that peppered the river and silenced the jungle.

(At that very moment, we later learned, Patricia, our placid German friend from Bangkok, was being robbed at gunpoint on a beach in Phuket. All she had, apart from her bikini, were a towel and sunglasses. 'Maybe you want my bikini,' she said. In the end the clever bandit took her sunglasses.)

There are points in life where you meet yourself coming back. You head off full of steam only to bump into your reflection striding towards you with a big *Maybe you should think about this*. Such a point was to be found at Banmai. It began when the mud of the track met the flip-flops of the feet. This mirrored the general state of our equipment. We hadn't a boot between us. Our map was an envelope. Dominique and Sindi were sharing a single sleeping bag. Our food consisted of a few tins of sardines and some sweet biscuits. And now a new thought...

'I wonder,' mused I, 'if there are tigers in the forest? They roam other parts of Thailand.'

'It's a bit late to be asking that,' Sindi said. She was smiling which suggested at that moment that she might not be the full shilling.

We decided to sit down and mull over these issues. Dominique rolled a smoke to help us along.

'After all,' Cora said, 'we don't want to do anything stupid, do we?'

But never let it be said. Deciding that we were as good as we were likely to be, we barged on through Banmai's rice-paddies and out into the forest. At the second dot on our map - the Lisu village of Cienka, a collection of bamboo huts at the base of the mountains - we stopped for directions; but the only signs of life were the pigs and chickens that wallowed in muddy spaces between the huts. 'Anybody home?' we shouted. Nothing. We spread out and called again. Nothing. Eventually a young boy peered from a crack in one of the doorways.

'Noyai?' Sindi asked. The boy pointed up the nearest hill. Fifteen minutes later we were hopelessly lost and had to retrace our steps. A second attempt and we found the track: a near-vertical slog that brought sweat and cursing in equal measures. We waded creeks. We crossed log bridges. We climbed again, rising above the green heat into the forests of the Shan Plateau. An hour out of Cienka the track deteriorated to a mudslide. Our flip-flops were useless, so we went barefoot, the mud squirting up between our toes, and poisonous, 10-inch centipedes scurrying by at our walking pace.

Late afternoon saw us high on a hill and still climbing, the forest silent except for the occasional startled bird, the river a silver vein far below. In a swidden of sprouting maize we checked our legs for leeches. Sindi nursed her feet, earlier stung by red ants. As she did, a loud buzzing rose from the forest.

'Chainsaws?' I wondered. 'It's hard to imagine anyone up here with a chainsaw.'

'Those are not chainsaws,' Dominique said. 'They are a kind of insect. Cicadas.'

'The map,' Cora said. 'Remember how it said saw-pits near Cienka? The "saw-pits" are up in the bloody trees.'

A confidence crisis: if saw-pits could become cicadas, did Noyai, the Lahu village in which we planned to spend the night, actually exist? And if it did, how far away was it? Without a tent, sleeping in the mire of the earlier rain would be unthinkable. Continuing through the forest after dark would be impossible. With no choice, we plodded on, exhausted and resigned to the possibility of sitting against some tree for the night.

'Perhaps it is not very wise to be walking around in the jungle without a guide,' Dominique said as we passed a clump of bamboo in the day's fading light.

'We'll be alright,' I said, although 'alright' was prone to interpretation.

'Wa-a-a-gh!' Dominique yelled. He jumped to one side and scared the shite out of the rest of us. Almost invisible against the bamboo, a man was hunched in a squatting position. He was cradling a flintlock rifle.

'Noyai?' Dominique asked after we had all recovered.

The man lowered the rifle and pointed straight ahead. I tried a bit of sign-language: forward-slicing of the hands, then spreading wide of the arms. The man extended both arms and with a smile brought the hands close together.

'Not far to go,' I translated. I was delighted.

Half an hour later, we arrived at a muddy hilltop village where we re-shod with the flip-flops to avoid picking up nasty intestinal hookworms through our feet. In the cluster of stilted bamboo huts, children, pigs and chickens scattered. Three men, coming out of the forest, stopped in their tracks. All shouldered flintlock rifles. Heavy machetes, like short-bladed Samurai swords, hung from their waists in bamboo sheaths. One man carried a section of bamboo on a rope - his water container. When we reached the centre of the compound, a young woman, probably in her late teens and wearing a blue shirt, green tunic and black sarong, came to the door of one of the huts. With the universal sign for sleeping and a corresponding mud-splashed wretchedness, we made clear that we would dearly love to spend the night in her home.

In the death of the day, we climbed the ladder to the hut, went inside and planted ourselves down on the split-bamboo floor in front of a small fire set on a stone flag. And as the young woman of the house began to prepare some food, we complimented ourselves on the success of day one and how fantastically we had conquered the jungle and the question of tigers.

'In bare feet and all,' I pointed out.

They looked after us well in Noyai. First came a meal of rice and unidentified greens, during which our clumsy attempts to eat with our hands brought dignified chuckling. Once we had eaten, a steady stream of villagers arrived. They felt our hair. They felt our clothes. They felt the weight of our packs. The women, wearing silver necklaces suspended from their ears and silver bangles on their wrists, were enthralled by Cora's and Sindi's jewellery. One with a baby to her breast wanted to swap silver for a plastic bangle of Sindi's. When Dominique dropped a water-purifying tablet into his canteen, you'd swear it was that wine business down at Cana all over again.

With each new batch of arrivals, our hostess would tell again how she had found us. Her husband, a powerfully built man in his early twenties who had arrived home after dark with a chopped-up banana plant for his pigs, would concur. The visitors would ask questions we didn't understand and we'd tell them things they didn't understand. Following my earlier success, I again tried sign language but it was hopeless. They just laughed at my antics.

After a couple of hours, when most people had left, an old man in a black tunic and trousers joined those of us still gathered around the fire. When a polite measure of time had passed, he edged in closer, pulled from his pocket a small silver pipe with a dark wooden bowl, and a ball of opium. And thus was the night laid to rest.

* * *

Back in the 1970s, the hills that bordered Thailand, Burma and Laos were uncharted wilderness controlled by warlords and their armies who ran a vast lucrative drugs trade. Deep in the jungle, fields of poppies farmed by the hill tribes bloomed each year from late December to early February. Once harvested, the poppies were converted to heroin in hidden refineries. The man at the top was a Burmese Shan separatist called Khun Sa who had become Opium King after the short-lived Opium War of 1967.

Prior to his rise in the opium trade, Khun Sa had been at the helm of an 800-strong militia supporting General Ne Win's Burmese dictatorship in its war against Shan separatists. But no sooner had his followers been armed by Rangoon than he seized large swathes of the Shan and Wa states and declared himself a Shan freedom fighter.

Simultaneously, he opened up a sideline in opium production.

This might have gone well for Khun Sa had his opium interests not clashed with similar interests held by remnants of the Kuomintang army that had fled China after their defeat in that country's civil war. Following months of tension and the occasional skirmish, the showdown came at Ban Khwan, a Laotian lumber village on the Mekong River close to where Burma, Laos and Thailand meet.

In June 1967 Khun Sa sent a column of 300 mules, 500 men and sixteen tons of opium on a 190-mile jungle trek from Ving Ngun in Burma to Ban Khwan. The opium was to be delivered to a refinery owned by General Ouane Rattikone, commander in chief of the Royal Lao Armed Forces and recent recipient of his nation's highest honour - The Grand Cross of the Million Elephants and the White Parasol.

The Kuomintang forces resident along the Thai-Burmese border were customarily paid to allow opium consignments through, but Khun Sa refused to cough up. Consequently, his opium train was harried by the Kuomintang who launched a first unsuccessful attack outside Kentung, about half way to Ban Khwan. On July 14th and 15th the two-kilometre mule train crossed the Mekong into Laos. Marching south, they reached Ban Khwan two days later.

The pursuing Kuomintang force, 800-strong, crossed the Mekong on July 24th and attacked Khun Sa's men at Ban Khwan on July 29th. In the ensuing battle more than 150 men were killed as both sides slogged it out with rifles, .50-calibre machineguns and mortars.

On the second day of the battle General Rattikone intervened. He sent six T-28 fighter planes to bomb both sides. Under the pressure of the bombing and the Kuomintang onslaught, 400 of Khun Sa's convoy retreated across the Mekong into Burma. The Kuomintang fled north only to be confronted by Laotian troops to whom they had to pay a levy of $7,500 dollars - big money in those days - so they could cross into Thailand. The Laotian army then made off with Khun Sa's opium and delivered it to General Rattikone. Although the general's Ban Khwan heroin refinery had been destroyed during the fighting, he reputedly had five more still in operation.

In 1969, Khun Sa was arrested by the Burmese and spent the next five years in solitary confinement while Chinese warlord, Ho Hsing Han, another of Ne Win's former allies, became the first 'Opium King' of what had now become known as The Golden Triangle. He in turn was arrested in 1973 by the Burmese who charged him with high treason. In the ensuing see-saw of events, the Burmese freed Khun Sa the following year after his second in command kidnapped two

Russian doctors as bargaining chips.

By 1976 Khun Sa had re-established himself along the mountainous jungles of Northern Thailand, replacing Ho Hsing Han as Opium King. With his headquarters on the Thai side of the border, he renamed his group The Shan United Army (which would eventually number 20,000 soldiers) and again began fighting for Shan autonomy while he and his fellow travellers produced seventy percent of the world's opium. In addition to his share of the trade, Khun Sa taxed the jungle mule trains of the weaker producers, adding hundreds of thousands of dollars a year to his coffers.

Due to the area's inaccessibility,[12] the easy movement between Burma, Laos and Thailand, the rampant corruption of generals and politicians, and the then political advantages to the West of having them there, the opium lords and their armies thrived. The harmony only suffered when one or other government made a half-hearted sortie against them, or when the opium lords themselves fell out as happened that June of 1976.

Lo Hsing Min, the younger brother of the imprisoned former opium king, had been kidnapped by the first commander of his jailed brother's army. The kidnapper, Wang Sing Hoh, known as 'White Elephant' and now believed to be in control of the Lo army, was demanding a one million baht ($46,000) ransom for his captive's release while moving him from hideout to hideout in the very country through which we were so nonchalantly wandering.

On our return to Bangkok, we also read in the *Bangkok Post* that a Thai border patrol had stumbled on a heroin refinery in the jungle, resulting in a firefight between the patrol and the refinery's operators.

* * *

We reached Lisu Banmai at noon on the second day, stopping long enough to fill our water canteens from a bamboo aqueduct coming down from the hills, and to have tea and eggs with a Lisu family in the village. Dominique and I got to pose with the smiling father of the family and his flintlock rifle.

In the afternoon, as the rain came on again and the track split in two, and Wanchardan's single-line map hit a new low, our expedition

---

12.   Most of the region could only be reached on foot or by mule.

discovered that Dominique and I were both natural-born pathfinders. This came as a surprise to Cora and Sindi. From then on, as the rain continued and the track broke into muddy ribbons winding off into the forest with no hint of which of them might lead to the Kuomintang village - known simply as Kuomintang - where we hoped to spend the night, we would have conversations.

'I think Kuomintang is this way,' I might say.'

'Look at the ground,' Dominique might say. 'That way looks more used.'

The women would look on, hands on hips. You know what I mean. No help at all.

Twice, however, we bowed to local knowledge, courtesy of two people we encountered. One of them, a sturdy woman galloping along with a heap of firewood on her back, stopped to laugh hysterically at our powers of locomotion.

'Hoo-hoo-hoo,' she went, mimicking Cora's panting as, barefoot and muck to the eyeballs, we slithered uphill through runnels of mud. Dominique and myself with drenched anoraks over our heads. Cora and Sindi huddling under a Thai umbrella of waxed paper.

In the end luck brought us to a high ridge from which we could see down to a valley with several small villages. Another half hour of skidding downhill confirmed our hopes. At the first village a half-naked Lahu woman, sitting on the ladder leading to the door of her hut, pointed the way. A bullock-trail led to the Kuomintang village.

'Thank you,' Dominique said. In that momentary lapse of concentration, he stepped into a nest of red ants.

'FUCK IT!' he yelled and hopped about like Rudolf Nureyev, a signal for the rain to stop.

The Kuomintang village boasted neat, well-stocked gardens, healthy pigs and chickens, and wooden corn-grinding 'mills' rigged up to the river. As soon as we landed we were greeted by a thirty-something Chinese man in jeans and T-shirt.

'You like Coca-Cola?' he asked. We were back from the hills. 'You visit Yappa? Yappa is village of free love.'

We never would discover the background to such a view of the Akha village that was also on Wanchardan's map.

Not surprisingly, the Coca-Cola man's shop doubled up as the village guesthouse, where Cora and I shared a bamboo platform with the mosquitoes and three other travellers who had arrived from some other direction - Mike and Kevin from Australia and an American woman called Chandra. Dominique and Sindi stayed with the family next door.

When Kevin heard that we had been through Lisu Banmai, he told us that he and Mike had also passed through a couple of days earlier.

'And there was this big German insulting the food he'd been given by one of the families. "Give me a piece of elephant, none of these fucking leaves" he was shouting. Until the father pulled down a flintlock rifle and stuck it in his mouth.'

We established that this was the same lovely man who, same rifle in hand, had posed with myself and Dominique.

As we ate that night, a mingling of subdued voices gathered outside the hut.

'People coming,' the Coca-Cola man said. At that, the door slowly opened and a sturdy barefoot woman with a face gracefully refined by fifty or so years stepped into the frame. In the dim light of two kerosene lamps she was the full visual sensation. Puffing on a pipe with a long, curved silver stem, she wore an indigo tunic and short skirt, silver bangles, multi-coloured leggings that ran from ankle to knee, and a spectacular, conical cloth headdress bedecked with tufts of fur and row upon row of silver discs and coins. Working her way along the far wall of the hut, she ran her eyes from one of us to the other without saying a word. And if that wasn't enough to root us to our benches, five more pipe-smoking women, similarly dressed, followed her through the door. At which point eating was done.

'Who the hell are they?' Cora whispered.

'I haven't a clue,' I whispered back.

'Akhas,' the Coca-Cola man said from the side. 'People of free love. Sometimes they are coming if foreign people are here.'

'Ooops!' Kevin said. 'Here comes the antidote to free love.'

Four men and a young boy, all in black pantaloons, tunic-shirts and brightly-woven hats, were filtering in through the door, each with a pipe, machete, and flintlock rifle.

While the Akhas settled on benches and leaned against the walls of the hut, Cora wondered if museum figures came to life.

'They would like to talk to you,' the Coca-Cola man said, breaking the spell. There then followed one of those remarkable conversations full of laughter, silences and short animated bursts where nobody knows what anybody else is saying. And where everybody gets to feel hair and clothes, and check out jewellery and sleeping bags and flintlock rifles and teeth. Until eventually, Chandra, Cora, the Coca-Cola man (as interpreter) and one of the younger Akha women built a side conversation that everyone seemed to enjoy. The Akha woman then took off her headdress.

'You like to buy?' the Coca-Cola man asked. 'Good souvenir.'

Chandra bought the headdress.

After an hour or so, the Akhas suddenly gathered themselves up, chorused goodbye in English and traipsed back into the night to leave behind an imprint bigger than the hut and as long as life.

Tomorrow, a young Akha man, leading a horse, would pass through the village. Dominique, Sindi, Cora and I would then walk with him into the cicada-shrilling hills to Yappa. Close to the village of low huts we'd be met by the grotesque leer of a dead dog stretched over a raised triangular frame. From the supports of the village gate, wooden carvings representing the animist spirits of the Akhas would stare down at us, the power of creation enshrined in enormous sexual organs. Above them, on an overhead beam, we'd find a miniature carving of a helicopter.[13]

But tonight would forever be the night the Akhas came through Kuomintang.

* * *

Dominique and Sindi decided to extend their stay in the bush. Cora and I decided we'd return to the Kok and follow it down to Chiang Rai. We left Kuomintang by the bullock-trail and stayed with it for most of a day through villages of the Lisu, Lahu and Karen, with only a brief stop for sardines and biscuits by a marsh of steaming vents and sulphurous springs. Reaching the river close to the village of Tamakang, we waited for a skiff to take us back down to Banmai.

At Banmai, we were directed to the house of headman, Mr. Koh. He wasn't at home, but Mrs. Koh, a slender, middle-aged woman with greying hair and skin like creased leather, signalled that we could stay the night, then busied herself to avoid awkward attempts to communicate. An hour later, a powerful, smiling man in shorts, T-shirt and machete, came striding out of the forest with the other men of Banmai to officially welcome us to his village and his home.

* * *

At eleven o'clock the following day, we were back at the river, waiting for the boat to Chiang Rai. On the muddy bank that served as a boat-

---

13. Somebody told us later that the president had visited the area in a helicopter. True or false, I have no idea.

halt we joined two other men, both of them Karens. The older of the two was in his late forties, lean and muscular with close-cropped hair. He was perched on a wooden rail like a bird. The younger, in his twenties, with an enormous grinning face, was an animated conversationalist unvexed by the limitations of sign language and mud drawings.

I asked to see the older man's machete - the sawn-off-shotgun version of the Samurai sword. This triggered a sign frenzy on the part of the younger man. From what we could understand, his friend had in the course of life's rigours, stalked and killed five men with that very machete. Men with guns. The older man grinned and nodded modestly, while his protégé ran a finger across his throat, threw his head back, closed his eyes and fell over.

I handed back the razor-sharp machete and attempted to show due respect. Really, we were just passing through, and minding our own business to boot, which wasn't much business at all. It was a great relief when the noon boat from Tha Ton swung around the bend to deliver us from the whittling skills of the birdman.

'Howdy folks.' The voice belonged to a lone, bearded white man, half-lost in the throng of the boat. He rose to his feet to help us get our packs on board as the crowded skiff spluttered to a halt against the mudbank. 'Name's Richard, all the way from Canada. I take it you're here to shoot the rapids.'

'Not good,' Cora said. 'The locals are sinking into the belly of the boat.'

But, apart from a couple of shudders on submerged rocks, a bit of a drenching at each set of rapids and much gripping of the sides of the boat, we coasted through with just a few pangs of doubt.

And so the day passed. A stop at a village where a boatload of dead and dying monitor lizards were being loaded on a boat for the markets of Chiang Rai. Shadows, shafts of light and a glimpse of working elephants. Dugouts going with and against the current. Wooden fish-traps. A house beside the river, then a half-hidden village, then forest again. And on our final approach to Chiang Rai, a set of cliff faces, riddled with caves where saffron-robed monks sat in silent meditation.

We stayed a day in Chiang Rai before leaving by bus for Chiang Saen, a small town of recent significance to us, located forty miles to the north-east, on the banks of the Mekong.

We had no idea that Chiang Saen would be inundated with Laotian refugees. After twenty-two years of war and the biggest bombing campaign in history during which the U.S. dropped four million tons of bombs on tiny Laos, the communist Pathet Lao had taken full control of the country the previous year. The Hmong, who had supported the Americans' 'Secret War', losing some 35,000 men in the process, were singled out for retribution when the war ended. Forty thousand had fled to Thailand and they were still streaming across the Mekong to places like Chiang Saen. But we were there for purely esoteric reasons.

Dodging whatever constraints were in place, we set off in high spirits from the town, taking a dirt track that hugged the right-hand bank of the Mekong. The six-mile walk remains as vivid as yesterday. The electrical storm that cleared to steamy sunshine. The smell of earth, flowers and trees, fresh and clean from the rain. The hum of insects. The mud that sucked at our bare feet. The coconut palms. The sweat soaking our clothes and packs. The children running in terror as we trudged through small villages. Mothers surprised to see us, smiling from stilted bamboo huts. Fishing boats on the river. Laos on the far side. Odd to be able to see the villages, people and soldiers of a country so thoroughly closed to us

From its source in the Kun Lun Mountains of China, the Mekong would have already travelled over 1,200 miles by the time it became the dividing line between Burma and Laos. At the southern extremity of this frontier, a little to the north of where we were trekking, it was already a mighty river when another of countless tributaries added its volume to the flow. The Ruak, a brook by comparison, was nonetheless significant in that it separated the hills of northern Thailand from the Shan state of Burma. This was where Burma, Laos and Thailand met. On the far side of the Mekong, the Battle of Ban Khwan had taken place nine years before.

Two hours out of Chiang Saen we reached the confluence of the two rivers, and the simple little village that stood there. But instead of the welcome to which we were accustomed, the villagers recoiled in bewilderment. Once they had recovered from the obvious shock of seeing us, the men began to gesticulate frantically. We should leave immediately. Pointing towards the dark forests of Burma, they fired imaginary guns, chopped us up with imaginary machetes and clapped us in imaginary irons. All a bit of a surprise after the pleasant walk upriver.

'We're going,' I said. 'Calm down. We just want to take a few pictures.'

Not knowing what I was saying, they became more frantic. However, when we had taken two photos with our Kodak Instamatic, one of the villagers agreed to take another, probably to speed us on our way. We then threw a few stones into the water, the way you might toss them on a mountaintop cairn. *Kilroy was here*. Very confusing to the villagers. A few minutes sojourn at the heart of the Golden Triangle and, job done, we shouldered our rucksacks and walked back down to Chiang Saen.

'Whatever was going on back there,' Cora said as we reached the outskirts of the town, 'those people fairly wanted to put the skids under us.'

'And look what's coming.' I nodded towards a low-sized cop with flaring nostrils who was striding our way.

'What the hell are you doing in Chiang Saen?' he bellowed in semi-Oxford English. 'Where upriver have you come from? Who the hell are you anyway?'

'We're from Ireland...' I started.

'Get out of Chiang Saen now,' he ordered.

'Okay,' I said and we went and booked in at a cheap guesthouse.

Forty years after our trek into the Golden Triangle I came across the piece of paper on which Sai in Mandalay had written the name of the Shan commander who might have snuck us from northern Thailand back into Burma. I checked the Internet to see if I could find any sign of a General Zhang Qifu. I was stunned. General Zhang Qifu was none other than the Opium King, Khun Sa.

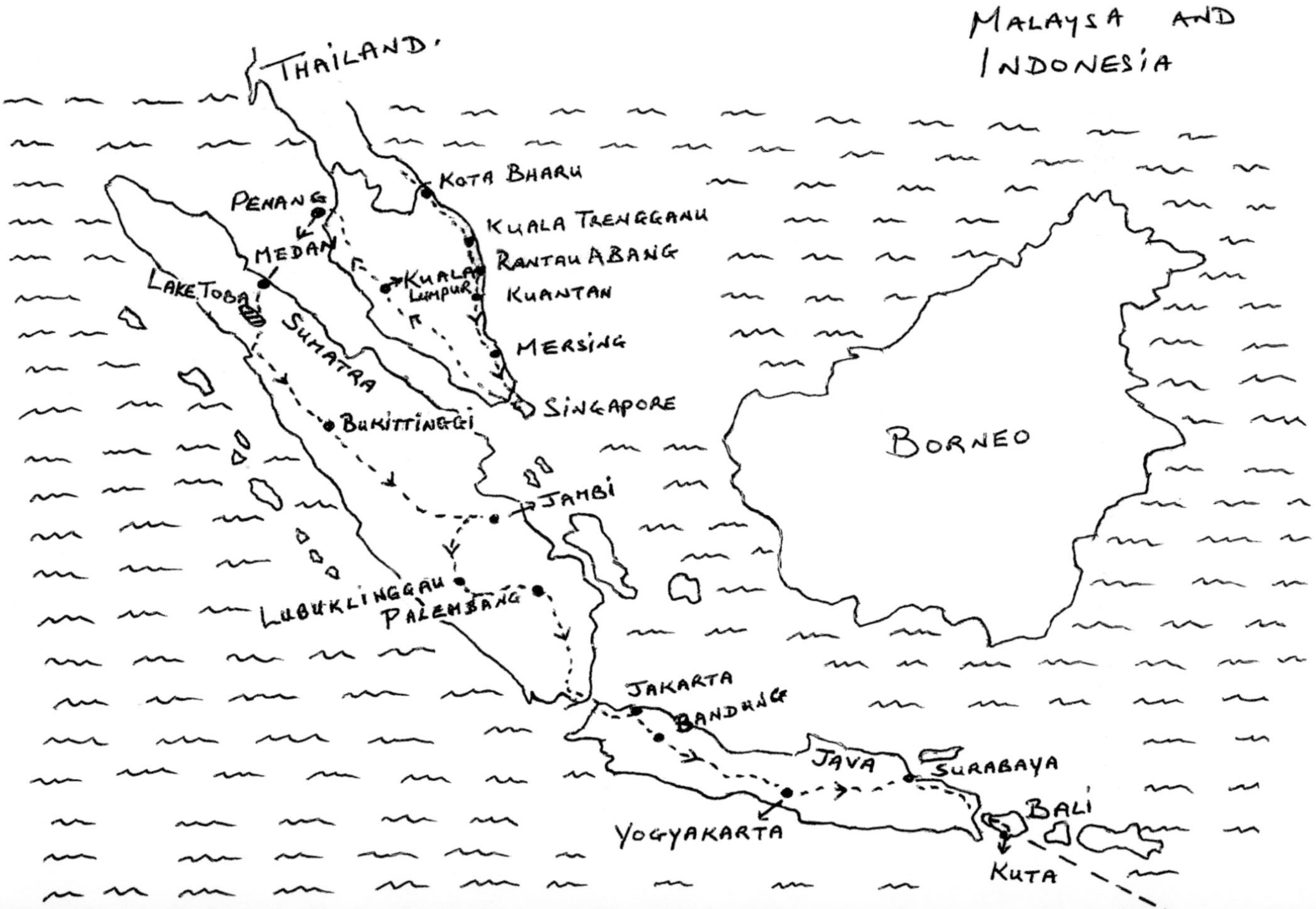

MALAYSIA AND INDONESIA

THAILAND

KOTA BHARU
KUALA TRENGGANU
RANTAU ABANG
KUANTAN
MERSING
SINGAPORE

PENANG
KUALA LUMPUR
MEDAN
LAKE TOBA
SUMATRA
BUKITTINGGI

JAMBI

LUBUKLINGGAU
PALEMBANG

BORNEO

JAKARTA
BANDUNG
JAVA
SURABAYA
BALI
KUTA
YOGYAKARTA

CHAPTER 5

The Turtles Of Rantau Abang

On the night of June 23rd 1976, in howling gales and slashing rain, we arrived in Kota Bharu, the state capital of Kelantan in north-east Malaysia, having crossed the frontier with ten minutes to spare on our Thai visas.

Overnight, we had travelled south by train from Bangkok to Hat Yai, with only a few hours of fitful sleep which was jarringly disrupted by cops who swarmed onto the train with carbines in the middle of the night.

'In case of attack,' one of them said. 'Last week, hundreds of bandits attacked the train with guns.' They were riding south with us, stationed in the body of the train and at the open windows between carriages.

The 11.00 a.m. onward train from Hat Yai to Sungei Golok took six hours to cover 122 miles, stopping at every bullock-trail along the way so that we ended up running the last mile with our packs on our backs along a hot dusty road towards a border post that closed at six o'clock.

We rushed through Thai customs and immigration and kept on running, arriving at a bridge over the Golok River that separated the two countries as two men drew a big gate closed across Malaysia. We banged hard and they let us in.

Formalities were few at the small border post. The customs people had all gone home and we were met by a single immigration officer, a humpy-faced man with a sardonic smile who carried big-time bullshit in the set of his shoulders. He pointed to a poster on the wall. It looked like a cross between a wanted poster and a warning against some contagion.

'You are hippies?' he asked. 'You see here what my government says: hippies are not welcome in Malaysia.'

The poster had illustrations of young Westerners with long hair, shoulder bags and sandals. Luckily my hair wasn't very long and Cora's shoulder bag and our flip-flops were safely tucked away in our packs. We thus avoided having the infamous Malaysian 'S.H.I.T.' (suspected hippie in transit) stamped in our passports.

'You have drugs?' the diplomat asked.

'Ha-ha, no,' I laughed. 'Drugs are bad for your health. They make you cough.'

I coughed for emphasis while the Buddha sticks in my jeans pocket grew by the second.

'We have very severe penalties here in Malaysia,' he warned. 'This is a Muslim country.' He then stamped our passports with a two-week stamp. 'Same as hippies,' he said. He rose heavily to his flat feet and went home for his dinner. We didn't make a scene but I cursed him to hell and back (when he was gone). And what I wouldn't do if I saw him again.

'Scaredy-ba,' Cora said. 'You're all gutsy when it's over.'

'We're not finished yet,' I thundered. 'We'll be back to sort this out. Sometimes you just have to make a stand.'

'I thinks that's a very bad idea,' Cora said.

We took a 27-mile tuk-tuk ride to Kota Bharu as the storm exploded, and booked into a cheap Chinese hotel where the bedroom walls started a foot from the floor and finished a foot from the ceiling. The shower was the now-familiar jug and tank of cold water full of wriggling mosquito larvae. Out on the first-floor veranda we watched the lightning and listened to the call to prayer from the mosques in town.

'We need to economise,' I said.

'It would be hard to economise any more than this,' Cora pointed out.

We need to hitchhike,' I said. 'Otherwise we'll run out of money and not be able to buy those air tickets to Darwin.' This was a new consideration.

As happened with every trip to date, our aspirations had exceeded our resources. But we had expected that. Our plan, if you remember, was to work our passage on a boat from Bali to Darwin. However, we had now learned that we couldn't get into Indonesia without an onward air ticket. Singapore sold relatively cheap air tickets from Bali to Darwin, but this would be no good to us if we reached Singapore without the funds to buy them. There was also a separate problem that we needed to work around: buying the air tickets would most likely leave us penniless, and Indonesia refused entry to paupers. And even if they let us in, we would first have to get to Indonesia from Malaysia - how was that going to happen? - then cross Sumatra, Java and Bali without a cent in our pockets.

'We could maybe get a working passage on a tramp steamer to take us across the Strait of Malacca,' was my idea. 'Then tell them some yarn in Sumatra about our money coming to Bukittinggi. Then limp our way to Bali.'

'Might as well go on,' Cora said. 'We've come this far. If Indonesia turns us back, they turn us back. Then we have a *real* problem.'

Amazing how seemingly perfect solutions can wither with time. I have no idea how we thought this might all work.

After two nights in Kota Bharu we stocked up with food at the outdoor market and began our economising. But, hitchhiking down the east coast of Malaysia was a dismal affair, mainly due to the dearth of vehicles. Between short lifts and long sweat-drenched walks along the coast or through plantations of rubber, palm-oil and coconuts, we'd sit for hours under a tree, watching buffaloes and bullock-carts go by, me strumming my guitar, Cora teasing the roadside clusters of the thorny fern-like 'sensitive weed' that folded over when touched.

In villages smelling of dried fish, we were repeatedly reminded that it was durian season. People would rush out to offer us big chunks of this spiky, yellow-green, football-sized 'king of fruits'. But the Western nose was finding it hard to get past an unfortunate smell of public lavatories, so penetrating that airlines and larger hotels in South East Asia refused entry to clients carrying durians. The pale-yellow flesh was also said to be so high in cholesterol that older people often died from it. And, true or not, there were rumours that if you drank beer within a few hours of eating durian - on account of some fermentation process - your bowels would explode.

After sixty miles we gave up on the hitchhiking and took a bus to Kuala Trengganu where the Sultan's birthday was in full swing - a huge extravaganza of music, fireworks, dance and theatre, depicting the cultures of the Malay, Chinese and Indian peoples of mainland Malaysia. By the time the night was done, we were among the last to leave the streets.

In the morning we took a shared taxi south along the coast to the village of Rantau Abang. To our right, the jungle crept towards the sea from the west where some of the oldest rainforests in the world - home to Malaysia's aboriginal *Orang Asli* - had been placed under national protection. There were, it was claimed, some 500 tigers still roaming the mountainous interior, the same tigers that once ran wild all the way from Wallace's Line to Siberia and Manchuria. The road was littered with enormous squashed reticulated pythons, a snake known to grow to thirty feet.

'Rantau Abang,' the driver said as we got out. 'Maybe tonight you will see the turtles.'

That was why we had come.

We plodded down a sandy track to the beach. After a night-long battle with mosquitoes we were a bit tetchy, but Rantau Abang dispelled all of that.

* * *

We ordered chicken fried rice at one of the thatch-on-poles restaurants that sat by the entrance to the beach and took stock of our surroundings. A row of thatched huts. A palm-fringed beach of golden sand that ran north and south as far as the eye could see. An amethyst-blue sky over the South China Sea. And the prospect of a tête-à-tête with the living representatives of an order of reptiles that had existed on Earth for the last 100 million years.

Each year, between May and September, giant leatherback turtles came here to nest. To help their survival, a fenced, government-controlled hatchery afforded protection from poachers to some at least of the eggs which would otherwise end up on local tables. The hatchery officials also hovered over the hatchlings on their journey to the sea when as many as nine tenths would otherwise fall to predators.

'Hi!' The voice shook us out of a state of somnolence. 'If you're looking for a place to stay, check out the restaurant just past those coconut trees. I think you'll find he's still got one or two rooms.' Tom, a deeply-tanned Englishman dressed in a sarong, was on his way home after three years in Australia. 'I've bought some land in Tasmania,' he told us. 'I'm planning to go back again to build a house.'

Like ourselves, he was in Rantau Abang to see the leatherbacks that could grow to nine feet and weigh 1,000 pounds and whose last major breeding ground was this steeply-sloping, 10-mile stretch of Malaysian coastline.

'Didn't see any last night,' he said. 'But then I was only out for an hour. Someone was saying that there were a couple further down the beach. I saw some tracks there this morning. Maybe tonight?'

In a five-roomed hut that served as visitor accommodation, we rented a room with a plank-bed, a table, a kerosene lamp, one shuttered window opening to the sea, a well-ventilated grass roof and plenty of geckos. With the drift of the afternoon more travellers trickled in: an Australian couple on their way up from Singapore; a French couple and two Canadian women coming down from Kuala Trengganu; a middle-aged German man who had a big glass bong in his rucksack; an Englishwoman Cora and I had met in Kathmandu; then three more Australians and a second German. Over the next ten days, we would become a little community of our own at Rantau Abang.

They were lazy days. The most taxing chore any of us could conjure up was to walk a few miles north to the wreck of a Taiwanese boat that had broken its back. At some stage during their stay everyone set off at least once to hike those few miles: only three ever made it. The expedition launched by Tom, Cora and myself got hopelessly side-tracked by scores of sand-coloured crabs that darted down ready-made holes in the sand, and hundreds of jellyfish that turned the sea to an opaque white.

'You got to watch out for the jellyfish all the time,' Tom said. 'And when they're not about, you got to watch out for the sea-lice.'

Out at sea a large white sailing ship headed south, one of the magnificent Macassar schooners called *pinisi* that still plied the South China Sea and the islands of Indonesia, and were plagued by old-fashioned pirates who also raided the shipping lines to Singapore. This was such a problem that Singapore later requested the help of the United Nations in dealing with it. In future years, the pirates would also carve a murderous reputation with the 'boat-people' fleeing Vietnam.

* * *

On our first night of turtle-spotting, we got up at three o'clock and went south along the beach, pocket lamp at the ready, ears tuned to the surf. It was a warm clear night full of stars, with a soft breeze off the sea. The only visible light came from a huddle of fishing boats out in the blackness and the iridescent blue footsteps that trailed behind as we disturbed minute phosphorescent plankton in the wet sand of the waterline.

Two hundred yards down the beach we came on a set of tracks, as if a small bulldozer had come out of the sea and ploughed up the beach. But we were too late: the turtle was already gone. We walked on but nothing more.

'Maybe we should go back,' I said. 'Try again tomorrow night.'

Before we had time to decide, Cora tugged on my arm.

'Look. There's something in the water...'

When it was still swimming it was hard to see; but when it reached the shallows, the massive dome rose from the surf like a mini Volkswagen beetle washed in phosphorescence. We stood rigid, partly in awe and partly in consideration, as the 1,000-pound bulk dragged itself clear of the sea and snorted its way up the beach, scattering a shower of sand in its wake. When it stopped, we followed, then sat back to watch it excavate the hole into which it would lay its eggs. We were so engrossed that we didn't notice the arrival of two Malays in sarongs and shirts until they were right beside us.

'No light,' one of them whispered when I flashed the pocket-lamp on the eggs. 'Light scare turtle. Only light when I say.'

'Are you from the government?' I asked.

'Yes,' he said. 'Government.' A few minutes later he gave the nod. 'Light now.'

Before we realised what was happening, he was in the hole scooping the eggs into his sarong. Then both men took off. By the time the real government officials arrived there were only seven eggs to be preserved. Then the turtle expended a huge amount of energy infilling the empty nest and disguising its location by stirring up half the beach.

Two hours after its arrival it turned, panting and coughing, towards the sea. The first rays of sunlight, shooting through bands of pink cloud, glinted on its back. Plunging into the surf it was afloat in two heaves, the horny head rearing up for a breath before it dived. A hundred yards offshore it surfaced for another breath. Then it was gone.

Back at our restaurant we had breakfast of coffee and banana fritters as the village men came back from their night's fishing, each carrying a handful of squid and a few small fish.

'Overfished by the Japanese,' the Englishwoman from Kathmandu said.

For a while there was a silence of the kind that needs no words as those who were awake stared out to sea, watching the sky colours change as the sun rose on the turtle's vast ocean. The silence was broken by English Tom, speaking mostly to himself.

'Old Matahari,' he said. 'The eye of the day.'

To the north, predominantly Chinese-Malaysian communists were operating against the Kuala Lumpur government from bases along the Thai border, the remnants of a rebellion that began in 1948 and cost 12,000 lives over the next 12 years. At its height 350,000 military personnel, including 100,000 British troops from sixty units, were deployed against a few thousand communist guerrillas. By using brutal tactics against insurgents and their supporters, burning homes, destroying crops and forcing Chinese farmers into so-called 'protected villages', the British and their Malay allies, and later the Malaysians themselves, eventually reduced the insurgents to small pockets of diehards who were still, in 1976, operating from their shrinking jungle bases. These were most likely the 'bandits' mentioned by the cops who had boarded our train on the way south.

That afternoon we read that an air and land assault by Malaysian and Thai forces had wiped out many of the bases, but the low-level war would go on until the final communist surrender in 1989.

A couple of days later, after several more turtle-sightings, we were again studying our dwindling finances while sitting under a coconut tree when a hefty nut thudded into the sand beside Cora. She picked it up, weighed it in her hand, looked up at the feathery canopy that had dropped it and made a decision.

'That nut' she said, 'could've busted my head.' Neither of us ever again sat under a coconut tree.

On the same day I took advantage of an absence of jellyfish and sea-lice and went for a swim. While dog-paddling in the warm water, I cupped a thick length of seaweed in my right hand. In an automatic reaction I lifted my hand clear of the water and tossed the seaweed away. Whereupon the seaweed became a banded sea snake that fell back into the water. I fled like an Olympian.

'That there thing,' I said to Cora, collapsing on the sand beside her, 'has venom ten times deadlier than a rattlesnake. Even a dead one can give a knee-jerk bite that would kill a person.'

'I never knew snakes had knees,' the smartass said.

* * *

Two days later we were run out of Malaysia. We had gone south to Kuantan to demand that our two-week visas be extended but had fallen foul of officialdom.

'Hippies do not get visa extensions,' we were informed by an officious young immigration officer with eyebrows that looked like blackberry bushes. 'And you are hippies.' He pointed at one of the hippie posters on the wall. 'You see here. Long hair, sandals, all signs of hippy people. Also, hippies stay in cheap hotels. What is your hotel please?'

'The Tin Ah,' I replied knowing instinctively that it would do us no favours. He looked it up in his book of knowledge.

'The Tin Ah,' he grinned maliciously. 'Ah yes, the Tin Ah... Under $10 Malaysian per night. This also means you are hippies. No visas for you. Only enough time to leave Malaysia.'

He gave us a three-day extension. In the morning we stormed back full of indignation.

'This is an affront to our dignity,' I said, well up now on my high horse, and mindful that I had a stand to make. 'We demand an apology.'

'Yes my friend,' the officious one replied. 'You may have the apology. And a reminder that your three days are running out.'

Cora said it was a great victory.

We travelled by bus to Endau where we crossed a wide estuary on a platform towed by a tug which broke down, causing chaos for an hour. From Endau we caught another bus to the small coastal town of Mersing where we spent our final two days in eastern Malaysia. In the evenings a muezzin sang from the minaret of a mosque close to our hotel. On the second day I managed to climb a tall coconut tree. Cora congratulated me, said I was the Missing Link.

Five years later Cora and I were back in Rantau Abang, on a return visit to Australia, but things were changing. There was talk of hotels, and the beach was being sectioned off so that a toll could be charged to anyone wishing to visit. We left after a day with a feeling that something terrible was taking place, and that we had perhaps been part of it.

Further south, an area that had been rainforest five years earlier was a brown, treeless dustbowl. There were no more reticulated pythons, dead or alive.

The floating platform at Endau had been replaced by a bridge.

* * *

Today, the leatherback turtles are all but gone from Rantau Abang. Where 10,000 a year came to lay their eggs in the 1960s, only one landing was detected in 2017 after a ten-year absence of the species. Scientists believe that five factors brought about the virtual extinction of the Malaysian leatherbacks. The first was the local market for turtle eggs. The second relates to inept hatchery methods that produced 100 percent female turtles because temperatures were not properly controlled.[14] The third was the drowning of thousands of turtles in the huge drift nets and long lines used by large fishing boats. The fourth was hunting for the turtle's meat, or use of turtles in religious rituals. And the fifth was the uncontrolled tourism that grew in the 1980s, with hotels and bright lights near the beachfront causing turtles to shy away, and up to 2,000 tourists camped in the area, building bonfires

---

14. Gender is decided by the heat of the sand incubating the eggs which is decided by the depth of burial.

and sometimes riding on the backs of the turtles. Chan Eng Heng, a professor and turtle conservationist at the University College of Science and Technology of Malaysia, summed it up in 2002 when only three landings occurred.

'It is very sad. Rantau Abang used to be the prime location for leatherbacks in the world. I'm not sure if anything can be done now. There are no more eggs to protect...'

For a hundred-million-year-old lineage, it goes beyond words.

CHAPTER 6

The Land Of Bugis Street

On July 8th, Cora and I breezed into Singapore. Four days later we left again with air tickets from Bali to Darwin and sixteen Malaysian dollars - virtually nothing. But, for the first time, our passage to Australia seemed secure.

One of the most welcome letters I have ever received had been waiting for us at Singapore's *Poste Restante*. It was from my mother. Pension contributions that I had reclaimed before leaving home, had arrived. Five hundred dollars was waiting for us in Georgetown in Penang, an island off the north-west coast of Malaysia. Seriously overdue reassurance that all would be well.

After celebrating with a meal of rice and various small dishes served on a banana leaf on the floor of a small Indian restaurant, we went back to our cheapie on Owen Road, where we came across Ivan and Danny, two Australians who had just arrived from Sydney on their way to Sri Lanka. Prodigiously culture-shocked, they were pacing the floor in shorts and T-shirts, trying to dredge up the courage to venture outside.

Ivan was the organiser of the outfit. Slightly-built with dark curly hair and a heavy moustache, he was fleeing a collapsed marriage and a lacklustre teaching job in Sydney. He was, however, overshadowed by the larger, blond-haired Jimmy, a barrel-chested slab of muscle with enormous hands and an appetite that would startle a bin-lorry. Jimmy had been a bricklayer back home. Next morning, as we toured the monstrous department stores of Orchard Road, the workings of the combination bared themselves.

'No mate,' Ivan advised, his right eye working a nervous tic. 'I don't think we should load ourselves down with all that shit on our second day out of 'stralia.'

Jimmy was buying stereos, calculators and cameras to beat the band. This caused Ivan to fidget a great deal as the duty-free bargains piled up in Jimmy's arms. Eventually he cracked. He too ended up with arms full of electronic junk. Later, when Ivan thought they were being conned by the guy trying to sell them 'growing stones', Jimmy bought them anyway. And Ivan followed suit. The 'growing stones', which they were told to water regularly, got a fine reception from the other travellers down on Owen Road.

As the days went by the rift between our companions deepened. Ivan thought Jimmy spent too much. Jimmy thought Ivan thought too much. Jimmy enjoyed a puff of whatever was going and was wild short on discretion. Ivan couldn't shake off the image of a Singapore gallows.

'I mean,' he complained, 'going out and buying smack from some guy you never met in your life on the corner of the fucking street.'

'Shaddup!' Jimmy snapped as he rolled a smack cigarette.

'He'll end up strung out on junk,' Ivan would confide to myself and Cora.

'Ivan's nerves are shot through,' Jimmy would confide.

But, leaving out the perils of being caught between Ivan and Jimmy, and the stifling sticky heat, our days in Singapore passed in relative calm. After the tough slog down through Asia, the cleanliness, efficiency and organisation of the city was a pleasant surprise. It was a place of vibrancy, commerce, excellent food served in huge emporiums, children and adults flying kites, and the order of Lee Kuan Yew.

Lee Kuan Yew, who led Singapore to independence and had repeatedly been elected as prime minister since 1959, ruled the island state with ultimate authority and a legendary zeal for law and order. Under his control, Singapore had become a financial and industrial powerhouse despite an abundant lack of natural resources. Enforcing a tight, oppressive regime of discipline, 'correct' public behaviour, English education, interracial tolerance, and draconian opposition to drugs, he had managed to transform a poor port into a wealthy welfare state with an economy heavily based on private enterprise, foreign investment and duty-free. The price for Singaporeans was the destruction of old neighbourhoods and their replacement by huge concrete blocks, the suppression of political dissent, and Big Brother at every corner. Tossing a cigarette butt in the street could land you in serious trouble. Jimmy's smack cigarettes were potentially lethal in more ways than one.

Out at sea the ships of the world's trading nations, strung out in a great anchored flotilla, saluted the success of Singapore. At night they became floating strings of light that grew from the dusk to merge with the stars.

Meanwhile, the inner harbour along the mouth of the Singapore River was choked with barges, bumboats, sampans and old schooners with folded sails. Among them, slaving away under the merciless heat, the city's 'coolies' carried the enormous burden of Singapore's riches on their backs.

In a further measure of progress, old Chinatown was dying. The low buildings, shuttered windows, wrought-iron balconies, carved eaves and tiled roofs, were fast disappearing, leaving an ever-shrinking cluster of sad streets where paper lanterns, canvas awnings, caged songbirds, and the bustle of outdoor markets pretended that nothing had changed. For the most part, the old communities had been exiled to high-rise tombs. In Sago Street, one of the remnants of Chinatown, we watched a man place two Siamese fighting fish in a tank so he could take bets on the outcome. It was said that old people came to die in this street. They sat in doorways and waited. Like Chinatown itself.

On our second night in the city, we were down at the harbour, basking in a cool sea breeze, enjoying the lights and tucking in to a feed of chicken satay and ketupat - cubes of glutinous rice steamed in woven palm-leaf pouches - when we rediscovered Nigel, a wide eyed Englishman we had previously met in Chiang Mai. He had crossed into Singapore the same day as us.

'Man,' he said, 'can you believe it? I was strip-searched for dope on the bridge into Singapore, and made to give a urine sample.'

'Wait 'til you hear what this eejit did...' Cora began. 'He walked through with a pocket full of ...' A gentle nudge under the table ended that one. It was one thing to do something stupid, another to have the whole bloody world know about it.

'Man,' Nigel said, 'this is a heavy town. I saw in the papers today that they're going to hang some guy for possession of smack.'

Funny how things change. In colonial times, half the city was built on the profits of the opium trade.

When we had finished eating, Nigel accompanied us back to Owen Road where we found four other travellers packed into Ivan and Jimmy's room, and everyone off the wall. Annie, a plump, dark-haired Welsh woman of about thirty was explaining herself.

'I mean, everything is possible, isn't it? Just look at how much we know now that we didn't know before. And if we didn't know it before and we know it now, then whatever we don't know now, we might come to know tomorrow. Isn't that right?'

Nobody was sure.

But, with that gem hanging in the room and Buddha grass flaming from a bong made from a bottle and a bamboo tube, Jimmy passed around a small tin of tiger balm. 'Just rub it under your eyes,' he said. A few minutes later, nine pairs of blinking, watering eyes were still pondering Annie's point as Jimmy got into another of his smack cigarettes. He then went out onto the balcony and vomited into the street.

'For fuck's sake,' Ivan yelled, 'Lee Kuan Yew will have a fucking fit!'

By the time Jimmy got back the topic had changed.

An American woman with hair to her waist and a Mona Lisa face was waving a joint in the air.

'Hey you guys,' she beamed, 'did anyone hear about this weird guy who's been going around bumping off freaks? It's been in all the papers...'

Everyone but Ivan and Jimmy had heard.

An Indo-Vietnamese French national and psychopath called Charles Sobhraj had been cutting a bloody trail across Asia, eventually leaving behind the butchered and charred corpses of as many as twenty victims. It would transpire that one of his haunts was Bangkok's Patpong, from which he preyed on travellers staying at the Malaysia Hotel. In all, Sobhraj was implicated in at least ten murders in Thailand in 1975 alone.

A month after we left Singapore, Sobhraj and three women accomplices - now in India - tricked a tour group of sixty French engineering students into accepting them as guides. Sobhraj then drugged them at a Delhi hotel with pills which he pretended were to counter dysentery. However, when the students started dropping off, three of them pounced on Sobhraj. He was arrested and subsequently charged with the Bombay murder of Frenchman Jean-Luc Solomon, who died from poison intended to knock him out during a robbery.

Conditions inside Delhi's notorious Tihar prison were horrendous, but Sobhraj arrived with precious stones concealed in his body and was able to bribe the guards into providing him with a life of luxury during two years on remand. Becoming known as 'Sir Charles', he had a TV and phone, the best of food, women companions and opportunities to give paid interviews to visiting authors and journalists. Instead of the expected death penalty, his trial produced a 12-year sentence, spawning rumours that he had bribed the court officials.

However, the 12-year sentence meant that a Thai extradition warrant for murder would still be valid when he was due for release, which would lead to almost certain execution. But that was not to be. In March 1986, on his tenth year in Tihar, he threw a huge party where he drugged guards and prisoners alike and waltzed out of jail. On his recapture, he was given an extra ten years. And salvation. In February

1997, 52-year-old Sobhraj was returned to France where he retired comfortably to the suburbs of Paris, charging thousands of dollars for interviews and photographs, and upwards of $15 million for a film deal based on his life. For Sobhraj, it appeared, crime had paid.

But in September 2003 he was spotted in Kathmandu, having drilled into a previously unsuspected seam of human arrogance or stupidity. Two days later, he was arrested in the casino of the Yak and Yeti Hotel, and in August 2004 he was sentenced to life imprisonment for the 1975 murders of two Dutch backpackers.

* * *

For a bit of night life away from the shadow of Lee Kuan Yew, you went to Bugis Street.

It was a madhouse. At midnight, the street went into a tailspin. In a blaze of coloured bulbs and fluorescent strips, impromptu restaurants, bars and food stalls threw up their awnings. Bugis Street filled with tables, chairs and incense burners. Fireworks exploded. Music blared. Drunks howled. Trishaws, delivering young foreigners, rowdy sailors, Malay, Indian and Chinese businessmen and opium-stoned old men, came trundling in. In the spicy steam and smoke, street hawkers, black marketeers and pickpockets further swelled the ranks. But the party only began in earnest when the *kai tais* made their appearance because that's what Bugis Street was all about, an outrageous nightly binge where pride of place went to the transvestites who arrived in an array of dazzling regalia.

Sashaying up and down the short street, they would pose for photos or try to hook up with drunk foreigners. Some of them were so stunning that the joke on Bugis Street was that you could easily tell the real women from the transvestites: the transvestites were the truly gorgeous.

There was also a well-patronised public toilet with a flat roof which doubled up as Bugis Street's stage. A hallowed tradition of the street was the 'Dance of the Flaming Arseholes' performed on top of the toilet's flat roof by stark-naked western sailors with rolled-up, lighted newspapers clenched in their arses. For some unknown reason, cheerleaders on the ground would chant, 'Haul 'em down you Zulu Warrior' while the lads put on the show.

The whole crowd from Owen Road went down together and had no sooner landed than out of the darkness came a bell-ringing, rickshaw-borne convoy of elderly Americans. Earlier in the evening, Cora and I had seen them bulldozing their way through Chinatown. As they settled in, four Englishmen climbed the street's only tree, to be photographed peering from the branches at the crowned Queen of Bugis Street.

'They're all women.' This in a slurring of vowels from a very drunk Australian called Dave who hadn't shaved in a week. 'I've spent the last six months in a mining camp on Groote Eylandt in the Gulf of Carpentaria. That includes a wet season when guys go troppo and go crashin' off into the bush in earth-movers and you never see them again. Me? I just kept dreamin' of three glorious months travellin' across Asia and findin' women like these.'

In Manilla, Dave said, the pimps were Peeping Toms. In Bangkok, a woman wanted to marry him. In Kuala Lumpur, another robbed him. And it was looking like he was going to wake up in Singapore to an awfully big surprise if his fixation on a shapely redhead in a miniskirt was anything to go by.

'I'll tell you something,' he drooled as a growing bawdiness encouraged the *kai tais* into arse-pinching forays among the tables. 'I bet she knows a thing or two.'

'She's a he, Dave,' I said to head him off at the pass, but the cause was lost.

Close by, a lanky Dutchman figured he might join the *kai tais*. He reached out and pinched a passing woman only to discover that she was the wife of a brutishly large German whose sense of humour fell far below the occasion. There ensued a loud crack of German fist on Dutch jaw and the Dutchman was taken away. The cops then hauled off two Chinese guys who were dancing on a table. Ivan and Jimmy left, citing a need to go to Chinatown to score some opium.

Cora and I would come back to Bugis Street every night of our stay.

For those who went there in its heyday, Bugis Street would always be the enduring memory of Singapore. It was eventually pulled down in the 1980s and replaced by a complex of shops, restaurants and nightspots which swept away the pulse of old Singapore, did for the Dance of the Flaming Arseholes, and delivered the end of an era. The Land of Bugis Street was no more.

* * *

Even if you are expecting money in Penang, being suddenly penniless in Singapore comes as a bang. Once we had bought our air tickets from Den Pasar to Darwin, we were left with nothing more than our bus fares back over the bridge to Malaysia, and sixteen Malaysian dollars

- enough to buy two meals each in a cheap restaurant. We needed to make a bolt for Penang.

Four days after arriving in Singapore we were on our way again. Sitting on the pavement waiting for a bus to the border, we were joined by three dainty Chinese belles, waiting for the same bus. Then a young Indian man arrived with a bag full of goodies.

'You like to buy a wallet?' he asked.

'No thanks,' I said.

'Fan?' he pulled out a portable, battery-operated hand-fan.

'Vibrator?' he tugged one from the bag and switched it on in my face. I growled and he left. When the bus pulled up, the three delicate souls beside us, in their bright floral dresses, bashed myself and Cora clear across the pavement, before sweeping onto the bus and claiming the last three places. They waved: tough shit buddy; better luck next time.

CHAPTER 7

Running On Empty

Over the next three days we made a frantic dash for Georgetown and our $500.

In contrast to the predominantly-Malay east coast of Malaysia, we were now travelling through the Chinese stronghold of western Malaysia, a legacy of bygone days when the Dutch and British colonists encouraged migration from China and India to satisfy the labour needs of the tin-mining and rubber industries.

It was clear from the people we encountered that the large Chinese, and lesser Indian, populations felt discriminated against by the dominant Malays. Many of the poorer Chinese lent qualified support to the campaign being waged from the northern jungles by the Chinese communist guerrillas. Two of them picked us up on the first afternoon in a beat-up truck. The driver, a tall, thin man with greying hair and a stringy beard, seemed affable enough. His mate, however, an aggressive, squat, heavy man with a shaven head and a threadlike moustache that spanned the edge of his upper lip, seemed to associate us with some international malaise that contributed to the plight of the Malaysian Chinese.

'You rich kids?' he enquired, sneering into our faces. 'Maybe you rich hippie kids from America?'

'No,' I explained. 'We are from Ireland, and right now we have no money.'

'Hylan?' the mate said with a quizzical gaze. 'Where Hylan?'

'Near England,' Cora said.

'Hylan poor?' he asked.

'Right now,' Cora said, 'very, very poor.

'O-o-oh,' he said. He spoke to the driver and they pulled over and bought us coffee.

Late that night we arrived in the village of Sungai Rambai to the south of Malacca.

'I'm whacked,' I said. 'We need to find somewhere to sleep.'

'Where?' Cora asked. 'In the trees? What about all the dead snakes which means live snakes as well? We just have to keep going.'

'No traffic,' I pointed out.

'Come,' a voice said. 'You sleep in my house.' An old Indian man materialised from the shadows. 'My name is Gurakana,' he said. 'Come, come.'

He led us through the darkness to a stone-flagged hut lit by an oil lamp. At a nearby café, we spent the last of our money on a very frugal meal before gratefully sharing the floor of Gurakana's attic with hordes of voracious mosquitoes.

The following afternoon, hungry and exhausted, we arrived in Kuala Lumpur and were about to ask a cop for directions to the city's northern exit when I was tapped on the shoulder by a dapper Sri Lankan man in his late thirties who had just finished work.

'Follow me,' he said. 'It is time to rest.' He brought us to his home where he and his wife fed us our only meal of the day and gave us their bed for the night.

On the third evening we arrived at Butterworth which presented a major hurdle. We needed to take a ferry to the island of Penang to reach our $500.

'We're going to have to ask someone to loan us the money,' I said to Cora.

'Does "we" mean me?' Cora asked.

Just as we considered how we could, with the least loss of dignity, beg the cost of the ferry, we found that all outward journeys were free - you paid on the way back!

Shortly after six on the evening of July 14th 1976 we set foot on Penang. In the leafy, colonnaded city of Georgetown, with Singapore 450 miles to the south, we just knew that nothing could now go wrong.

Except the money.

Fifteen hours into credit at the Yeng Keng cheapie on Chulia Street, we found that our $500 was missing. At the First National City Bank, named on my mother's transaction, they had never heard of us. At the words 'No money for you here...' I had a terrible urge to vomit over the teller.

'You're joking,' I said.

'He's not,' Cora said, 'which reminds me of this bad feeling I haven't mentioned...'

However, our reluctance to loosen our grip on the counter prompted much consultation in the bowels of the bank and the teller came back with a suggestion.

'You must try the Public Bank Berhad,' he said. 'They have an arrangement with the Irish bank that sent the money.' In a fever we did as bade, and lo and behold a fluff-faced clerk unearthed the relevant documents.

'Yes,' he said. 'The cheque is here.' We collapsed in relief. 'But we cannot pay you.'

'What!' we both squeaked.

'The wording of the papers,' he said. 'It says American dollars. We cannot pay you American dollars without first the clearance of the United States. It will take one month.'

You're not fuckin' serious, I nearly said.

'Can you pay us in Malaysian dollars?' Cora asked.

'Not possible,' he said.

'Can we sign something to say we accept an alternative transaction?' I asked.

'Not possible.'

'Can we make a new arrangement with the Irish bank that forwarded the money?'

'Not possible. The Irish banks are on strike.'

'Oh no,' Cora groaned. 'The last bloody bank strike lasted six months...'

It took five days, multiple and assorted bank visits, and two trips to the British High Commission (no Irish diplomats anywhere nearby) before we finally got our money released in Malaysian dollars which we then had to convert back into American dollars so we could buy travellers' cheques.

However, thanks to the laid-back nature of the Yeng Keng manager, and a small loan organised by the British High Commissioner, we were able to sleep in a bed and eat sparingly during those days. We also paid regular visits to the Indian man at the corner who revolutionised the making of Milo drinks, pouring the mix back and forth between two containers with such speed that he created the illusion of a pale-brown tube. Cora also managed to top up her cholera vaccination.

'They did it down in the post office,' she said when she came back. 'A line of people all being jabbed with the same needle. I wonder where they sell the stamps?'

Shortly after dusk on our third day in Georgetown we ran into Ivan and Jimmy. We had started the day with a dawn visit to a Confucian temple to watch a tai-chi group of older people welcome the day. We had then called at the city's snake temple with its sleepy vipers, and followed this with a Lion dance rehearsal that we stumbled on in a hall in town before going off to Batu Ferringhi beach to see the sun go down over the Strait of Malacca. We were on our way back to the night markets when we met our old pals who were in the company of two Australian heroin addicts. All four had come from one of Georgetown's opium dens. Jimmy was off his head and Ivan was looking rough.

Ivan shooed off the two junkies and invited myself and Cora back to their place where Jimmy produced his heroin stash and rolled a long smoke.

'He carried that fuckin' smack from Singapore.' Ivan said. 'He'll be dead before we reach Sri Lanka.'

We were joined by a Swedish couple from an adjoining room and Jimmy passed the smoke around to any takers. Ivan, funny enough, sucked on it each time, then threw up spectacularly in a sink in the corner.

'Man,' he said, 'this shouldn't be happenin'.'

'Shhh,' I said. 'Drums. We should maybe go and check it out.'

'Might be a wedding',' Jimmy said as we neared the narrow street from which the sounds were coming, 'Maybe we could get a beer.' We then rounded the corner.

'Chinese play!' I shouted like a lifeboat captain in a gale. Just before it dawned that it was a Chinese wake.

'Why put your foot in it,' Cora said, 'when you have two.'

The focus was a long-haired priest in red robes and a golden crown. His body, undulating from a raised dais, moved to the rhythm of a flute and a collection of bamboo and coconut drums. His arms formed slow arcs that ran from his shoulders to his fingernails which were so long that they had curved inwards. He was presiding over a black coffin that stood uncovered in a doorway.

The music changed and he picked up two metal balls. Moving them up and down, he produced sharp chimes, still undulating to the music. Along the street, monstrous cylinders of incense burned among the mourners' chairs as the relatives of the man in the coffin provided tea and food of which we were invited to partake.

Ivan and Jimmy agreed that the coffin was an omen. Jimmy went so far as to flush his smack down the loo. 'So the fishes out at Batu Ferringhi can get whacked,' he said. An act he instantly regretted.

Later, under the colonnades of Chulia Street, the four of us drank green tea in a small restaurant. Outside in the street a car hit a truck and some of its passengers were injured. The five Chinese men at the next table thought it was the funniest thing ever. They laughed so hard that two of them rolled to the floor.

On Thursday, July 22nd, Cora and I bought air tickets to Medan in Sumatra, having failed for two days to get tickets for the previous Tuesday's boat, which might or might not leave on the Friday.

CHAPTER 8

Slowly Walking

In the soupy heat of Medan's bus station, Christine Hakkers put her hand to the man's forehead and calmly pushed the forehead and a headful of greasy hair back out through the open window.

'Piss off,' she said, drawing the glass across. 'I do not want you leering in my face.'

Twenty-five-year-old Christine, a Dutch nurse who spoke English with a Canadian accent was, like ourselves, ultimately on her way to Australia. A tall woman with long fair hair and a freckled complexion, she had nursed in Canada and didn't suffer fools lightly.

'As you are the only other non-Indonesians on this bus,' she said as we waited for the completion of the passenger roundup, 'we are probably going to the same place. Perhaps we can travel together?'

Cora sat in beside Christine and we set off for a hole in the Earth left behind by the greatest volcanic eruption of the last two million years.

When Mount St. Helens exploded in 1980 it spewed out .7 cubic miles of material: when the Toba volcano erupted some 74,000 years earlier, its total deposits came to 670 cubic miles. The eruption dumped an ash layer up to fifteen feet deep over the Indian subcontinent, carried ash as far away as Africa, and triggered a 1,000-year deep freeze. Studies of mitochondrial DNA would also suggest that the number of modern humans dropped cataclysmically to a few thousand survivors at roughly the same time as Toba's eruption, although it's impossible to prove a link.

When the volcano finally collapsed in on itself, it left behind a caldera that is fifty-four miles long, seventeen miles wide and 1,700 feet deep - Lake Toba in northern Sumatra. Further volcanic activity pushed up our destination, a plug that became Samosir Island.

The bus ride to Lake Toba was much horn and little brake. At each bus-halt we zoomed around the pick-up points with a man hanging out the back door yelling 'Parapat! Parapat!' (The village that was the ferry-point for Samosir.) We then sped off down lanes and dirt tracks to collect those who had sent couriers rather than attempt the walk to the bus with their baggage. Eventually, enveloped by the smoke of clove-laced cigarettes, we were firmly wedged into our wooden seats by the boxes, bags, chickens, and flour and rice sacks, of the other passengers. And still we zoomed around towns and villages yelling 'Parapat! Parapat!'

Gradually the lowland humidity melted away as we climbed through stepped rice-paddies and plantations of coconut, banana, pineapple, rubber and palm-oil. At the pretty hill town of Berastagi, home to the Karo Batak people, we passed under the twin peaks of Mount Sinagung and Mount Sibayak, two of the 127 active volcanoes that form Indonesia's Ring of Fire. Local music, which had lost its cultural novelty in the first hour, crackled from battered speakers while the driver maintained a death-race to Parapat.

At dusk we swung around a twist in the road and began to drop to the lake - spiritual centre of the Toba Batak people - lying at 2,950 feet above sea level. A string of tribal villages ran along the enclosing forested cliffs while the scattered lights of mountainous Samosir were reflected along the island's shoreline.

The Bataks, long feared as one of Sumatra's most warlike people, had once been renowned as powerful wizards who could kill by magic, and cannibals who ate prisoners of war and their own criminals. Marco Polo claimed in 1292 that they also ate their parents when they became too old for work.

True or not, it was all in the past as we wheeled downhill to Parapat and booked into a triple room at a lakeshore losmen. We later sat outside, mesmerised by distant flashes of sheet lightning and a howling wind that whipped the lake to a frenzy.

They say that Sumatra has two seasons: the wet and the wetter. One of them was massing over the lake.

* * *

At eight in the morning, after a night of fierce rain that battered the tin roof of the losmen, the jolly, middle-aged woman who ran the place appeared unannounced in our room with banana-porridge and coffee.

'Gut mawning,' she said. 'Ferry come soon.'

We rose to a fresh morning, completely devoid of the coastal humidity. The storm had passed and the sky had cleared so we ate outside. We then went for a short stroll. We then had a paddle in the lake. We then had more food and another stroll. And still the ferry was coming 'soon'. Finally, after three hours, an old, cumbersome, 30-foot wooden tub, converted to a double-decker and powered by an inboard motor that sounded like a doctored car engine, bobbed into view. As soon as it berthed, four other travellers and seven young Batak men, three in red turbans, shirts and blue sarongs, appeared from nowhere. We were all dragged aboard and we set off across the lake.

'Music?' one of the Bataks asked, pointing to my guitar. I handed it over and two minutes later the boat was rolling and pitching to the strains of an impromptu concert, the crew joining in with the singing and hand-clapping while one of the turban wearers rolled a massive joint. Christine said there was just no escape from the old ganja.

'We dedicate the joint to Si Raja Batak,' the turban man announced. 'He was the first human, who was born in the time of a great earthquake on the holy mountain of Bukit Pusuk on the western side of Lake Toba.'

'Whatever you say,' Christine said.

The helmsman, unable to steer and clap at the same time, abandoned the steering. A fisherman in a shallow dugout paddled away from our wash. Although I am loath to admit it, it reminded me very much of home.

'Where do you go?' a slim teenager with short curling hair wanted to know as we approached the island. He had come from below deck.

'Tuk Tuk Timbul,' Cora said.

'Very good,' he smiled. 'I am Kornel. I live at Tuk Tuk Timbul. You are very welcome.'

On shore, three naked children tossed pebbles into the water. One of them, a boy of about six, had pushed the tail of a dead snake down its throat and was swinging it on his arm like a hula hoop. In the fertile belt between the shoreline and the mountains, buffaloes wandered through a patchwork of terraced hills and gardens. Women in bright sarongs, blouses and cloth headdresses shouted greetings from houses with saddle-shaped roofs, some of sugar-palm fibre, some of tin. Rising behind the houses, the peaks and forests of the island's mountains were shrouded in a swirl of white mist. Below in the water, we could see what looked like a shoal of goldfish.

One of the un-turbaned Bataks rolled another joint. 'Welcome to Lake Toba,' he grinned, like a marsh mongoose with a crocodile egg.

* * *

The Siallagans - the family of 17-year-old Kornel - had built a simple tin-roofed house on stilts in the tiny secluded cove of Tuk Tuk Timbul. Recently they had added the losmen - a long hut split into six rooms, each with two narrow beds and just enough space to walk between them. Twenty yards away, an open restaurant faced the lake.

On arrival, Kornel introduced us to his parents, a slightly-built, elderly man in shorts and T-shirt, and a barefoot woman of about forty in a sarong and blouse, her hair tied back from a face both strong and benevolent. We then met the three oldest sisters: Nurmin, nineteen with a shock of wavy black hair and a wide smile; Remin, eighteen years old with long flowing hair; and Lormen, sixteen and thin with a permanently quizzical expression. All beautiful young women. Then came 12-year-old Bontel. Bright-eyed, with a shiny black fringe and a cheeky smile, Bontel, was known as 'Boss'.

'Hi man,' he chirped. 'You stay here. Very good place. You like it very much.'

An hour after our arrival, after we had met several other younger Siallagan children, a tall Australian with stubbled jaws and drooped eyelids came weaving down the track to the cove and plonked himself down in front of us.

'Hi,' he said. 'Name's Tony. I'd like to invite you guys over to my place in the next village for tea and ganja cookies. You can see the inside of a traditional Batak house. Only problem is that I accidentally burned half of it down. I was stoned and fell asleep, and knocked over an oil lamp.'

Christine, Cora and I followed Tony up the cliff track and down along the foreshore to his village, where he was the sole foreign visitor. The house in which he was staying was the standard, massive Batak structure of wooden beams on stilts, painted in red ochre and chalk, built entirely without nails, and supporting a saddle-roof of corrugated tin that curved up to pinnacles at both ends, although one end was badly burnt.

'The pinnacles of the saddle symbolise the buffalo's horns,' Tony said. 'The Bataks see it as a link between Heaven and Earth. The carvings on the gable are of Naga Padoha, the giant serpent on which the Earth rests. And you have lizards and the head of the *singa* [a bulging-eyed monster that was part human, part buffalo, and part crocodile].'

'Seen the church?' Tony asked as we climbed the steps leading to the raised doorway of the house.

'What church?' Cora asked.

'The one that got blown down in last night's storm. You'd think an elephant sat on it.'

'No. We only came about an hour ago,' Cora said.

'Oh yeah,' Tony said. 'Well, you should go take a look some time. Some houses down in the village too - mostly lost their roofs. Seen any of them?'

'No,' Cora reminded him. 'We just got here.'

In the semi-darkness of his new room, smelling strongly of the charred embers of his old room, we squatted on the floor. Tony dished out the tea and cookies. He scratched a mosquito bite on his neck and chomped into a cookie which pretty much put Tony out of circulation for the rest of the day. Christine, Cora and I went back to our cove and another electrical storm that bounced across the rim of the ancient caldera purely for our entertainment.

The next day was Sunday; and on Sundays Tuk Tuk Timbul was consumed by religion. As a result of the missionary work of late 19th century Rhenish-Lutherans, the Toba Bataks were Christians, albeit with the odd animist belief thrown in. The Siallagans were regular churchgoers, with 19-year-old Nurmin of the wavy black hair and wide smile being chief advocate.

'You come too,' she invited all at the losmen. 'We go to Ambarita. Very nice.'

In no time she had mustered a major god-seeking expedition. Nurmin, Remin, Lormen and a younger sister named Lastri, led the way in an array of bright dresses. Christine, Cora and I followed, while Philip and Gerard, two bearded, ever-smiling French cousins took up the rear.

'Slowly, slowly walking,' Nurmin advised as we moved at tortoise-pace up the cliff path and past the tombs of the Batak ancestors. She was particularly distressed by my own pace which she considered life-threatening and in need of her special attentions. From then on 'slowly walking' became a Nurmin refrain, synonymous with life on Samosir where tension and stress were dangerous killers looking in vain for a foothold.

At Ambarita, we stopped at the 300-year-old royal court of Raja Siallagan, a circle of stone chairs where disputes were once settled and the punishments of criminals ordained. At tribal trials the chief would sit in the stone armchair, while the lesser elders occupied the surrounding chairs, with the accused sitting on the smallest one closest to the table. Anyone sentenced to death was then blindfolded, tied hand and foot and carted off to a large stone execution block, where he or she was, according to Nurmin, sliced, seasoned and pummelled with a mallet until tender.

'Also eating tourists,' she added. 'Tourists very delicious.'

The church, a modest structure of beams, bamboo and a tiled roof, turned out to be a place of worship for what my mother would have called 'the holy rollers'. Ten minutes after we'd all been ushered into the appropriate male and female aisles, the service began with some forty people joyously singing and clapping hands. But, without warning, the tenor changed with a series of impromptu speeches where nobody seemed to be in control. The men, however, were the principal speech-makers, directing reams of fiery rhetoric at the women and children, clearly the island's principal sinners.

'Jesu Christu!' people shouted from left and right as the speeches grew in ferocity and the congregation broke into loud, passionate sobbing and crying. One by one they dropped to their knees, wailing, chanting and pounding the earthen floor with their fists, shoulders heaving in infectious fervour, until the only people upright were the foreigners. Whatever old Pastor Ludwig Nommensen had told these people, he had told it well. When the big wooden door at the back of the church began banging and crashing in the wind, the French cousins, Philip and Gerard, fled.

We foreigners should go to church more often, Nurmin said as we made our way home. Otherwise, come the day, we'd all be bloody sorry.

The coming ten days blended into images of cloud puffs, glorious sunshine, or ferocious storms, with eagles diving for fish, Nurmin and her mother chasing snakes through their vegetable patch, and small red-and-green lizards darting through the flowers and chilli bushes. We would sometimes sit for hours gazing out over the silver sheen of the lake, undisturbed unless a fishing dugout was to break the water. Or, during an occasional energy surge, we might walk to the market at Ambarita or climb into the central mountains.

* * *

'Let thy step be slow and steady, that thou stumble not.' So said Tokugawa Ieyasu, 16th-century founder and first *shōgun* of the Tokugawa *shogunate* of Japan. Chief among his 20th-century devotees, undoubtedly, were the Bataks of Samosir Island.

This drove our next-door neighbour, a skinny, thin-lipped German-Brazilian called Rolf, into a state of severe aggravation, greatly enjoyed by the Siallagans. It was the second Saturday of our stay. Rolf, Cora, the French cousins and I were waiting for the ferry - already an hour late - to take us to Parapat market. Nurmin, who was swimming in the lake, and young Boss, were also planning to go.

'Hey Rolf,' Nurmin would call from the water as Rolf paced the shore, 'Batak people no keep time, eh? Maybe ferry come one hour. Maybe two. Maybe no come today, eh? Maybe already gone.'

Two hours late, the most overloaded tiny ferry in the world pulled up at the rocks that were Tuk Tuk Timbul's wharf. We all squeezed on board and off we went.

'Stay on deck,' I advised Cora. 'If this thing topples, we at least get a second chance.'

Cora said I was Job's comforter and not a great swimmer.

'I have a medal,' I argued.

'True but irrelevant,' she said. 'Two lengths of a swimming pool when you were thirteen is a far cry from the distance between Samosir and Parapat.'

Crammed below deck were all those people, swimmers or not, who would never get that second chance if the boat went down. You hear about them all the time.

In Parapet, Cora and I had a mission: post some cards to Ireland. We located the post office and politely stood in line. When we reached the counter, we stood for twenty minutes while a dour-looking man in his early forties growled away to himself, scribbling on pieces of paper and ignoring us. He then looked up and checked his watch.

'Twelve o'clock,' he said in a monotone. 'Stamps finish.' And slammed down the hatch. I thought I was dreaming.

Boss, who had come along to do some family shopping, said that I should do something terrible. I still find it hard to believe that I didn't punch the living daylights out of that hatch.

Back in the restaurant that evening, the Siallagan girls were cooking and singing and the usual lightning was streaking the sky when, behind the backs of Christine and Cora, 16-year-old Lormen nabbed a brute of a cockroach. After quietly roasting it over the cooking fire, she handed it to her mother who was eating rice and vegetables further down the communal table.

'Cora! Christine!' the mother called, holding high the cockroach. When the two women turned, the mother closed her eyes and crunched down on the beast with a forced moan of pleasure.

'Yum-yum,' Lormen said.

You could hear Christine's screams all the way to Ambarita.

* * *

Sunbathing baffled Nurmin. 'No good!' she'd exclaim whenever she saw anyone peel off their clothes to lie in the sun. On the hottest of days, she'd appear wearing sleeves and a broad straw hat. They only came off when she went for a swim or worked in the restaurant. She would then, at the end of each day, inspect the damage self-inflicted by the crazy foreigners.

'This very good,' she'd say of Rolf who was white as a cellar ghost. 'This not so good,' she'd advise Christine whose fair complexion was not so prone to darkening. 'And this no-o-o good,' she'd conclude sadly at the ruin brought upon ourselves by myself, Cora, the French cousins, and amorous Jacques and Michelle from Quebec who were already in residence when we arrived.

Foreigners' names were another source of wonder. She had no difficulty pronouncing any of them and found it hilarious that Jacques couldn't pronounce mine.

'Why?' she ridiculed. 'Why you no understand? And you tourist. Me understand and me no tourist.'

Of wars she had this to say: 'Why people fighting? In how long it take my father to dig garden for feeding only one family, his life over. So, why fighting?'

She also wanted to know if, beyond Lake Toba, girls had the same access to education as boys.

'Me never go to school. Too poor before. Before, this family eat only rice and tapioca and my father working like this [digging]. So he make small Batak house for tourists. One house only in one week, and he sell for 500 rupiahs, only so we can eat vegetable. But, other man, when he hear, he come to my father and he say stop. So we no eat vegetable again, only tapioca. Now we have losmen - only three and a half month - now good. Eat vegetable again. My father no have to work so hard. Remin and me always only cooking for tourists, but now life good. Now eating tomato and vegetable. Now, Kornel and children go to school. Me only work. Why girls always only work.'

What could any of us say? Other than it happened, Nurmin, when patriarchy transitioned from stupid to stupider.

Eventually, a morning came when it was time for Christine, Cora and myself to leave Tuk Tuk Timbul and take a further step towards Australia. We went looking for Nurmin to say goodbye but couldn't find her. The others were all there and there were kisses and handshakes all around.

'You come back again,' 18-year-old Remin with the long flowing hair, translated for her mother. 'She cook you good cockroach.'

Then the Toba ferry rolled into view.

Christine, Cora and I were dragged on board the old wooden tub and we pushed off from the rocks. Jacques and Michelle blew kisses from the losmen and called to Remin that they wouldn't mind breakfast in the customary two hours' time. Too late, we saw Nurmin. She was standing by a solitary papaya tree on the brow of a small hill behind the restaurant, a hoe in her right hand, her hair erupting from a red bandana. Looking taller in the new sarong the French cousins had bought her at Parapat market, she neither waved nor called.

When the ferry pulled away for Parapat, she wiped an eye and turned away. It's a moment that lingers still.

CHAPTER 9

The Trans-Sumatran Highway

'Prepare for the roughest journey of your life,' was the warning posted in the newly-published *South-East Asia On A Shoestring*, encountered for the first time in Bukittinggi in western Sumatra.

'Whoever wrote this,' I said, 'has never gone third class on the Erzurum Express from Istanbul.'

'It's a bit worrying all the same,' Cora said, 'If you talk to anyone who took the bus in this direction, they tell you take the boat from Padang to Java, that it couldn't possibly be worse: if you talk to anyone who took the boat, they tell you, for the sake of your life, take the bus.'

'The bus would probably be more interesting,' I suggested. 'And we could always break the journey with overnight stops.'

Cora went along with this. Christine opted for the boat. And *South-East Asia On A Shoestring* had it right: no journey before or since has equalled the nightmare of the Trans-Sumatran Highway of 1976. It was to cost me a fractured coccyx and the general diffusion of my scepticism of the written word.

The journey from Parapat to Bukittinggi was a sort of evolution. As the road wound its way through high mountains, teeming rainforests and spectacular gorges, the general discomfort of being cramped and buffeted was initially almost tolerable. However, as the hours passed and the potholes enlarged and the bus became more crowded, the conditions became the journey. The hard, green, cigarette-scarred seats either drooped so you had to brace against the seat in front, or tilted and cut into the backs of your knees. Wooden stools in the aisle accommodated extra passengers who added exponentially to the sacks, boxes, and bags cluttering every available space. High-pitched, sad-bastard music, piped over a tinny sound system, screeched relentlessly until an American guy in the seat in front cracked at two in the morning.

'TURN OFF THAT SHIT!' he roared, which silenced the speakers for all of two hours.

Meanwhile, throughout the day, those around us who weren't

smoking clove cigarettes were busy throwing up into plastic bags and towels, while fruit peelings, peanut shells and vomit-bags mounted on the floor. On a road that endlessly twisted on itself, the driving veered between brutal and more brutal. Screeching halts would signal near misses of livestock or horse-drawn carts. Intermittent stops for coffee and food (fuel for the next round of puking) happened at roadside shacks with toilets from Dante's Inferno. After six rattling hours, night fell and the scenery vanished, and it was still twelve hours to Bukittinggi. This, we had been assured, was the best part of the ride to Java.

At four o'clock in the morning we crossed the Equator and stopped briefly so that the passengers could get out and pee by the side of the road, or finish throwing up from the last round of eating. Then, despite the conditions, Cora and I managed to doze for a couple of hours, waking up to a magnificent morning that almost made the bus tolerable again.

The early greyness, accompanied by a chilling haze, was gradually dispersed by shafts of watery sunlight that opened up a lush land of canyons, ravines and volcanic peaks, with the distant, 9,486-foot Mount Merapi smoking away a year after its last major eruption. An hour later we arrived, gravel-eyed, in Bukittinggi. As we approached the town the American guy who had taken the screaming fit, gave myself and Cora a brown, scaly fruit each.

'Snake-fruit,' he said. 'Good stuff.'

I ate mine and threw up within minutes. Twenty years later I came across the same fruit growing wild in the rainforests of Borneo. I ate it again and threw up again. I would appear to be snake-fruit intolerant.

Ringed by the three peaks of Merapi, Singgalong and Sago, Bukittinggi was a relaxed mountain town of wooden houses, verandas and tin roofs, many again designed in the buffalo-horn shape. As a centre of the matriarchal and matrilineal Minangkabau people of West Sumatra, it combined Islam with a matrilineal society in which the oldest living female was the most powerful member of the household. Ancestral property was passed down the female line, and women were deferred to in all matters of family politics, finances and prospective marriage alliances. It was also the town of cinnamon trees and regular minor earth tremors that felt for all the world like a heavy truck passing by.

We arrived, drawn and pasty-faced, to the clip-clopping of horse-drawn bemos and the voices of traders pushing massively overloaded carts to market. Exhausted and wanting nothing more than to eat, sleep and gather our wits, Christine, Cora and I booked in to the Grand Hotel, the local travellers' haunt. A fortuitous move as it transpired.

Sometime around mid-morning, Cora and I were sitting in the

common area of the hotel when we struck up a conversation with a couple who were among a dozen other traveller guests. Alan Dodds, tall, with collar-length curling hair, a light moustache, a quick sense of humour, a keen interest in the writings of Carlos Castaneda, and a frame thinned down by eleven months of travel, came from London. Alan had a thirst for adventure that was written all over his face. Christina (Chris) McGuinness, rosy-cheeked with long dark hair, was Scottish. A strong calm woman, Chris called Alan 'Allie', tempered some of his more adventurous ideas, and laughed in rippling bursts at life's more ridiculous turns. Alan was twenty-nine. Chris was thirty-six but looked ten years younger. Seasoned travellers, they too were on their way to Australia.

Very occasionally in life you meet people with whom you strike up an immediate, inexplicable bond. And so it was with Alan and Chris. We opened our mouths - *Hi, where are you from?* - and they never shut. On through the rest of the morning. Into the afternoon. Through dinner, shared with Christine Hakkers and Philip and Gerard, the French cousins from Samosir who had also made it to the Grand Hotel. And on into the night. From topic to topic, with this in common and that in common. And where would it go next? Maybe we could meet up in Bali?

In the morning Christine went to the market and returned with the makings of guacamole to find the conversation was in overdrive again. All five of us shared breakfast, then went off to visit Ngarai Sianok Canyon at the edge of town where Christine, Alan and Chris discovered that they were all on their way to Perth.

'We can stay in touch,' Alan said. 'Then we can all go and visit our Irish cousins [us] in Sydney.'

You just knew that something more would come of this.

'The world's biggest flower grows down in that canyon,' Chris said. 'They call it the *rafflesia arnoldii*. It can grow to three feet across and weigh up to fifteen pounds. It's supposed to smell like rotting meat and that attracts the pollinators. Shall we go and look for it?'

We didn't. We fed monkeys on the canyon rim. And the conversation rattled on - through a trip to the market and on through lunch. And back at the hotel while Alan and Chris waited for the three o'clock bus back to Parapat.

As bus time approached Chris was laughing.

'You know,' she said, 'coming here was totally weird for us. We'd been hanging out in bliss on Samosir Island when, for reasons that neither of us could fathom, we condemned ourselves to two 18-hour bus rides that cost forty dollars, for one day in Bukittinggi. It made absolutely no sense, until now.'

Less than two years later, that chance meeting in Bukittinggi would lead to a wild and scary brush with the Shoalhaven Gorge of New South Wales that Cora would later call one of my 'great ideas' (sarcasm, I suppose), and where the hell did I pick it up.

* * *

We left Bukittinggi at noon on a Monday with tickets to a spot on the map called Muaratebo where we planned the first break on the journey to Java. Christine Hakkers waved us good luck and promised to see us in Australia.

Our bus was an antiquated Chevrolet. Our seats were indeterminate spaces on a hard bench. The usual horn-blasting flourish accompanied our departure. A short way from town and the 'Trans-Sumatran Highway' became dirt. On a crowded bus, long bereft of its suspensions and carrying half a ton of rice on the roof, this marked an alarming turn of events. As we crashed and shuddered into the first ruts and potholes, bouncing up and down on the wooden benches to the omnipresent smell of clove cigarettes (soon accompanied by vomit), and the screeching, crackling music that had bawled us out most of the way from Parapat, it was suddenly a long way to Java.

'Maybe we should have taken the boat,' Cora said.

Too late now as, coughing and spluttering, we wrapped our faces in T-shirts against the brown dust that swirled in through the windows.

South-east of Bukittinggi the road climbed above cultivated valleys into dense rainforest that draped the mountainsides in a dark shroud, from which troupes of monkeys burst onto the road. On what had now become an altogether savage surface, we convulsed along, hour after hour through the heat and dust, each twist tossing passengers on top of one another, every narrow bridge requiring a careful lining up of the bus so we didn't topple off the rough planks. Whenever we slowed down, we were caught in another choking cloud of our own dust.

Although we had left Bukittinggi with a full bus, we continued to gather passengers until forty-five people, and a mountain of baggage, were crammed into, between, underneath and on top of thirty seat-spaces made for people far smaller than us two who sat with our knees jammed into the seat in front, me with my guitar upended between my knees. Eventually, the driver's three assistants couldn't hack it anymore: they flashed out through a window and up onto the roof. A short respite on a potholed, but surfaced, section of road allowed us to smoke without fear of jamming the cigarette into someone's ear. We were then back on the dirt, being pummelled and bludgeoned again, the jungle having closed in conclusively with only a few small villages of bamboo and thatch, and little else but ourselves on the road.

We were in the mountains when the sun went down and the bus, with its glassless windows, became a chill box. When we dropped back to the lowlands we had the heat again. And there were new threats. A couple of hours after dark, when we stopped in a desolate stretch of forest we were warned that the night cacophony wasn't all benign.

'Do not walk far,' one of our travelling companions called after us. 'Tigers are very dangerous in the night.'

'It's a good job we're getting off this wreck in Muaratebo,' Cora said. 'At least we'll have a night's sleep.'

As Donald Trump would have put it, bigly wrong.

Twelve hours out of Bukittinggi, after a series of breakdowns and punctures, we trundled into a torpid wood-and-bamboo settlement enclosed by dense jungle. This was Muaratebo. Caked in dust, with bloodshot eyes, we fell into the village's one open restaurant, although restaurant is an over-statement.

At a glance it was obvious that there wasn't much to Muaratebo other than the greatest assortment of bugs on Earth. Every creation that walked, crawled, hopped, flew, wriggled or scuttled, did so in that restaurant. The owners who owed much custom that night to myself and Cora for diverting the bus from its normal route, wondered what terrible folly had prompted us to be dropped off in the back end of nowhere.

'We have a plan,' I explained. 'We are going to travel by river over two days from here to Jambi. On a rubber-boat.'

The locals seemed amazed. Maybe there was no rubber in Muaratebo?

'Crocodiles, monkeys, fireflies, the lot,' I assured Cora.

Twenty minutes later, when the bus pulled out, we were given the only accommodation available - the floor of a doorless room behind the restaurant where the walls stopped an arm's length from the roof. This, we quickly sussed, was where all the biting bugs that tired of the hooley out in the restaurant came to retire.

'It's not really amazing that nobody else got off,' Cora said as we spread our sleeping bags on the floor. 'No sleep with this lot.'

'Try,' I said. 'It'll all look better in the morning.' But it didn't.

For one thing, there was no boat for three or four days, until an enormous cargo of logs (not rubber), still arriving at the river, was loaded on board. Three or four days in Muaratebo was out of the question. For another, the bus only stopped here on passenger request, not too often in other words. But never let it be said... Down at the river, crisscrossed by a few dugouts, I had a brainwave.

'Look,' I said to Cora. 'All that bamboo.' It hung out over the river in huge clusters, as thick at the base as a human thigh.

'Yes?' Cora said. 'What about all that bamboo?'

'We could make a raft. That bamboo would float us down to Jambi. We could lash a platform together, maybe even build a hut...'

'That's a great idea,' Cora said. 'See you in Jambi.'

We were still arguing the piece over lunch, and bracing ourselves for at least a day in the screaming heat of Muaratebo when a truck rolled in. The driver, a bony man in grease-smudged shorts, was on his way to Jambi and agreed to take us: Cora in the cab along with himself, his mechanic and his brother, me in the open body of the truck with the packs and an assortment of spare parts for earth-moving equipment. Ten minutes later Cora and I almost lost our packs, along with the entire truck, on an unsecured boarding-ramp at a jungle ferry-crossing. Then we were off again into the vast tangled forests of southern Sumatra on an atrociously corrugated and potholed track, pythons slithering into the undergrowth and monkeys cascading through the trees. In the wilderness beyond, the forests were home to Asian elephants, tigers, Asiatic golden cats, clouded leopards, tapirs, monkeys, orang-utans, rhinos, and a huge diversity of other creatures, many of them virtually unknown outside of Indonesia.

Conditions on the open truck were not the best. It was extremely hot and, without water, I was dehydrating badly, a situation further exacerbated by the wind generated by our momentum. To this was added the clouds of dust and the independent manoeuvring of every loose object on board as we swung around bends with me being battered by the heavier pieces. My seat was a roll of caterpillar tracking that was brutal on the potholes. It wasn't so bad when we were in agreement as to whether we were going up or down; but more often than not that wasn't the case. On just such an occasion, as I came down, we hit another enormous pothole and the cylinder of tracking and I collided in mid-air with a crack that sent a shooting pain right through me. I had just fractured my coccyx. The pain would follow me, on and off, for weeks. In Sydney I would be told by a doctor that nothing much could be done; and to this day, sitting for long periods, such as on a plane, becomes uncomfortable.

In the middle of the afternoon, we passed a family camped on the roadside. A wrinkled, bare-breasted woman with long matted hair stood beside a young boy in a loincloth. A little further on, a man in tattered shorts, carrying a long knife, and a group of other men in loincloths, were half-hidden in the forest. They were *Orang Rimba* (people of the forest), nomadic hunter-gatherer descendants of the first wave of Malays to colonise Sumatra.

'Kubu people,' the driver told Cora, 'they steal your mind, so you follow them in the forest. When somebody dies in a village, they move to another part of the forest.'[15] (Over the coming decades the *Orang Rimba* would be driven from their traditional lands by logging companies, palm oil plantations and government 'resettlement' schemes that would devastate them, their culture and the rainforests of Sumatra.)

In Jambi we again broke the journey and checked into a cheap hotel, desperate for sleep. But the heat and the mosquitoes put paid to that. In the morning, half out of our minds with exhaustion, we discovered that Jambi was the Sumatran centre for psychological warfare. Its version of white noise was ever so simple.

'Hello mister, what is your name? Where you come from?'

At first, it appeared as a friendly gesture. It then began to hover under a question mark. It progressed to an irritation. And finally it drove us insane. I can see your face: what was the big deal? Today I also find it hard to imagine how something so trivial could have so badly affected us at the time but it did. When we fled to the balcony of our hotel, it congregated down in the street. So we hid in the room - until the heat drove us back outside.

'Hello mister,' a voice began again...

Someone's gonna be sorry, I said to myself, although I had no idea how that was going to happen. Or how I'd explain it in court.

'You must come to my house,' the voice went on. 'You will please stay the night with my family. You will meet my parents and my brothers and sisters.'

I've cracked, I thought. *I'm hearing things. Any minute now and I'll be talking to the dead.* But no. There was a real speaker, a smiling 18-year-old student who had earlier noted our plight. 'I saw that you were not happy,' he said. 'I told my father that you must come to our home.'

---

15.   'Kubu' was a Malay exonym ascribed to the *Orang Rimba*.

We gathered our bags and followed. And there in Jambi, in the home of the Wage family, plied with food and coffee, we re-established a tenuous link with sanity as the old father rocked his cane chair and tapped his feet to Beatle tunes rapped out on my guitar by our saviour.

In the morning however, when we turned up at the bus station an hour before the departure of the Lubuklinggau bus, life became unpleasant again. Passing close to a group of six station loafers, all in their early twenties, I had my hat whipped from my head by a lad with pinched eyes and a half-wit grin. A lad who thought he was a hoot but couldn't differentiate between a travel-emaciated foreigner who might provide a spot of entertainment, and one reduced to an unstable wreck.

'Could I please have my hat?' I said.

His reply in Indonesian drew howls from his mates and a gathering crowd, delighted by the diversion. Although love of humanity's foibles was now running thin, I forced a smile. He should now, I figured, hand over the hat. But instead, he pulled out a magazine photo of a naked white woman, waved it at Cora and, still playing to the crowd, began to prod her with his index finger.

That, I said to myself, *is assault.*

Almost immediately I became keenly aware that I grew up in a place called Evergreen Road where Micky L who lived up the street could handle this kind of thing with alacrity, but that I myself wasn't doing very well right now.

One of me was saying, *No way is this guy getting away with that.* Another was urging caution: *Now, don't be rash. There are six of them.* Then in marched the ghost of Micky L. His real name was Michael Sullivan. His nickname was a reference to the Irish-American boxer of the late 19th-century, John L Sullivan, the world's last heavyweight champion of bare-knuckle pugilism under the London Prize Ring Rules. Cora claimed that there was a loud guttural discharge that she couldn't repeat and out popped 'the mad eyes' that must have belonged to Micky L.

The long and the short of what next occurred was that the hoot's mates stepped back to give him the field; I retrieved the hat; there was a swift moment of mild disorder; the hoot hit the ground and a very irritated Cora gave him a kick in the arse for good luck.

'Don't take his hat again,' she said into his stunned face. When we walked away, the onlookers gave us a wide berth. No more messing with the Irish, compliments of Micky L.

Between Jambi and Lubuklinggau we bounced and hammered along a hopeless jungle track for fifteen more hours, dust blinding and choking, knees banging against the seats, heads banging on the roof, me and my guitar wrestling for the same space, the screeching music, the cram of sweating bodies, exhausted neighbours who had travelled non-stop from Bukittinggi falling asleep on top of us or throwing up on their shoes, glaring sunshine and nerves frayed to a frazzle. At every stop, Cora and I were stoned by village children or followed by 'Hello mister, what is your name...?' In the end even the monkeys couldn't cheer us up.

By late afternoon, the atmosphere on the bus was sour and sullen. The two drivers, (taking turns at trying to catch some sleep in the underside luggage compartment) and the Bukittinggi passengers, were extremely touchy. We weren't far behind. The crumpled T-shirts through which we were breathing, our every stitch of clothing and our hair, were plastered in dust, and our eyes were bloodshot and stinging. And nine more bone-crushing hours to go.

'I'm getting off!' I told Cora after hitting my head while spitting a mouthful of dust out through the window. 'I've had it! I don't give a flying fiddler's about tigers, scorpions, snakes or anything else out there. I'll sleep by the side of the road. I'll sit there all night if I have to. Anything but this. Either I get out or I have a nervous fucking breakdown!'

'Are you sure you're not having one now?' Cora said.

Passengers stared. We smashed into another pothole. A shattering sound emanated from above. Presently, a dark slimy liquid gushed in through the glassless window and sloshed all over me. There was nothing to do but laugh. Hysterically.

Later in the night, we stopped to eat in a small jungle oasis where, out of the blue, a cup of tea was thrown over Cora. We were both shocked, as indeed was the hallowed ghost of Micky L who was about to rise to the moment. But it became clear that it was an accident when the culprit was smacked in the gob by one of the drivers at whom the tea had been badly aimed. Two more fights flared in the mugginess of the restaurant before the exhausted crew and passengers slumped back onto the bus to thump and rattle into the night. At two in the morning, Cora and I flopped into the Subur Losmen in Lubuklinggau, shaking from fatigue and wondering what next.

Four and a half hours later the heat and mosquitoes had driven us out into the street to greet a crimson dawn through raw and swollen eyes. By eight, the harassment and stone-throwing outside had driven us back in, forcing us to ground until after sunset and another night with the mosquitoes. From now on we were in full flight for Java. All through the next day and all through the night. And the next day and the next night. And the next day again. Sixty hours without a wink of sleep. At Tanjang Karang we cashed our last forty dollars. (The flights from Penang to Medan had been a bit extravagant.) At Panjang we boarded a ferry for Java, leaving lowland Sumatra behind - forever we swore. At Merak we found a bus to Bandung and from there a train to Yogyakarta. A burly, curly, bearded Englishman and his petite Australian partner joined us in the carriage as we collapsed, face down, onto our packs.

'Jesus Christ,' Barbara said. 'You two look like you've been through the mill.'

'Sumatra,' Paul said. 'We're flying over it this time.'

* * *

At the Africa Asia Hotel, the backpackers' haunt of Yogyakarta, we slept for thirty-six hours solid. There was then a big reunion. Over a feed of frogs' legs and rice, we were reunited with Christine Hakkers and Philip and Gerard, the French cousins from Lake Toba. Then, a massive intrusion! Amid the celebrations, and the exchanges of Sumatran horror stories, a small black monkey came bolting down the hotel courtyard and bounced into my lap. I sprang to my feet with a courageous shriek and the little bugger fell off. For a second or two he didn't know what to do, but he rallied and bounced up into Barbara's lap. 'Poor baby,' Barbara said, stroking his head. He buried a cheek in her chest and gave me a dirty sleekit look.

August 17th was Independence Day. A great parade took place through central Yogyakarta. Gamelan orchestras. Traditional costumes. Floats. Hundreds of men dressed up as Indonesian freedom fighters and Dutch colonial soldiers. Christine was disgusted at the unflattering images of the 'Dutch', who were mostly dead or maimed.

'Hey John,' one of a group of men shouted, 'You got prostitutes?'

Christine, Cora and Barbara were the target. We ignored them.

'Prostitutes!' the boys called again.

Then the great procession ground to a demoralising halt. Somewhere down the line, nobody had planned for the procession's arrival.

'Another great Indonesian fuck-up!' Paul shouted at our tormentors.

We legged it back to the hotel for bongs, coffee and biscuits.

'Time for bed,' Barbara said when teddy-bear Paul couldn't keep his eyes open any more. 'You know how hard you are to shift when you fall asleep.'

'I know,' Paul said. 'A sixteen-stone wardrobe.'

After a few more days in Yogyakarta, during which we managed a classical Javanese dance performance and a gamelan concert at the 18th-century royal complex, Cora and I travelled with Paul and Barbara to Bali. Across the stinking-hot, fertile plains of Java it was rice-harvesting time and the flooded fields and terraces were full of women in sarongs and conical hats. In Surabaya, where the mosquitoes were particularly bad, Cora and I wrote to Tony Lee, an old friend from Afghanistan days, asking him to forward $150 to Darwin to ease our passage to Sydney. We then chugged on east on an ancient train, skirting around the imposing mass of smoking Mount Bromo into a rose-flecked evening that brought people to bathe in the streams and rivers. Overhead, giant fruit bats came in such waves that the flapping of their wings overrode the rocking clatter of the train.

CHAPTER 10

Before The Deluge

'A busy day on Kuta Beach would have been twenty young travellers out of their heads on magic mushrooms.'

How many times down the years have I thus described that idyllic haven?

The fungi - of the psilocybin order - would have been woven into omelettes by beach chefs, kings and queens of the genre who could also rustle up a mean 'Kuta cookie' (high in Buddha grass, low in cookie). The graveyard shift on the beach would consequently find grown men and women staring out to sea for the Second Coming. An Australian walking by would say *Hail Caesar*. A French woman - a nun in a delusional moment of an earlier life - would see the devil lurking in the shrubbery.

Fuddle-de-doo.

Strenuous activity for those browsing on the exotic would rarely stretch beyond a spot of body-surfing. We gave it a go and learned that if ever you brace yourself against a nine-foot wave, you lose. Full stop.

Washed up on the shore as battered flotsam.

A handful of young Western women would lie naked in the sun. Young Balinese women in sarongs, tunics and broad straw hats would sell them massages and skinless pineapples on sticks. A small number of Balinese men would come to gape at the phenomenon. Other Balinese women would while away idle times by de-lousing one another's hair, a pastime common across rural Asia.

We were here because a loan of forty dollars from Paul and Barbara had allowed us to extend our Indonesian visas in Yogyakarta and stretch our stay in the country. Otherwise our time in Bali would have been little more than a dash to Denpasar's airport. Now we were ensconced in the Kherdi Lodge among the coconut palms at the back of Kuta Beach.

Accommodation at Kuta Beach was mainly to be found in fishermen's huts that doubled up as basic lodges, connected by quiet, sandy walkways. The 'rich tourists' - who seemed to be mainly Japanese -

were to be found nine miles away in Sanur. They had the hotels. We had the sunsets. At night there were no clubs, no discos. Only the stars and the moon through the fronds of the coconut palms.

Bali before the deluge.

* * *

In contrast to the Islam predominant in Sumatra and Java, Bali was Hindu. But a Hinduism spawned by a unique history. The first settlers, who arrived by sea more than two and a half thousand years ago, brought with them a set of beliefs that worshipped dead ancestors and the spirits of trees, rocks, mountains and rivers. These beliefs governed life on the island until the arrival in the 9th century of Buddhist and Hindu influences. The Hindu influences were further reinforced by three significant events: the marriage of the Balinese King Udayana Warmadewa to the Javanese Hindu Princess Mahendradatta at the end of the 10th century; the conquest of Bali by the east-Javan Majapahit empire in 1343; and the fall in 1515 of the Majapahit empire itself which led to a mass exodus from Java to Bali of Hindu priests, artisans and nobility.

Similar to what happened to Buddhism in Burma, the resulting hybrid of Hinduism and animism spawned an army of demons, goblins and spirits who appeared frequently in the human realm to taunt and terrorise. This religious format dominated every aspect of life on the island which, according to its people, was loaned to them by the gods on condition that beauty be the essence of human endeavour.

The Balinese effort to fulfil their side of the celestial bargain was on wide display. In every village, rows of slender bamboo poles, curled on top like upturned fishing hooks, were hung with woven figures of Dewi Sri, the rice-goddess. Every house had its own altar where offerings of food sat beside burning incense. Stone gods and demons were equally placated. Processions of women streamed to the island's temples, with masses of richly decorated offerings balanced on their heads.

Having strolled around to the closest village temple - a serene structure of tiered pagodas, tapering to a pinnacle and thatched in black palm-fibre, Paul had an idea.

'We could have a *real* religious experience. We could visit one of those temples that have legions of macaques.'

'We did that in Kathmandu,' I said. 'A woman threw rocks at us.'

'The closest monkey temple to Kuta,' Paul went on, 'is Bukit Sari in Sangeh village, about twenty-one miles away. We should go there.'

'And be attacked by monkeys?' Barbara said. 'Or women with rocks? Why not?'

On our third morning in Kuta, Paula's suggestion took hold: we travelled to Sangeh by bemo, an old minibus with the seats removed and replaced by wooden benches arranged along both sides so that passengers faced one another. Stools on the floor accommodated the extras.

On arrival at Bukit Sari, the eldest of three temple keepers handed us sarongs and sashes. 'You must put these on,' he said, 'before you go inside. Also, please read here.' He pointed to a sign.

> *'Your attention please, during menstruation, ladies are strictly not allowed to enter the temple, thank you.'*

'Here we go again,' Cora said. 'But how can anyone tell?'

'It's like "on my scout's word of honour",' Paul said. 'Or maybe the monkeys suss it out.'

'Anyway, we're not ladies, are we Cora?' Barbara said. 'We're women. So it doesn't matter.'

'It will if the monkeys jump us,' Cora pointed out.

The three monkey tribes of Sangeh, descendants of the monkey god, Hanuman, made a living robbing tourists and skedaddling up the trees with their loot. Cameras, sunglasses, hats and handbags were all fair game. The only hope of retrieval was to lure the robbers back down with nuts or bananas, sold, conveniently enough, by the locals. When the greedy brood of Hanuman went to grab for the food, they dropped the loot. Not good for a camera dropped from forty feet up.

As soon as we entered the complex, on our way to the temple shrines and pagodas, they swooped down from the nutmeg trees of 'Thieves Alley' and snatched every loose object they could find which, fortunately, were attached to an American woman who had travelled with us on the bemo. Although one of the monkeys jumped onto Barbara's neck, grabbed her by the hair and held her hostage, we had nothing to trade. Seeing this, the monkey pounced from Barbara to a Swiss couple carrying silos of peanuts.

We learned from a local elder that, if you're focussed enough in prayer, you can hear the monkeys talk. And if you're even more focussed, you can see the trees of the forest walking about the place. Like the Ents of Middle Earth.

'For "focussed",' Paul said, 'we should read mushrooms.'

* * *

We were on a dirt road onto which our bemo had diverted when we drove into the procession. At first we thought we had run into some kind of exuberant political rally, until we saw the funeral towers: we had run into a double cremation. We paid the bemo man, hopped out and waited beside the village temple. Cremations were the most important event in the Balinese cycle of existence, an experience not to be missed if happened upon. By all accounts, what we were now witnessing was a relatively unelaborate affair but spectacular none the less.

To a backdrop of gongs, drums, cymbals and xylophones, the procession was led by twenty barefoot men in shorts, some in T-shirts, some bare-chested, who were trotting the road with the leading funeral tower. A white coffin with a large pagoda-like canopy that made it look like a narrow four-poster bed was held at shoulder height on a platform of bamboo poles. Violently shaking and spinning the tower, the pall-bearers were yelling and charging into the crowd, while people appointed to the task splashed water over them. Once the tower had gone by, a more sedate column of mourners followed, led by five young women who appeared to be relatives of one of the dead. Dressed in orange sarongs, yellow sashes and elaborate golden tiaras, they were carried on sedan chairs strapped to bamboo poles. A bent old priest in a loincloth, brandishing a dead chicken and a garland of flowers lashed to a wooden staff, danced alongside while scores of women followed, carrying on their heads pyramids of rice, incense, fruit and flowers. In general tone, the occasion seemed oddly joyful, ushered on by oddly joyful music

The second tower, carried by thirty pall-bearers and shaded by white parasols, looked like a giant swan with outstretched wings. As it passed we were invited to join the mourners by a long-haired teenager who was a nephew of the body in the four-poster bed. Walking to the field that was the crematorium, the nephew explained the significance of the event.

To the Balinese people, death freed the soul so it could go on to the next birth. It was therefore a happy occasion. But it was also important that the departed felt appreciated. To ensure the best send-off, a family sometimes had to wait for years until they had gathered enough money. The bodies we were following had been buried for more than a year. Now they had been taken from the ground and washed before the families put them in the *wadas* [funeral towers]. The tossing and spinning of the towers was designed to confuse the souls so they couldn't come back to haunt the living.

The feasting and revelry that followed at the crematorium as the corpses were consumed by the funeral pyres, seemed more appropriate to a dignified harvest festival than a funeral. The cooled ashes were then gathered into coconut shells to be tossed into the sea down at Kuta at a later date.

The decorum of the event was in sharp contrast to some Irish wakes. When the mother of a friend of mine died, a cousin had to be robustly escorted from the premises after bursting into a raucous rendition of *Knees Up Mother Brown...*

That night, Kuta hosted a cockfight followed by a performance of the Legong dance. Tightly wrapped in golden dresses and wearing crowns of gold and frangipani flowers, three young girls played out the intricate tale of King Lasem who abducted the beautiful Princess Rangkesari and ultimately paid for his folly with his life.

Accompanied by the percussive music of the village gamelan orchestra, the dancers put on an incredible display of mime and gesture, with body, eye and eyebrow movements that belied their average age of seven. At one point the dancing was so well synchronised that two of the girls mirrored one another's steps. The Legong was performed, as it had been for centuries, on a little, dimly-lit platform to a formula passed down through generations of dancers whose brilliant careers generally ended at puberty.

* * *

Over the coming days Paul, Barbara, Cora and I developed one of those friendships that owe much to the environment in which they sprout. When you travel you are what you are there and then. There are no expectations, no demands, no overloads, no yesterdays; and in this case there was significant harmony.

We strolled along the beach to Legian, separated from Kuta by two miles of sand. We visited Ubud with its rice terraces and artists' villages. We called at the night markets of Den Pasar and ate their street food. And we sat on the beach, watched life go by and waited for those Kuta sunsets.

'You're hitchhiking from Darwin to Sydney?' Paul said on our final evening as Cora and I ran broke for the third time. 'Here, take this.' He handed me four dollars and fifty cents in Australian coins. 'An extra hamburger when you're starving is an extra hamburger.'

Down on the beach it was sunset again. The Japanese tourists, swaddled from head to toe to avoid the rays, had all gone back to Sanur and the *rombongs* had arrived for the day's grand finale. Pushed along by hawkers in sombreros, these contraptions consisted of a large tin box on a couple of bicycle wheels, with a little fire-heated oven and some storage space. They provided cooked fish, roasted corn and cold drinks to Balinese and foreigners alike.

'Stop!' Paul called after one of them. 'This guy,' he said through the side of his mouth, 'makes the finest magic mushie omelettes in Indonesia.'

Paul, Barbara, Cora and I then sat on the sand with a group of Balinese women and their children. Nobody spoke. The sun, already low, smeared scarlet, yellow and pink across bars of puckered cloud, and created on the wet foreshore an illusion of firelight on burnished bronze. A lone fisherman, returning from a day on the Indian Ocean, hauled his outrigger *perahu* above the high-tide line of seaweed, shells, broken coral and bleached crab carapaces.

A young German woman, fair of form and bare of pelt, strode down to the surf and stepped out into the sunset.

'I'm hallucinating,' Paul said. 'Whenever I see an ice-cream man, I always know I'm hallucinating. And, oh dear, here comes the ice-cream man.'

AUSTRALIA:

① HITCHHIKE FROM DARW
TO SYDNEY. 1976.

② CAPE YORK PENINSULA 1

③ BLUE MOUNTAINS AN
MT. KOSCIUSZKO 1

DARWIN

MATARANKA

LARRIMAH

GULF OF
CARPENTARIA

COEN RIVER

ROKEBY

COEN

MUSGRAVE

LAURA

COOKTOWN

MOSSHAN

MAREEBA

CAIRNS

CORAL SEA

TENNENT CREEK.

CLONCURRY.

WINTON.

ROCKHAMPTON.

TOOWOOMBA.

BRISBANE.

GLEN INNES.

BLUE
MOUNTAINS.

SYDNEY

CANBERRA.

MT. KOSCIUSZKO

TASMAN
SEA

CHAPTER 11

The Track

Black mud sucked at my feet. Mosquitoes and sand flies attacked. Fiddler crabs scuttled over the mud, the large 'fiddle' claw raised in defence. Small stubby fish with big heads and goon-eyes flipped out of shallow pools and hauled themselves along on pectoral fins. I was stumbling about among the aerial roots of mangroves in cut-off jeans. I had my Instamatic camera at hand should crocodiles appear.

Back on the riverbank, Cora was sunning herself when I emerged from the swamp, covered in mud.

'Did you have a good time?' she asked without ever opening her eyes.

Stretching down the river bank, I reached my legs into the murky water and sloshed about for a while to wash off the muck and cool the mosquito and sand-fly bites. Further upriver, I checked out a rough wooden sign that had been hammered into the ground.

'Do not swim,' it warned. 'Sharks and crocodiles in this river.'

Although I'm sure no crocodile could have leapt from that river, I jumped back.

'Did you do something silly?' Cora asked, having now opened her eyes.

'No,' I said although that wasn't the full story.

She and I then went for a short stroll through the bush - a mix of open eucalyptus forest, Pandanus palms and bamboo - only to narrowly miss being run over by a charging herd of water buffaloes.

'That does it,' Cora said. 'Let's go before we get killed.'

We pocketed the camera, went back to the motorbike and scattered before us cranes, herons, parrots and cockatoos as we made a run for the sanctuary of Peter and Audrey's.

Where, I asked myself, *are the fields of sour-faced sheep?* This, after all, was Australia.

* * *

The bush country south of Darwin was more like what we would have expected of East Africa. Skies and waterholes teeming with exotic birdlife. Huge herds of buffalo. Vast forests of gum trees. Palms and bamboo. Broad wetlands inhabited by crocodiles. Twelve-foot termite hills. Giant monitor lizards. And the Australian bushflies that buzzed in our faces, climbed into our eyes, noses and mouths and resisted all attempts to shoo them away. However, no kangaroos.

Since morning we'd been driving through this wilderness, making short forays on foot into the bush, then retreating again before we got lost. The Adelaide River, to the east of a place that some joker had named Humpty Doo, had given us something of a line that we could follow in relative safety, or so we thought.

Now we were heading back to the home of people we had never met until the day before, the day we had flown from Denpasar to Darwin, a city recovering from the devastation of Cyclone Tracey.

The hurricane that did the damage had gathered over the Arafura Sea on Christmas Eve 1974 before barrelling southwards with category four winds that ripped Darwin and its environs to shreds. The most compact hurricane ever recorded, with gale-force winds reaching no further than thirty miles from the eye, it killed seventy-one people, caused A\$837 million (A\$5 billion in 2020 dollars) of damage, destroyed more than seventy percent of Darwin's buildings, left 41,000 out of 47,000 inhabitants homeless and caused the evacuation of 30,000 people. We had heard about this storm from an Australian we met in Rangoon.

'Earlier in the day, my mate had taken acid. As he lay on his bed on Christmas Eve, the windows came in around him. Then the roof came off the house and the bed started moving towards the door. By Christmas morning the guy's brain was fried eggs...'

Another guy told how he had fallen into a drunken stupor at a basement party. When he woke up in the morning the city was gone.

We had landed in Darwin with one thought: find us a feed of milk, white sliced pan and cheddar cheese. It had been such a long time.

As soon as we hit the centre, we charged into a supermarket, bought the said commodities and fulfilled on a pavement bench the dream of months. We then went to the post office where the requested $150 had just arrived at the *poste restante* from Tony Lee. Flush again, we wandered the streets taking in the scenes of ruin that still haunted the town despite a Trojan effort to rebuild. Steel or concrete stilts were all that remained of some houses whose fibro and weatherboard cladding and tin roofs had disappeared in the cyclone. Telegraph poles, made of steel to thwart termites, had been bent to the ground. We briefly considered spending the night in the remains of a cinema which had been colonised by a bunch of 'hippies', but too many of them looked like serial killers.

In mid-afternoon we walked to the outskirts of Darwin with the aim of hitchhiking to Sydney, 2,500 miles away, roughly the distance from Dublin to Ankara in central Turkey. The reason for not taking public transport was that paying to travel, if hitchhiking and meeting the locals was an option, was like Jack's beanstalk: we didn't believe in it.

We stood for an hour in the sweltering humid heat and waited. But other than a smattering of local traffic and three road-trains that would have taken a mile to stop, not much was happening on the road to Sydney.

Two guys in a pickup did stop but when we ran towards them with our packs, they laughed and drove off again. 'Bastards!' I shouted after them. 'Hope you get the mange!' A bit over the top, I know. Anyway, half an hour later they came back. I couldn't believe our luck: it was time for the guy who laughs last...

I stooped down, scooped up a pretend rock, ran onto the road and hurled the pretend rock at the oncoming pickup. The lads swerved into the trees. Ha-ha-ha! I can't stop laughing.

'You're madder than mad,' Cora said. 'One of these days you'll be up for manslaughter.' But deep down I was pretty sure she saw that justice had been served. I must also assume that she or I looked like a condensed version of the Incredible Hulk to the lads as they made no attempt to retaliate.

Eventually, we were about to head back to the serial killers when a battered blue Holden pulled up.

'I am only going forty kilometres,' the driver said. 'But I live out in the bush and you are welcome to stay.' Peter, a 26-year-old, bearded, shaggy-haired German full of lean muscle, had just finished work and was covered in building dust. 'I was travelling just like you,' he said, 'until I arrived in Australia and met my girlfriend, Audrey, who is Scottish. And now we have a daughter called Penny so we have to stop for a while. I have a motorbike you can use tomorrow to see some of the bush before you leave for the south where it is very different.'

'Thank you very much,' I said, glad of such good fortune.

That night we sat on the floor of Peter and Audrey's home, a compact wooden house with a tin roof. To the chirruping of crickets, slim, sandy-haired Audrey cooked a staggering meal of steak, baked potatoes, salad, and freshly-ground coffee. Peter produced a bong and I pulled out the guitar. Under a ceiling-fan that made little dent in the humidity, we drank beer in frosted cans and had such a good time that Cora and I, having grown unused to high protein diets and alcohol, got the roaring trots. But the most memorable, and most disconcerting, part of the evening came in the form of large hairy tarantulas that moved at will about the floor, patently unnoticed by Peter, Audrey and delightful five-year-old Penny who treated everything with relentless logic.

'They are too small to eat you,' she said.

On our second evening, after we had returned from the Adelaide River, Cora officially complained to Peter about the lack of kangaroos in Australia.

'Never mind,' Peter said. 'Let's go for a swim.'

In the rocky pools of nearby Berry Creek we washed off the heat and grime of the day in deliciously cool water.

'There are crocodiles in this river,' Peter shared as we swam among the fish. 'But only freshwater ones.'

'Well, that's a *great* relief,' Cora said.

'They mostly eat fish,' Peter smiled.

'Mostly isn't what you'd really want to hear,' Cora said as she exited the water.

By the time we had dried off, to be again assailed by the clammy heat, the sun had dropped behind the trees.

'So,' Peter said, as we pushed our way back through a thin line of eucalypts to where he had parked the car, 'no kangaroos today?'

There they were - fifteen of them standing upright in a grassy clearing like they were at the races. We moved forward and they were gone, leaving us with an insect-humming twilight and the last of the birds.

Back at the hut it was more steak, beer, bongs and tarantulas.

'Don't worry about them,' Audrey said. 'By the time you get to Sydney, you'll be used to them. Then you can start worrying about the funnel-webs. They're the *real* spiders.'

'And take care in the outdoor toilets,' Peter warned. 'There you have the redbacks that will bite your ass.'

* * *

Three days after arriving in the Northern Territory, we left Peter and Audrey and got back on the road. 'The Track', the locals called it. For the next four days we would discover concepts of open space and distance that had never previously held any comparable meaning. If you leave out the odd 'small town', invariably no more than a roadhouse cum petrol station with maybe a wooden, tin-roofed house or two, there was only wilderness, merging gradually from one eco-system to the next.

The deep green of the open forests and wetlands of the north gave way to blue scrub and stunted trees, then to red desert around Tennant Creek. East of Three Ways, the junction of the Stuart and Barkly 'highways', limitless plains of saltbush crept across the desert until it in turn gave way to the prairies. Then the bush closed in again as we neared the Great Dividing Range and the fertile coastal belt of eastern Australia.

Much of the road was unsealed red dirt where vehicles and people were scarce. Outside of the 'small towns' there were a few scattered Aboriginal settlements, and cattle stations lost in the interior but carefully marked on our map. (Sometimes the station owners had left roadside signs inviting passers-by to visit.) That was pretty much it.

In places the land was so poor and dry that a single cattle station could cover hundreds of square miles and host several air strips without being considered a grossly enviable asset.

At the pub in the tiny, dusty settlement of Mataranka we had our initial encounter with the hardy breed who dragged their carcases across this land. We had stopped because Carlo, the hawk-nosed Italian who had brought us from Katherine in the open back of his pickup, had done so. In the bar, where nothing but the fan moved very much, a bunch of cowboys and jackaroos from surrounding cattle stations were unanimous that a hitchhiking ambition such as ours revealed an unbalanced relationship with reality.

'Could take ya weeks, mate,' one guy declared.

'Months,' another mumbled under a hat that had pieces of fly-chasing cork dangling on bits of string.

Five others agreed. An older man in the corner said nothing.

'He's troppo,' the initial speaker claimed. 'He's been plannin' to go for the past two hours. But he's waitin' for his swag to make the first move.'

'You should-a come in de bush,' Carlo invited. 'You could-a work wid us to build-a de roads. And de girl, she could-a cook us de food.'

I'm not taking the piss: he really did talk like this.

Carlo and the drivers of two accompanying pickups earned a living pushing tracks into the bush and sleeping under the stars. As little as the idea appealed to me, Cora was even less impressed by her proposed role in the scheme. So, having slaked a ferocious thirst, she and I returned to the road. We were still there, arms cramped in dehydration, when the boys rolled out of the bar three hours later. Communication with Darwin had seemingly ended in Katherine, with only eight vehicles through Mataranka in those three hours, a predicament that marred judgement. When Larry, one of Carlo's two friends, pulled up and offered us a lift to Larrimah, we jumped aboard.

'It's a bit of a squeeze,' Larry belched, referring to his dog and a large cooler of beer already occupying most of the double passenger seat. 'But she'll be roight.' It was later to be affirmed many times that whenever an Australian said 'She'll be roight', the chances were that 'she' most definitely wasn't going to be 'roight' at all.

'No problem,' Larry assured us as he knocked back can after can of Fosters. 'Do it all the time. In this heat, the alcohol just evaporates off in sweat.'

Yeah, I thought, *mine,* as he slurred his words and we howled down the Track in a reckless, sixty-mile-an-hour pursuit of Carlo's truck. We eventually overtook on the inside, carving a furrow along the verge and shrouding Carlo in dust. The inevitable happened when Larry took both hands from the wheel to rearrange his dog and the cooler of beer. He hit the wheel with his elbow which sent the pickup careering towards the bush on our left. He would have ploughed us into the trees if Cora, who had never driven in her life, hadn't caught the wheel and swung us back onto the road. Larry then grabbed it back as two fifty-gallon drums of fuel, crashed across the back, throwing us into a crazy slide towards a culvert on the far side of the road.

'Shorry...' Larry blurted after pulling us clear. 'Sho shorry...'

With the heat, lack of water and lack of vehicles leaving us no choice but to stay on board, we sat on our nerves, listening to Larry's apologies until the three of us collapsed into the pub in Larrimah. It took double brandies, tossed back in one gulp, to restore composure.

Five minutes after our arrival Carlo burst through the door in a rage of drunken indignation.

'You are-a de shit driver!' he roared at Larry. 'You shouldn't-a be on de fucking road! You are-a de stoopid, stoopid, shit driver!'

Larry reared up and swore he'd break Carlo's 'wog neck'.

'Fuck you!' Carlo shouted. 'And fuck-a-de Waltzing Matilda.'

As the two squared up for battle, Cora and I slipped our rucksacks out the back door and stayed well out of sight until Carlo and Larry were safely out of Larrimah.

Despite a 22-hour wait for our next lift, we were in Sydney within six days, thanks mainly to a balding, middle-aged businessman named Doug Potter. One minute we were standing on the desolate roadside, burnt and dehydrated, not a vehicle in sight. The next, we were sitting in an air-conditioned Volvo, drinking coffee and eating sandwiches.

Doug, a round-faced man with a big heart, was on his way to Melbourne.

'I've had a promotion in work,' he said, 'which has meant a transfer from Darwin to Melbourne and a chance to drive the sunburnt country. For myself and my family, the move signals completion of the life we knew in Darwin, a life that was pretty much obliterated by Cyclone Tracy.'

Their home had been ripped apart, he said, 'like cardboard'.

'As I lay in one corner with one of the children, my wife was huddled under what remained of the staircase with the other, and neither pair knew if the others were alive or dead. We were like that all night until the wind started to die down a little towards morning. When we were finally able to come out, finding the others safe and well was the greatest moment of my life. But we had lost everything. The only thing left of our home and possessions was the cooker. Everything else we had ever owned was gone: ornaments, wedding presents, even the photographs of the children. It was like starting your whole life all over again. But at least we were all alive. And we even got to celebrate Christmas.

'Along with the cooker, the turkey had also survived as it had been in the oven when the cyclone hit. So, on Christmas morning, we gathered together some of the neighbours, and with whatever we managed to salvage from each other's homes, we made a meal and thanked God we had come through safely.

'But enough of that. Tell me what's been happening in Belfast...'

The journey down the Track introduced us to an ever-changing glimpse of Australia's wildlife. Kangaroos. Emus. Families of wild boar. Herds of brumbies (feral horses). Huge monitor lizards. And two locust swarms that left the windscreen splatted in goo. We also encountered a bushfire that burned on a 10-mile front and could be seen from twenty miles away. Hovering above the flames were dozens of raptors, watching for animals that were fleeing the flames or had been too slow to get out alive.

We stopped for a drink in Cloncurry, a town replete with swing-door saloons, cowboys leaning against wooden verandas, horsemen with rifles, and the classic drunk snoozing against the walls of the General Store. On the edge of town a dilapidated shanty-town was home to a small Aboriginal community.

I remembered them from books at school: native Australians who lived in a vast country and hunted with boomerangs and spears. That was now the stuff of history. The black hunter, who was perhaps the greatest of all bushmen, had since been 'pacified', Christianised, 'civilised', alcoholised and dehumanised. From an original estimate of some 300,000 on Cook's arrival, their numbers had been decimated to 46,000.

Over a seventy-year period the colonists of Tasmania, on Britain's watch, systematically perfected one of the few successful acts of absolute genocide in recorded history. In a final insult, they made a museum exhibit of Truganini, the last of the Tasmanians. Within two years of her death, her skeleton was exhumed by the Royal Society of Tasmania and later placed on display. It remained so until April 1976 when, approaching the centenary of her death, Truganini's remains were finally cremated, and scattered according to her wishes in the D'Entrecasteaux Channel off the south-east coast of Tasmania.

The Aboriginals encountered in every town since Darwin had shared the haunted look of the survivors of catastrophe.

Our lift with Doug spanned four days of hard driving from early morning to dusk, with one day extended into night to conclude a long unsurfaced nightmare of bulldust, road kills, and potholes that would swallow a cow. Two thousand and fifty miles down the track we bade him goodbye at Toowoomba on a cold, wet afternoon and turned south along the Brisbane Valley towards Sydney. A truck rolled by, festooned in stickers. *Eat more beef, you bastards,* one said. *Loose chicks tightened,* said another. The cerebral end of the market. As we walked out of town, Cora let out a squeal.

'That magpie has just bitten me in the head,' she said, pointing at a bird that was swooping around her.

'No way would a magpie bite you in the head,' I said in my best ornithological voice. 'Maybe it dropped something.'

'So what's that?' she said as a trickle of blood ran down her forehead.

It was the one and only time in all our travels that either of us was wilfully attacked by a wild animal. And it was a bloody magpie.

To the south springtime was bursting out over the New England Tablelands in plumes of yellow wattle. We were closing in on Tony Lee and his Irish wife, Colette. We had last seen them in London five years earlier, the day after Tony's father had died suddenly.

'The home run,' said the amphetamine-popping trucker, who had driven us the 400 miles from Glen Innes on our final day of travel. 'I love the home run.'

We were thundering down the Putty Road in the gathering darkness with a driver who hadn't slept in three days and looked like a man possessed. He dropped us off in Windsor on the outskirts of Sydney and wished us well in 'stralia. Over the next four hours, as we crossed from Windsor to the northern suburb of Newport where Tony and Colette lived, the city swam by in a flood of neon and speckled high-rise. It would have been a terrible place in which to have landed cold.

Instead, we arrived to a red-carpet welcome from Tony and Colette, who now shared their lives with their two-year-old son, Aaron, who was soon to have a baby brother.

'I knew it,' Tony shrieked when we arrived at the front door at half eleven at night. 'I said it to Colette last night, that any time now, you two would just walk up and come knocking on the door.'

Colette made a pizza and Tony cracked open some bottles of Guinness he'd been saving for that very night.

'It's not every day the Irish turn up in force in Newport,' he toasted. 'Here's to Belfast and Feakle in the County Clare [Colette's home village].'

September 9th 1976. We were in Sydney. Broke, in debt and in need of work so we could fund the next leg of our journey. But we had made it.

CHAPTER 12

Cape York Peninsula

'No learner's permit for you,' the man said. He wasn't a nice man at all.

Down at the vehicle licensing office, he had asked me some dopey questions and failed me.

'Well,' I said to Cora, 'who gives a shite? We have the bike [a 250cc Honda XL] and we'll just have to do without the license.'

Down below our 'flatette', in the calm waters of Mosman Bay, Tom Dunlop and I tested the rubber raft. We blew it up, ignored the label that read: 'Use only under adult supervision', and launched out into the narrow inlet with the plastic paddles. A few minutes later the Mosman ferry rounded the headland of Cremorne Point and bore down on us, whistle screaming, as we went around in circles. Bruce Penn and Cora were watching from the kitchen window of the flatette.

'Captain Ahab!' Bruce shouted at Tom. 'Look out behind ya.'

Glenys Kitchingman, who was to head off to Cape York Peninsula to take that rubber raft down the Coen River along with myself and Cora, was meeting with an opal fossicker acquaintance. She wanted him to run his eye over our equipment list. He couldn't improve on it, he said, it must have been put together by someone who knew what they were doing. That was me, who was down in the harbour in mortal danger of being run over by the Mosman ferry.

'You really plan to take this thing down some crocodile-infested river up in Queensland?' Tom asked.

May 1977. Eight months had passed since we had arrived in Sydney.

* * *

Within three days of reaching the city, Cora had found work at the Manley-Warringah Rugby Leagues Club and we had refunded Paul's $40 via Singapore's *poste restante*.

We had also been warned again about the Sydney funnel-web, possibly the world's deadliest arachnid, that was to be found only within a sixty-mile radius of Australia's largest city.

'They're especially dangerous after rain,' Colette said, 'when they go into people's homes. They're aggressive and their bite is a deadly neurotoxin. One day Aaron was out in the garden and I heard him scream. I ran out and saw that he'd been bitten by something. First thing that ran into my mind was a funnel-web. So I grabbed him, ran into the house and phoned the emergency number. It took ages to get through and when I finally did, the woman on the other end asked, "Is he still conscious?" So I said, "Yes." "Oh don't worry" she said. "If it had been a funnel-web, he'd be dead by now."'

'What about redbacks?' I asked.

'Redbacks?' Tony said. 'Come and take a look at this.' He led us into the garden, lifted a piece of tin and there they were: Australia's version of the Black Widow. That evening we found an enormous brown Huntsman Spider in our bedroom. 'Harmless,' Tony said as he struggled to persuade me that it wasn't a funnel-web.

Cora's job at the leagues club was the first step towards finding our feet in Sydney. We now needed to repay Tony and Colette, get me a job, and move to a place of our own. In the meantime, we would continue to enjoy the company of our old friends in all its vagaries.

On the second Sunday of our stay, Tony led a fishing expedition to nearby Pittwater where the only thing we caught was his thumb. (Colette had to use a blade to extract the barb which caused Tony to briefly faint.) We then decided to rent a Hoby Cat. Relying on Tony's limited sailing skills, he and I took off with gusto - mostly due to a strong wind - and were soon careering across Pittwater in the small catamaran towards an ominous wall of rock.

'Oh dear,' Tony mused, stroking his curling moustache, 'I wonder what the book would say now.'

But lucky us. We avoided the rocks by nose-diving into the water and turning the catamaran upside down in what Tony had earlier described as 'a renowned breeding ground of grey nurse sharks'. I was back on one of the upturned hulls the way a penguin bounces out of the surf.

'What we need to do now,' Tony said, 'is grab at the sail and tip ourselves backwards into the water so we can right the boat again.'

'You're joking,' I said as the water cleared to reveal the word *S-H-A-R-K-S!* (complete with exclamation mark) in red, oscillating, three-foot letters. 'Could we not, sort of, be rescued?'

My eventual compliance in this matter would forever remain Tony's greatest act of bewitchment.

On October 23rd, after several more minor misadventures, we all sat in the Lees' garden through an almost total eclipse of the sun when the confused birdlife went into a frenzy. We then went for self-barbecued steaks at the Oaks Pub in Neutral Bay. Two weeks later, it finally came time to move on. Based on my community-work experience in Belfast's war-torn Ballymurphy, I had landed a job as a Youth Officer for the municipalities of North Sydney and Mosman, working alongside Jillian Salz and Cathie Hull, two stalwarts of local community development. During the second week of November, having repaid Tony and Colette the $150, we left the comfort and camaraderie of their home, and moved to the so-called flatette in Boyle Street, Cremorne Point, close to the city centre.

Our new home consisted of a single room with a bed settee, and a small adjoining kitchen, glass-fronted on two sides and looking out over Mosman Bay. But what was lacking in size was present in form. Through one of those windows the sun rose each morning. The city's red sunsets drained out through the other. On full moons, sunset was immediately followed by the appearance over the bay of a huge bone-coloured disc that illuminated the moored boats, the trees, and the houses trapped in their little pockets of light. Later, during the sweltering weeks of February we'd wait at the open windows for the Southerlies, the sudden rise of cool wind that would rush through the flatette, dissipating the day's humidity and heralding one of Sydney's spectacular electrical storms. Downstairs, a little drummer boy whose ceiling was our floor had a set of amplified African drums; and depending on who carried the night's monopoly on induced euphoria, we might ask him to for Christ's sake knock it on the head, or we might lie back and enjoy it.

We also had the wildlife.

Directly across the street, a set of steps led down to a wooded bush reserve where we traded the possums, lizards, rainbow lorikeets and laughing kookaburras of Newport for the possums, lizards, rainbow lorikeets and laughing kookaburras of Cremorne Point, also home to a large, stubby Blue-tongued Lizard.

And we had the passing parade.

'Watch this,' Cora said one Saturday afternoon. We were leaning out one of our kitchen windows to catch the breeze. Just before diving flat to the deck, she wolf-whistled at a passing chap with a thick neck, shoulders out to here, and a T-shirt that proclaimed *Pommy bastards*. When Muscles looked up there was no one to see but me. Not exactly a pommy, but how was he to know?

Within a week of moving to Cremorne Point we had bought a map of northern Queensland which included Cape York Peninsula.

* * *

Ever since that day south of Darwin, when we drove out to the Adelaide River, we had been considering going back up north. We had looked at Arnhem Land, east of Darwin, as a possibility but much of it was Aboriginal land and therefore off-limits. It was also a long way from Sydney. But northern Queensland was another story. A train ran directly from Sydney to Cairns; and beyond Cairns an enormous wilderness, partly accessible by four-wheel drive or trail bike, stretched all the way to Cape York. Several rivers flowing towards the Gulf of Carpentaria could provide further access. It looked the ticket. Trail bikes and a rubber raft would do the job.

All we needed now was to find a couple of others to join us. To go alone into such a wilderness would be foolish. But when I put the idea to a youth-work colleague over in Balmain, the reaction was, well… cool. Bushy-bearded Paul Caddy, who spent much time in the wilds with his English wife, Barbara, said he wouldn't even think of it.

'You realise you're stark raving mad,' he said with his big staccato laugh. 'Anywhere else in Australia and I'm your man, but not the Cape. It's like this: that's the last place on Earth to be conquered by humans, and all the monsters have gathered there. You've got sharks and barracuda; stingrays, stonefish, sea-wasps [box jellyfish]; sea-snakes, river-snakes, taipans and death adders; crocs, spiders, leeches and centipedes. What if a croc hits the dinghy? You might as well be a million miles from nowhere.'

Paul and Barbara Caddy were off the list.

Ignoring what I considered a hasty rejection, I continued to look for Cape York enthusiasts among the handful of people we had so far met. In the end there was only one taker: Glenys Kitchingman, a cheerful, 27-year-old woman who ran the Duke of Edinburgh Award Scheme at the New South Wales Department of Youth & Community Affairs which was paying my salary through North Sydney Council.

I had met Glenys at the end of November during a visit to the department. She was at her desk applying her considerable organising skills and exuberance to the latest round of awards. Although the trip up north was already taking form, it never struck me at that point to mention it as Glenys, sharply dressed and in high heels, with her light-brown hair tied in a ponytail, didn't seem the kind of person who might go charging into the bush. However, sometime in early December, I thought: *Well, I might have that wrong. Nothing ventured, nothing gained.*

'You wouldn't by any chance fancy a trip to Cape York Peninsula in June?' I asked. 'Motorbikes from Cairns to Coen, then a rubber raft down the Coen and Archer rivers.'

Glenys looked surprised, then thought about it for a minute.

'You know,' she said, 'it sounds like something I might fancy doing. I've never driven a motorbike but I can learn.'

The friendship thus ignited has lasted to the present day.

'You're out of your head attempting this,' Paul Caddy told her.

'Maybe,' Glenys said. 'But if you don't try, you never win.' That, it would transpire, was the measure of Glenys.

Six days before Christmas, while Glenys was camped on wild, barren, treeless Broughton Island, mentally preparing for the trip, Alan Dodds and Chris McGuinness, our companions of Bukittinggi days, turned up from Perth for a visit. Christine Hakkers, they said, would be along at the end of January. After recounting the horrors of the Trans-Sumatran Highway, we laid before them our growing plans for Cape York Peninsula, hoping that they too might join us.

'We've modified it a bit since the initial plan...' I explained.

'*His* initial plan,' Cora emphasised.

'Originally,' I outlined, 'we had planned on rafting down the Coen River, from Rokeby, an isolated cattle station about two thirds of the way up the peninsula, then on down the Archer River as far as the Aboriginal settlement of Aurukun on the coast, then turning north and paddling along the edge of the mangroves to Weipa. But, given the time limits...'

'*And* the sharks and crocodiles,' Cora added as I opened the map and Alan and Chris threw odd glances at one another.

'The time limits *and* the monsters,' I went on. 'We're now thinking of destroying the dinghy here at the junction of the Archer River and Mistake Creek - a name everyone seems to find funny - and doubling back along Mistake Creek. We can then use a compass to find our way back to Rokeby which is where we'll have left the motorbikes.'

'Tell them about the balloon,' Cora said.

'Balloon?' Chris asked.

'Yeah,' Cora said. 'For a while he was thinking of using a helium-filled balloon to float our gear and the dinghy back through the bush to Rokeby, pulling it behind him like a donkey on a lead.'

'Yeah,' Alan laughed. 'Good luck with that one.'

I firmly believe that mention of the balloon extinguished all hope of the participation of Alan and Chris in the venture but there would be another day. On mature reflection, the balloon was probably never going to work anyway. What with the trees and all that.

* * *

Christmas arrived and we spent the day with Tony and Colette and Tony's wider family. Hiding from the blistering sun under an open marquee, surrounded by postcards of robins and snowmen, we tucked in to the full traditional fare and outlined the plans for our trip up north.

'Good on ya cobber,' Tony said. 'That's the funniest thing I've heard for a while.'

A week later, while we considered how we might now learn a bit about the Australian bush before heading into its extremes (if Paul Caddy was to be believed), our life in Sydney took a bounce. Cora and I went out to celebrate New Year's Eve with Tom and Susanne Dunlop who had emigrated from Belfast seven years before.

Cora had met Susanne at the rugby leagues club. She had also said hello to Tom on occasions when he had collected Susanne from work. Two days before Christmas, she came home with the news.

'Another Irishwoman, a friend of Susanne's, is throwing a party out in Narrabeen on New Year's Eve and we're all invited. Tom and Susanne will pick us up. I think you'll get on well with Tom. He's really easy-going and he plays the guitar. They both seem to be our kind of people.'

At 9.00 p.m. on New Year's Eve, the Dunlops arrived in their Mini Moke, a small, front-drive utility vehicle that looked like it was made of Meccano and contained, in the second part of its name, an archaic term for 'mule'.

Tom, twenty-seven years old, with broad shoulders, thinning fair hair, John Lennon glasses and a wild beard, was a misplaced Belfast wit. His multifarious resources had made him a truck driver, joiner, mechanic and sociology graduate of Macquarie University.

'Nowadays I'm taking a rest,' he said en route to Narrabeen. 'Catching rays along the north shore beaches and thinking about life.'

'My job at the leagues club,' Susanne explained, 'is only short-term. Come the end of summer, I'm off to university to study vet science...'

Susanne, in her mid-twenties, soft-spoken, slight, with close-cropped mousey hair, and a wry sense of humour, went on to tell how life had changed since they first moved to Australia.

'When we first arrived, we lived in Perth and went through a period when Tom was a smart car salesman dressed in suits and ties and earning really good money. I used to drive a sports car at the time. Then one day we both suffered some kind of grave moral reproach and abandoned the lot overnight. Tom grew the beard and swapped his suit for a pair of jeans. I sold the fancy car and bought a pair of dungarees. Tom got his guitar and I got my bags and we started to look for something else. Later, we did a trip around Australia with our friends, Bruce and Jenny.'

'Anti-clockwise,' Tom qualified. 'In an old VW Kombi that trundled into Perth in such shape that even the wreckers refused to take it...'

A spiffing salvation, we all agreed.

'You'll have to meet Bruce and Jenny,' Tom concluded. 'They're on their way back from Queensland and should be turning up in Sydney any day now. The four of us are planning to get a house together... Bruce will make you laugh: he's about the most laid-back guy in Australia...'

'I like it,' Tom said when we recounted tales of our recent travels. 'Yous are both a bit bonkers.'

Out in Narrabeen, the New Year's party was an attempt to consume a bath of iced booze in a single sitting. Then it was back to Tom and Susanne's flat in Manly for two days of languorous sing-alongs. By the time the singing was done, we were friends for life.

'You wanna go see the Fairy Bower?' Tom asked as we were about to leave. 'It's in the Blue Mountains. We'll come and pick yous up in the morning.'

After seven weeks of near-isolation in our little flatette (it was now a three-hour return bus ride and a long drag up Wallumatta Road to reach Tony and Colette), we had found a niche in Sydney.

Months later we would find another in a place called Taldumande.

* * *

With the advent of January came the sweltering days of midsummer. Temperatures soared as hot winds swept in from the desert bringing swarms of bushflies. In the city the wind blew like a furnace-blast while it whipped up raging fires in the Blue Mountains and in Sydney's outer suburbs. Then, at the end of the month, as things calmed, we had a second encounter with the Blue Mountains: a weekend in the Grose Valley, sleeping under the stars with Tom, (Susanne was studying), their Australian friends, Bruce Penn and Jenny Zohn who had turned up at the beginning of the month, and Christine Hakkers who had arrived from Perth. We saw this as a kind of preparation for the Cape. Bruce and Jenny said good on ya mate.

Tall and lean, with blond hair, chiselled features and a bald crown, 26-year-old Bruce was a man who cared deeply about Australia's environment and had no time for its consumerism. He harboured an incisive sense of humour, and in later days made his own special contribution to the debate on his country's future national anthem. One of the songs proposed was *Come on Aussie, Come On,* so Bruce designed a cartoon postcard. It was an aerial view of a guy about to jump from a skyscraper. Away below, at the base of the tapering skyscraper, was a crowd of spectators, all looking up and singing 'Come on Aussie, come on'.

Bruce had spent time in the bush up north. During our visit to the sandstone canyon of the Grose Valley, he drilled home an old saying about camp-fires: 'The bigger the fire, the bigger the fool.'

Twenty-three-year-old Jenny, spirited eyes and short dark hair, walked with the gait of a panther and was as much at home in the bush as Bruce. As we climbed down into the Grose Valley from Govett's Leap, she named for us the red-bellied black snake that slithered across the track, the lyre bird that could imitate any sound, the whip birds with their loud cracking note, the bell birds that tinkled like wind chimes and the yabbies (freshwater crayfish) that studied our feet when we dipped into Govett's Leap Brook.

'You'll be fine,' Bruce said of our plans for the Cape. 'Respect the bush and the bush will respect you.'[16]

On our return to Sydney, as our plans continued to develop, Cora and I divided our free days between the Harbour beach at Balmoral and the surf beach in Manly. However, we confined our aquatic adventures to the safe side of Balmoral's shark nets. Neither of us could quite share the view of our new friends that, if a killing machine, backed by no sense of humour, rows of big teeth and 350 million years of bad faith, hits a crowded beach, it's likely to get someone else.

Over the coming months we made several more trips into the bush, sometimes alone, sometimes with our friends, becoming familiar with its various environments and falling in love with its diversity of wildlife. Nothing intimidating at all, apart from one moment of panic.

While unpegging our tent one morning at Kangaroo Creek in the wilds of the Royal National Park, something got my right hand. *Funnel-web!* was my first thought (always start at the top). But I found instead a beautiful yellow and purple caterpillar with small tufts of stinging hairs.

Then of course there was that ill-judged assault on Mount Kosciuszko.

---

16.   In later years Bruce would move to Tasmania where he became a renowned poet.

During one of many nights spent in the house that Tom, Susanne, Bruce and Jenny had rented in French's Forest, we were listening to Leonard Cohen and J.J. Cale and discovering new ways of making bongs, when we decided that a trip to the Snowy Mountains would greatly help with the acclimatisation for the Cape.

Easter came, and we left for the mountains with Tom, Bruce, Jenny, Glenys, Veronica from South Africa who worked with Cora, and Veronica's boyfriend Tony. Destination: the 7,310-foot summit of Mount Kosciuszko, Australia's highest point.

At eight o'clock in the evening, as we left Sydney by train, the thermometer read thirty degrees centigrade. When we woke up in the morning, we were snaking along a plateau coated in frost.

In the out-of-season ski resort of Thredbo, at the foot of Crackenback Ridge, we assessed the situation. The sky didn't look too good and it seemed cold enough for snow and we weren't equipped for that. That might deem that we should go home. However, it might also blow over. Let's be optimistic. On Jenny's suggestion, we bought gloves and woollen beanies and considered ourselves sorted. We then had a group photo taken by some passer-by and set off up the face of Crackenback along the line of the ski lift. It was a tough climb to the exposed top where we were met by a gale that sucked away all body heat. But we were undaunted. On go the legions of the lost. Minutes later we had the first flurry of snow. And in behind rolled a 22-hour blizzard.

All these years later I look at the slides we took that day as we trudged across the Ramshead Range towards Mount Kosciuszko in the shrieking wind and stinging snow, and I think I might give it a miss if it came up again. There's one of Tony helping Glenys to rock-hop across a stream as the snow swirls around them. There's Cora after slipping in the same stream. There's Tom, his right side caked white from the horizontal lashing of winds so fierce that our anoraks cracked like gunshots and facing into the snow was impossible. There are people trudging through tiers of white with scarfs and hankies around their faces. And there's one of the whole group, huddled together along with eighteen others, on the cramped floor of Seaman's Hut, a survival hut just 650 feet below the elusive, and never to be reached, summit of Kosciuszko, a hut built in memory of Laurie Seaman, a young skier who died in a winter blizzard at this very spot in 1928. The body of his companion, Evan Hayes, was found two miles away.

When I went outside in the dark that night, to fetch water from ten yards away, the wind, shooting frozen snow into my eyes, drove me back inside again.

'Here mate,' Bruce said, his eyes sparkling with delight, 'make sure you keep us informed of any little trips you're planning for the future. Assuming of course that there is a future.'

* * *

'Crocodiles!' Tom said a few weeks later during one of our weekends at French's Forest. 'Never mind yer bloody crocodiles. Take a look at this.'

He laid out a cutting from the bikers' magazine, *Two Wheels*. It was an account of a motorbike trip up Cape York Peninsula. One of the accompanying photos showed a bike axle-deep in mud. Another showed an engine in a dozen pieces as repairs were carried out. 'These guys are bikies,' Tom chortled. 'And look at the hassles they had without ever going off the main track.' He tossed his head, gave a long whistle, looked out over his glasses and grinned.

Out in the street, Glenys was learning to drive her 175cc Honda XL trail bike.

* * *

'Sorry, no bikes,' the station master in Cairns said. 'They were left behind in Brisbane when you changed to the Sunlander; but no worries, they should be here on the next train, day after tomorrow.'

Sunday morning, June 5th 1977.

We exploded. After two nights and a full day on the train with virtually no sleep, we were in no mood to forgive a stupid decision to build the New South Wales and Queensland railways on different gauges.

Furious at such addle-headed blundering, we dragged our rubber raft and seventy pounds of gear, packed into two rucksacks, around to the nearest campsite, erected our two-person cocoon of a tent and slept for a couple of hours - two up, one down, with a sheet below and an open, shared, single sleeping bag on top. (We had economised on everything.)

The immediate plan was to fly our gear to the isolated cattle station of Rokeby, about 410 driving-miles north-west of Cairns, chosen because of its proximity to the Coen River. We would follow on the two motorbikes - to be left at Rokeby while we rafted down the river. Once we reached the Archer River, we would loop back via Mistake Creek, then track across the bush to Rokeby and the return journey to Cairns. A big debate had taken place back in Sydney about whether or not we should tell them in Rokeby that we were coming. We had decided against. Don't give them a chance to say no.

Now, all we had to do was forward our gear to Rokeby's airstrip.

The Bush Pilots' Airways had a Tuesday morning flight that touched down, if required, at Rokeby. We deposited our packs and the raft at the airport on Monday afternoon. A note stapled to the equipment explained its enigma to whoever lived at the other end. We ourselves would leave Cairns on Wednesday, the day after the bikes arrived. But, on Monday night, we had more bad news: a railway strike at Rockhampton had disrupted all northbound services.

'And what exactly does that mean?' I asked the Cairns station master.

'Your bikes,' he replied, 'are delayed indefinitely.'

'Great,' Cora said. 'Our bikes in Rockhampton, our gear gone to Rokeby, and us by the looks of it stuck in Cairns. Can anything else go wrong?'

Oh yes, it could.

That night we were woken from a deep slumber by a deafening crack of thunder. The heavens opened and the rain avalanched in, to be trapped in neat pockets by a groundsheet that would have made a terrific roof.

* * *

To pass some time, we took the Tuesday boat to Green Island, a coral cay fifteen nautical miles out on the Great Barrier Reef. In an underwater observatory we looked out at large fish that looked in at us. From a glass-bottomed boat, we saw the marvels created by such a tiny creature as the coral polyp. On a structure that ran 1,400 miles from end to end, and contained 3,000 separate reefs, an enormous living labyrinth of every shape, colour and disposition imaginable had evolved. After his first visit to the Great Barrier Reef back in 1957, natural historian, David Attenborough, described it as 'the most magical experience of my life'. One could only concur.

Good news greeted our return to the mainland. The rail strike was over. Our bikes would arrive in the morning, bringing us back on schedule.

'I'll collect my bike first,' I offered Glenys as we celebrated with a flagon of wine. 'Then I'll drive you over to collect yours.'

'Good idea,' Cora said. 'We can get on with the packing while you're away.'

But hangovers and bikes are a bad mix.

I arrived at the train station early in the morning. Without thinking, I hopped onto the saddle of my bike which was waiting on the platform. I kick-started the engine and opened the throttle. And forgot to check if I was in gear. Up shot the front wheel and I rocketed across the platform, narrowly missing a couple of station hands. I then bounced with virility off a concrete pillar and fell to the ground. On the second attempt the station hands had gone to ground. Wednesday, June 8th 1977.

We spent the rest of that morning trying to squeeze everything we needed onto the bikes while Glenys tied her hair into its familiar ponytail.

'We still have two apples and four oranges that just won't fit,' I pointed out.

'We'll eat them dear Henry...,' Cora sang to the tune of *There's a hole in my bucket*.

The tent, machete, sleeping bag, sheet, three empty five-litre cans and a few items of clothing were strapped behind the seat of Glenys' 175cc Honda XL. On our 250cc bike, also a Honda XL, Cora and I carried a small rucksack with cooking utensils, some food, a diary and a two-litre water-bottle. A tank-bag held more food, our repair kit, which amounted to three spanners, two tyre levers, a (later discovered to be useless) spray for mending punctures, and a replacement throttle cable as the cable on the 250 was fraying.

Cora stood back to inspect the bikes.

'There's nothing like being ready,' she said. 'And this looks nothing like being ready. But, it seems that this is it...' After six months of preparation, we were firmly on our way.

We left Cairns in jubilant form and climbed into the mountainous rainforests of the Atherton Tablelands, home to cassowaries, tree kangaroos and fantastic butterflies. Once we had cleared the rainforest, we moved out into more open forest on a sealed road that ran to the little town of Mareeba, patrolled on its perimeters by large numbers of wallabies and emus. We then turned north to Mount Molloy where the light traffic we had experienced so far melted away. We topped up with fuel and, as insurance, I sat a five-litre can of petrol on my right thigh, held in place by a loop of rope running around my neck, the cap loosened to allow for expansion.

Immediately north of the mining settlement of Mount Carbine the sealed road came to an end and we hit the dirt. We took it easy, no more than thirty miles an hour. Then, piece by piece our confidence grew. We began to laugh at the occasional pothole and stretch of loose gravel. We inhaled the perfume of wattle and eucalypt flowers. We whooped and punched the air. We were sucking diesel.

The sun had slid into the trees when we pulled up at the McLeod River. Close to a high bridge of sliced tree trunks, we struck camp for the night. Black cockatoos, galahs and honey-eaters screeched from the trees. Clouds of insects hovered over the river. Kingfishers swooped on the fish that came to feed.

Night slipped in unnoticed, our campfire transforming the forest into flickering tree trunks and shadows. Sitting on the ground by the fire, we talked about what might lie ahead and picked out patterns in the flames. The burning wood was a face, then a dragon, before collapsing into the flames. Cora poked the embers. Glenys added a log. The sky was an inky black with the Milky Way in crystal definition. Then CRASH! The world exploded in a bombardment of rock.

Upriver a few hundred yards we found the culprits: Jeff and Angie from Townsville. Smashed out of their minds, they were laid out like corpses along with their dog, Knackers, in front of a Volkswagen Kombi.

'This is as far as the Kombi can go,' Angie explained. 'So we're having a blast.'

Not so long afterwards, we were laid out like corpses beside them.

* * *

In the morning we found we had pitched the tent under a green ants' nest. Living leaves had been stitched together by the ants using a substance taken from their larvae. The nests were hard to spot. But we learned to look carefully. Brush against the wrong leaves, and vengeful soldier ants showered down like poison darts.

After a leisurely breakfast we said goodbye to Jeff and Angie and set off again.

It was a beautiful morning as we crossed the Great Dividing Range, the two bikes riding together along a well-graded track. At intervals we slowed down to allow for a hesitant wallaby or emu. Overhead there were parrots, cockatoos and solitary eagles. Not another human in sight. From the top of a pass, we looked north across an interminable blanket of forest to where the track faded in a horizon of smoky hills.

'With a road like this,' I declared as we sailed downhill towards the plain, 'we'll be in Rokeby in two days.'

'Don't...' Cora warned. 'Whenever you say stuff like that, things go horribly wrong.'

Around the next corner, a black-headed python crossed the track. We stopped to take a couple of photos. And, just as Cora had predicted, we spun around a bend and ploughed into every obstacle that the track could throw at us. Runs of sharp rock. Loose boulders. Massive ruts. Even more massive potholes. Deep gullies gauged out by the rainy season. As sudden braking would have thrown us off the bikes, we hit the obstacles hard, the bikes tossing us clear of the saddles several times.

'Oh Jesus, Mary and St. Joseph,' Cora said. (Weird. She said that a lot.)

A white patch shot towards us. It looked solid but turned into bulldust that caved away before the wheels. We skidded through, not daring to brake and hoping the bike would pick its own way. On the far side, we regrouped.

'My word,' Glenys said, 'that was about the hairiest thing I've ever experienced.'

'I hope there's no more of it,' Cora said. 'I nearly bounced into the bloody bushes.'

There was. In fact there was little else. From there on, the track was a continuation of rocks, gravel, sand, potholes, bulldust, mud, corrugations and gullies. Glenys and I suffered aching hands from the near-constant drag of the clutch and front brakes. Welts rose on our palms from the friction, and our arms were numbed by the pounding of the corrugations. Cora took a pummelling on the back and suffered acute affright syndrome from having no control over our bike's next move. Half way through the afternoon, we wrapped our midriffs in the crepe bandages we had brought along as kidney belts.

Four hours after seeing the python, we had covered forty-five miles to the Palmer River.

'Forty-five miles in a day,' Glenys said, 'and I'm stuffed. The Coen River is suddenly an awfully long way off.'

'It just goes to show,' Cora said, 'that you should double the amount of time you think something will take and divide your target by two.'

'Then you'd never get anywhere,' I argued.

'No,' Cora said. 'You'd always get everywhere.' It was an argument that she won over time.

At the Palmer we slapped the red dust from our clothes, spat it out through our teeth and undid the ropes of our gear. We waddled to the river, waded across in the shallows and planted ourselves on a sandy bank. We pitched the tent. We made dinner of instant mash, dried cabbage and sardines. We lay back by the fire and closed our eyes as the sun went down and frogs, crickets and fruit bats claimed the forest.

As did the ghosts of the Palmer.

Just over a hundred years earlier, the Palmer River had been the centre of a gold rush that was the last of its kind. In the ten years following September 1873, 35,000 European and Chinese diggers flooded into Cape York Peninsula. They would take 100 tons of gold out of its rivers and slaughter much of its indigenous population. Many of the diggers also died - of fever, hunger, thirst, and by the bullet and spear of the violence that plagued the goldfields. When the fields were done, the diggers left and their camps and towns reverted to bush.

But old bushmen claimed that, late on stormy nights, the dead returned. That you could make out the muffled crunch of heavy boots. The rasp of wet gravel on tin. The cries of excitement as pay dirt was struck. And the joys and agonies of men and women who laughed and loved, fought and died, over the right to ancestral lands versus the right to a dirty yellow rock with a life-giving energy less than that of a single green leaf.

* * *

At the tiny township of Lakeland Downs the track branched in two. The main arm went to Cooktown on the coast. We intended to stop there on our way back. The other went north to the tip of the peninsula, with a few minor branches to isolated homesteads and Aboriginal settlements. Reminding ourselves that we had so far been on the 'highway' to Cooktown, we dropped in at the local pub.

'Excuse me,' Glenys said to the cheery woman behind the bar. 'What are road conditions like between here and Coen?'

The cheery woman behind the bar laughed. This drew the ponderous attention of an old-timer sipping a beer.

'Hasn't been graded yet,' he grunted. 'And the rivers are runnin' high. Ya might be okay to Laura, but from there on...?' He turned slowly to face the door, looked blankly out at the bikes, already considerably worse for wear, then back at us. 'Jesus Christ,' he said. 'Two bikes! Between three? D'ya have any idea what that track is like...?'

The woman behind the bar laughed again, sympathetically this time.

'Road?' she said. 'Ain't no road up there. Road ended other side of Mount Carbine.'

On that note, we rewound our crepe bandages and left the Downs, bouncing off into open bush littered with tall, 'magnetic' termite hills that faced north-south, affording each colony maximum protection from the midday sun.

'Like tombstones,' Cora shouted from behind. 'I hope we don't add to them.'

From the Downs onwards the track was homicidal. All previous hazards now assumed more monstrous proportions and were added to by sloughs of heavy black mud, streams bedded in varying degrees of instability, and huge troughs chewed out by the rains. However, as the day progressed and our luck held, our strategies improved.

Racing along the walls of ruts and ripping over the corrugations dramatically increased our average speed and gave more control, particularly on the corrugations. It also increased the numbness in our arms, the rattling of our teeth, the popping of our eyes and the risk of hurtling haywire into a sudden expanse of bulldust or mud. A few miles of graded track south of Laura allowed myself and Cora recovery time after a near collision with the grader itself which had been swinging its scoop like a wrecking ball.

A lack of protective barriers on rough bridges called for a delicate balancing act to avoid being chucked overboard by the gaps between the logs. Then north of Laura (one pub, one garage, a few houses, a general store and a small Aboriginal settlement) this problem ceased - along with the bridges.

The Little Laura, north of the settlement - the first river without a bridge - was running high. At the sight of two men winching a half-submerged Land Rover from the middle of the flow, we pulled up at the water's edge. At the sight of us, they stopped dead.

'Where in Christ's name are you folks off to?' one of them asked.

'Coen,' we said.

'Well, I never... But if you want to cross here you'll have to carry those bikes above your heads.'

'We can double back,' Cora suggested. 'A guy in the shop in Laura mentioned some track that goes to another crossing further upstream - if we can find it.'

'By the way,' Glenys added, 'he also asked where we were headed. When we said "Coen", he asked "Ya goin' down the river?" The news of our coming has preceded us.'

After ten minutes we located the barely discernible alternative track and had the first of many mishaps. Glenys' front wheel went into a rut and she was thrown. She got up cursing and covered in dust. She looked funny, but laughter was suppressed in the greater cause of harmony.

Then came the crossing of the Little Laura, and a test of theories.

'If we get back as far as we can,' I figured, 'and take a buck charge, we should get across before the bikes cut out.'

'Oh,' Glenys said, not quite with that programme. 'So, you reckon that all the people you see crossing rivers that are far wider than this are relying on momentum?'

'No,' I said. 'They get stuck and are winched across like those guys back there.'

'Okay,' Glenys said. 'You go first. I'll watch how it's done.'

'Hang on!' Cora yelled, jumping from the saddle. 'No way am I staying on the back for this.'

Leaving behind the doubters, I wheeled the bike back to the last rise, lined it up and charged. With an almighty splash I landed in the river in a butterfly of water and ploughed through like Moses at the Red Sea. Glenys hit the water a few minutes later.

'I still think there's some other way,' she said but she had to admit that my tactic had worked.

We rolled on, banging and bumping through the rest of the day, the 250 out front and Glenys far enough behind to avoid its dust. Whenever she dropped from view, Cora and I would wait until she appeared. If she didn't, I'd go back to invariably find her cursing some muddy creek or gully where her bike had gone over. After we had pulled it clear, Glenys would mount the bike and purposefully kick the engine back to life.

Wallabies, snakes, lizards, wild boar, brumbies, birds and insects would stare in respect.

An hour before dark on the third day of the ride to Rokeby, we reached the Kennedy River, still a long way from our destination, to find the river swollen. The fact that it was thirty yards to the far side and that all the rivers were reputed to harbour crocodiles means that I still feel a tad guilty about asking Cora to wade in and check for depth.

'Hips,' she called. 'And a soft sandy bottom.'

You have to be tough to be that casual.

Evel Knievel wouldn't be in it. I again charged the river, throwing the bike into a magnificent flying leap that propelled me half way across. But half way was no good. The back wheel burrowed into the sand, and most of the bike went under.

'That was brilliant,' Cora called. 'I don't suppose you need any help.'

I did my best to ignore that.

'Don't worry,' she said. 'We're coming.'

With one dragging, one pushing and one lifting the exhaust clear, we coaxed the bike to the far side.

'You know what,' Glenys said, 'when we were out there in the middle I couldn't quite get the crocs out of my mind.'

With the crocs still on our minds, we had to wade back across and repeat the process while keeping the smaller bike hoisted clear of the water.

We then discovered the remarkable qualities of the Honda XL and why it was called the Thumper. After being buried in the river, we stood the 250 to dry for ten minutes and, hey presto, one kick and it had life again.

Washing in the Kennedy River that evening, we counted the bruises collected in the late afternoon when the track was splashed in shadow, hiding obstacles that would have best been avoided.

But, confidence was burgeoning.

'What about the exhilaration of beating the bulldust,' I said, 'and riding the walls of those erosions and gullies. There's a kind of pleasure in tightening all the loose bolts, and knowing that we'll be hammering up the track again tomorrow.'

'Oh dear,' Cora said. 'Not that again...'

We cooked the evening meal and dried our clothes under an enormous paperbark gum[17] that hung over the river, its uppermost branches catching the setting sun. On the river itself, a blue-grey hue settled on the sand bars in a silence broken only by the gurgle of water and the last of the settling birds.

'Sh-h-h-h,' Cora said. Then we all heard it: somewhere out in the faraway, the long-drawn, plaintive howl of a dingo.

Shortly afterwards, a Land Rover crossed the river and pulled up. It was one of four vehicles (bar the grader) that we would encounter in the four-day run from Laura to Coen. The driver, a guy in his early thirties from a cattle station further north, got out to shake hands.

'As we don't get too many strangers up here,' he said, 'I thought I'd make your acquaintance. Where the hell are you for? And is there any way I can help?'

We boiled a billy of tea and he stopped the night with us.

'Be careful where you camp,' he warned. 'The salties come a long way up the freshwater rivers and it only takes one croc to do the business. Best to stay away from where the river is deep.' He then resolved our river-crossing debate. 'Charging the river? No sir,' he said. 'You need to ease in slowly and idle the bike across.'

Glenys, to her eternal credit, said bugger-all.

---

17. These trees, generally found along riverbanks, were the largest in the forest and were characterised by bark that peeled in thick pulpy layers.

* * *

Cora's *Oh dear* of the previous night hadn't been misplaced. Almost as soon as we broke camp, the track deteriorated into a continuum of ruts, gullies and corrugations so severe that the pummelling brought headaches. To avoid some atrocious corrugations, Cora and I bombed along a roadside screen of tall sword grass and were very lucky to avoid a termite hill that sprang up out of nowhere. Hitting it would have been akin to hitting a wall. I also had to consider the fact that I was now carrying two fume-seeping cans of petrol, hanging from my neck and sitting on my thighs. Although they remained amazingly stable, I was a flying petrol bomb.

At Musgrave telegraph station, a single house that was the one oasis in the 168 miles that separated Laura from Coen, we topped up again with petrol from a pump that came out of Noah's Ark and had to be worked by hand. Inside in the living room the woman of the house was teaching her family the primary-school curriculum with the aid of the Bush radio that provided daily lessons. She was amazed by our arrival, our minimalist baggage and the cans of petrol hanging from my neck.

'Wait till you hear who I've got here...' she said to whoever was on the other end of the wire. And that was how word of our journey began to spread the length and breadth of Cape York Peninsula. By the time we got to Coen they would all be waiting.

North of Musgrave we hit a 30-mile span that combined lengthy runs of bulldust and the worst corrugations so far. For long stretches we were forced to idle the bikes through the dust, straddling the saddles with the engines barely ticking over but burning up lots of fuel. Even at this pace, however, we would still skid sideways into potholes hidden under the white powder. In a 200-yard stretch Glenys went over four times. On the fourth fall, she lay on the ground, pummelling the earth.

Then, with stubborn tenacity she raised herself from the dirt, brushed herself down, got back on the bike and continued.

At noon on the fifth day, after a night at the Annie River, we dropped down through densely-wooded hills into Coen, a frontier post of four unpaved streets and a scattering of tin-roofed wooden houses. In the creaking red-roofed bar of the Exchange Hotel, we found that we were famous. Jim Scanlon, the local cop - who was away in the bush - had heard about us from a man in Cairns, who had heard about us from a man in Brisbane who knew Glenys. Mrs. Scanlon, who joined us from the cop shop, had heard about us on the bush radio.

'You'll never make it,' she said. 'The dinghy will be snagged: the river is full of submerged logs and fallen trees. And do you know about the crocs?'

The rivers of the Cape were home to the relatively harmless, fish-eating Johnstone's crocodile that grew to six feet and might bite you for a laugh, and the estuarine or saltwater crocodile that could pull down a buffalo, and could, according to Mrs Scanlon, be found as much as sixty miles inland.

'There's supposed to be five channels to the Coen,' Harris, the big barman, said. 'And three of them vanish in the swamps somewhere.'

'You don't understand,' Mrs. Scanlon went on. 'There's been nobody on that river for a hundred years, not since the gold rush.'

'I'd watch out for them salties,' a bearded barramundi fisherman from Port Stewart added. 'They come roarin' up to my back door every bloody night. I shot one of them one time that was twenty-seven feet long.'

I don't know if he did or didn't shoot that crocodile. At the time I sensed a big dollop of poetic licence and that was probably about right. It seems that the largest saltwater crocodile ever recorded was four feet short of the fisherman's tale - albeit a 23-foot monster that weighed in at two metric tonnes.

'And what about the snakes?' Harris went on. 'Have you got a gun...? What? No gun? Jesus, you're bloody game. Ya wouldn't catch me down there without a bloody gun in a hundred years...'

Just then Jim Scanlon walked in, slim, serious, about thirty-five and casually dressed in shorts, open-necked shirt and battered bush hat. When he realised that all the arguments had been presented to no avail, he made the final effort.

'If ya get bushed in there,' he said, 'ya're on yer own. There's no goin' in after ya. That there country is too rough for horses, we can't land a chopper, and search parties on foot wouldn't be able to carry enough supplies.'

However, having failed to shake our resolve, the welcoming party bade us the best of luck, still harbouring a hidden conviction, confided to us on our return: nobody in Coen seriously believed that Jim Gordon, the owner of Rokeby cattle station, would for a single moment entertain the idea of our attempting a journey down the Coen River.

The track to Rokeby, they told us, branched off about ten miles up the road. Look for the sign to Meripah (cattle station). Rokeby was about two thirds of the way to Meripah.

'At least,' Mrs. Scanlon said as a parting shot, 'there's a *man* along. We were really worried when we heard it was three *girls* on motorbikes.'

Cora and Glenys snorted white heat.

A short way out of town we found the Coen, clear and rocky as it splashed down from the mountains. We set up camp, threw ourselves into a deep hole and lay back to dry against some rocks. ('Deck chairs,' Glenys called them. That other world had clearly slipped away.) We were some 350 miles north of Cairns and sixty short of Rokeby.

That remaining distance took the guts of the following day. At first we couldn't find the track as the sign was lost in the grass, forcing us back to Coen for clearer directions. The track itself then turned out to be little more than two wheel indentations running through the bush in a variety of ambush positions that floored us several times.

'Coming out of one sharp bend,' Glenys would write in her journal that evening, *'I saw two helmets, two petrol cans and two bodies lift into the air like puppets in slow motion, and land a yard from the bike. Ciarán was cursing but when he saw the funny side we sat on the track and laughed. Still, the fall had shaken them and within ten minutes they were over again. This time it wasn't funny. As the bike lost it, Ciarán jumped clear but it landed heavily on Cora's ankle...'*

Cora still has the scar to prove it.

Late in the afternoon, eight hours after we had set out, the ordeal was over. The bush broke away to reveal a collection of buildings on a slight rise in the middle of a clearing.

As we trundled up the slope, petrol cans slung from my neck, my rear number-plate hanging loose and our bodies caked in dust, a sturdy-looking man of about forty-five, who was mending a harness, drew to his full height. He pushed back a battered hat and scratched his head.

Jim Gordon was the only person north of Mareeba who hadn't heard we were coming.

* * *

Our equipment had arrived safely despite sitting for two days on Rokeby's airstrip, two miles from the house. It had been discovered by the station's Aboriginal workers.

'It was a stroke of luck,' Jim said. 'If the wild pigs had found it first, there wouldn't be much left.' Our explanatory note, however, had been torn off in transit.

'I just thought the stuff must belong to the army,' Jim said. 'Maybe some soldiers were comin' on manoeuvres.'

He stared as we explained our plans. He'd study the map, ask another question, study the map again, then scratch his chin, not quite sure what to think.

'Well,' he said in the end, 'I sure hope you know what you're doin'. It's rough country, and the Archer has big crocs. They can get into the Coen too. Anyhow, the river is a stretch from here. If you want to get there before dark, I'll drop ya down in the truck. You can leave the bikes in the shed there.'

As we undid the gear from the bikes a scream shattered the peace. Jim tore off into the station house. Seconds later a shot rang out.

'What in Christ's name...?' Cora said.

A minute later Jim reappeared with a six-foot snake draped over a stick. Its neck had been almost severed by a shotgun blast. Strolling over, he dropped it at our feet.

'Could be eastern brown or taipan,' he drawled. 'But probably taipan. Mum found it in the bathroom. We don't usually get 'em in the house in the dry season.' Using the stick he bared the fangs and venom sacs. 'A man don't live too long if they get into him.'

Growing up to nine feet, with half-inch fangs that carry massive doses of neurotoxin, the taipan is one of the world's deadliest snakes.

'If ya get bitten in the leg by one of these,' Jim said, 'best to chop off the leg.'

He then introduced us to his wife and we loaded our gear into the back of his four-wheel-drive. Half an hour after arriving at Rokeby we were on our way to the river, watched by a mob of grazing wallabies.

'There's been a cattle station here,' Jim explained, 'since it was set up by the Massey brothers back in 1884. The station covers what used to be the tribal lands of the Mungkan and Kaanju people. Many of them still live and work with us. Most of our workers have been born here, either at the station or out in the bush at our Jabaroo outstation, one of the bases we use for musterin'.

'The cattle run wild in the bush until they're brought in for transportin' by our Aboriginal stockmen and trackers They go out on horseback and combine their cattle work with their traditional way of life, gainin' experience as cattlemen and preservin' their own customs.'

Dusk was already settling when Jim dropped us off at a murky hole about ten yards wide and guarded by giant paperbarks. Along its banks, massive tangles of roots groped the water. The plopping of small fish as they rose for insects added to an eerie silence. We took stock and decided to camp on the far side on a sandy flat, half hidden by some small trees and well away from the water's edge. We then tied a whistle each around our necks in case any of us got lost and prepared to cross the river.

'Well folks, this is it,' Jim said as he helped us unload our gear. 'Nothin' but crocs from here to the Gulf.' He climbed back into his truck, leaned out the window and grinned. 'I hope to see you again some time.'

Then he was gone and we were alone with two rucksacks and that raft of rubberised canvas that said 'Use only under adult suprvision'. Downstream, where the river curved out of sight, all was waiting.

We inflated the raft and loaded on the packs, noticing for the first time how little space remained for people.

'Well, come on,' Cora said. 'We're not going to get anywhere by looking at the bloody river.'

'Maybe two runs?' Glenys suggested. 'First the gear and then the people.'

I was appointed paddler in chief.

Wobbling out from the bank I discovered that my lack of control over the raft was not confined to Mosman Bay. Many circles later, I thumped backwards into the sandy slope on the far side.

'Sinbad,' Cora called, 'don't forget to come back.'

'Be brave,' Glenys added. 'You're our fearless leader.'

The swishing of the paddle, however, was the only sound that accompanied the second crossing: the storm troopers were too busy keeping their limbs in the middle of the raft. As for disembarkation, it was an act of such single-minded calculation that raft, packs and crew were twenty yards from the riverbank in the time it would take to strike a match. We pitched the tent as darkness closed in and, after we had eaten, hung the packs from a tree to protect the food from the wild pigs and avoid waking up in the middle of the night with a mad boar in the tent. We then sat around the fire and rolled up some Queensland heads to chase away the mosquitoes while every hoot, howl, croak, shriek, clunk and plop imaginable filled the forest.

'I'm having awful visions of the crocodile that guy from Port Stewart told us about.' Cora said, shining a flashlight towards the river.

'People say that the salties come out of the rivers,' Glenys said, 'and use their tails to knock flying foxes from the trees.'

'Too much information,' Cora said. 'I'm glad it's my turn in the middle tonight.'

'Tomorrow evening,' I swore, 'we'll build a stockade.'

* * *

In the morning everything was rosy. The sun was rising. There were blue and red dragonflies and butterflies of every colour, hovering over the river. The birdsong was jubilant. Breakfast was good and the ominous black hole of the night before looked cheery and harmless. Wearing shirts and rolled-up jeans, we loaded the dinghy, squeezed ourselves on board and set off in high spirits, idly paddling along with an eye open for crocodiles while trying to keep the raft pointed in the one direction. The only problem was that, with all our gear on board, we had to sit on the walls of the dinghy. Any crocodile lying in watery ambush would have had a great laugh.

Immediately past the deep hole, however, progress was dented. The river widened into shallow channels, divided by sand bars and tangles of trees. We hadn't figured on this. A river, you'd think, would be a flow of water running unimpeded between two banks. Over the next couple of hours we waded, paddled, dragged the boat, lifted it over fallen trees, and fought a generally cheerful, but slow, battle downriver.

'At least,' I pointed out, 'we didn't bring the guitar.'

'That would have been stupid,' Cora pointed out.

Sometime around noon, we rounded a bend to a scene that cut the morning dead. A long, still, murky hole with high muddy banks stretched beyond the next bend. This was deep, silent, dark water. Overhead, the canopy became a tunnel, smothering out most of the sunlight and replacing the chatter of the birds with silence. Tangles of wood and grass hung from the trees where the rainy season had left them.

Cautiously, we let the raft drift, then started to paddle with our three plastic oars. The raft went in every direction it chose as the invisible claws of the hole groped and scraped at the rubber bottom, reminding us of Mrs. Scanlon's words: *The dinghy will be snagged: the river is full of submerged logs and fallen trees.*

Mud and exposed roots slithered in from the banks. Giant cobwebs hung from the foliage. Huge grey trunks, rising from the deep, suddenly changed position to block our path. They twice knocked me into the water - to flights for dry land that were astounding.

Then the silence broke, first a whisper, rising gradually to become a glut of strange sounds, welling up from the depths of the forest to fill and shake the overhead canopy before receding into the distance again, leaving a feeling of what-the-*fuck*-was-that?

In the middle of the afternoon, a little more relaxed about the river (having not yet been eaten - always a good sign), and reduced to a pair of cut-off jeans each, we emerged from another deep hole into a curve of shallow rapids lit by slashes of sunshine.

'Let's pull over for the night,' Cora suggested. 'Remember how that guy back at the Kennedy River told us that crocodiles don't like shallows.'

'Great idea,' Glenys said. 'And to make it even better, I'll bake some damper [a kind of basic bread]. My word, we're getting into the swing of things now.'

On that high note we made camp, gathered a generous store of firewood, washed away the grime of the previous day, and took careful note of the position of all green ants' and hornets' nests. And while Cora and Glenys stretched out in the sun, I went into the forest with a long stick in search of game to supplement dinner supplies that relied heavily on untested hunting skills to provide the main course.

If you ignore the Golden Triangle escapade, this was the first real expedition that Cora, Glenys or I had ever organised, and despite what the opal fossicker had told Glenys back in Sydney, the menu was wanting. Breakfast wasn't too bad: we had muesli, porridge, dried fruit and dried milk. The rest of our food consisted of starches (flour for bread, and instant mashed potato) along with some packets of processed cheese, dried cabbage, dried eggs, dried peas and a few tins of sardines. The notion was that we would supplement this with copious catches of fish and duck. Now it was time to get the fish and duck. Based on the belief that if you throw a stick often enough you're sure to hit something in the end, I was optimistic. False hope is better than no hope at all.

Barefoot, I stalked through the bush, ready to pounce on anything that moved. An exhilarating moment of communication with the ancestors suggested I change to a gallop. Dodging branches, thorny 'stay-awhiles' and green ants' nests, I ran deep into the forest, no thought of snakes, spiders or scorpions. At a point where to have continued might well have been forever, I skidded to a halt beside a quiet billabong dappled in rafts of reddish-pink water lilies.

I sat down to apply the mind. Needle-like fish played in the water, stalked by a darter and two herons. I was engrossed in the fish when a lightning move scared the living daylights out of me. With a splash, a small crocodile hit the water. Contemplating the possibility of mama lurking nearby, I slowly circled the waterhole and got a severe shock when a wallaby broke cover. Nerves in tatters, I backtracked to the river to find Cora and Glenys thigh-deep in the water.

'I found freshwater mussels,' Cora shouted. 'You just grope in the mud with your feet and you'll feel them moving.'

'Good tucker tonight,' Glenys said. 'Did *you* catch anything...?'

Breaking all the rules of crocodile country, we waded deep into the water and filled a billycan. That evening, as the river purpled, we ate our first bush food, me with one ear pricked in the direction of that muddy billabong. And when night settled and we sat around our fire and shooting stars lit the sky and we listened to the gurgle of the river and shadows flickered on the water, I made a promise.

'Tomorrow night, we'll build that stockade.'

* * *

Over the coming days the first navigation of the Coen River since the Palmer gold rush ground its astonishing way downriver, moving freely through the long, spooky, deep holes, and being keenly obstructed elsewhere. Broken and uprooted trees, and tangled tapestries of bushes and driftwood, would regularly force us to get out of the boat. Sometimes we could haul it over or under the blockage, or slash a path through with the machete. Other times we'd have to unload the gear and carry it and the boat to the next clear piece of river. Some days we'd work the river well into the afternoon, leaving just enough time to make camp. Other days we'd stop early and explore the surprises that the forest had in store.

We could find ourselves sitting under a palm watching a family of wild pigs forage, the old boars flanking with their razor-sharp tusks. We could study a colony of bull ants, or a praying mantis or stick insect. We could walk among clouds of butterflies. Or take in the diverse and extensive birdlife of the river and the bush. Blue-winged kookaburras. Azure kingfishers. White cockatoos. Black cockatoos. Palm cockatoos. Wedge-tailed eagles. Bitterns, herons, egrets and swamp hens. Rainbow bee-eaters, Blue-faced honey-eaters. And countless others of the 321 species recorded in Cape York Peninsula. Or we could climb into the branches of a paperback and watch the river or, void of botheration, lie back in the sun, close our eyes and listen to the forest.

And every day would end with the campfire, the darkness, the stars, the forest chorus, the river, and puffs of pungent smoke as we recounted the day's events and drew designs for that stockade.

But, no matter how we tried, our hunting efforts were producing nothing. Nor had there been any more mussels. We were now burning far more calories than were going in and needed to catch something. We tried line-fishing with insects but to no avail. Net-fishing with a converted pair of knickers bagged three tiddlers. We hunted snakes but couldn't find any. The scrub fowl so painstakingly stalked always flew away. We threw sticks at the egrets and missed. We tried to spear the large crayfish that came to investigate our feet but they were too fast. With the futility of our efforts, desperation drove us to low thoughts. Lizards? Maybe if we caught enough of them?

'Gee,' Glenys said after our umpteenth plate of instant mashed potato, 'this stuff is doing terrible things to my guts, upon my word. There used to be a time when food was food and wildlife was wildlife. Now there's no such thing as wildlife.'

'We need a concerted effort,' I said. 'What about putting tomorrow aside to do nothing but hunt. We could decide on what we're after.' We agreed and decided on snake.

We brought our entire arsenal: the machete, a long sharpened stick and three shorter 'throwing-sticks'. Leaving the small island on which we had spent the night, we crossed the river on a fallen tree-trunk and in bare feet and cut-off jeans headed into the bush.

'Reminds me of the first play I was ever in,' Glenys said. ''Dashing around in skins after being marooned on a desert island. But I never imagined I'd be doing it for real.'

A short way into the bush we came across the threads of a track. This, we guessed, might or might not be the track that continued from Rokeby to Meripah. Either way, it allowed us to draw an arrow that pointed to our camp.

After some further wanderings we arrived in a clearing with clumps of Pandanus palm, isolated gums and grass that grew to chest-height in places. We wound our way along animal tracks, ever watchful for the sluggish death adder, notorious for being stupid and stood on.

As ever, the bush was a constant diversion of birds, lizards, frogs and insects. And wildflowers as diverse in shape and colour as the trees, vines, palms and plants on which they grew. In a cluster of bushes, we came on two curious spiders: one that made its home in a folded leaf attached to its web; another fantastically daubed in red and yellow with a flat, shell-like abdomen that tapered into six spikes, two at the back and two on each side. Further on we arrived at a secluded billabong encircled by termite hills. Cora perched herself by the water while Glenys went off to photograph dragonflies. In this patient spot where human feet may have never bent a stem, you got the feeling that the hunt was being hopelessly sidetracked.

I had just about given up myself, when a massive reptilian head reared up from the grass. *Christ!* I thought. *This is one BIG snake!* I then saw the shoulders.

'Goanna!' I yelled to my co-hunters. 'Grab your sticks and we'll surround it!'

I let fly with the long stick I was carrying but I was too far away. It spun in an arc and struck home, but without force. Six feet of goanna took off through five feet of grass, chased by five-foot-eight of Irish extremism roaring *Get him* like a bedlamite.

Cora and Glenys joined the chase. We cornered our dinner in a thicket of grass and bushes. We closed in. The goanna made a break. Straight at Cora.

'I would have dived on it' she later explained. 'But Glenys had just told me that a cornered goanna climbs the nearest vertical object, that it has sharp, powerful claws, and that it puts up a ferocious fight.'

The goanna bolted past.

Several unrewarded hours later, we turned for camp only to find that everything looked the same and nothing looked familiar. Lots of running around and a vast wilderness were poor bedfellows. In bare feet and cut-off jeans, with a machete, half a box of matches, three whistles and a compass, we were lost in the middle of Cape York Peninsula. The river had been our guide. We had no idea where it was.

'This is anything but good,' Glenys said in the understatement of 1977. 'We all have to get back to our work.'

Our first reaction was for each of us to head off to search for clues in the direction we believed to be correct. We were fifty yards in different directions, when the logic of that hit home. It was bad enough being lost together: separately was going to be a total disorder. We sat down and considered the predicament.

The river couldn't be that far away, half a mile at most, and probably not to the south: all we had to do was find it.

We looked at our options and decided to hold our position and work from there: at least that way we wouldn't make matters worse. The plan, therefore, was that Cora and Glenys would stay put while I set off with the compass and machete, and my whistle, to check all possibilities in 800-yard trajectories. We'd draw an arrow in the ground and I'd take a bearing to a distant tree. When I reached the tree, or began to lose sight of the women, I'd use the compass to maintain the bearing. As a precaution I would cut notches in the trunks of trees at regular intervals so I could follow them back if needed, like Hansel and Gretel. After each attempt, another arrow would be drawn at a 30-degree tangent and I'd try again. If I found the track or the river, it was two blasts on the whistle.

It took over an hour, but eventually it worked. I hit the track. Five minutes later, two smiling women came sauntering through the grass. Chastened, we arrived back at camp, grateful for a cup of coffee and a piece of processed cheese.

'Sometimes you've got to laugh,' Cora said.

'Indeed,' Glenys said. 'People may think we're mad. But to be this mad takes effort.'

Dinner was curried noodles, sardines and a Glenys treat: baked bread-and-butter pudding laced with dried fruit.

We had finally accepted that our hunting skills were sadly wanting when fate doled out a celestial gift. We were wading through an awkward stretch of river, littered with fallen trees and tangles of driftwood when a Nankeen Night Heron with a damaged wing fell from above at Glenys' feet. Quick as a flash, she was on top of it, grabbing it by the wings. That, in its simplicity, was how we secured our second bush dinner. Which in turn led to further good fortune.

We had stopped where the river dropped from a run of shallow rapids into a dark nadir into which Cora and Glenys had temporarily vanished while trotting the dinghy through the shallows. Cora was pitching the tent. Glenys was lighting the fire. I was crouched in the shallows cleaning out the bird. Absent-mindedly, I tossed some of the innards into the deep water. Immediately, the surface churned to a froth.

'Did anyone see that?' I yelled, backing away from the river. 'Something just grabbed the guts. We have bait at last.'

I took a fishing line, stuck a strip of intestine on the hook, threw it in, and zap! A large bream. Cora threw a second line and zap! Her first ever fish. We came, we saw, we conquered. We were sailing with the wind. In the space of minutes, we had ten bream, two catfish and a perch. And something severed Cora's 40lb line without as much as a quiver.

'Time to get away from the river,' I sussed, 'and get out the tinfoil.'

'Moby Dick,' Cora said during the fish-bake. 'I nearly caught Moby Dick.'

'Whatever it was,' Glenys said, 'it's still in there. And not a stockade in sight.'

'Tomorrow night,' I promised.

From then on we used the innards of one day's catch as bait for the next, and ate regally every night. Our only problem was protecting the bait overnight from very clever ants. This we did by hanging it from tree branches in plastic sandwich-bags full of water, hoping that morning would come before the ants figured out what we had done. Most mornings, we'd get up to find a circle of ants merrily cutting their way through the plastic just above the water line.

'Amazing,' Glenys said one night as we sat around the fire. 'I wonder why everyone gave us those wild stories about how dangerous this place is. Just imagine how foolish they'd feel if you could land them right here at this moment.'

'On the other hand,' Cora said, beckoning towards the din of the forest, 'they might feel totally justified.'

The night beyond the camp was the usual deafening chorus of shrieking, howling, croaking and droning. Demons presented themselves in brief glimpses of owls, small marsupials, crickets and flying foxes. The trees around the camp had come to life as they did every night, pulsing in flickering gowns of yellow, orange and violet, beyond which pillars of ash-grey gave shelter to phantoms. It was the kind of night when a person alone might have pulled closer to the fire and covered up with a blanket or coat. And maybe whistled, but not too loudly. Through gaps in the trees, shooting stars disintegrated in a thousand fragments. We could hear pig grunts somewhere close by and a dingo in the distance.

'The river looks so eerie in the firelight,' Glenys said. 'And yet, I don't feel at all afraid.'

'Okay,' I said. 'One, two three!' We let out a long shrill blast on our whistles. The result: total, absolute silence. Not a peek from any living thing. Then a tentative croak or click as, one by one, the animals realised it was only a joke. The exchange of insults could start all over again.

* * *

We never did make it to the Archer River. After the first three or four days of exhausting ourselves against the Coen's obstacles we redrew the boundaries. We would go as far as we could at our ease and enjoy our surroundings.

A week downriver we turned back for Rokeby and the long slog upriver, dragging the dinghy behind us in the shallows and paddling through the deeper sections. At one juncture I found myself pulling the boat with Cora and Glenys still inside.

'Bad things happen,' Cora said when I complained.

But there were also times when we broke the slog to relax in the bush. Using the tree-notching technique piloted on the day we got lost, we could now meander at will, then pick our way back to camp whenever we chose.

We'd turn over stones or break open dead wood to reveal centipedes, scorpions or large bird-eating spiders. Or we'd stand and watch a praying mantis with a cricket, or a goanna on a dead tree trunk, or termites repairing a damaged mound, or a fly laying live maggots on a fresh piece of dung. We gave a wide berth to a 1,000-cubic-foot web inhabited by a colony of social spiders where each individual was responsible for its own section of the gruesome communal home.

And we wandered through without a scratch.

* * *

Ten days after he had dropped us at the river, we were back in Jim Gordon's place, giving him a renewed hold over his sleep. He fed us beef, chips, home-brew and rum, put us up for the night, and shared some good news.

'Mum's in Musgrave. She told me over the radio that the grader's been over the main track, all the way to Cairns. She ain't no beauty, but she's a hell of a sight better than what you had on the way up.'

After dinner, Jim pulled out a large store of books on the Australian bush. Although a cattle man all his life, he held the bush in an esteem rare among his peers and would have no part in the widespread endeavours to exterminate the dingoes by dropping poisoned meat from bush planes.

'Nature looks after itself,' he said. 'The cattle men are always moanin' about the roos and the dingoes: the roos are eating all the grass and the dingoes are killin' the calves. But it's not true. The roos and dingoes and the cattle can do well together, with the roos keepin' down a lot of the stuff the cattle don't eat, and the dingoes keepin' the roos in check. The cattle men's argument is really just an excuse to go around killin' everything.'

'What about the pigs?' Glenys asked. She herself had occasionally hunted them.

'The pigs is a different matter. They were introduced, same as the rabbits and cane toads. They do a lot of damage to the bush, so I got no objection to huntin' them. But I won't let anyone else in to do it. For that matter, if you folks had been carryin' a gun, I wouldn't have let ya past the station.'

'If we'd written to you in advance,' Glenys asked, 'would you have given us the go-ahead for the trip?'

'No way,' Jim said. 'Every night you were on the river, I kept askin' myself why I hadn't turned ya back. Last request I had was from a full-blown expedition and I turned them down flat without even considerin' it.'

'So why did you agree to us going on?'

'I suppose,' Jim said, 'you had the element of surprise and you must've looked looney enough to make it. And to be truthful, lots of folks around here wouldn't have fared as well as y'all did on that river.'

When we told Jim of our mussel-hunting in the deep water, and the fact that we had only come across one small crocodile, he laughed.

'Before it was made illegal,' he said. 'I used to hunt crocodiles in the very holes you were paddlin' through. They'll go under when they hear ya comin'. But if ya go out at night with a strong beam, the red eyes are on the water. And you know of course about the sawfish?'

'Sawfish?' That was Cora.

'Yep. Get them with beaks up to four foot long. And the water-snakes are good and plentiful too...' He may at this stage have been winding us up.

There was more rum, and more again, before Jim tuned into the bush radio to announce to one and all in north Queensland that he had us back under his roof, safe and sound. We had even brought him a billycan of fresh mussels.

'All you folks down in Cooktown' he said, 'you'll see them in a couple o' days, 'cos that's where these crazy folks are headin' next.'

Jim offered to transport the dinghy and the two rucksacks to Musgrave as he was driving there to collect his wife. Terrific, as flying them out of Rokeby would not have been easy. He also provided a petrol top-up which we insisted on replacing in Coen, something we would arrange with Harris, the big barman at the Exchange Hotel.

From Musgrave we made further arrangement to have the dinghy and packs relayed back to Cairns.

* * *

If we hadn't been over the track on our way north, we would have undoubtedly considered the journey back south a tough one. The corrugations were still severe enough to cause headaches. Many of the gullies, erosions and sand patches remained. And the gravel left on the graded sections was treacherous, as were the long shadows of evening. But, by comparison to our journey north, it was sheer joy.

There were also a few more vehicles on the track. At one point, two four-wheel-drives came towards us - two families on an adventure. Surprised to see us sitting by the bikes, they stopped.

'Are you driving one of these?' one of the women asked Glenys. 'Gee, and I thought driving a car on these roads was pretty difficult.'

'You know what,' Glenys said afterwards. 'It's beginning to sink in that we took on quite a lot on this trip.'

At the Morehead River, south west of Musgrave Telegraph Station, Glenys flagged down a truck that was following in our wake.

'We could maybe ask the driver to take our cans of petrol,' she suggested, 'and drop them for us at the Kennedy River.'

'No problem,' the truck driver said. 'More than happy to carry your petrol. But where are you from, ay?'

'Sydney and Ireland, 'Cora said. 'But we've just come from the Coen River.'

'Then I'm pleased to meet ya. My mother is expectin' visitors from the river any day now. I can let her know that they won't be comin'.'

The driver, who was bringing cattle to Cairns, turned out to be young John Wetherspoon whose home was Meripah cattle station, the station that sat twenty miles east of Rokeby. (If Rokeby was isolated, try Meripah.)

Once John had left we headed south again in a style of driving that was feisty to say the least, with speeds of up to fifty miles an hour. Until our ardour was doused, along with our engines, in three feet of the Little Laura. We had a hell of a time extracting the wheels from the mud while simultaneously trying to pull the bikes up a thirty-degree slope on the far side of the river.

It took two hours this time before the bikes would start again. (We really didn't deserve the luck we had with those machines. In almost a thousand miles of dirt riding, and a combined mechanical ignorance that was total, we never once had as much as a puncture.)

It was a propitious delay. As we sat by the river a four-wheel-drive arrived with three anthropologists on board. They also had difficulty getting across; but while they were working on it, they gave us directions to an Aboriginal gallery of rock paintings at a place called Mushroom Rock

'On condition,' our informant said, 'that you don't tell anyone. So many of these sites have been defaced by knuckle-draggers that the locations are kept under wraps.'[18]

'No problem,' we said and wrote down the details.

Our initial attempt to get there proved a fiasco. We missed the track, slipped backwards on hills of bulldust, bogged to the axles in mud, fell

---

18.   I wouldn't have written about this location except that I'm aware that there are now Aboriginal-run tours to Mushroom Rock.

over in a creek, and took an hour to cover two miles in the scrub before turning back, caked in mud and wrecked.

'Those Aboriginals would need to put their fuckin' paintings where people can fuckin' well see them,' I fumed. I know, a bit much; they were painted thousands of years ago; they couldn't have known we were coming; but it had been a long day.

'Ouch!' Cora said. 'I've just been stung by a bee.'

'I've never in my life been stung by a bee,' she had just told Glenys.

'Ciarán,' Glenys said, 'I think that might have been the Aboriginal ancestors aiming at you.'

In the morning we left the bikes behind, found the correct track - a foot track that looked like an animal trail - and walked half an hour to the rock.

Underneath the sandstone 'mushroom', in black charcoal, and white, red, orange and yellow ochre, the people who had lived in this area had left behind a pictorial record of the world they had known and understood. There were spirit quinkans, goannas, a crocodile, an emu, a shark, a horse-like animal, hand-stencils - and a white figure wearing what looked like a peaked cap.

We sat for an hour under the rock alongside the ghosts of the gold rush massacres. We then drove south on an ever-improving track where the rattle of the bikes decreased by the mile. Nevertheless, we had to stop twice to tighten chains. And Glenys had the bolt that held her clutch handle in place pop, making it impossible to use the clutch. However, a Land Cruiser arrived in the nick of time to solve the problem with a nail and a pair of pliers.

We had one close shave. Having branched off for Cooktown at Lakeland Downs, Cora and I had crossed the second arm of the Annan River, spanned by a wooden bridge, when a truck came screaming at us on the wrong side of the road.

'Oh Ciarán,' Cora pleaded, 'stop the bike...' She then closed her eyes for the impact.

Any attempt to brake, and we would have skidded on gravel and gone under the truck, so I did the only thing I could. I went over the edge into the bush. For the next few seconds I was driving blind, eyes stinging from the truck's dust. We shot into a gully, ran along the bottom, rose and, finally through some freak accident, found ourselves back on the track. Miraculously, we had missed the trees. A tenacious legacy of luck had once more served us well.

Glenys appeared from the still-billowing cloud, relief all over her face.

'Jesus Christ,' she said. 'That was bloody close. I thought you were goners for sure. I saw you go off the road and then there was only dust.'

Four days after leaving Rokeby we were in Cooktown. Cloaked head to toe in dust, we drove into its camping ground and pitched our tent among some coconut palms next to the campervan of a loveable lunatic with bulging eyes and a dishevelled beard who was permanently stoned and took an instant shine to Glenys.

'Welcome! Welcome!' the lunatic roared as soon as we landed. 'Have you heard the news? The Japs are bombing Darwin. With Toyotas!' He almost choked on his own laughter. 'Anyway,' he went on, 'pleased to make the acquaintance. My name is Psimaux. P-s-i-m-a-u-x. It's French, you see.'

We later found that his name was Simpson, shortened to 'Simmo'. Simmo loved our stories of the trip.

'Tell me again about the mussel-fuckin'-fishin',' he'd say. 'An' about how y'all went down into that river in yer bare fuckin' feet. Far out, man. Far fucking out.'

Simmo had a wild tongue on him.

Sitting on the mangrove estuary of the Endeavour River, Cooktown was unexpectedly small: three parallel streets, hemmed in between the mountains and the sea. A tiny cluster of shops and houses were all that remained of the once-booming gold rush town. In its heyday it had boasted ninety-four hotels and as many brothels, gambling halls, strip clubs and opium dens. Its Chinatown alone had boasted 2,500 residents.

The morning after we arrived, Cora and Glenys called in at the history museum to learn more about the town's past and the region's associations with Captain James Cook.

On June 17th 1770, Cook had landed here when it was a stretch of unexplored coast with plants and animals unknown to science. Having grounded his ship on the Great Barrier Reef, he had pulled in for repairs and had subsequently accomplished a brilliant navigational feat by climbing nearby Grassy Hill and charting a safe passage back to the open sea.

'We could go up there later,' Glenys suggested on the second morning.

'I'm bored lying around,' Cora said. 'Let's do something now.'

'We could check out the mangroves,' I suggested. Some people never learn.

'Good idea,' Glenys said. 'See some more of the birdlife.'

Very soon, when we could have been enjoying the company of Simmo and looking up at the coconuts, we were toppling around through black mud and tangles of aerial roots, reminiscent of that day back at the Adelaide River outside Humpty Doo. Again we had the fiddler crabs, mudskippers (those fish that hopped about the mud), mosquitoes and sand flies. And the green ants that showered down from their camouflaged nests with a vengeance. But we also had plenty to laugh about and press to our hearts as we relived a journey that would be a harbinger of times to come.

In the late afternoon we climbed Grassy Hill and stood where Cook had stood all those years ago. The panorama was spectacular: a commanding view of Cooktown, the Endeavour estuary, the Coral Sea and the mountains to the north, west and south. We were still there at sunset when the sky burned a violent red and a fresh breeze trembled across the waters of the estuary. June 29th 1977.

By the time we had descended to sleepy Cooktown, moonlight had crept across the wild lands of Cape York Peninsula.

Back at the camping ground Simmo was welcoming two hippies from Cairns who, along with ourselves and a long-haired, bearded Richard from Perth, were the night's only other occupants.

'Have you heard the news?' he roared. 'The Japs are bombing Darwin! With Toyotas!'

All that now remained on our itinerary was to visit the rainforests of Mossman Gorge and ride back to Cairns.

* * *

On our return to Sydney, I got the bike ready for resale. One of the things to be sorted was the dodgy throttle cable that had been fraying when we set off for the Cape. Tom Dunlop changed the cables.

'Look,' he said, holding up the old one. 'It was hanging on by a thread.' He bent it back and forward twice and it snapped.

He shook his head and chuckled. 'Lucky bastard,' he said.

* * *

In 1994 Cora and I went back to the Cape, this time with our daughters, nine-year-old Tríona and five-year-old Áine. Starting in Cairns, we drove to the McLeod River in a hired car. By then a whole industry had grown up around four-wheel-drive vehicles and off-road travel and it was heart-breaking to find that the banks of the beautiful McLeod had become a shit-laden latrine where those going north also dumped the first instalment of their rubbish. The wheels of their tyres had also spread the disastrous rubber vine, an invasive species that was strangling the great gum trees along both sides of the road.

A week earlier, at Wilma's Country Kitchen on the Bloomfield track, we were told that Rokeby was now a national park and that Jim Gordon lived in Mareeba. We went to look for him but, as luck would have it, he was visiting his son in Musgrave. However, when we got back to Cairns we managed to track him down through the old Exchange Hotel in Coen and speak to him by phone. His herd, he told us bitterly, had been diagnosed with bovine TB and put down. Then the old station was taken by the government.

'But I still have those photos you sent me,' he said. 'I sometimes look at them and they remind me of the time you all came to stay and of the only life I ever really knew.'

A few days later we took the recently established Cairns to Cooktown four-wheel-drive bus service, passing through Lakeland Downs. The old track had been vastly upgraded and replaced in many parts by a new dirt road that now made travel to Cooktown possible in a standard vehicle. I guess nothing stays still.

But here and there the old track remained. We could see it at intervals, rolling over the contours of the land in all its dilapidated, uncompromising glory.

'It's all flooding back,' Cora said.

'I know,' I said. 'When the Cape belonged to the monsters.'

'What do you mean dad?' Tríona asked.

Some distance away, on the line of the old track, two motorbikes rose from the haze of late morning. At first I wasn't sure, but there they were. Riding along side by side in the manner of friends, they were hauling dust and heading north.

To where the Coen River was waiting.

CHAPTER 13

Taldumande

We were woken by persistent banging on the front door. It was just after two in the morning and there was that feeling you get when you wake up in a dark room where nothing is familiar. Where the hell were we? Then it dawned. We were no longer in our little flatette in Cremorne Point. Last night we had moved to 30 Walker Street, North Sydney.

Taldumande Youth Refuge.

'Maybe somebody has the wrong house,' Cora said.

That wasn't something you'd bet your shirt on.

I dragged myself off the bed - a double mattress on the floor – threw on a pair of jeans and wheeled down the stairs, eager to neutralise the pounding that had already woken half of North Sydney.

'Okay! Okay!' I said, opening the door - and wishing that I hadn't.

'Hi Ciarán,' came the chirpy greeting. 'Is Ross at home...?'

'No,' I said. 'Cora and I run the place now... Come on in.'

It was Elaine, a regular at Walker Street. I had met her during earlier visits to the refuge when Ross and Christine Booth, both in their late twenties, were the resident house parents and I was a humble member of the management committee.

'This is my friend, Mandy,' Elaine said. 'We both need somewhere to stay for a few days.'

I brought them in, made them something to eat and settled them into one of the rooms. I then crawled back to bed.

'You won't believe it,' I said to Cora. 'Guess who our first guest is? Elaine...'

'Oh no,' Cora said. 'What a start...'

So, why and how did this come about?

Returning from the Cape, we had been expecting the final outcome - apart from medicals - of our application to extend our one-year working visas to permanent residency. If successful, we could stay indefinitely and use Australia in the future as a second home. If we failed, we would be turfed out of the country.

Our initial application had been turned down, a decision conveyed to us in a blunt letter dated February 22nd. Signed by G. Dilworth of the Department of Immigration and Ethnic Affairs, it said: *'Your case has been thoroughly investigated but it has been decided that it is not one for approval. Permanent residence is only granted to those persons who possess skills and expertise not available in Australia'.*

Obviously not us. But we had appealed.

As they now had our passports, we were stuck. We couldn't quietly go to ground. (In those days you could have worked legally in Australia without being legally in the country.) But, from the most unexpected quarter, life was turned around. Late one afternoon, I was down at the youth refuge with Ross and Christine discussing their plans to leave at the end of the summer.

The refuge, providing emergency, short-stay accommodation and resettlement assistance to teenagers, was among the first three to be opened in New South Wales. For the previous five months, it had been run by Ross and Christine, along with Christine's 25-five-year-old brother, Paul, who looked like a reduced version of Oliver Reid and had recently come back from driving truckloads of travellers around South America.

'It's beginning to affect Katie,' Christine said. 'We need a place of our own.'

Two-year-old Katie, however, seemed far less affected than the parents. Ross, tall, thinning on top, with a huge handlebar moustache, large wire-rimmed glasses and a drawl the length of Baja California, was outwardly calm and philosophical, but the bloodshot eyes gave it all away.

'I got a call the other day,' he told me, 'from this deadshit, Billy, who ripped off all sorts of stuff belonging to us before he disappeared. "Hi," he says. "Is that you Rossie baby? Up your nose with a rubber hose." Then he says, "Is Chrissie there?" and makes a big dirty slobbering sound and hangs up.'

Christine, a slim attractive woman with big eyelashes and dark hair bobbed in a Marilyn Monroe style, was equally harassed-looking.

'It's the parents you really have to worry about,' she said. 'Some of them are quite mad.'

Since December I had been a member of the management that had been formed when the original management fled. In that capacity I had watched Ross, Christine and Paul steadily approach the margins of the unsound. Finally, in February, they had announced their intention to head for the hills.

'No chance of a change of mind?' I asked during my fateful visit.

'No way,' Ross and Christine chorused.

When I was about to leave, I mentioned my bad news about the visas. We appealed,' I said. 'But it's not looking good. No reply in five months. They seem to be holding our passports until our visas run out so they can see us to the airport.'

'Hang on there,' Ross said. He took a swig from a stubby of Foster's and pulled on his big moustache. 'I'll phone my uncle.'

Two weeks later a letter, signed by the same G. Dilworth of the Department of Immigration and Ethnic Affairs, arrived. *'Further to my letter of 22nd February,' it said, 'your case has been reconsidered and it is now one for approval subject to the usual conditions of health and character...'*

I make no link between that second letter and Ross Booth's phone call to his uncle, the Attorney General. But Cora and I became Australian residents just as Taldumande, despite advertising and interviewing, ran out of house-parents in the first week of September.

'What about it?' Tom Wilson asked at the next management meeting. 'Would Cora consider it?'

Tom, an Irishman from County Down, was the local District Officer with the Department of Youth & Community Affairs. At thirty-five, he was among the most respected District Officers in the state, and was responsible for the care of homeless young people on Sydney's north shore. Silver-haired, with a bright, ruddy complexion and a droll sense of humour, Tom was possibly the most capable youth worker in Australia. A silver tongue accompanied the silver hair. By the afternoon of the following day he had convinced Cora to become Refuge Manager. I would be some kind of voluntary 'house father'. A week later, at the beginning of October, we left our Cremorne flatette, our lovely home with its glorious views and quiet evenings, and moved to Walker Street.

The refuge was sited at the top of the street, a cul-de-sac connected to Blue Street by an enclosed concrete stairway, smelling strongly of urine and harbouring the cerebral droppings of many an alley philosopher. *Help*, cried one. *The paranoids are after me. Death,* assured another, *is the best buzz of all: that's why they keep it till last.*

The house itself was a solid build, three storeys high with an enclosed first-floor balcony that was connected to our bedroom, offering stupendous night views of the green-glowing Harbour Bridge, the gliding ferries and the skyscrapers beyond. Five steps led from a small front garden to the door where two glass panels had become hardboard by the time we arrived. Inside, it was dreary as a dungeon. Having been empty for almost a month prior to our arrival, its life had wilted, leaving a cold, dank feeling of dereliction, and echoes that reverberated like the knocking in a vault.

Paradoxically, however, the whole house would periodically tremble, then rumble, then shake violently as trains pulled in to North Sydney station, immediately next door. The station had five platforms. Those in the know called Taldumande 'Platform Six'.

'You should spend the first week settling in,' Tom Wilson had advised. 'Then gradually, you can begin the short sweet road to madness.'

Elaine and Mandy put paid to that.

Elaine was fifteen, with long black hair, an almost convincing smile, a scar down one cheek and a butcher's knife, whittled down to a stiletto, tucked into one of her boots. At twelve she had found heroin, prostitution at thirteen, and tattoos, motorbike gangs and hell-raising ever since. Mandy was an unknown quantity who told many versions of who she was and how she became homeless. Despite angelic features and curls like Shirley temple, she would in the long run prove every bit as capable as Elaine.

By lunchtime we had two more guests. The first was a dark, thin Italian lad called Joe who brought to everyone's attention the fact that it was easier to leap from the roof of the refuge to the patio of the Travel Lodge, which cut off the top of Walker Street, than it was to come down the stairs. The second was Shirley, an edgy 16-year-old with straw hair and one blind eye - the result of a battering from her father. Shirley's reality was locked in by two fixes a day.

On the heels of that lunchtime there never was a moment when the chaos subsided. Within two days the house had filled to its capacity of seven and a bout of pilfering broke out. In the evening Mandy walked in stoned and spilled the beans on Elaine. Elaine subsequently charged upstairs in a rage and buried her stiletto in the bedroom door.

'I'm going to kill that fucking tart!' she screamed as I tried to explain the unreasonable nature of doing that.

Mandy, wise to the possibilities, didn't show for three days, by which time a dozen other crises had passed. Joe's leaping from the roof was causing consternation in the neighbourhood, not least with the management of the Travel Lodge. When we suggested he use the front door, he threatened suicide, a position we might have taken lightly had not Michael, another of our guests, taken an overdose the night before. A heavy thump had brought Cora running upstairs to find him on the bedroom floor, eyes rolled back into his head.

A month after opening, the burden was somewhat lessened when we were joined at the refuge by two day workers. Ian Gilbertson and Arthur Wilson would also do some evenings and the odd weekend so we could get out to the pub or over to our friends in French's Forest or out into the bush.

Ian, lean, with a light moustache and a shawl of sun-bleached hair, was a surfer. Dedicated to the last fibre, he would often arrive to work at 8.30 a.m., having already spent two hours in the sea.

'My dream, mate,' he'd say, 'is to find me a beach with a good surf, a nice climate, a steady flow of food and booze and a good woman so I can retire from this crazy planet.'

He lived about as close to the water as was possible without getting drenched, sharing a flat at Narrabeen Beach with his demure, blonde girlfriend, Claire. In the summer he rarely wore more than a T-shirt and shorts and always went barefoot. He was also the personification of Australian republicanism, with a passionate hatred for royalty, the Australian Liberal Party, bureaucracy, multinationals and John Kerr, the British Governor-General of the time who, in November 1975 had ousted the Labour government of Gough Whitlam and replaced it with Malcolm Frazer's conservative Liberals.

'A bloody coup, mate,' Ian would say. 'We had a bloody coup d'état, and not a shot was fired. Can you imagine what would happen in so-called Great Britain if her bloody majesty pulled a stunt like that?'

Ian read Kafka and Dostoyevsky to while away the more idle hours and quoted freely from the Existentialists to illustrate a brand of ultra-cynicism blessed of its own beauty.

'A god?' he'd say. 'Of course there's a bloody god. Who else could've given us Rome and two World Wars?' 'People are fucked, mate,' he'd conclude. 'All people are fucked.'

Arthur was less inclined towards philosophy. A bearded, long-haired imitation of Jesus Christ who roared around Sydney in a souped-up banger of his own design, he gave his spare time to his girlfriend Julie, his car and his two favourite pastimes: skin diving among the sharks of New South Wales and walking in the bush. He was also the host of outrageous parties where people dressed up in strange costumes, bounced about on his water bed and juggled with eggs (that was me, and I can't juggle). Arthur was the most resilient of refuge workers. After more than two years at Clifdon Lodge hostel and the eight months that Cora and I spent at Taldumande, he went on to stay a further two years. When we last heard of him, it was reported that he was slowing down, his boundless energy on the ebb and his mind fixed on buying two horses so he and Julie could ride into the sunset.

* * *

Vicki, a plump 15-year-old with short blonde hair and rosy cheeks came directly to Taldumande from a girls' institution where she had spent six months for theft. The condition of her release was that she had an address to which she could go. Seventeen-year-old Denis, a swarthy lad with dark, collar-length hair and a freckled face, had been kicked out of a halfway house for destructive behaviour.

Denis was an expert car thief and had recently completed a spell inside following a joyriding accident in which his best friend was killed. Vicki, who had an open prescription for barbiturates which she mixed with alcohol for stunning effects, was also a dab hand at shoplifting. Their respective talents would eventually land them both back inside, but not before they left their mark on Taldumande.

After bringing Michael of the attempted suicide on board, the three of them managed to sniff out Shirley of the blind eye who had just moved on to a flat in Crow's Nest with some mysterious mates from up around King's Cross. In the new partnership, Denis was the chauffeur, Vicki and Shirley supplied the drugs and Michael, a cold, callous, heavy-set bully, was the muscle. Some months later after he too had landed in the clink, we heard from a former friend of his of a mugging in which Michael had afterwards gratuitously stabbed the semi-conscious, middle-aged victim.

A few mornings after the teaming-up I came downstairs to investigate strange noises. Denis was pouring yesterday's gravy over the living-room chairs. It was the first I had seen of him since he and Vicki had gone off together the previous afternoon. I rang Tom Wilson.

'I think we have a problem, Tom. We might need an extra pair of hands. Denis is now jumping up on the mantle piece, trying to climb out the bedroom windows and picking the spiders off himself and the walls.'

'Large or small spiders?' Tom asked.

Tom landed to the door as Denis came onto the first-floor landing wearing a blanket and straw hat and talking loudly to the wall. Vicki, who had been in his company all night swore he had taken nothing.

'Could this be a nervous breakdown?' Cora asked.

We rang the psychiatric clinic up in Chatswood.

'We'll be with you in a jiffy,' one of the nurses said.

'He took five tabs of acid,' Vicki said.

When the two female psychiatrists arrived, Denis danced about the room, talked some more to the walls, climbed back onto the mantle piece and laughed hysterically to himself. They were flummoxed.

'Coffee?' Denis asked, climbing down from the mantle piece. They both nodded. Denis placed a shoe on the mantle piece, took an imaginary spoon and coffee jar, carefully undid the lid, shovelled out the coffee, poured the non-existent water, stirred and added imaginary milk. 'Sugar?' he asked.

'Two please,' one of the women said.

'None thanks,' the other said.

Denis complied and handed them the shoe. The psychiatrists fled.

By eight that evening, Tom Dunlop and Bruce Penn had arrived to give a hand, but Denis was worse than ever, racing around the upstairs rooms and attempting to climb out the windows. Vicki's story had changed several times, but she was now telling us that Shirley had brewed up some 'tea' made from the hallucinogenic datura, or angel's trumpet, a highly toxic wild plant that had already caused several deaths. Cora rang the drug referral centre.

'Two or three days,' the reply came. 'You can't handle it yourselves. It's a job for the psychiatric unit.'

We bundled Denis into Tom Wilson's car and carted him off to the psychiatric hospital in Chatswood where we found that Shirley had already been committed by the cops who'd found her, stark raving mad, weaving through peak-hour traffic in Crow's Nest. When we returned from the hospital, Joe - the Italian lad - was on the roof with his suitcase packed.

'How long more can you guys survive this?' Glenys wondered during a social visit. 'If I wasn't here to see for myself, I'd think you were making half of this up.'

And on it went. We had gang feuds, uninvited guests who entered via Joe's exit route, car chases around North Sydney, police visits, a wrist-slashing in the bathroom, stolen vehicles, and the perfect crime when a group of the boys went up onto the Harbour Bridge and dropped a boulder on a house below. A couple in their living room were watching TV when it crashed through the ceiling. The alerted cops had to do little more than seal off both ends of the bridge and wait.

Despite the chaos, Taldumande had its benefits. With no living expenses, we were saving A$1,000 a month and freewheeling towards the day when our travel coffers would be full. The more the coffers filled, the more the future called.

Finally, drained to exhaustion, we decided in March 1978 that we would leave Sydney at the beginning of June and make Papua New

Guinea the next step of our journey, a plan inspired by a book of photographs I had come across in our local library.

By June we would have lived with 120 young people who had found their way to Walker Street. Despite the above impression, the majority were a pleasure to have known. For some, the refuge was a breathing space until some row at home was patched up. For others, who had come to Sydney in search of the bright lights, it was a place to rest their destitute heads, get a feed and the train fare back to the old familiar. But for many it was their only link to any semblance of stability. Victims of chance and an affluent, depersonalised society, they had been kicked out by parents who couldn't cope, or they had fled drunkenness, abuse and violence. They came from squats, park benches, juvenile institutions, welfare agencies and the beds of pimps and prostitutes, a world in which everyone was a potential enemy, conman, thief or cop, and where survival was a protective shield against the 'thems', a category into which many automatically slotted the refuge.

To people who had been beaten with too many sticks, it was just another kip where the heavies were sure to lean on you sooner or later. When the heavies didn't materialise, they were doubly suspicious. Then gradually, the tough exteriors would melt away to reveal young people who had been robbed of the love and security others took for granted. Lone travellers looking in confusion at the milestones that pointed in every direction and ultimately in none at all. Deborah, raped by her father for having made love to her boyfriend. Alex who woke up screaming at night with nightmares of an attempt to drown him in the bath. Nina, almost strangled by her mother. Shirley with her one blind eye.

In long evenings of card schools, pool tournaments, endless rounds of coffee and cigarettes, and a TV and record player vying for the one audience, those who had passed through came back to visit, an ever-expanding extended family of remarkable characters who became a support network for the newcomers. There was Roger of the fair curly hair, the undisputed statesman of Taldumande. Thoughtful, level-headed, respected by the others, Roger was the philosopher, the avid reader, the good-humoured big brother, even to kids who were older than him. If he had a dark side, it was his hero worship of Charles Manson. From the day he arrived, he was a consistently reliable strength at number thirty. Then one day, as Cora and I neared the end of our stay, Roger vanished under regrettable circumstances. In our subsequent attempts to trace him, we discovered that he didn't exist.

Everything about him up to the moment of his arrival at the refuge had been a blind. To this day, Cora and I wonder who Roger really was and where he went.

After Roger, the most prominent face to emerge is that of Small Eddie, who was only small by comparison to the six feet of Big Eddie. A terrific, droll 16-year-old with dark hair that fell into his eyes, and a little melancholy in his soul, Small Eddie was the proud owner of four pages of typed Irish jokes bequeathed to him by his grandfather. When he finally moved out - to return on four or five nights of every week - he went to live at a boarding house in Neutral bay, run by a kindly Mrs. Rex who unofficially adopted him. Shortly afterwards, he arrived at Walker Street with Thomas Pelika, a 23-year-old police sub-inspector from Papua New Guinea who had also moved in with Mrs. Rex.

'I am on a placement,' Thomas told us, 'with the School of Pacific Administration. Part of my studies for the police. I will then go back to Papua New Guinea. If you come to my country, you must visit me.'

We would meet again down the road under nerve-wracking circumstances.

Big Eddie was a different kettle of fish. Tall and well-built for his seventeen years, he was the cool, manipulative and hilariously funny lad with the beaming face and loud laugh. When he arrived at the refuge in Tom Wilson's car, he made an immediate impact by first interrogating myself and Cora, then inspecting the premises, including the larder and back yard, to ensure that all was in keeping with his standards. Eddie had just spent six months in a young offenders' centre after a judge took a dim view to him 'living off immoral earnings'.

No sooner had Big Eddie settled in than the most unexpected and shady visitors began to show up. One was an older man, immaculately dressed and groomed, who drove big cars and often whisked Eddie away to King's Cross where he picked up some work as a bouncer. Another was a squat guy of about forty, with sleeked-back, black hair, rough skin and a permanent five-o'clock shadow who looked like a hitman from *The Godfather*. This man, who often accompanied the older guy, would always arrive in a baggy suit, braces, white shirt and broad colourful tie, with his coat neatly draped over one arm. A little shy and speaking quietly, he would ask for Eddie with the utmost of politeness. Shortly after Cora and I left Australia, this man disappeared, never to be seen again. Rumour had it that he had fallen foul of the underworld, of which he was reputed to have been a member. He was lying, it was said, at the bottom of the harbour in a concrete jacket.

At one stage, Big Eddie fell for one of our other guests, a young

Italian woman named Sue who was another rock at the refuge. Eddie took issue with one of the lads who vowed 'to get into Sue'.

'I'll kill the bastard,' Eddie said.

He stood outside the refuge, calling on the petrified Romeo to come out and die. He then barred Cora's exit from the house when she tried to leave for the shops. At this I discovered that I could take the five outside steps and vault the garden gate in a single move. By the time I hit the ground on Walker Street, Eddie was half way up the steps to Millar Street. For the next few weeks word was out that he was carrying a knife 'because a mad Irishman is after my blood'. Then he returned one night, reformed and in a mood for a cup of coffee, and we were all pals again.

Then there was Ned who fancied himself as a bit of an actor and approached a local television station for an audition. He was knocked back, but the station was very interested in Ned's unusual home. We became serialised, incognito, in *The Restless Years* soap opera, with Tom Wilson as programme advisor. What we experienced in real life one week, we could revisit on TV the next. Later, as I tried to console Ned, I found him looking at me sadly.

'Ciarán,' he said, 'you don't understand. I'm going to make it.'

And indeed he eventually did.

I should also mention Gary, a speedy, skinny kid who went everywhere on his skateboard, and came home ashen-faced one afternoon after bowling over some old woman up in Millar Street. He had been charged by the cops with what he called 'dangerous driving' and what they called being a public nuisance. After one particular night out, Cora and I arrived home just as Gary did.

'Loan me that thing for a minute,' I said.

Seconds later I was whizzing down Walker Street on Gary's skateboard, gathering considerable speed and balancing wonderfully, when two thoughts hit me. One was that Walker Street ended in a long flight of steep steps that led straight into Sydney harbour. The other was, *How the hell do you stop this thing?* I could neither stop, slow down nor turn, so I simply stepped off. It took weeks for the scars to heal and four months before I could again lean on my right elbow.

Among the trials of Taldumande, parents made a number of contributions.

One evening a huge 16-wheeler pulled up across the street and an equally huge driver came pounding on our door. Ian opened up and calmly explained that, sorry mate, you can't come in. Cora, meanwhile, spirited the trucker's petrified daughter and her friend out the back door to a temporary hideaway.

'Well mate,' the father boomed. 'Nothin' for it then but to bust a few fuckin' heads. Who's this bastard Wilson?'

After weeks of delicate negotiation, during which Tom Wilson lived with the premonition that he was going to be run over by a 16-wheeler, the daughter went to live with one of her sisters, a compromise reluctantly accepted by the father. A month later a man called from the probation service. The father had been charged with 'carnal knowledge' of the daughter's friend and everyone was on the run again.

'And what,' the more naïve of our visitors would ask, 'would you say is your success rate?'

'Well,' Arthur would say with that deadpan look of his, 'we haven't had any loving parents to the door now for three weeks.'

In the beginning of May we had our youngest guest. Eight-year-old Graham grew up too fast and fell down too young. Freckle-faced, thin and wiry, Graham, whose world was refracted through his own unique prism, spoke in garbled clichés.

'That's the way the crumble cooks,' he'd declare as he played poker to rules that were indecipherable.

On the second day he slipped outside unnoticed. An hour later the phone rang.

'Is that the youth refuge?' an anxious male voice asked.

'Yes,' Cora replied.

'This is North Sydney police station. We have a young lad here named Graham and we would like somebody to come quickly and collect him.'

In the background, Cora could hear a shriek of 'Look out! He's got the ashtray!' followed by a crashing sound as the ashtray found a target. Graham had been caught trying to steal a motorbike.

By the time Cora reached the station, the main office had been reduced to rubble, but one of the detectives had succeeded in locking Graham into a room. When Cora and the detective went to get him, they found that he had barricaded the door by forcing a chair against the doorknob.

Finally, after much cajoling by Cora, he came out, fists raised. Then, sidling into the protection of Cora's arms he turned on the cops.

'Tomorrow,' he promised, 'I'm comin' back here with a can of petrol to burn this place to the ground. With every one of you fuckers in it.'

Back at Walker Street he curled up on the sofa and dozed off, cradling a black and white terrier that belonged to Taldumande's fluctuating menagerie, a loveless assortment of dogs, cats and hamsters that caused Ian untold distress.

'Look,' he'd say, chalking arrows on the walls above sinister payloads. 'The house is succumbing to the cosmic vibes of cat shit.'

Upstairs, Benny, one of two giants who stalked about the house, punching doors and walls to impress one another, was growing dope under his bed.

* * *

It wasn't all crazy. Through the final months of 1977, Cora and I had spent a great deal of free time in the Blue Mountains and the Royal National Park, developing our bush skills and experimenting with different combinations of equipment and food, having swapped the mash and spam for brown rice, dried fruit, beans and lentils.

At year's end, we rang in 1978 with Bruce and Jenny on the banks of the Murrumbidgee River in the foothills of the Snowy Mountains. We were there with 15,000 New Age visionaries at a Festival of Alternative Lifestyles, organised by former Labour Deputy Prime Minister, Jim Cairns, and Junie Morosi, part Italian, part Portuguese, part Chinese, and all-attractive hate figure for the Australian gutter press.

Jim Cairns was best remembered as chair of the Vietnam Moratorium. In May 1970 he had led an estimated 100,000 people in a sit-down in the streets of Melbourne, the largest political protest ever seen in Australia. Along with other similar protests across the country, it greatly changed attitudes to the war. Junie Morosi was his former Principal Private Secretary, and their relationship got fully up the noses of the Australian establishment. A devotee of the ideas of the German sexologist Wilhelm Reich, she stubbornly rode out the tumultuous years of media spotlight and brought Jim Cairns to his belief in the alternative lifestyles movement.

On the banks of the Murrumbidgee, other devotees flounced around naked, smoked acres of grass and made love in the sun. Over the weekend, a bout of dysentery broke out; the hessian toilet-walls blew down leaving nothing but a line of pits and bare arses; a water tank burst and washed away a row of tents; a guy almost died of anaphylactic shock from a bee sting; some people made a huge parachute and were lucky they weren't blown to Taiwan; and a guru of the movement told us in sweet words how best to live off pine nuts.

* * *

Until the rains of February 1978, which came on the heels of weeks of stifling humidity, the youth refuge had been functional. In February it began to die.

After a weekend of hiding from thunderstorms under a sandstone overhang in the Royal National Park, five of Taldumande's residents and I returned to Walker Street to find tubs, basins and bowls scattered about the floors. Water was dripping down walls and glistening on light-bulbs.

'It was pretty bad,' Cora said. 'At one point we had to shelter to one side of the house. We rang the landlord but nobody has come near us.'

A week later it rained again, soaking many of the residents in their beds and forcing us to punch holes in one of the ceilings with a brush-pole to prevent a total collapse. Catching the water in an old bath, we emptied it out a first-floor window into Walker Street. In the coming weeks, as the dampness persevered, the decision was made to move the refuge. After some cajoling, Councillor Carol Baker and I (as Youth Officer) managed to convince North Sydney Council to make available a section of semi-derelict flats at Ridge Street.

In May 1978 we closed the doors of Walker Street for the last time.

Shortly before the refuge days came to an end, Alan Dodds and Chris McGuinness turned up again from Perth, having driven across the desert wildernesses of Western Australia and South Australia in a newly acquired Land Rover. And that previously mentioned brush with the Shoalhaven Gorge stepped from the shadows.

* * *

Back in January, Cora and I had walked five miles of the lower gorge, having slithered 1,500 steep feet into its depths from Badgery's Lookout.

'This river,' I said, 'looks ideal for a gentle cruise in our rubber raft.'

'It does,' Cora said. 'But how the hell would we get the raft this far.'

'Maybe there's a place where a road meets the river?'

'Then it would be no bother, would it?'

Returning to Sydney, we bought detailed maps and found that the Shoalhaven was accessible by vehicle at a place called Oallen Ford, more than 100 miles inland from where the river reached the Tasman Sea some nine miles east of the town of Nowra which was itself about 100 miles south-southwest of Sydney. Perfect. We'd give a month to paddle from Oallen Ford to Nowra. Logistics yet to be sorted.

'Remember the last time Alan and Chris were here,' I reminded Cora, 'they said to give them a shout if we had anything coming up. They might be interested.'

'Maybe,' Cora said. 'But no mention of helium balloons this time.'

Within days of Alan and Chris turning up in Sydney, we were a four-strong expedition with the makings of a plan. We would ask Greg McManus, who lived with a colleague of mine at Hyman's Beach near Nowra, to come with us to Oallen Ford in Alan and Chris' Land Rover. Greg would then drive the Land Rover back to Nowra. We'd bring two rafts, and float gently down the Shoalhaven. In a month's time, we'd arrive at Nowra, collect the Land Rover from Greg and drive back to Sydney. Ever so simple.

'Between Oallen Ford and the sea,' I said, proud of the homework, 'the river drops about 1,900 feet. Just under nineteen feet a mile.' That, we should have sussed, was most likely not the case, but in the buzz of the moment any question mark was lost in a cloud of vanishing-dust. And the plan grew in shape and stature.

As this was going to be a leisurely run with no worries about weight, we could treat ourselves. Along with two tents, two cameras and my guitar, we would bring some onion bags of fresh vegetables, and a couple of cardboard boxes of tinned food, not forgetting dessert puddings. And a bunch of books for good measure, to be read as we casually bobbed downstream, myself with guitar serenading us along.

The more Alan studied the plan, the more his eyes danced across the maps with the kind of vigour and abandon that invites the unknown with open arms and gives life a sharp edge. It can also get you killed.

'Yeah,' he repeated as we hardened the details. 'We'd be up for that. Wouldn't we Chris?'

'Birds of a feather,' Chris said as Alan and I bored holes in the maps.

Alan and Chris would be staying in Sydney until Cora and I returned from New Guinea, at which point we would leave for the Shoalhaven Gorge.

Soon after their arrival, the four of us, along with several other friends, spent a couple of days in the bushland of Yalwal Creek, a tributary of the Shoalhaven River. Among those who joined us were Greg McManus and his partner, Averil Fink, both of whom had now been fully co-opted into the Shoalhaven plan.

During moving time at the refuge, the four of us also drove to the dizzying Kanangra Walls in the Blue Mountains and it bucketed on us for two days.

'Is this an omen on the Shoalhaven?' Chris asked. 'Should we be taking note?'

If only...

Cora and I finally laid the Taldumande days to rest and said goodbye to our Sydney friends at a three-night, two-day, party at the Lavender Bay home of tall, bearded Mark Ierace and slim blonde Kay Trulove.

Mark and Kay lived in a boathouse that sat over the water and was a regular bolt-hole of ours when we lived at Walker Street. Their friendship and sense of humour had cushioned many a period of Taldumande chaos, and the idyllic setting of their home provided the perfect location for that crowning event.

Everyone was there: the French's Forest crew; Glenys who was planning to move to Darwin to work in Aboriginal affairs; Steve, Ann, Sandy and Jake from the next-door boathouse; Alan and Chris; Tom Wilson; Arthur from the refuge and his girlfriend Julie (Ian and Claire had gone off to Bali); fellow Youth Officer, Seamus O'Brien who was belting it out on his guitar; Kay and Dan from Canada who ran a youth refuge at Cronulla; Paul Caddy who had advised against the trip to Cape York peninsula; Andy Sos from Canada who reckoned, as the sun rose on Monday morning, that we should never come back. His health couldn't take it. Sixty people in all - Irish, English, Scottish, German, Australian, French, Kiwi and Canadian - singing, dancing and playing music until the pot plants bounced off the shelves and Mark had bad visions of his boathouse home breaking free and sailing out into Sydney Harbour.[19]

Although Cora and I would be back in Sydney after New Guinea and again in 1981 and 1994, we would never see most of those people again. Time and the great spaces of the world would swallow them up.

Tony and Colette Lee weren't there for the final fizz. They had moved to Melbourne some months before, but we would catch them up again and again down the road.

After the party, we moved to Alan and Chris' flat in Neutral Bay while we made final preparations for Papua New Guinea and our planned raft ride into the Shoalhaven Gorge. We then had a final, final farewell the night before we left for New Guinea.

'Please go this time,' big Andy Sos from Canada pleaded. 'My liver is collapsing.'

---

19   Mark, who had been with us at the Festival of Alternative Lifestyles and again at Yalwal Creek, was studying to be a barrister. He would later go on to be one of the Chief Prosecutors at the U.N. War Crimes Tribunal in The Hague, and would eventually return to Australia to become Chief Public Defender for New South Wales.

AUSTRALIA:
① HITCHHIKE FROM SYDNEY TO COOKTOWN AND BACK 1978.
② SHOALHAVEN GORGE.
GULF OF CARPENTARIA
CORAL SEA
TASMAN SEA
COOKTOWN
CEDAR BAY
BLOOMFIELD
KURANDA
MAREEBA.
CAIRNS
EUNGELLA NAT. PARK
MACKAY
ROCKHAMPTON
WOODGATE NAT. PARK
BRISBANE
ARMIDALE
PORT MACQUA
BARRINGTON TOPS
NEWCASTLE
SYDNEY
SHOALHAVEN GORGE
NOWRA
MURRUMBIDGEE RIVER.

CHAPTER 14

Lord Of The Flies

We gave ourselves two months to travel at our leisure from Sydney to New Guinea. First stop: Myall Lakes. Then on to Barrington Tops. Beyond that, nothing was fixed.

Alan and Chris accompanied us with their Land Rover as far as Myall Lakes National Park, 150 miles north of Sydney. On our way through Newcastle, we were joined by Seán and Brenda Strain, old friends from Belfast, and their infant son, Dáire. During the months of Taldumande, before Dáire's birth, Seán and Brenda had been regular visitors to Walker Street and we had paid them a visit or two in Newcastle where they now lived.

'You'll be eaten by the cannibawls,' was Brenda's take on our New Guinea plans.

After a weekend with the swamp-hens and pelicans in the wetlands and palm forests of the national park, Seán and Brenda went home to Newcastle. Alan and Chris then drove myself and Cora to the home of Denis Burt, a friend of theirs who owned a property outside Alison, close to Barrington Tops. Denis, bushy-bearded with thick shoulder-length hair, worked in the mountains at a hydrology research station run by the Forestry Commission, and had agreed to take us beyond the station to where we could begin a trek across the mountains.

In the bitter frost of the following morning, we said our goodbyes to Alan and Chris and set off in Denis' four-wheel-drive. After months of virtual inertia it felt good to be moving again.

Half an hour into the mountains, we stopped at a hut where a heavily-built old man with a massive hernia and an undersized hat was slicing logs into railway sleepers.

'You're looking,' Denis said, 'at the last broadaxe cutter in New South Wales.' 'Any thought of retirement?' he asked.

The old man looked up at the sky and tipped back his hat.

'Yeah,' he said. 'I reckon it won't be long now. But I'm bringing the axe with me.'

At the research station Denis demonstrated some of the technology deployed to determine the effects of logging on the drainage of the temperate rainforest. Interesting as all this was, it meant that it was eleven o'clock before he dropped us off high on one of the ridges.

'That species got left behind by the last Ice Age,' he said, pointing to the scaly trunks of a stand of moss-draped Antarctic Beech. 'Those particular trees are about 800 years old. I'll leave you in their good hands. Enjoy the rest of your stay in Australia.'

He then turned back for the research station.

Barrington Tops is the habitat of an enormous diversity of plant and animal life. In the lower valleys, there are subtropical rainforests and sub-forests of tree ferns while the plateau is covered in sub-alpine woodland. The whole area is believed to have once been the home of the Gringgai clan of the Wanaruah people prior to European colonisation. It is believed that the nearby town of 'Dungog' (place of thinly wooded hills) takes its name from their language. In the early 1800s the area was also the domain of celebrated bushranger, Captain Thunderbolt.

Frederick Wordsworth Ward, the son of a convict, was born at Wilberforce in New South Wales around 1833. One of eleven children, he became an accomplished groom and horse-breaker while still a teenager. By the age of twenty, however, he had also become involved in horse-*stealing* and was eventually arrested in 1856, earning himself a sentence of ten years with hard labour at Cockatoo Island in Sydney Harbour. After four years, he was released with a ticket of leave to his sister's property at Mudgee, whereupon he fell for Mary Ann Bugg, a part Aboriginal woman, whom he followed to Stroud and married. All went well until he arrived late for a monthly muster at Mudgee a few days before the birth of his first child and was accused of stealing the horse he was riding. He was returned to prison to finish his sentence, with a further four years added for stealing his mount.

On September 1st 1863, Fred and another prisoner escaped with the help of Mary Ann who had swum across the shark-infested waters to Cockatoo Island, carrying with her tools for the escape. All three then swam to the mainland. Shortly afterwards, Fred robbed the tollbar at Campbell's Hill near Maitland. Pounding on the wall of the office to demand the toll money, he earned the nickname 'Thunderbolt'. He and Mary Ann went on to become notorious bushrangers, engaging in hotel and highway robbery and horse-stealing, also somehow managing to have three more children.

One of the many Thunderbolt stories tells how his love of good horses led him to Tenterfied races in March 1868. Mixing freely with the other patrons, he was impressed by the racehorse, Minstrel, from the Warwick district which took the Maiden Plate of forty sovereigns. Determined to acquire it for himself, he waited in ambush at Boonoo Boonoo Gap. To pass the time, he stopped a German Band who had played at Tenterfield and robbed them of their £16 takings. Considering this a piddling amount, Thunderbolt forced the band to play for him on the roadside.

So pleased was he by the performance that he handed back a small amount of money as the band was leaving. He also asked its leader for a forwarding address. Weeks later the band received a letter from Thunderbolt, with the balance of the stolen money.

On May 25th 1870 Thunderbolt is said to have been shot dead near Uralla on the northern tablelands of New South Wales by one Constable Walker following a highway robbery and horseback chase. Family tradition held that the man killed by Walker was Thunderbolt's brother, Harry. Thunderbolt himself rode off into legend.

* * *

We followed the Glowang trail over Mount Nelson, dropped a little, then climbed again to 3,900 feet. The wind was crisp and dry despite the cloud. Birdlife was second to none. There was just one snag: we had no water and couldn't find any on the trail.

By nightfall we were speeding along the heights in the hope of finding even a muddy puddle that would provide two cups of coffee while our thirst was derided by the roar of the Gloucester River far below.

Eventually we couldn't take it anymore. We went over the edge in the dark and slid down a steep slope of scrub, friable rock and fallen trees. Under the forest canopy, it was pitch-black, adding to the risks, but the sound of tumbling water drove us on. Until I stepped off a ledge into space, to be saved from the torrent by an overhanging branch. We called a halt. Using a billycan on a rope, we hauled water from the river and managed to cook the semblance of a meal.

In the morning, we crawled out of our tent, poorly erected in a hollow left by a fallen tree, and were greeted by a sheer drop and the marvel that we hadn't killed ourselves.

'Shortly after we dragged ourselves back to the ridge,' Cora would later tell people, 'we had to wade knee-deep through the Gloucester River before it dropped into the gorge...'

* * *

The sky had been black since first light. A biting wind had been cutting across the ridges. It was to last all day, building in intensity as we trudged through the forest, and prompting us to strike an early camp. We stocked up with a store of firewood lest the intermittent flurries of sleet should fulfil their threat of a full-on blizzard.

No snow fell that night. But the wind, and the cold seeping from below kept us awake. When we rose at dawn, the sky was a mass of thunderheads.

We packed up, checked our maps and, chased by a confetti of falling leaves, took the shortest route downhill. Other than a few wallabies and the only koala we would ever see in the wild, we were on our own.

At Sharpe's Creek at the foot of the mountains the storm broke. Banshees howled. Trees shook like metronomes on speed. Frisbee-birds sailed through the air. In sheets of hail and sleet we cut the day and threw up our tent in a clearing, engaging all our efforts to prevent its arrival in New Zealand. Rocks were employed to hold the guylines.

'If this tent lasts the night,' Cora said, 'we should buy it a medal.'

Through the whole of that night the storm wailed. Lightning flashed. Thunder boomed. Our tent - a new three-person ridge tent - cracked like a football rattle. Sometime around midnight, the first tree came down. A loud creaking was followed by crashing and splintering as it tore branches from its rainforest neighbours. A terrifying prospect when you're lying in a dark, wet, flimsy tent.

In the conversation that followed, we did our best to decide whether the next falling tree would land on us or land somewhere else. We concluded that we would just have to hope that it landed somewhere else.

Then the next one came down, and the next. We didn't sleep. The only respite was an hour's break from the rain that allowed us to light a fire, cook a rushed meal, and share some dried apricots with a visiting sugar glider and a cheeky possum.

By morning Sharpe's Creek was in flood and the hail and sleet were still lashing down. Exhausted, hungry, and shivering in wet sleeping bags, we stared out through the fly screen. With seven unbridged rivers between us and the nearest town, walking out wasn't an option.

With the dread of another night looming, a mirage drove into our clearing in the afternoon: a pickup driven by a tired-looking, middle-aged man who worked for the National Parks & Wildlife Service.

'Can you take us out of here?' Cora called. 'We're stuck.'

'I don't know what made me stop here,' the man said. 'But if you want to go, we need to go now. The rivers are rising fast. There's going to be no coming or going in another hour.'

We packed in a flap and jumped aboard the pickup. Swaying violently in the gales and dodging falling branches, we thrashed the muddy track and the concrete fords of the seven unbridged cascades, sliding badly in two, and got a puncture a mile from Gloucester. That was the afternoon before one of the most bizarre experiences of our lives.

* * *

After a night of listening to the storm from a cosy bed in the B&B of a Gloucester pub, we woke to a fine day, and with a spry step, set off for the coast. We would keep moving, we decided. North towards warmer climes.

We had walked some distance along the Bucketts Way, a road virtually void of traffic when a yellow Morris Minor pulled up. The driver, fortyish, thick-set, with ruffled blond hair and a puffy complexion, told us that he was Herman and could only bring us a short distance as he was on his way to fly a small plane to Port Macquarie. In further conversation, he mentioned that he had in the past flown bush planes in Africa and Papua New Guinea.

'What a coincidence,' I said. 'Right now, *we're* on our way to Papua New Guinea. Is it easy enough to get around there?'

'It can be difficult,' he said. 'But you'll manage if you persevere. But watch out for the kanakas. They'll put an arrow in your back as soon as look at you.' Not really what you'd want to hear even if it sounded like racism.

After ten minutes he dropped us off and we began to walk again. But we hadn't gone far when he reappeared, said the flight was off and would we like a cup of coffee.

'I live just off the road not far from here,' he said. 'You'd be more than welcome.'

I checked with Cora. No problem.

We turned off the main road and drove about a mile of bumpy dirt track to a farmhouse surrounded by a fence, over which were draped the drying pelts of foxes. Herman shot foxes at night.

'The place is a bit of a mess,' he said as we stepped through the front door. He wasn't kidding.

Inside, we were greeted by the slaughterhouse stench of a further dozen fox pelts spread across the floor of the parlour, and a wall draped in trophies bagged on the African veld. Leaving us to our own devices among the rotting fox pelts, Herman disappeared into the kitchen. For a few minutes there was no sound which made us feel a little uncomfortable. Then, to a sudden clatter of crockery, Herman began to rail against his former wife who had left him, and now he couldn't clean the fuckin' place, and all 'sheilas' were leeches, and did we take milk.

'We need to get out of here,' Cora said.

I was myself wondering whether or not I wished I was somewhere else when the next instalment nailed it.

After handing us the coffee, Herman left for his bedroom. When he came back, he had a high-powered rifle tucked in the crook of his right arm and a sheaf of papers in his left hand. I will now state without fear of contradiction that I very near choked. Was this what our Aussie friends had warned us about: the bush looney who shoots you dead and buries you out in the sticks? Nobody, but nobody, knew where we were. I used to always think that in a situation like this you might be able to distract the guy and grab the gun; but I realised as Herman strode towards us that I first needed to practise the move on small unarmed children. And, even if I got the gun, what then?

Cradling the rifle, Herman stopped in front of us and began to read from the documents, produced by some crackpot organisation of which he claimed to be a member. The more he read, while interspersing his own commentary, the more he resembled Hanging Judge Roy Bean about to shout 'Guilty!' It's funny now, but back then it wasn't funny at all. When grabbing the gun isn't an option, it's hard to nonchalantly sip coffee while the guy with the rifle is pacing the floor, threatening doom on all the people you like and some of those you don't.

'It's like this,' he said. 'Our organisation is committed to saving Australia from the commies, the druggies, the poofters, the Masonic Lodge and the Rockefellers. We have all the facts, far more than those deadshits in ASIO [the Australian Security Intelligence Organisation]. Our people are more efficient and dedicated. See that big drugs bust up at Port Macquarie a couple of weeks ago? We were responsible for that.'

I didn't dare look down to see if I was wearing my *Australian Marijuana Party* T-shirt.

'We're fighting for the good of Australia,' Herman went on, 'to rid the country of all those undesirables.'

I was waiting for him to say 'and the Irish.'

He then produced a clip of bullets. 'I make them myself,' he said.

Untraceable, I thought as I tried to keep my cup steady during a ten-minute tirade that ended with Herman waving the rifle about like Sitting Bull in a bad Western.

Needless to say, we came to no harm. But the incident was a shake-up. As soon as we extricated ourselves from that house, we drew us up a rule of thumb, the only rule we would share with our daughter, Tríona, many years later when, at the age of nineteen, she was leaving to travel in South America: never allow anyone to make you lose control of your environment. (It's okay if you do it yourself.)

Back on the main road, with Herman and his rantings behind us, we speed-walked away, hoping someone would come along quickly and get us out of there, all the time glancing back in case the Morris showed again.

'Oh Jesus,' Cora said. 'He's coming. He's flashing the indicator.'

'Drop the packs and be ready to bolt.' That was me as the Morris came closer. Where to, I have no idea.

But, in a ridiculous coincidence, the yellow Morris Minor coming down the road was driven by a beaming, bearded student from Port Macquarie who was offering us a lift.

'Drive!' Cora said as we threw ourselves in. 'You won't believe this but...'

'Holy shit!' the student said. 'Sounds like *Psycho*...'

After an overnight in Port Macquarie, we headed north-west to spend a few days with Bruce and Jenny and a bunch of their friends who had all recently enrolled at Armidale University. We found them living without electricity in a long bare hut that had once served as the shearers' quarters of an old sheep station called Loch Abba. The toilet was out the back - a 'dungie' full of redbacks! But based on recent history in this neck of the woods, redbacks could be the least of your worries.

In a bog close to the hut, a dead cow stood upright in the mud, crows and buzzards pecking out its brains through holes that once were eyes.

*   *   *

We hitchhiked north again, stopping in southern Queensland at Woodgate National Park where we camped behind a deserted beach among wallabies, possums and emus. When the tide was out, the beach was covered in hundreds of tiny, blue soldier-crabs. When the tide was in, dolphins drove mackerel onto the sand and provided us with dinner.

At Rockhampton, we caught a northbound freight train to Mackay, following the general advice not to hitchhike the 210-mile stretch unless we wanted to be murdered by a suspected serial killer. We travelled in style: forty-four wagons and a fine old engine winding the lines ahead of our own six-benched passenger compartment. The only other people on the train were the driver and guard who made us tea in the morning as the sun rose in a flaming aureole over the silver rim of the Pacific.

West of Mackay, we entered the sugarcane country of the Pioneer Valley on our way to the tropical rainforests of Eungella National Park. It being the crushing season, they were scorching the cane to clear unwanted foliage and vermin. Trainloads of blackened cane - as many as a hundred wire-box carriages pulled by two engines - crossed the road at level crossings.

This was so-called blackbirding country. Over a forty-year period during the second half of the 19th century, large schooners prowled the Pacific islands in search of young men and women who could be forced into slavery in the sugar plantations of Queensland. The ships would arrive offshore, offering muskets, axes and mattocks to seduce the islanders on board. Once on board they were shoved into putrid hulls and shipped to the cane fields of Australia.

One of the most notorious blackbirding voyages involved the brig *Carl* which set sail from Fiji for the New Hebrides in June 1871. Following a well-established trading route, the brig arrived in the Solomon Islands some eight or nine days later, where part-owner, Doctor James Patrick Murray, devised a novel technique to get his natives on board. After making a few overtures by holding trinkets over the ship's sides, bars of pig iron attached to ropes were dropped on the circling canoes which either sank or were overturned. Any occupants not quick enough to escape were fished out by the *Carl's* crew and thrown in the hold. Then Murray sailed on to other islands, perfecting the pig-iron technique as he went.

By the time he reached Bougainville, Murray had taken some seventy islanders. After heavy fighting with the Bougainville men, another forty were captured. The following day, forty more were taken at Buka Island. Internecine fighting based on traditional enmities then broke out below deck, with the Bougainville men fighting the others. They also tried to set fire to the ship. At this point, some of the captives were allowed on deck while those left in the hold were fired on during the night by the ship's crew. In the morning the hatches were removed. Fifty dead and twenty wounded were brought on deck and thrown overboard.

Blackbirding continued until the late 1890s when the worst of the hard work had been done in the cane fields, paving the way for white labourers. When the new nation was federated in 1901, the deportation of kidnapped islanders who were still alive became one of its first acts. And blackbirding was wiped from the history books.

At Finch Hatton, at the foot of the mountains, we were dropped off by a man who worked in the sugar industry.

If you ever saw what sugar does to concrete,' he said, 'you'd never eat another grain.'

No, he had never heard of blackbirding.

From Finch Hatton we walked a steep road into the rainforests of Eungella (the Land of Cloud) to see the duck-billed platypuses that lived in Broken River. The only other person up there was Jim Shields from Reading in Kansas. An amateur ornithologist, Jim had once been chased up an aspen by a grizzly bear and had recently stood and watched what was then the last seventeen whooping cranes left in the world.

'I'm the guy out here with his hands in the air,' he said when he came knocking on our tent.

* * *

We hitchhiked on through Cairns to Kuranda in Cape York Peninsula and stopped off with Val Segboer, a long-haired, flower-power woman in her mid-twenties, and her young daughter, Bidi, who lived in a tin-roofed house in the rainforest. Val and her partner Don, who was away at the time, were friends of Alan and Chris. Val welcomed us with the smile of an Italian model, showed us to one of the bedrooms and pointed at the open window with a caution.

'Close the window before you go to sleep. The last people who slept in this room woke up in the middle of the night to find a python swallowing our cat at the bottom of the bed.'

'Sobering,' I said. We checked under the bed and locked the window.

Over lunch, we swapped yarns, Val caught up on the latest news of Alan and Chris, and we talked about our plans for the Shoalhaven Gorge. Val then suggested a drive to nearby Barron Falls, often a dramatic cascade but not in full spate when we arrived. Nevertheless, the short scenic walk through the rainforest to the viewing point was its own reward.

'If you're interested,' Val said on the way back, 'the Mareeba rodeo is on tomorrow. We could drive over in the morning.'

The Mareeba rodeo of 1978 will forever be associated with a rare highlight never considered by the Romans: a Brahmin-bull chariot race. Unfortunately, the chariots and bulls crashed on takeoff and flew into the air. In the aftermath, broken bulls and chariots were carried from the arena by burly cowboys. Val, a vegetarian and pacifist, was disgusted, and even more so when we met a friend of Don's outside.

'Did y'all enjoy the rodeo?' he asked.

Like asking Mrs. Lincoln: *Apart from that, how was the play?*

We left Val the following day and hitchhiked further into Cape York Peninsula, stopping at the Palmer River for a night of nostalgia before going on to Cooktown.

We then retraced our steps to the junction with the Daintree track, walking twenty miles before camping at the Annan River in the company of freshwater turtles. On the way we ran into a stoned Simmo. He drove by on a trail bike, recognised us, and promptly plunged headlong into a creek. Where was Glenys, he wanted to know, and drove off perplexed when we said 'Sydney'.

Our intention now was to follow the Daintree track to Bloomfield, then pick up a walking trail through the world's oldest living rainforest until we reached civilisation again somewhere down near Cape Tribulation. We gave ourselves a week to complete the journey.

On the afternoon of our second day's march, we were sitting under a tree, looking down over the forest to a tranquil sea when a four-wheel-drive pulled up. It was the first vehicle to pass all day.

'Can we offer you a lift?' the driver said.

'No thanks,' I said. 'We're planning on walking.'

An hour later, a battered Holden station wagon pulled up in a cloud of dust and its entire covey fell out, spluttering and coughing.

'Petrol fumes,' the driver gasped. 'We can't close the windows. It's fumes or dust. We're a bit crowded. We've got five in the car, but if you want a lift we can take you to Bloomfield.'

The battered jalopy and the cut of the dust-caked crew, whom we'd first mistaken for Aboriginals, won us over. Throwing our packs in the boot, we squeezed into the back seat beside a big burly man with thinning brown hair.

'Whereabouts are you from?' he asked - in an Irish accent!

Forty-four-year-old Brian Griffin had emigrated from Limerick twenty-two years earlier. He had been sailing up the coast with his 27-year-old partner, Jonelle, and their two-year-old daughter, Erin, when they had met residents of the famous commune of Cedar Bay. Ken, an eccentric Austrian with a Van Dyke beard, jeans and what used to be a white T-shirt, had abandoned a restaurant in Sydney to go to the bay. George, the Polynesian who was driving the Holden, was an old bay hand.

'If you'd like to join us,' Brian offered, 'we're sailing to Cedar Bay in the morning.'

* * *

Cedar Bay hit the headlines in August 1976, when the right-wing regime of Joh Bjelke-Peterson, Queensland premier and peanut farmer from Kingaroy, launched a land, sea and air assault on a group of hippies living at the bay. Armed troops and cops hit the beach in boats launched from a naval attack ship, while others were dropped by chopper. Others still arrived through the forest. Hoping to find a massive drugs haul and perhaps an escaped murderer or two, all they got was thirty near-naked hippies and a few ounces of marijuana. Arresting everyone, they then burned down the commune humpies along with their inhabitants' belongings, shot holes in water tanks, destroyed the gardens and chopped down the fruit trees. Shortly afterwards the police commissioner, who had opposed the raid, resigned in disgust.

In a subsequent court case the commune members were cleared of all charges of trespass when it emerged that Cedar Bay Bill, an old hermit living at the bay for the past forty years, had a long-forgotten tin-fossicking lease on the land. The communards [of sorts], Bill said, were his esteemed guests.

Civil liberties lawyer, Terry O'Gorman, was pleased with the outcome. Just beginning his career, he had been one of the first to trudge into the bay to offer legal support to the bewildered hippies who were taking a case of wilful destruction against the Queensland cops. He had cut quite a dash, it appears. When walking through the forest in his safari suit and encountering several naked women, he stripped to his underpants as a concession to his clients.

'It's really the only time I've ever conducted interviews like that,' he later explained to the media.

* * *

The mountain tops were shrouded in mist as we rounded Rattlesnake Point at the southern tip of Cedar Bay. The 28-foot yacht lurched and pitched. Cora was sick.

'The best cure for seasickness,' Brian said, 'is sitting under a coconut tree.' He pointed towards the north of the bay. 'That one over there.'

We tacked across.

Maggie Apples, who had joined us in Bloomfield, indicated the location of the various commune camps, hidden by the forest: South Camp, Top Gardens, Centre Gardens and North Camp. Maggie, in lime-green cheesecloth shirt, blue jeans and navy-blue waistcoat, was in her early twenties, petite with darting eyes and long, corn-coloured hair.

'The placid people,' she explained, 'all live at Centre Gardens. The pig-killers live up at North Camp.' There were issues here. 'Even the animals know it,' she went on. 'In the creek at Centre Gardens the jungle perch come right up to nuzzle you when you're in the water. Over at North Creek, the fish are paranoid.'

Maggie was a vegetarian and the people at North Camp were evidently not. She was on her way back to the bay with her young daughter after going to Cairns for commune supplies - four months ago. Maggie lived at Centre Gardens.

It was easy to see what had brought Maggie and the others to Cedar Bay. In a huge sweep between Rattlesnake Point and Obree Point to the north, a magnificent, palm-fringed scimitar of sand swept down to the surf. Directly behind the beach, the rainforest backed away over a compressed coastal plain before climbing sharply into the mountains. To get there, you either walked or sailed into what was still 'Crown land'.

At the top end of the bay, Brian manoeuvred the yacht towards the entrance of North Creek, drawing up the keel to avoid running aground on an inshore reef. As we closed in on the creek, two guys emerged from the forest, both starkers.

'Nobody wears much clothes around here,' Maggie explained.

Another guy, in green dungarees and puffing a big joint, appeared at the head of the creek. Brian threw him a rope and we berthed close to a pocket of mangroves. Cora crawled to the nearest tree and slid backwards down its trunk.

Maggie Apples and her daughter left immediately with the two naked lads. George went off to his home under a rotting upturned boat. Brian and Jonelle prepared for nightfall. And the figure in the dungarees - an emaciated guy with long black hair, hooded eyes and a straggly beard - welcomed Ken and his Irish guests.

'This is Colin,' Ken said. 'Colin is a fruitarian.'

Cora pulled herself upright and we followed Colin to a clearing, 100 yards from the creek. Patches of garden surrounded two half-completed humpies constructed of wood and palm fronds. One was the kitchen, a skeleton of branches supporting a roof. The other, which had the addition of a single wall, acted as a bedroom. Colin had a hammock in the bedroom. Ken slept in a one-person tent behind the kitchen.

'This is North Creek Manse,' he said. 'Make yourselves at home.'

'Thanks very much,' I said.

After Cora and I had pitched our own tent close to the creek, we returned to the kitchen. Ken was brewing tea on an oil drum converted to a stove. On crude wooden tables flanking each side of the stove, he had laid out cups and a plate of fruit.

'You can sit here,' he said. He brushed off sections of tree trunk that were the kitchen chairs.

Cora and I supplemented the victuals with bread, cheese and a tin of fish. Ken leaned up to a box suspended from the roof to pull down a can of condensed milk. The box, and pieces of fishing net nailed to the kitchen uprights, provided North Creek with larders.

'Keeps things away from the rats,' Ken said. 'Marsupial rats of course.'

Colin dipped in to the fruit. Neither Cora nor I had ever encountered a fruitarian and were astounded by Colin's sudden pronouncement.

'Fruit,' he said, 'is the only food fit for human consumption.' Ken grunted audibly.

'Is it not lacking in some very essential proteins?' I asked, being careful not to offend one of our hosts.

'Capitalist propaganda,' Colin claimed.

'Oh...' I said, trying not to appear too sceptical.

In ramblings devoid of logic, Colin went on to dismiss all evidence in support of other foods, including that of his own famished frame and the dizzy spells and mild hallucinations he'd been having of late.

'Cleansing pains,' he explained. 'My body is rejecting the mucous and other toxins deposited by all the bad food I used to eat before.'

Looks to me mate, I thought to myself, *that your body might be rejecting you.*

'I don't lay my food trip on other people,' he said after another half-hour of doing exactly that. Meanwhile he was digging deeply into the stockpile of wood and pulling ever closer to the stove.

'Cleansing pains my arse,' Ken said in a guttural Austrian accent. 'The cleansing pains don't stop you from burning all my wood. And you are suffering so much from malnutrition that you don't have the strength to collect any of your own.'

Lord of the Flies was the thought that came to mind. Then something moved in the darkness that had crept in on us. A small marsupial. Followed by another. And another. Ken's 'rats', all bouncing about in the shadows, hoping someone would drop a morsel. Then a massive cane toad hopped across the middle of our floor. Beyond the firelight, the chorus of the rainforest was deafening.

* * *

'We have potatoes, carrots, pumpkins, spinach, cassava, tomatoes, sweet potatoes, Chinese cabbage, pineapples, rock melons, parsley and five spice growing here,' Ken said as he and Colin showed us around the gardens in the morning. 'And over there in the orchard there are bananas, mangoes, passion fruit and paw-paws [papaya]. Even though the rainforest soil is poor, they don't do too badly.'

'The paw-paw trees look a bit dubious,' I said. 'I've never seen Y-shaped ones before. It's not the fallout from those French nuclear tests over in Mururoa?'

'No man,' Colin answered. 'Just those heavy Queensland pigs. When they smashed up the bay and chopped down the fruit trees, that's what happened to the paw-paws. Everywhere there was one, now we have two.'

After breakfast we had visitors; and from then until the day we left. It was inevitable as the track connecting the camps went through the middle of our kitchen.

Graham from North camp was first to pass through, on his way to the boat. A hard-looking guy in his early thirties with a scraggy beard and ponytail, Graham was a bit of a mystery, a man of few words who avoided being photographed and whose background began with his arrival at the bay. A skilled bushman, he provided North Camp with regular pig kills. He was also the commune horticulturist when it came to growing dope.

'His plants grow eighteen feet high,' Ken told us.

Graham was followed by the old man of the woods himself, white-bearded, Cedar Bay Bill on a rare visit (it was the only time we saw him). Bill Yale Evans, an agile, fit man despite being in his early seventies, had been living at the bay for over thirty years. He mostly kept to himself, but had run out of tea. Ken did the introductions and Bill shook hands with myself and Cora before sticking the tea in his shirt pocket and disappearing back into the forest. Though we never saw him again, we heard many years later that Bill had lived to his nineties. When we went back to the Cape in 1994 with Tríona and Áine, we camped overnight at The Lion's Den, a remote pub at the beginning of the Daintree Track. In the bar, they told us that Bill had died ten months earlier.

'He married a 22-year-old,' an old hippie from Portsmouth told us. 'At his age the excitement must've popped his ticker.'

After Bill, came Maggie Apples to collect her supplies from the boat.

She in turn was followed by Earl the Dane who, like ourselves, was a transient. A few minutes later we were joined by a guy with black curly hair who was dressed from the waist up and looked to be about thirty-five. He had a naked six-year-old boy in tow.

'Hi,' he said. 'Rainforest John is the name and this is Rainforest,' He immediately gave us the lowdown. 'I have this theory, that children get inferiority complexes from being named after their parents, so we've kind of reversed the process.'

John and his partner, Rainforest Jane, lived at Centre Gardens under the collapsed remains of their humpy which had fallen in a storm and was now virtually indistinguishable from the surrounding bush.

'At least if the pigs come back again,' John said, 'they'll not find me.' He then confided in Cora that he didn't think too highly of Colin's fruitarianism. 'Wonder how it would cope with a pick and shovel?'

Then came an astonishing declaration: after four months out in the world collecting her supplies, Maggie Apples decided to go on a fast along with Colin.

'I've often fancied it,' Colin said.

'Me too,' Maggie replied. 'How long would you think of doing it for?'

'Forty days,' Colin announced. 'Forty days and forty nights.'

'I'd be into that,' Maggie said. 'Let's go for it.'

Ten minutes later they were both off down the beach, leaving what Colin called the 'food areas'. As they left, he hoisted his box of fruit onto his head, wished us all healthier eating and hoped we'd mend our non-fruitarian ways.

'Has everybody gone mad?' Ken wanted to know.

George gave a sad shrug but couldn't care less: he just hopped into Colin's hammock space.

'Shit,' Ken said. 'I had a jar of honey here before I went to Cooktown and now it's gone.'

Gloom descended on the bay: this was a slight to communal integrity.

'Can't say I remember anything like it happening in years,' Rainforest John declared.

When the visitors had left, Cora and I went upriver for a swim and found the jungle perch, contrary to Maggie Apples' story, every bit as friendly as their alleged counterparts at Centre Gardens. We spent the remainder of the day on the beach, listening to the sunbirds and parrots, and looking out at manta rays leaping over the surface of the Coral Sea.

Cora and I were never commune people. But sitting that night on Brian and Jonelle's boat and listening to the steel guitars and voices of Billy and Sandy, North Camp's first family (both in their mid-twenties), we considered it.

Gentle, bearded, long-haired, Billy with the black cowboy hat, reckoned we had nothing to lose by coming back. Sandy, his petite tempestuous partner who had a beautiful singing voice, ran her hands through her long dark tresses and threw us one of her penetrating gazes.

'Thing is,' she said, 'you might want to travel instead.'

'I saw a double-eyed fig parrot today,' Earl the Dane broke in. Earl, tall with fair curly hair and a stubble, looked like he might be having us on.

He may not have been. The double-eyed fig parrot really exists.

* * *

On the third morning, Cora, George and I found ourselves attached to makeshift brooms. At Ken's request, we were sweeping the kitchen floor and surrounding areas to banish the anarchic disorder of bare clay.

'What on earth are you at?' Jonelle asked. She had snuck up on us. 'Brian isn't well today,' she said. 'A case of the coconut blues so he's taking it easy. But is anyone coming to see Tarzan?'

Tarzan...?

'Yes. Tarzan. There's a crowd of us down on the beach, and we're off to see Tarzan. Drop your brushes and come on.'

Cora, Ken and I joined the expedition. The other members were Maggie Apples, Earl the Dane and Karen from North Camp, a shapely blue-eyed woman with long blonde hair who generally walked about in an open, waist-length, cheesecloth shirt and wore it well. Half way down the beach, a search had to be organised: Maggie had lost her child.

Child found, we walked a few hundred yards more before turning into the forest. The sound of wood-chopping led us to a small clearing. Tarzan himself, displaced by a fantasy warp, stood in a cylinder of light that beamed down from a rip in the forest canopy.

Except for the pair of runners, a blanket and the rifle he kept by his side, he looked exactly as you'd expect Tarzan to look: a tall, athletic man with greying curls, a fierce chin, a broad nose and several days' growth on his face. Wearing a standard Tarzan loincloth, he was hacking a dugout from one of the biggest trees in the forest with the kind of hatchet you'd normally use to chop kindling.

When he heard us coming, he stood up, legs slightly apart and hatchet hanging by his side. Behind him, a second, partially completed dugout taken from the same tree lay in a bed of shavings. Beyond the dugouts, he had built a triangular sleeping platform from branches and leaves. The kind of thing a gorilla might build. It was supported by two poles and the great buttressed stump of the despatched tree.

'Tarzan...?' Earl enquired, as if it might be someone else.

Tarzan looked at Earl with an obscure, nervous expression.

'I hope we have not come at a bad time,' Earl went on. 'Only we heard you were making the canoe.'

'That's correct,' Tarzan said, visibly relaxing. 'Come and have a look.'

We gathered around.

'The big boat,' he explained, eyes darting from one of us to the other, 'will be a five-man, or maybe three-man and three-woman. I'm gonna take it to Dutch New Guinea. She'll be good for a long voyage on the open sea. It'll take a while to finish her off; then I'll need a hand to get her to the water, but she'll be right for New Guinea.'

It had taken eight days to bring down the tree with the hatchet. Describing the final moments, he grimaced, smiled, furrowed his brow and chuckled.

'From then on you, understand, it was gettin' dangerous, with what was left of the stump about the size of a saucer. I kept hittin' her another tap with the axe and runnin' well back in case she came. She was a real clown of a tree, one of them that you never know which way she's gonna go. Then I hit her one last time and heard the creakin' and knew she was comin' down. I took to my heels fast as I could and kept runnin' till all the crashin' had died down... She was as big a tree as you'll ever get in this jungle and I didn't want her landin' on my head.'

Stories of Tarzan's dugouts were legion: one was said to have sunk on launching; a second had been built on top of a mountain and couldn't be moved; and Cora and I had come across a third, waterlogged in North Creek. Yet he was adamant that he had once sailed one of his bigger creations through the Torres Strait to 'Dutch New Guinea' (West Irian), of which more will later be said. Turning to the works in progress, he explained that the smaller model, resembling a deep wooden bathtub, was 'a one-man job that will take a mast and sail'. The other would be 'an eighteen-footer'. Looking at Karen and Maggie, he offered a new crew variation for the big canoe, having sussed that Cora and Jonelle were already part of other crews.

'Maybe four men and two women. I reckon that's what I'll need.'

Ushering us over to his sleeping platform, he showed us his current store of food: a few tins of fish, a bunch of wild bananas full of black gritty seeds and a handful of 'walnuts' that you couldn't crack with a sledgehammer.

'I'm forty-five now,' he said. 'and in the twenty-five years I've been livin' in the jungles of north Queensland, I've found this kind of platform to be the most comfortable arrangement. Keeps you safe from the pigs too.'

He handed Ken one of his 'walnuts'. Ken broke two hefty lumps of wood in his effort to crack it and had an eyelid sliced open by the springing nut.

'Here,' Tarzan said, offering him a fistful of moss. 'Bandage it with this.'

Whatever about Tarzan's boat-building skills, he was well liked by all at the bay. Smithers and her boyfriend Roscoe, two recluses from the next bay who could never organise being fully clad or fully nude, made special trips to visit him. The only complaint came from Rainforest John.

'He's dangerous. Stray bullets from his huntin' expeditions are strippin' the bark off the kitchen supports at Centre Gardens.'

On the boat that night this was deemed 'vegetarian hysteria' by the carnivores of North Camp.

* * *

North Creek had been battening down the hatches. By midday the gusts had become gales, tearing leaves from the trees, whipping through the shoreline palms and churning the sea to a black swell. Everyone was wondering if we were in for an out-of-season cyclone. Cora, Ken, George and I joined the Griffins on the deck of the yacht, drinking coffee and rocking with the tidal surge that was swelling into North Creek. Late in the afternoon, the creek burst its banks and the sky began to rumble.

'A boat,' Ken said, 'coming from Rattlesnake Point.'

Half an hour later, as North Creek's population watched, a catamaran dropped anchor 300 yards offshore. Twenty minutes later a punt carrying a man, woman and child pulled for shore.

'I wonder,' Polynesian George said, 'if the family has planned this stop, or if the gales have forced it.

'My money is on the gales,' Brian said.

'It's weird and ominous,' Maggie Apples said, looking surprisingly robust for a woman one week into a forty-day fast. 'Like something out of a thriller. The boat forced to pull in on some undiscovered coast where King Kong waits in the mountains and we're the natives watching from the jungle.'

Ken, who had spent several hours piecing together the scraps of evidence that he hoped might lead to the still undiscovered honey-thief, laid down his pen and paper to agree with Maggie's observation.

'I hope they know where they are,' he said. 'Because if they don't and they run into Tarzan, they'll freak out of their minds completely.'

'Well,' Maggie said, 'I guess it's cooler than landing up at North camp. Rainforest John came back just a while ago, and he reckons things are going fairly crook up there. Someone cocked a shotgun at someone else. Over one of the chicks, John says, but I don't know the details...'

'There's been quite a bit of that sort of thing recently,' Ken said.

Moments later, two figures broke from the forest close to Centre Gardens and walked towards the shoreline. They called to the family in the punt. The punt was dragged ashore and the family followed the two figures back into the forest.

'Got it,' Ken said scribbling down another clue and returning to the problem in hand. Another elimination was applied. Another cross-reference. He stroked the Van Dyke beard. 'Eventually. Eventually, I will get the bastard.'

He said nothing more. Keep 'em guessing.

It was a terrible night: fierce gales, torrential rain, thunder, lightning, and a threatening roar from the ocean. Although the trees sheltered us from much of the wind, it was still enough to lash the tent with a violence that blotted out the hammering of the rain. In the morning, the catamaran was gone; and the guy who had arrived in it the previous afternoon had left an enduring mystery at Cedar Bay.

At the height of the storm, he had woken everyone at Centre Gardens as he and his partner argued. She was pleading, don't do anything stupid. He was insisting that their boat would be smashed to pieces; he had to get it to Cooktown. Shortly afterwards a dark, rain-sodden huddle of people, framed against enormous streaks of lightning, could be seen at the shoreline. They were trying to reason with the catamaran man who was dragging his punt towards the sea while one of the others helped and simultaneously advised against.

The catamaran man hurled the punt at the surf. It capsized. He tried again. It capsized again. After the third attempt he abandoned the boat and surged into the surf. He was bowled over but he pushed on against the breakers. Then he was swimming, swamped by the waves, until he was swallowed up by the blackness. His partner was screaming. The others had to hold her back as she tried to follow him into the sea.

Outside, the twin-hulled catamaran was momentarily illuminated, a tossing silhouette in the storm.

Another bolt of lightning, and a cheer went up from the beach: there was a second silhouette, a man climbing onto the boat. A few minutes later the engine kicked to life, barely audible above the whistling of the wind and the roar of the surf. Another cheer. Soon the sound was lost in the storm and there was nothing out there but a boiling, empty ocean. An hour later someone went back to the beach and found the woman still sitting there, rain and tears streaming down her face.

By morning the storm had spent itself; and while unsubstantiated rumours of a drugs shipment ran around the bay, the emptiest spot in the Coral Sea was where the catamaran had been. I have no idea if it ever reached Cooktown. In such a storm it was a hell of a long way.

* * *

It was Sunday night. North Creek and North Camp had combined to throw a banquet up at Billy and Sandy's place. No vegetarians were invited. But even then, harmony wasn't guaranteed. When Cora and I arrived at North Camp just before dark, two of the lads were threatening one another with shotguns.

'Put the fucking guns away!' Sandy shouted. 'There's bulk food to be cooked here.'

In the afternoon, Brian, Graham and a clean-shaven ex-ringer called Lee, also a resident of North Camp, had killed a pig in the forest. While they were out hunting, Cora and Ken had collected oysters and *bêche-de-mer* off the reef. I had speared a crab and stingray and caught a large cod on a hand line. Added to this bounty were the fruit and vegetables of North Camp and North Creek, and a couple of offerings brought from the next bay by Smithers and Roscoe.

As half a pig roasted over the fire, Billy and Sandy settled down with their guitars, the guitar wood glistening in the light of a kerosene lamp. Lee stoked the fire, coaxing a sheen from two guns hanging on the wall. Karen stood by the hearth in her cheesecloth shirt. Graham mixed flour and water for chapattis. His assistant was a woman called Feather, who was six feet tall if she was an inch. Earl the Dane rolled joints. Jonelle, Cora, Brian and little Erin worked the salad. I played the odd song along with Billy and Sandy. The hut smelled of cooking food, wood-smoke, kerosene and grass. Outside in the darkness the forest was a riot.

'Has the reverend left?' Feather asked.

He had materialised out of the bush the previous day, a grey man in grey shorts, grey shirt, bush-hat, camera and bible, pursuing the crusade of the righteous.

'I wonder,' Brian mused, 'if Tarzan eats missionaries?'

'That's nice,' Sandy said to Ken, putting a forkful of food in her mouth. 'What is it?'

'*Bêche-de-mer,*' Ken said.

'What the fuck is *bêche-de-mer*?' Sandy said.

'Sea slugs,' Ken said.

Sandy's eyes raked him for a few seconds.

'You ever do that again,' she said, firing her plate at the wall, 'and I'll fuckin' kill ya.'

She then picked up her guitar and sang like an angel.

And so the night passed. Good music. Good food. Stories of the raid by the Queensland cops. Stories about Tarzan and Cedar Bay Bill. Ken still trying to solve the honey theft. The mystery of Graham hanging over it all. And an evening that mellowed to the point of inertia. But at the back of it all, Cora and I still agreed that we weren't really commune people. In the big world, you could still dissent and serve *bêche de mer*.

With the banquet over, we of North Creek trudged home in the flickering of glow-worms and fireflies. A line of decaying logs, put down by the North Camp residents, gave off a blue luminescence that guided us through the darkness.

* * *

A few days post banquet, Cora and I sailed back to Bloomfield with the Griffins and half of North Camp. Brian anchored in the estuary of the Bloomfield River. Cora and I pitched our tent close to the high tide mark where we had seen sea snakes on our arrival. A couple of hours after dark, we caught sight of a bonfire and went to investigate. A group of Aboriginals were having a party.

'Do you mind if we join you?' I asked. 'We're from Ireland.'

It always works. Nobody hates the Irish.

'Welcome. Come,' one of them said. 'You drink wine?'

We shared flagons of the stuff until the early hours, singing songs, swapping yarns and swapping shirts. By the time we all went home, one of the men was wearing a bright yellow T-shirt with twin red dragons emblazoned on the front. I was in a cowboy shirt several sizes too small. Afterwards, Cora and I lay in our tent, far too close to the water, and listened to the thrashing and barking of estuarine crocodiles down in the mangroves. Sleep wasn't easy.

Our final contact with Cedar Bay came a couple of months later. We were hitchhiking back to Sydney after our time in Papua New Guinea and got a lift from a Rockhampton man who had been to visit one of the islands of the Great Barrier Reef.

'I met this strange character,' he said. 'His name was Colin. He was a fruitarian - ate nothing but fruit. He turned up, saying he was there for the mango season. Trouble was, there wasn't a mango tree on the whole of the island...'

In Search Of Eldorado

PAPUA NEW GUINEA

Port Moresby

MARAWAKA
WONENARA
TO'OKENA
CHUAVE
GOROKA
KUNDIAWA
NONDUGL
KOINAMBI
JIMI VALLEY
BANZ
KURUMUL
MOUNT HAGEN
TAMBUL
IALIBU
MENDI

CHAPTER 15

Heads We Go, Tails We Don't

On the morning of Thursday, August 10th 1978 we nose-dived into the steamy heat of Port Moresby with a pilot who had learned his trade in low-level bombing raids. It was the first step in a journey that had been months in the making and would probably never have crossed our minds had it not been for the book of photographs I had come across in our local library in Sydney. Now it promised to be one of the highlights of the entire round-the-world trip. We were planning to stay two months in the Highlands of Papua New Guinea, spending time with as many as possible of the tribal groups that still lived a traditional way of life in this most remote of lands. As there were no road connections between the capital and the Highlands, we changed to a smaller plane to climb across the coastal swamps to Mount Hagen, a tiny outpost high in the central massif. Mount Hagen would be where we'd harden our plans.

For centuries this seemingly impenetrable mountain barrier had led to the belief that the Highlands of New Guinea were uninhabited. The existence of an extensive upland civilisation remained unknown to the outside world until May 26th 1930. On that day, Irish-Australian gold prospectors, Mick Leahy and Mick Dwyer, and their team of fifteen lowland Papuan porters, had scaled the heights of the Bismarck Range in search of payable deposits in the upper reaches of the Ramu River. At the top they expected densely forested ranges. Instead, they found themselves staring across vast open grasslands. As darkness closed in, countless pinpricks of firelight were the first indication that they had stumbled on a population of hitherto unknown people. What followed was the last major collision of Western and pre-technological civilisations. Until the morning of May 27th 1930 the million inhabitants of New Guinea's upland valleys were unaware of the outside world. When they later saw the white men panning for gold, they speculated that they were reincarnated dead sifting the gravel for their own bones.

New Guinea's rich highland culture had remained free of outside influences until well into the 20th century. When we arrived in 1978, the central administration in Port Moresby was still making contact with new groups in the interior where isolation had been so compounded over the centuries by inter-tribal fear and hostility that 800 different languages had developed on the island. Whatever inroads had so far been made were generally confined to the valleys traversed by the 'Highlands Highway'. This dirt road connected the coastal town of Lae to Goroka and the two minor outposts of Mount Hagen and Mendi.

In mid-afternoon we landed in Mount Hagen aerodrome to a warm, dry breeze and a reception party. Tribal people from the mountains had come to see the plane land. They stared as Cora and I - the only white people on the flight - disembarked. We stared back. Walking past the line of tattooed women in grass skirts, and men in bark aprons and 'arse-grass' (bunches of cordyline leaves), some carrying spears and bows and arrows, was like finding the moon occupied.

We collected our packs and walked into Mount Hagen, little more than a few bougainvillea-draped dirt streets that acted as an administrative centre for government officials, missionaries and a handful of Australian coffee-plantation owners. Sitting at the head of the Wahgi Valley and surrounded by the heavily forested Central, Bismarck and Kubor ranges, the township had until recently been the last outpost of the Highlands Highway. Although the track now ran to Mendi, the frontier feeling remained.

We booked into the Red Cross hostel, went for a stroll, landed in the only pub in town and were immediately bombarded by all the reasons for not proceeding with our plans.

'If you go into the bush like you're planning,' an Australian coffee-plantation owner told me at the bar, 'you'll both be robbed, she'll be raped and you'll probably be killed. Do you know that the Highland tribes are at war?'

This was not reassuring. As the day progressed the same message was presented again and again by Mount Hagen's whites, mainly other coffee-plantation owners.

'Colonial paranoia,' I said in the end.

'Those people might have a point,' Cora said when a street brawl between two tribal groups erupted outside our bedroom window that very night.

In the morning the woman running the hostel, the only person who didn't try to fill us with dread, confirmed that wars broke out without warning across the Highlands.

'But you'll be relatively safe,' she said, 'unless you're accidentally caught up in the crossfire. However, you must be aware that your safety depends on the behaviour of the last whites who went through a given area. To the village people we whites are all wontoks - one-talks, people of the same tribe. Under the payback system, that makes us answerable for one another's actions. So if the last whites through have misbehaved, or maybe knocked someone down with their vehicle, you could be in trouble. Out in the bush, it's an eye for an eye, a life for a life...'

On the Friday night we met Robert and Helen, two Americans in their early thirties on a whirlwind tour of Asia. They had driven from Lae in a hired car, terrified of having an accident and being summarily executed.

'The advice from the Papuan cops,' Robert said, 'is that if you have an accident, keep driving, report it to them, then get the hell out of the country if you don't want to end up like a porcupine.'

'We're planning to walk about in the mountains,' I said.

'That might be insane,' Robert said. 'You hear all sorts of bad stories. However, Helen and I are going for a run tomorrow to look around the countryside. If you'd like to join us, it would give you some idea of what you're taking on.'

'On the other hand,' Helen said, 'there's always the option of travelling back with us to the coast.'

The tranquillity that greeted us on Saturday morning was encouraging. Mountains crowned in puffs of cumulus. Green valleys with clear rivers. Foraging pigs. Villages of pit-pit (cane-grass) huts with kunai-grass roofs. Gardens protected by pig fences. Butterflies, dragonflies, birds. Here and there along the vehicle-free, dirt road, we passed groups of people engaged in the mundane tasks of daily living. Whenever we stopped, the sounds were those of the birds and insects. Nothing threatening. Until the first attempt to stop the car.

A group of five ring-bearded men stood out in front of us. In their bark belts, aprons, arse-grass, woven caps and feathers, they looked splendid. The axes and spears looked less so.

Robert veered around them, but we were unnerved. A mile down the road it happened again. This time we were forced to stop. Three men had blocked the road.

'Let's see what they want,' Robert suggested. We got out to chat. They seemed friendly at first. Nevertheless, one threatening gesture from the young axe-man among them was enough. A quick U-turn, and we fled.

With hindsight, they were probably the most innocuous highwaymen ever imagined: an old bearded man on wooden crutches, another with shrivelled skin whose bark apron and arse-grass were complemented by a leather helmet that had once belonged to a Japanese airman of

World War II, and the man with the steel axe. After all, there were four of us...

'None the less,' Helen said, 'you guys should really consider that lift to the coast.'

Back in Mount Hagen, the weekly market had drawn people from the mountains to sell and barter. Tattooed women ran the show - one with the words 'Coca Cola' across her forehead. Sitting on the ground in grass skirts, beads, shells, and maybe the occasional strip of possum fur, they traded in fruit, sweet potato, taro, cassava and the bright Hagen capes that were a recent addition to local women's attire. Generally small and slight in stature, many of the women would have walked for days over the mountains, carrying produce in *billums* (string bags of bark-fibre), strapped to their foreheads. Some would have carried a second *billum* with an infant inside, and another child on their shoulders.

The men strolled about in bark aprons and arse-grass, or mission handouts. Headgear varied. Spectacular feather headdresses and bark caps would vie with anorak hoods, underpants, and even half a rubber football. Bristling with weapons, they kept an eye on things. Some chewed betel nut. Others drank beer and whiskey.

'Oh dear,' Robert said. 'A murder in progress.'

Three spearmen came charging through the marketplace. A fourth man ran before them. The quarry escaped but the incident did nothing for confidence. Back at the Red Cross hostel Cora had a question.

'What to do now? We're getting very mixed messages.'

'We could flip a coin,' I suggested. 'Heads we go, tails we don't.'

Heads it was. Many a dilemma in the coming years would be resolved using this scientific method.

'If that's a decision,' Robert said, 'we'll drop you out the road in the morning. We'll wait until you're out of sight. If you change your minds before that, you can turn around and we'll bring you right back to town.'

* * *

When we said cheerio to Robert and Helen the following morning we had no fixed plan other than a vague idea that we might, in a few days, end up in Mendi. We therefore resolved to simply shoulder our packs, walk out into the bush and see what happened.

Around noon we passed our first village, a compound of cane-grass huts with spirals of smoke seeping through the thatch, an arrangement that kept the huts free of vermin and left their inhabitants smelling sweetly of wood smoke. The village was enclosed by a pig fence of sharpened stakes. A similar fence protected the gardens which were laid out like the squares of a bar of chocolate. We glided past as silently as we could. So far, so good. Until we rounded the next bend.

Six men were heading our way. Bark aprons, arse-grass, shell necklaces, grass armlets, headdresses of parrot and bird-of-paradise feathers, pig tusks through nasal septa, faces and bodies daubed in ochre. Spears, axes, machetes, and bows and arrows. The full calamity.

'Whose idea was this?' I said rhetorically out of the side of my mouth. Cora still believes I was trying to blame her.

As we drew level the men stopped with an expression that was hard to box.

'That was nerve-wracking,' Cora said when we had slid past. 'Where the hell do you think they're going?'

'I don't know,' I said. 'But I'd like to be a long way from it when they get there.'

Not relishing any more encounters with armed warriors, we branched off along a narrow foot track. Only to be confronted by an armed warrior.

He stepped from a solitary hut, a square-shouldered man with a ring beard, powerful arms, big spear and the full kit. His pig tusks were so large that they encircled his chin. And in a new twist, bones ran through his ear lobes.

He faced us square-on, spread his feet and thumped the shaft of his spear into the ground. We considered making a run for it. But then something I remembered hearing about many years before...

'Good afternoon,' I said.

'*Apinun!*' the great menace boomed. The crown of feathers shook as he took each of our hands and pumped away. '*You go we?*' [Where are you going?]

'Mendi,' Cora said. 'We go to Mendi.'

'A-a-a-agh,' he exclaimed. '*Longwe.*'

The spell was broken although nothing akin to ease had entered the story. In fact, half an hour later we were in bother again.

We were approaching a village. Through the gaps between huts we could see a central compound in which warriors in full regalia were dancing, chanting and waving weapons. Around them in a circle, half-naked women and children were ululating. We had no idea what was going on, but we figured it best to be sneaking past.

We were mincing our way around the perimeter of the village when we were spotted.

'Aye-e-e-e!' came a woman's cry. In a total diversion, every woman and child was coming our way. Behind them, warriors with painted bodies, headdresses and lots of weapons, came to a standstill. Thunder stolen.

'Aye-e-e-e! Aye-e-e-e!' A couple of the women threw themselves to their knees and hugged us around the thighs, threatening to topple us. We tried to extricate ourselves before the warriors, having lost their audience, might also lose their cool.

'Tenkyu tru,' I said. [Thanks a lot in Pidgin.]

We dragged ourselves loose and hightailed it down the track, and were greatly relieved to find ourselves back on the main road. A jeep trundled into view, slowing down as it approached.

'Wanna lift?' the driver asked. Although we had planned to walk all day, we jumped in, grateful to be temporarily insulated from warriors and weapons.

The driver and his friend, both young Australians, owned a coffee plantation. Two young American women in the back were visiting. The atmosphere was one of instant cultural harmony in the face of an enormous cultural chasm.

'They were getting ready for a payback in one of the villages back there,' the driver said. 'One of their people was killed by some other crowd and they were getting ready to go and take revenge. Did you see any of it?'

'We did,' Cora said. 'We were nearly part of it.'

'Don't worry,' the driver said. 'In the seven years I've been in the country, I've learned that the bark is worse than the bite. So long as there's not about to be a bust-up. And so long as it ain't Thursday - government pay day - when everyone rips into the booze and people get axed.'

'But how can you tell?' I was very anxious to know this.

'What you have to watch for is the *meris* - the women. When things get really serious, the *meris* take themselves off. That's the time to make yourself scarce. If the *meris* run, you run.'

This piece of advice would come in handy in the not too distant future.

'Did you see Danny Leahy's house?' the driver asked. 'Danny was one of three other brothers who followed Mick Leahy into the Highlands. He's still alive and living in Mount Hagen. He's an old man now, but he can still spin some hair-raising tales about the early days.'

I was sure he could. I wouldn't have done so badly myself after three days.

By early afternoon we had crossed the Kougal River into the

Southern Highlands, passed through a vast plantation of red-berried coffee trees, and climbed into the Vakari Range. The jeep dropped us at a small village where we were immediately surrounded. The people were fascinated by the driver's explanation (in Pidgin) that we were walking about the Highlands for no apparent reason. We shook dozens of hands, wishing everyone an *Apinun*. An old man stepped forward, his face etched with concern. Were we *longlong* [crazy], he asked the driver. Why did we not take a PMV [public motor vehicle]? The PMVs were Toyota Stouts that occasionally came ripping around bends, packed to capacity and not beyond nosedives down mountainsides. To myself and Cora, they were a much more *longlong* option that walking.

'*Dispela man na dispela meri laik go long wokabaut,*' the driver explained [this man and this woman like to walk].

'A-a-a-ah,' the old man exclaimed, his eyes widening in tender comprehension. He put a finger to his mouth, shook it in the air as though he had burnt it, and sighed: a gesture of compassionate astonishment that would follow us across the Highlands.

'*Sorri tru,*' he said with a hesitant shake of his head, '*Sorri tru.*' We had been consigned to the realm of the *longlongs*.

We left the village and found ourselves skirting the base of 14,327-foot Mount Giluwe, the second highest mountain in Papua New Guinea. In a secluded glade we stopped for a bite to eat.

Somebody had told me you could purify water with Milton sterilising fluid. I did. I then drank some and instantly vomited.

'Ciarán,' Cora said after a while, 'you know the way we stopped here because there's nobody about?' I nodded. 'Well,' she said, 'there's six somebodies behind you and they don't look friendly.'

I turned to find a semi-circle of glaring warriors materialising from the forest.

'*Apinun!*' I said full of fervid *joie de vivre*. And it worked again. The glaring melted into unsure smiles and hands were shaken in all directions. But the nerves were getting the better of us. Once friendly relations had been established, we didn't hang about. Besides, it was already late afternoon and we needed to find a place to camp. But where? All land seemed to be tribally owned and either cultivated into gardens or covered in impenetrable, snake-infested jungle.

Then providence lent a hand in the person of Neil Taylor, an Evangelical Bible Missionary from the southern United States. Thin, neatly dressed, in his mid- thirties and wearing a bush hat, he thundered over the brow of a hill in a Toyota Land Cruiser and screeched to a halt.

'Would you care for a ride?' he asked. 'It'll be dark soon and pretty cold.' His two passengers, men from his village base of Pagluge, were demoted to the back. 'Maybe you'd like to join us for something to eat?' he said. 'My wife, Edith, would love to meet you. Maybe you'd even like to stay with us for a few days?'

'That would be so nice,' Cora blurted with a haste that was indecent.

For the next eight days we slept at the Pagluge mission guesthouse, a wooden hut close to the mission house. And as the days passed, we slowly came to terms with this mind-boggling land.

* * *

'The tribes are indeed at war,' Neil told us over dinner. 'The Hagen clans are of a particularly warlike temperament and are threatening the Western Highlands with chaos. There's also upheaval in the Wabag district of Enga Province. In my own area, I've had to withdraw a missionary whose life had become endangered. But they'll not kill a white if it can be avoided. We're not part of their wars. If you stumble in, they'll let you pass. I was on my way to Mount Hagen one time when I drove into a battle. Some houses were burning and the track was full of fighting warriors. When they saw me they all held fire until I'd passed, then got down to business again.'

Edith Taylor, a tall, resolute woman with fair skin and a great southern drawl was probably in her early thirties. Her style of dress and the way she tied her blonde hair in a bun gave a first impression of severity. It melted on contact to reveal a friendly, happy pioneering spirit.

'We came here three years ago with our six children,' she told us, 'because Neil had a calling to fill the position previously occupied by his father who founded this mission. Since then we've been lucky. God has guided us through all the tasks he has set for us and the children are growing up healthy and strong. Neil has even built us this home with God's help.'

The house, a wooden building with a stone chimney and tin roof, was surrounded by a protective wire enclosure. It stood away from the village. The mission church, a structure of cane-grass and thatch, was further down the track. The whole setup seemed remote from the other life of Pagluge, a remoteness reciprocated in the distance the villagers placed between themselves and the mission.

'They don't tell us very much,' Neil said during our first visit to the village. 'Most of what we know we've learned from anthropologists who have visited the area.' He nodded towards an older man who came out of one of the huts. 'Ah, here comes an old friend, a true rogue if ever there was one. He's probably despatched a few souls in his day.'

We were introduced to a middle-aged man with leathery skin, bad teeth and a grizzly beard. He wore a tatty jacket, bark belt, apron and arse-grass. A keen-looking axe rested on his shoulder. The relationship was friendly, respectful and awkward. But he didn't mind showing us around. He pointed to the gardens being worked by women with digging sticks and crude spades, to the pig fence that had recently been repaired, the hatch that was the entrance to the windowless *haus man* (the men's longhouse), the *tugi,* a log lying full length across the doorway to prevent women from entering, and a *haus meri* where the women, children and pigs lived.

'The division,' Neil explained, 'is partly due to the men's concern about menstrual "pollution". Women mustn't cook or touch men during the time of a period. But, it's also based on the need to be ready for sudden raids by enemy clans. All weapons and wealth are stored in the *haus man*... This area is now Kewa land although the other clans around are of the Embongu people. They once owned this land until they were driven out by the Kewas. So the Kewas are especially distrustful of the neighbours.'

Once we had seen the sights and were assured as an aside that sorcery was no longer practiced in Pagluge, we were cordially escorted back to the mission fence.

'Our guide,' Neil said, 'is a *bikpela man*. The *bikpela man* is the power figure in the social structure of Highland clans. He's charged with holding together the family groups and alliances in a world that had, prior to Australian intervention, recognised no autocratic rulers. It's a position earned by guile and the ability to mediate. The *bikpela man* must be a diplomat and skilled orator, and be central to raising, giving and receiving wealth. He must also settle disputes, plan warfare and negotiate peace. You noticed the length of his *moka* tally. Every little stick represents a debt owed to him which makes him a man of great status.'

Under the Highland system, wealth was based, not on what you owned, but on what you had given away. Each gift, generally in the form of pigs or pig meat - the hub of Highland commerce - was publicly announced by a small hardwood stick, added to the tally and suspended from the giver's neck on two rattan thongs like a miniature, collapsed rope bridge. A man of substance could extend his influence by placing many people in his debt. Clans could do likewise by hosting extravagant *mokas*, feasts at which dozens or hundreds of pigs were killed, placing other clans in debt. The *moka* season occurred during August and September, the main reason we had chosen those months for our trip to New Guinea.

'Over there,' Neil pointed back towards a clump of trees growing out of curious barrel-shaped mounds of earth. 'That's where the *haus tambaran* - the spirit house - used to be. The seat of the sorcerer. Nowadays, it's all illegal and in most accessible areas the *haus tambarans* have been pulled down, but the practice is far from dead. For instance, when somebody dies suddenly, sorcery is blamed as it's believed that there's no such thing as natural, sudden death. Counter-sorcery is then employed, tapping the body with sticks or whispering in its ear until the culprit is "named". Then off to war with everyone unless compensation is paid.'

On our second morning, Neil invited us for a run in the Land Cruiser to some nearby villages. It was an hour's drive along an atrocious swamp track to the first village, at the edge of which we were confronted by an angry mob armed with axes and machetes.

'The taxman,' Neil explained after checking the situation. 'He comes once a year to the accessible villages to collect taxes. The people here are refusing to pay this year because no work has been carried out on the track.'

The mob was milling around the Land Cruiser, shouting furiously about what they were going to do to the taxman, whose jeep could now be seen making its unsuspecting, merry way down the track. Suddenly, one of the men broke from the mob, threw his axe into one of the village huts and jumped onto the open back of our Land Cruiser.

'One of my pastors,' Neil said with a hopeless kind of smile.

The next pastor we collected was armed with a large *billum* of sweet potatoes destined for his brother's widow. We found her perched on a rock in another village. Covered head to toe in light-blue mud, and wearing a grass skirt, bark cape and a necklace of large white seeds that circled her chest and neck dozens of times, she looked like a ghost with a stiff neck.

'The pastor has adopted the family,' Neil explained. 'This will strengthen his line and entitle him to claim the bride price for the girls in the family. The widow has been sitting there, dressed like that for three months now.'

By the time we had reached Ialibu, the largest village in the area, we had collected a total of nine pastors. In the village compound the pastors showed us the *ples tambaran*, an oval of spirit houses, preserved they told us, as a reminder of how things used to be in the time of sorcery. Shortly, they began to outline the 'old' superstitions. Lined up one behind the other, hands on shoulders, feet shuffling and voices chanting, they gave a fulsome demonstration of that moribund past with a fervour that was astoundingly convincing. They then reverted to being Neil's pastors.

'The Highland tribes,' Neil said, 'hold the belief that everything comes from the ancestral spirits. Everything the black people have and everything the white people have. As the white people have more than the black people, the logical conclusion is that there's another set of untapped spirits up there somewhere to whom the black people haven't yet tuned in. Christianity has thus been embraced in the spirit of acquisition, and assimilated in accordance with the old beliefs. Some families would send one son to the Catholics, another to the Lutherans, another to the Baptists and so on, to ensure maximum coverage of the new terrain.'

A parallel development, designed to arrive at the same end, were the cargo cults. These were religious movements based on the belief that western goods ('cargo') were created by the Papuan ancestral spirits and intended for the Papuan people. The whites, however, had mysteriously and unfairly gained control of the objects that produced the cargo so these were reconstructed at the local level to correct this imbalance.

World War II brought a rapid rise in cargo cults. During the Pacific campaign against the Japanese, it was observed that the whites enacted certain rituals which caused clothes, tinned food, tents, weapons and other extraordinary goods to rain from the sky. As the war receded from the Pacific, and the abandoned military bases attracted no further cargo, the cultists attempted to jog the spirits' memories by imitating what the whites had been doing, believing that the airborne riches would come again from their ancestors, the only beings capable of such miracles.

They built symbolic runways and mock bases and wore headphones carved from wood while sitting in 'control towers'. They staged drills with sticks and painted their bodies with military-style insignia and the letters 'USA'. They waved landing signals from their 'runways' and lit fires and torches and waited for the cargo to fall from the sky. By the late 1970s, when the goods hadn't appeared, many of the more extreme manifestations of the cargo cults had faded away; but in parts of Papua New Guinea, some enterprising geniuses were still selling little black boxes to villagers, telling them to recite specific incantations into them to induce those riches from the sky.

On our return from Ialibu we were met by one of the Evangelical Bible Mission's most successful conversions, a rotund, bearded man of about thirty with a compelling concern for the world's souls. Pilibu had just come back from four years of study in the U.S. where he had collected a store of the more tinctured political analyses of the Southern bible belt.

'Martin Luther King and John F. Kennedy,' he told us over dinner, 'were both in the pay of the Kremlin. You could see it in their eyes.'

'Pilibu will be taking the evening service,' Neil said.

Cora and I, obedient to a policy adopted after the remarkable Batak service at Lake Toba, were there early.

The cane-grass church was filled to capacity. The congregation consisted of women and children, with a mottling of older men who were taking no chances on what might lie beyond the grave. Informality was stretched to its outer limits by the cacophony of disorder that governed the proceedings. The exceptions were the brave efforts of Neil and Pilibu to bring a modicum of gravity and decorum to the building. The nine pastors, in jeans and T-shirts, sat behind Neil and Pilibu. Facing the congregation, the pious gravity of their expressions would periodically crumble into bewilderment.

Like El Cid at the gates of Valencia, Pilibu thundered forth. But despite his rigorous extolment of the virtues of Christianity, and the glowing account of the wonders he had beheld 'in London, England; in Tokyo, Japan; and in New York, America' nobody much gave a damn. Far more pressing enticements were to be found in breast-feeding the children, chatting furiously, coming to shake hands with myself and Cora, or rearranging the bundles of dried cane-grass that would later act as lanterns. Each time there was a gap in the preaching something akin to heckling would break out: people shouting at one another; babies crying and peeing on the floor; women, who had missed the earlier hand-shaking opportunities running from the front to where Cora and I were seated.

The dim oil lamps of Pagluge's church pleaded for the Lord's assistance in bringing just a little smidgen more light to this forlorn outpost of Christianity.

* * *

Neil woke us early next morning.

'There's to be a big pig kill at Warababe,' he said. It's a village in the mountains. I have just got word from one of the other missionaries.'

Shortly after sunup we were off, Neil, Edith, Cora and myself. At Ialibu we turned into the mountains, climbing narrow jungle trails cloaked in a freezing fog. At a number of high points, warriors could be heard on the ridges and crags, transmitting messages across the mountains in a form of yodelling. They were telling of pig kills that were taking place across the Southern Highlands. PMVs came rollicking around the bends, jam-packed with armed, painted warriors heading to the pig kills. Two miles from Warababe we parked the Land Cruiser and went on foot down a steep muddy path.

'That there,' Edith said, pointing to a mound in the earth as we reached the first village, 'is the grave of a woman who was recently axed to death by her husband for infidelity.'

We squelched our way through the village compound and pegged on uphill to Warababe. A group of women in the throes of self-adornment, raised a wild hullaballoo as Neil and Edith were recognised.

'Dayla! Dayla!' they shouted. The cry echoed across the village. The Taylors were well liked. However, apart from some Western clothing, there were precious few signs of past missionary successes.

Twenty pigs had been clubbed to death for a big *moka*, enough to return many favours and place a multitude of new recipients in debt. They were being butchered in a clearing at the lower end of the village. Further afield, pit fires were heating mounds of stones. Smoke from the fires drifted through the village, obliterating one scene, then another, in a tapestry of shifting images. In one image, men with axes and bamboo knives hacked at a carcass. In another, a group of women prepared mounds of vegetables. In a third, two men were stuffing intestines with scraps of pork and vegetables to make sausages. In a fourth, hot stones were being transferred from the burning-pits to pit ovens. A platform of hot stones was then layered with banana leaves in preparation for the food. (A 'lid' of more hot stones would go on top and in two hours the food would be ready.) Smaller pieces of pork had already been cooked in bamboo tubes and were ready to be eaten.

'People stuff themselves with pork every year at these events,' Edith told us. 'Then they suffer what they call *pik-bell* [pig belly] when they all get sick from the deluge of meat-eating.'

Over the next couple of hours Neil introduced us to a large number of villagers, including the village 'councillor', Pua, a tall man with a full beard and an impressive *moka* tally who was the local administration's link to the village. Attached to his bark-fibre cap was a badge that denoted his position. Pua in turn introduced us to his wives and children, crowds of them. One of the women came forward, dropped to her knees and threw her arms around my legs in that hugging embrace of the first day.

'That's reserved for friends,' Neil said as he stopped me from toppling backwards.

Then, through the smoke, Neil spotted Kukumbu, the most important *bikpela man* in Warababe. At about the same time, Kukumbu spotted us. Dropping the bamboo knife he'd been using to carve up a side of pork, he rose to his feet as we came coughing and spluttering out of the smoke. With a whoop of surprise he leapt on 'Dayla', throwing two gory arms around him. He then opened the embrace and dragged me in as well, knocking our three heads together in his enthusiasm. He looked like he was in his sixties, a small man in an open, grubby yellow shirt, bark belt and arse-grass. A straggling ring-beard disappeared into the strands of his bark-fibre cap. A kina shell hung around his neck. A deceiving image for the most powerful man in Warababe.

'How come he's not wearing a *moka* tally?' I asked Neil afterwards.

'Kukumbu?' he said. 'When a man has fought as many wars, killed as many men, married as many women, sired as many children and raised as many pigs as Kukumbu, he doesn't need to wear a *moka* tally.'

Before continuing his festive preparations, Kukumbu skewered a large hunk of pork on a stick and handed it to Neil. At each of five more fireplaces, it was added to, leaving the Taylors in heavy debt around Warababe.

Down at the bottom of the village, groups of armed warriors and their families, had arrived and pork was being distributed. Then a row broke out. Someone not happy with their share of the cuisine. Kukumbu was summoned to sort things out. There followed a round of shouting and men grabbing at bows and axes before it was all settled, with handshakes all around. Then the four white *wontoks* were introduced to all the guests in another epidemic of hand-shaking. And as Warababe repaid its debts, forged new alliances, strengthened old kinships and created new debtors, the men on both sides lined up their women in a display of corporate strength while clan orators enumerated the gifts given and received, praised their friends and denounced their enemies.

High above on a ridge, two village men were letting the world know that *moka* was being made at Warababe.

'When the first whites came here,' Edith told us on the side, 'and the women wore nylon stockings, the people thought that white women could take off their skin.'

* * *

They say that cricket is cricket wherever you go: not so with rugby.

Neil and Edith and all their children drove us from Pagluge to Mendi, the last stop on the Highlands Highway. They settled us in at the Menduli Mission Guesthouse before dropping us down to the village to watch some rugby. As part of the provincial government's annual festival, the Mendi people were playing against the Huli Wigmen of Tari. Both had amassed large bodies of armed supporters. It had all the makings of football hooliganism at its best.

'Apinun.' The greeting came from a semi-naked warrior with bow and arrows and ceremonial Hagen axe. The latter comprised a black stone head fitted into a pocket of woven cane-grass attached to a curved wooden handle.

'Apinun,' I said and we shook hands. 'Can I see your arrows?' I asked, making the appropriate signs. The arrows were typical of highland arrows. Cane shafts but no feathers or guides of any kind.

'Dispela,' he said, proudly lifting a four-pronged, barbed variety. 'Dispela kilim pisin.' [Kills birds.] 'Dispela [a broad, razor-sharp bamboo arrowhead] kilim pik.' [Kills pigs.] 'Dispela,' he said, removing, with a theatrical flourish, sheaths of cane-grass from two arrowheads of bone. 'Dispela kilim man.'

A placid fellow with a bushy beard, a colourful net cap, a red flower in his left ear, a necklace of cowrie shells, a respectable *moka* tally hanging from his neck, and an average respect for life. In another place he might have been a politician.

Wild horses wouldn't have dragged us away from that match. When the opening whistle blew, we positioned ourselves beside one of the goalposts among a circle of Wigmen. Some were engrossed in the match. Others played *Jack Change It* on the grass. Instead of the usual headdress of feathers, these warriors wore large wigs of woven human hair, shaped like a thick banana. The wigs were topped in soft orange plumes, with some further embellished by parrot feathers and rows of canary-yellow 'everlasting' flowers. Jewellery included beads, necklaces, split-cane armlets, nasal tusks, shells, and sets of tusks that hung on their chests. The beak of a hornbill was slung between each man's shoulder blades. A bone knife hung at the waist. To confound the opposition, one man carried a neatly-folded, black umbrella.

The Huli Wigmen of Tari in full ceremonial dress.

Other fans, who clearly considered the Wigmen eccentric, gathered around. A man with a face blackened in sump oil, cradled a Hagen axe. A young woman in a grass skirt smiled through streaks of red and yellow paint. A child in furs and grass skirt hugged her mother's knee while Cora crouched down to talk to her. An old man in bark belt, apron, arse-grass, earrings, grey beard and a head painted black and white, removed a pair of incongruous sunglasses and pushed back his baseball hat. Bemused, he smiled and nodded towards the Wigmen. *Would you ever have a look at them there boys!*

There was a score. A section of the crowd went wild, waving their weapons at the silent section on the far side. Another score and the far side waved their weapons back.

A match like that could only have ended as it did. With every rule in the book broken, the final whistle blew and an avalanche of armed warriors invaded the pitch as the referee fled. Simultaneously, sections of the crowd dived for cover as a small plane came in low to land at the nearby airstrip.

Games Day at the provincial government's festival in Mendi.

Afterwards, the victorious team, chanting and waving spears, did a lap of the jungle outpost on the back of a truck.

* * *

The next stage in our loosely constructed itinerary was to walk from Mendi to a place called Kandep, then cut across the mountains to Wapenamanda in Enga province. Our only problem was that we had three maps and they disagreed with each other.

Regardless, we left Mendi feeling remarkably relaxed, having shed most of our apprehensions during the eight days spent in Pagluge. The paint, headdresses and artillery that had so alarmed us in those first hours out of Mount Hagen no longer posed a threat. Nor did the fierce glares. In a country where warfare had been a way of life for centuries, how else do you greet a stranger?

However, our *longlong* status was being reaffirmed at almost every encounter with the Highlanders. Where were we going? they would ask. Kandep, we'd say. Squeals of laughter. Why didn't we take the plane like the other whites? We wanted to walk, we'd explain. *Sorri tumas* [Sorry too much], they'd sadly intone. At one encounter, an older man wanted to help. He had arrived on the scene carrying nothing but a machete. Accompanying him was another man carrying an axe, and a woman weighed down with a *billum* of sweet potato.

Having grasped that we were bound for Kandep, he scratched his head with a pig-bone taken from his hair. He was also *sorri tumas*, but the problem was simple as far as he could discern: a carrier had to be found for my pack. He turned to the woman with the *billum*, and suggested that she carry it. He was extremely puzzled when I explained that it was okay, I'd carry it myself. After all, who in his right mind would want to carry a 50-pound pack when a woman could be found to do it? Cora, being a woman could damn well carry her own. *And mine*, you could hear him think, *if she was worth her salt.*

Our first decision was thrust upon us at the village of Korn. According to the map we had chosen to follow, our track forked left from here. But, according to the entourage we had now accumulated - two muscle-shouldered warriors in traditional dress, a third man in green dungarees who spoke a little English, two boys in bark belts and arse-grass, and a woman in a grass skirt carrying two *billums*, one with a sleeping infant - we should turn right. We tried again.

'This is Korn, okay?' I asked.

'Yes,' the man in the dungarees agreed.

'Here on the map,' I said, tracing a finger along the left hand of the fork, 'it says Kandep is this way.'

'No,' he insisted. 'This way.' He pointed up the right hand track. Sure, wasn't he going that way himself?

We double-checked the map and the track definitely went left. But the maps we had didn't inspire confidence with their three conflicting versions of Papua New Guinea. And here were the locals, positive beyond doubt.

'Maybe this is a new track,' I said to Cora. 'Maybe it's been recently built and the map is out of date.' Cora shrugged. We went right.

'Me Catholic,' the man in the dungarees informed us as Cora and I wheezed our way up the side of the first mountain, leaving Mendi and the Lai Valley far below. 'Me name Gary. You have no fraid. I help you.'

Gary, a small 21-year-old man with a thick moustache, smiled continuous encouragement as Cora and I panted along under the midday sun and the weight of our packs. Periodically, we sought assurance that the track still went to Kandep. Assurance was given. Undoubtedly, we hindered the general progress but our companions showed great patience. The three men had a casual smoke each time the foreigners showed signs of collapse.

'Magic mountain,' Gary the Catholic declared after several more steep climbs and no left turns. 'We go magic mountain from my village when man or woman die. We go for dreaming when somebody die from sorcerer. We dream with *bikpela man* from village and we find who *kilim* man or woman. Then we go *kilim* too.'

The clergy of these parts seemed to have none too good a grip on the congregation.

In the afternoon a nagging drizzle crept down from the peaks as Cora and I attempted to coax one foot in front of the other for the assault on what Gary assured us was the final slope before his village.

'You stay my village,' Gary offered. 'My house.'

We were climbing out of a 7,000-foot valley, many hours and many miles from Mendi. Thoroughly drained from the steep tracks, the packs and the sticky heat, I once more put to Gary the day's abiding question.

'Kandep?' I asked. 'This is still the way to Kandep?'

'No,' he replied without ever a blink. 'Kandep other way.'

'Oh no,' Cora groaned whereupon Gary quickly deployed a spot of damage limitation.

'This not Kandep way,' he said. 'But Kandep possible this way. This short cut.' He stretched a finger towards the forested mountains to our left. 'You go up in mountains and through bush three days. No village. *Longwe* [long way]. And many, many hills. But you no have worry. My village *klostu*. Soon we come my village.'

Even the *klostu* village was no solace. Gary had been assuring us that his village was *klostu* for the past hour and a half. In the Highlands, we were discovering two sorts of distance: *longwe* which could mean anything from the horizon to Tierre del Fuego, and *klostu* which was apparently without definition.

'Longhouse,' Gary said as we plodded through the mire of a village compound. 'Men use for pig kill.'

He was trying to cheer us up but we were beyond reach. We then topped a pass and were looking down on a broad cultivated valley.

'This my village,' Gary beamed.

Leaving the main track we slid downhill through cane-grass and kunai for another hour before re-emerging close to a boundary of rocks denoting village perimeters. We had arrived in Ekari, a tight lakeside settlement 7,200 feet above sea level. It was three o'clock in the afternoon. We had walked over the mountains for six hours with three five-minute breaks.

In Ekari, Gary introduced us to his family. We met a considerable number of brothers, sisters, aunts and uncles. We also met three of his fathers and six of his mothers. He then showed us his father's grave. All in all, a bit confusing.

In the evening we made tea. Gary raised a fire in his hut by rubbing two sticks together and a large pot was put to boil. We were joined by yet another of his brothers, a lad of seventeen in a red sweater and pink shorts, and one of his uncles, a middle-aged, bearded man with dark eyes who carried a Hagen axe in a broad cane belt and complemented his bark-fibre cap, feathers and arse-grass with an old, grey tunic-style jacket. We took a photograph of us all, using flash and a cable extension, and you'd think the Earth had opened up.

As tea was a rare commodity around Ekari, the whole village turned up once the pot was boiled so we dished out endless cups in bamboo sections and added a couple of our 1,500 saccharin pills to each, careful to maintain the pecking order of bikpela men, sorcerer, and other dignitaries. Afterwards, the women and children of Gary's household went off to sleep with the pigs; Gary and his brother dossed down on the floor; and Cora and I were given their plaited cane bed for the night. It was a gesture neither of us would ever forget.

'There's something crawling in my sleeping bag,' Cora signalled shortly after we had settled down. 'Lots of somethings.'

'I feel them too,' I said. 'I think it might be fleas. I'm being bitten.'

'One of these days,' Cora said, 'I'll sleep in a hotel.'

'That would be no fun. You couldn't tell about the night you were eaten by fleas.'

'You're a howl,' Cora said. 'I'm in convulsions.'

Apart from short periods of dozing, we lay awake until dawn. At first light we fled, having collected in excess of 500 bites apiece. It took three days to rid our baggage of the legions that rode out of Ekari on our backs.

* * *

We spent several hours skirting Ekari Lake and a large swamp, until we connected with a track than ran to Tambul. At a village that straddled the junction, we tried to find out how far we had to go. We found a man who spoke a little English and Pidgin.

'How far to Tambul?' I asked.

'*Longwe,*' he said. I gave up on distance and tried time.

'How many hours to walk?'

'Twenty-five. Tambul *klostu.*'

I tried again.

'How many minutes?'

'Thirty minutes.'

We gave up, filled a billycan with water from a leaf spout[20] and left

---

20.   A leaf or bamboo spout anywhere in the Highlands denoted drinkable water.

the village. A few hundred yards later we sat down and ate breakfast, quickly drawing several onlookers. We passed around some processed cheese. The wise villagers spat it out. Exhausted from the previous day's walk and the lack of sleep, we packed up and headed off again, climbing a steep twisted trail into dense rainforest and a descending mist.

Up ahead we could see the ridges we had to climb, tiered up one behind the other until they crept into the clouds. Soon we were enveloped in the mist that stilled the jungle into eerie silence, the stillness broken only by dripping trees festooned in creepers and moss. An occasional break would allow a glimpse back to the valley; then the mist would close again until it soaked through jackets and jeans and left us shaking with the cold. Our spirits, however, were briefly lifted by the appearance of two birds of paradise: the Lesser Bird of Paradise, with its emerald-green throat, maroon chest and wings, and sweeping flank-plumes of deep yellow and white; and the black-and-yellow, nine-inch King of Saxony, with its twin, 20-inch, scalloped, enamel-blue brow-plumes that could be erected at the bird's will. (Abundant food and the absence of predatory mammals has allowed the evolution of this extraordinary family of birds whose females select the gaudiest males who do little more than eat, drink and engage in bizarre courtship displays.)

Battling on, we dropped into a gorge, crossed a wooden bridge, then climbed again towards the daunting Mur Mur Pass. When the mist became rain we tried to shelter under the trees. As we did, a hypnotic chanting rose from below, followed by yodelling. Then silence, apart from the dripping of the trees, the call of a bird and the muffled sound of running water. Then more chanting. More yodelling. Then a figure appeared, and another, and another. Nine in all. They crossed the bridge and came into clearer view. Then a great burst of yodelling when they saw us.

The leading warrior wore a headdress, carried a bow and arrows and held a massive leaf above his head to ward off the rain. His face was streaked with fierce black lines, two running from nose to ears, and a third vertically dissecting his forehead. He was followed by two young men, also wearing headdresses and carrying axes. The next two were carrying a live pig strung by vines to a wooden pole. Then came two older men, both with fancier headdresses than the others and pig-tusks through their noses. Each carried a Hagen axe. One of them also sported a bow and arrows - and an umbrella. The last man carried a large machete. The ninth member of the band was a young woman carrying a *billum* of sweet potato. She was a wife of the man with the umbrella who turned out to be the leader of the group.

They told us they were on their way to Tambul, that it was two days' walk, and that we could walk with them.

'No have fraid,' the woman said as two of the men hoisted our packs onto their backs and the man with the brolly linked my arm and dragged me off. He then switched his Hagen axe to the other side, opened his umbrella, flung a proprietorial arm around my shoulder and with a short low whistle to every second step, marked time up the face of the mountain. The slow, bedraggled, chanting procession slugged on behind through squelching mud and pelting rain, headdresses, bows, arrows, pig and all.

'I think Chiefy fancies you,' Cora said.

Towards the top of the pass, a PMV came from behind. The brolly man hailed it down. He said something to the driver, a man in a headdress, carrying a bow and arrows, then bundled myself and Cora, our two packs and his wife into the middle of the crowd on the already overloaded pickup. He waved and we took off over the muddy pass on skidding bald tyres that swerved horribly over terrifying drops. The other passengers looked ready to jump at a moment's notice.

At Tambul we stayed in a mission house with friends of the Taylors who were growing cabbage out the back to supplement the village diet. One of them, in conversation, described the locals as 'the heathen pigs in the village'. (Some people say that the last true Christian died on a cross.)

In the morning, they put us on a mission pickup. It was driving to Mount Hagen.

CHAPTER 16

Banz Payback

A truck dropped us at the village of Kudjip, twenty-six miles east of Mount Hagen. It was a beautiful sunny morning. Two days of heavy rain had left the Wahgi Valley smelling fresh and alive. We shouldered our packs and headed off. Destination: nowhere in particular. Until we saw the two warriors. In full ceremonial dress and carrying spears, they were turning left off the main track.

Figuring that they were most likely making their way to a *sing-sing*, the highlight of village life, we followed at a discreet distance. We now knew that marriages, betrothals, births and wars all gave rise to the singing and dancing that we had encountered and fled from on our very first day out of Mount Hagen.

'We might be able to make good the loss,' I said. 'Speedy up,'

'Speedy up yourself,' Cora said. 'Or else carry my rucksack.'

We reached the next bend to find that the men had vanished.

However we walked on and, five miles later, arrived in a riverside village tucked away among trees and clusters of bamboo. This was Banz; and Banz, we saw on arrival, had a Catholic mission. Disappointed at having lost the two men, and mindful of the dense cloud now massing on the peaks to the north, we diverted to the mission.

'Hello,' Cora called to a bearded, dark-haired guy in his early twenties wearing a bush hat, blue shorts and white T-shirt. He was perched on top of a ladder, carrying out minor repairs to the mission-house roof. 'Do you think we could camp in your garden?'

'Oh Jaysus!' he yelled. 'Hang on a minute. I'll be straight down. Where in the name o' Christ did you two come from?'

'Mount Hagen,' Cora said. 'Before that, Belfast. Before that, Cork.'

He came spinning down the ladder and threw his hat in the air.

'I'm Tony. From Mayo... Jaysus, I don't believe it. Wait till Chas hears this... Chas! Chas! Are you there Chas?'

Chas Duggan, a big, affable, balding man in his late fifties, appeared at the door in a brown check shirt, white shorts and sandals. He was the local priest, all the way from Ballycastle in County Antrim.

'Well,' he said, 'whatever else, you're just in time for a Guinness. As for camping in the garden, I wouldn't hear tell of it. Not while there's a perfectly good spare room you can use. As long as you don't mind the mess.'

And soon to arrive was Joe, a younger, fair-haired priest from Limerick who had his own mission in Karap village in the Jimi Valley.

'Myself and Tony are building a church in there,' Joe said. 'You'll have to come and visit.'

One minute we were pissed off because our *sing-sing* had evaporated into the bamboo thickets of the Wahgi Valley; the next we were swilling cold Guinness with three Irishmen, listening to music and watching huge butterflies flit around the mission garden. (Five years later, I was returning one night to my tent on a beach in County Donegal when I came across three young women around a campfire: one of them turned out to be Chas' niece.)

After lunch, Joe left for Karap in a Land Rover loaded with building materials. Chas and Tony went back to work and Cora and I read in the shade of the garden's gazebo.

'Listen,' I said. 'Chanting. Coming from the direction of the river.'

'It's the radio in the house,' Cora said.

'No, it's not,' I said. 'It's the *sing-sing*. Grab the camera.'

We streamed off down the track, through the trees, towards the river. The sound was unmistakable now, waves of ululation and chanting swelling up into the afternoon heat: our *sing-sing* for sure. Then came the shock of our lives.

Rounding a bend, we were confronted by hundreds of armed, charging warriors. Angry-looking men in full ceremonial dress, coming straight at us. Worse than that, five *meris* were running panic-stricken before them.

'If the *meris* run,' the young Australian had warned us that first day, 'you run.'

The panic of the women was instantly outstripped. Cora and I vaulted a pig fence and shot through a field of sweet potato, bouncing over the mounds, until we were absolutely sure that we were of no interest to the sea of mayhem descending on hapless Banz.

'*Sing-sing* my arse,' Cora was panting. 'Try war-war... And to think that I was happily reading my book a few minutes ago.'

It took some time for us to muster up the courage to venture back towards the track and follow in the wake of the small army. Up ahead, the warriors had stopped. They were yelling, dancing, and waving above their heads an arsenal of spears, axes, machetes, lengths of sharpened bamboo, and bows and arrows. We had almost reached the rear of the column when there was another charge. We fled again, not stopping until we reached the sanctuary of the Banz Club.

Inside, slumped over the bar, were seven drunken, grunting white men. Australians and New Zealanders who owned, or worked on, coffee plantations. Two young black women sat in a corner. Cora and I burst through the door.

'Two whiskies!' I called to the barman. There was an astonished silence.

'Now, you two don't live about these parts,' one of the men said.

'We're from Ireland,' I said. There was a guffaw of mock approval. We had left the better company out on the track.

'Seen the fuckin' *kanakas*, mate?' It was the talkative one again. 'Thievin' bastards are out there stealin' our coffee.'

At the bar, we gleaned among the grunts that the people we had fled from were Talus. They had come to Banz demanding revenge for a clan member killed by one of the Banz people. In the past this would have meant the automatic taking of life (a man or two women for a man; women and children were one for one). Nowadays, it could mean that or, in an alternative devised during Australian 'protectorate' times, it could mean a negotiated payback settlement which was likely to be massive. The chosen option would be decided over the coming hours.

The opportunists among the offended Talus had taken time out to add some beans from the expats' coffee trees, a kind of fringe benefit to top up whatever else might be reaped from their threat of mass extermination.

Relaxed by an assurance from the barman that we were looking at a show of strength rather than the opening shots of a massacre, we drank up and went back outside. By now the ululating Talus had massed at the bush airstrip at the edge of the village. In a sea of swirling headdresses, headbands of iridescent green beetles, bones, shells, pig tusks and great bailer-shell breastplates, they waved their weapons and looked every bit as threatening as they were meant to. The Banz people stayed in their huts. Yet, this was just the beginning, a prelude to the climax of delicate negotiations that had gone on for weeks to prevent all-out warfare between the two tribes. Tomorrow would be Saturday, August 26th, the day of the great Banz payback when the score would be settled.

* * *

We were woken at first light by a slow, repetitive ululation resonating over the village. It spread like a cloak out into the valley and up into the shrouded folds of the mountains. Although the sun had risen, it was still cold when Cora and I arrived in the marketplace where the Banz people and their allies had been mustering since before dawn. In a fever of excitement, hundreds of plumed and painted men, women and children periodically broke the ululation to greet new arrivals. A thunderous roar would signal more weapons being added to the military might waiting for the Talus. The Talus, meanwhile, were arriving by the truckload and forming up on the northern end of the village in another avalanche of welcoming roars. Having been warned of the possibility of an outbreak of fighting, Cora weighed it all up and decided to return to the mission until the elders of both sides had taken control of their respective armies.

'Hang on,' I shouted after her, brave as ever. 'Don't be going without me.'

The build-up lasted several hours. Just as we finished lunch, a roar rose to the north. A few minutes later, the Talu clans swept past the mission and exploded onto the airstrip a short distance away.

By the time Cora and I reached the airstrip, the Talus had fanned out in a huge, spear-waving, ululating, crescent, a thousand strong, around the grass runway. Behind them milled another thousand women and children in all their finery. We were ushered in among the spear-waving warriors.

'*Banz man, em I dai pinis,*' one of them asserted to Cora.

'What's he saying?' Cora asked.

'I think he's telling us that the Banz man is 'die finish' - dead.' The little Pidgin I had picked up seemed to elucidate greatly on matters of destruction.

We were both digesting this morsel when the most blood-curdling roar I have ever heard drowned out the Talus. A howling sea of painted bodies swept onto the airstrip from the far end. The Banz men had arrived. Bristling with feathers, and waving their weapons, they fanned out across the runway and charged at the Talus who included the honorary us, caught on the wrong side of the line.

They were fifty yards away when Cora's nerve cracked.

'I'm outta here,' she said.

She took off to the shelter of some trees where Chas had arrived along with Mayo priest, Mike Wallace, who ran the Catholic mission down at Nondugl. Mesmerised, I stayed put, though the closer the charge came, the surer it seemed that negotiations had gone south. However, six feet from the massed ranks of the Talus, the charge abruptly stopped, and two thousand yelling warriors, jabbing their weapons at one another, pounded the airstrip. I will never, ever, forget the sense of salvation.

After two further false charges, the Banz warriors drew back into a second crescent. Their women and children flooded in behind. And the payback began.

The best orators from both sides - *bikpela men* carrying Hagen axes - stepped forward and began to ream off all the slights and slanders perpetrated down the years by each group against the other, culminating in the Talu version of the events that had led to the day's gathering. A Banz woman had killed a Talu with a knife. Others of her clan had then attempted to dispose of the body in the nearby river. This had been reported to the Talus and war would have resulted if the wisdom and restraint of the *bikpela men* on both sides hadn't prevailed. But agreement had been reached: 23,000 kina (about A\$25,000, a colossal sum), one hundred and fifty pigs, twenty cassowaries, one goat and one cow, would be paid to the Talus. There would be *pik-bell* for weeks in Talu villages.

A long procession of Banz warriors paraded in with the compensation. The vanguard carried the money pinned to woven discs, five feet across, decorated with red flowers, and held aloft on bamboo poles. They were followed by the cassowaries, gift-wrapped in woven bamboo pouches with only the blue heads and feet protruding. Then came the pigs, the animals central to highland culture. Some were strung on poles and carried between pairs of men. Others were led on leashes by women, many of them crying at the loss of the animals they had reared from birth and perhaps breastfed as piglets, a custom common across the Highlands. Last came the goat and the cow, the latter a rare sight in these parts. It was a massive amount to pay; yet, there seemed to be no malice borne towards the person who had visited such ruin on Banz and its allies.

By now Cora and Mike Wallace had ventured back into the Talu crescent. Mike, a droll, easy-going man of about forty, with swarthy features, dark, slicked-back hair, and long tapering sideburns that made him look like a leftover from the benevolent wing of the Teddy Boy era, was paying a social visit to his colleagues at Banz. Harbouring a deep understanding of Highland culture, he seemed to be not fully at ease with the missionary role. When we later visited him at Nondugl, whiling away the evenings with whiskey and chess, I got the distinct impression that Mike would have been just as happy growing coffee.

'The money on those boards doesn't mean a lot,' he explained.

'Money is a bit like kina shells, something to show off. Besides, not too many here could count to 23,000. Everyone can see that there's a lot of money, and that's enough. The figure was probably chosen because it sounds impressive. You even hear at times that a million kina has been paid over at some payback.'

Maybe so, but I estimated 18,000 kina at least spread across the displays.

Once the compensation had been publicly inspected, it was announced that the transfer of wealth would begin with the pigs. What followed was an afternoon of choreographed mock violence from which other societies might learn a great deal.

Eight spearmen broke from the Banz side and raced across the airstrip to the Talu ranks where they pounded the earth with their feet and shook their spears. Retreating back to their own lines they were chased by an equal number of Talu spearmen who in turn pounded the earth and shook spears. A pig was then brought forward and presented to the Talu spearmen who danced triumphantly in front of the Banz warriors before sweeping the 'conquered' prize back to their own side. Eight more Banz warriors then charged the Talu lines and the ritual was repeated. And so it went, first the pigs, then the cassowaries, then the goat and the cow until only the money remained. At which point the whole show began to unravel.

A grizzled *bikpela man* with a headdress of red feathers stepped forward from the Talu ranks. He climbed up on an old oil drum and a hush rippled across the airstrip. He had this to say: the Talus had been patient; they had come in good faith to accept the reparation being offered by the offending Banz people, and what had they got? Small cassowaries. Skinny pigs that had never seen a decent meal. A cow that wouldn't get into their truck. The Talus were angry. The Banz people had insulted them. Now the Talus were going to *'kilim man'*. At this, the *meris* on both sides began to scatter. Mike Wallace, Cora and I followed suit.

However, the tension was defused by an old man who was an even greater orator than the grizzled one. A flurry of comings and goings ensued and the matter was resolved, buoyancy returning to the fold. The female relatives of the dead man, their bodies caked in the brown and blue ochres of mourning, appeared to be the only people maintaining any consistency of feeling. For the others on both sides, the most benevolent and malevolent of feelings seemed to hinge on the most volatile of pivots.

Five hours after the Banz warriors had charged onto the airstrip the last of the money displays was handed over. But the Talus were still struggling with the cow. Four warriors, having run two poles under its belly, were trying to hoist it onto the back of the Talu truck. Each time the cow turned its head, the four and a following of spectators broke in panic. The poles were ditched until courage could again be mustered for another go. In the end the cow was totally spooked. The last we saw of it, it was running across a field of sweet potato with a dozen Talus in cautious pursuit.

'One time some Australians brought an elephant up the Highlands Highway from Lae,' Mike told us afterwards. 'They did it for a laugh and stopped off along the way to show it to the villagers. Can you imagine the scenes? When they got to Banz, a huge crowd gathered, but every time the elephant moved or waved its truck, there was a scatter into the woods. Then it began to eat and people were shouting "It's sticking the food into its arse!" The Australians then had to explain that it shouldn't be killed as it couldn't be eaten. "You know how bad *pik-bell* can be," they told the crowd. "Well, elephant-bell is far worse".'

On Sunday, the day after the payback, we attended mass at Chas' church. It was another bizarre religious occasion, topped by a disapproving visit by the *bikpela men* and sorcerers of Banz. In full ceremonial splendour, replete with billowing headdresses and a full complement of weapons, they paraded up and down the aisles, glaring in contempt at the assembled 'Catholics'. Inspection complete, they loped out the door shortly before Chas, in his own ceremonial robes, made his appearance. When mass was over, a young man in shorts and T-shirt came up to us. He shook hands, then held up a small black wooden carving of a human head with a headdress.

'You like?' he asked Cora.

'It's beautiful,' she said.

'For you,' he said.

With its tiny beaded eyes, it looks at us today from a wall in our home: a mute relic of a bygone age of *bikpela men* and stalking warlocks.

The ghats at Varanasi, April 1976.

Elephant 'toll-gate' between Agra and Kanpur, April 1976.

The Grand Trunk Road, east of Allahabad, April 1976.

Some of the magic bus passengers with Baba Fiji, Indian-Nepalese frontier, April 1976.

Cora with fellow travellers at Trekkers' Retreat, Pokhara, Nepal, April 1976.

The author, Durbar Square, Kathmandu, May 1976.

Golden Buddhas, Sagaing Hill, Mandalay, Burma.

The author, Cora and 'homestay' family, Fang, Thailand, June 1976.

Our Lahu hosts, Noyai village, Golden Triangle, June 1976.

Sindi, Dominique, Cora, leaving Tha Ton, Golden Triangle, June 1976.

Sindi and Cora, Lisu Banmai village, Golden Triangle, June 1976.

Akha woman and child, Yappa village, Golden Triangle, June 1976.

Cora, Yappa village, Golden triangle, Thailand, June 1976.

At the Mekong where Burma, Laos and Thailand meet, June 1976.

The author with leatherback turtle and government officials, Rantau Abang, Malaysia, June 1976.

Hitchhiking down the east coast of Malaysia, June 1976.

Tuk Tuk Timbul, Samosir Island, Lake Toba, Sumatra, July 1976.

Christine Hakkers and Cora with Batak women, Samosir Island, July 1976. Fire-damaged house in background.

Lake Toba ferry at Tuk Tuk Timbul, Samosir Island.

Nurmin (left) and Lormen Siallagan, Tuk Tuk Timbul, July 1976.

Cora with the Wage Family, Jambi, Sumatra, August 1976.

A busy day on Kuta Beach, Bali. The author with Paul, September 1976.

Funeral procession, Bali, Sept. 1976.

Tom Dunlop, Bruce Penn, Cora, Jenny Zohn and Christine Hakkers, Sydney, January 1977.

Glenys Kitchingman and Tony as blizzard begins, Snowy Mountains, NSW, Easter 1977.

Tony, Veronica, Jenny, Tom, Bruce, Cora, saved by Seamans Survival Hut, Snowy Mts., Easter 1977.

*Glenys Kitchingman and the author after Glenys had come
off her bike, Cape York Peninsula, June 1977.*

We find the sign to Meripah, Cape York Peninsula, June 1977.

Cora and Glenys, Coen River, Cape York Peninsula, 16th June 1977.

Cora and Glenys, in one of the shallower parts of the Coen River, June 1977.

Jim Gordon, Glenys and Cora, Rokeby Cattle Station,
Cape York Peninsula, June 1977.

Cora, Glenys, Aboriginal paintings at Mushroom
Rock, Cape York Peninsula, June 1977.

Tarzan outlines his plan to sail his dugout to 'Dutch New Guinea', Cedar Bay commune, Queensland, July 1978.

The author with Huli Wigman from Tari, Mendi rugby match, Papua New Guinea, August 1978.

Talu warriors, Banz payback, Western Highlands, August 1978.

Talu 'bikpela man' threatens to 'kilim man' because of quality of payback compensation, Banz payback, Western Highlands, Papua New Guinea, 26 August 1978.

Banz warriors sweep onto airstrip for payback, Banz, Western Highlands, Papua New Guinea, August 1978.

Cora, and Tony from Mayo, as the beer stocks diminish, Jimi Valley, September 1978.

Cora with Thomas Pelika, Daulo Pass, Chimbu district,
Papua New Guinea, September 1978.

Our bush plane from Goroka to Marawaka, September 1978.

The widely feared warriors of Marawaka, September 1978.

Kukukuku women and girls with bark capes, Marawaka, September 1978.

Cora, heading down to Lamari Valley, Papua New Guinea, September 1978.

Gathering of Highland clans, Goroka, Papua New Guinea, September 1978.

Cora, Averil Fink and the author, leaving Oallen Ford, Shoalhaven River, NSW, 22 October 1978. White water ahead!

Chris McGuinness and Cora as we bypass waterfall, Shoalhaven River, October 1978.

Chris and the author as the helicopter with Greg McManus on board weaves into view, Shoalhaven Gorge, 1 November 1978.

Cora, the author and Alan Dods, having made the first of three runs across the flooded river, Shoalhaven Gorge, 2 November 1978.

*Alan relaying the last of the equipment to the rim of
the Shoalhaven Gorge, NSW, 2 November 1978.*

*Cora, above tree line, Hollyford Valley, Routeburn Track,
South Island, New Zealand, December 1978.*

Mt. Ngauruhoe, North Island, Jan. 1979.

Climbing Mt. Ngauruhoe, North Island, New Zealand, January 1979.

Maria, preparing the refried beans at our restaurant,
Isla de Las Piedras, Mexico, February 1979.

Angélica, Cora and Marisa, Sierra Madre Occidental, 28 February 1979.

Cora and the author, trekking across the Sierra Madre Occidental, February 1979.

Cora Indian home with grain stores, Sierra Madre Occidental, March 1979.

Angélica, high up in the pine forests, Sierra Madre Occidental, Mexico, March 1979.

Cora, Huichol Indians, Sierra Madre Occidental, March 1979.

All eyes on us as we enter the Cora Indian village of La Mesa, March 1979.

Cora family, La Mesa, Sierra Madre Occidental, March 1979.

*Cora family fording the river outside Jesus Maria,
Sierra Madre Occidental, March 1979.*

'High noon' Jesus Maria, March 1979.

Our minus-5-star room at Campeche, Yucatán, March 1979.

The descent of Kukulcán, Chichén Itzá, Yucatán, spring equinox, March 1979.

Maya women in huipiles, Tulum, Yucatán, March 1979.

Cora, Rod and Roberta, Tulum, March 1979.

Cora, Guatemala City market, April 1979.

Cora, Lake Atitlan, Goatemala, April 1979.

Morning departure from San Pedro La Laguna for Santiago Atitlan, April 1979.

Santiago Atitlan, Lake Atitlan, Guatemala, April 1979.

Indian market, Chichicastenango, Guatemala, April 1979.

Santo Tomás Church, Chichicastenango, Guatemala, April 1979.

Palenque, Mexico, May 1979.

CHAPTER 17

The Relief Of Koinambi

By Monday Tony was ready to return to Karap where he and Joe were building their church. Chas was driving him home and using the visit to bring in supplies and another increment of building materials.

'You might as well make use of the lift,' Tony advised. 'Joe will be looking forward to seeing a couple of new faces for a change. And it's a hell of a way to walk.'

Early in the afternoon, under a glorious sky, we left Banz in Chas' four-wheel-drive. Cora travelled in the cab. Tony and I climbed into the back, wedging ourselves into the hollows of the tarpaulin used to cover the supplies. Almost immediately we were winding up a tortuous dirt track, a twisting, crumbling ribbon eaten away by the regular rains of the high country. We passed some villages of smoking thatch and noisy children and climbed on through potholes and ruts until we were in dense jungle. Ahead on the peaks, dark clouds were massing. We ignored them. Similar gatherings over the past few days had come to nought. However, as we crawled towards the faraway pass, the sky darkened to a deep purple.

'Have you ever been to Killarney?' Tony asked.

'Lots of times,' I said. 'Why do you ask?'

'You know the way it rains in Killarney? Well, Killarney is shag-all compared to what's about to happen now.'

He had hardly spoken when freezing sheets of rain forced us under the tarpaulin and turned the already atrocious track into a mudslide.

At the top of the pass, we were hit broadside by a cataract of mountain run-off. The impact caused a violent skid, but the vehicle righted itself and we went on. Tony and I bounced out from under our cover to find that we were in the clouds.

'Now you can see why parts of the road are missing,' Tony said. 'By the way, just along here a few weeks ago one of them PMVs went over the edge. But everyone bar the driver jumped clear. They must have been sitting on their nerves the whole shaggin' way.'

'Thanks Tony,' I said. 'A pity Cora isn't here. She'd *love* a story like that.'

Twice more we were hit by water, threatening us with the fate of the PMV. We then cleared the cloud and the rain stopped as we descended along the side of a mountain.

'Look at that for road-building,' Tony said. Where half the track had been ripped away by landslides, tree trunks had been rammed into the mountainside at thirty-degree angles. A bed of rough planks had then been laid to support the new 'road'. The sudden sinking of a wheel into the mud as you crossed that creation was not to be forgotten.

The first glimpse of Karap was impressive. Sitting on a narrow ridge, the village commanded a view over two valleys, one of which was the Jimi Valley. Joe's church, a triangular corrugated-iron monstrosity, towering up from the ridge, looked even more incongruous than it might have in another setting. We wound down the mountainside through moss-covered trees and near-vertical gardens. At the doors of small settlements, semi-naked people hugged their shoulders against the cold, their bodies glistening in the pig grease used for insulation.

Joe and the entire population of Karap were on the ridge to greet us. It had taken two and a half hours to cover twenty-one miles.

After a meal of steak and beer, consumed with lip-smacking relish in Joe's mission house, Chas and Joe settled down to mission talk. Cora and I followed Tony to a small wooden guesthouse perched on the lip of the ridge and looking west towards the sunset.

'What the hell is that?' Cora asked as the tranquillity of the ridge was shattered.

'Joe's generator,' Tony said. 'He gets electricity for a few hours in the evening and that keeps the freezer cold for the rest of the day.'

The generator was positioned close to the village, away from the mission house. The villagers got the noise: the mission got the juice.

For the next two days Cora and I explored our surroundings while Joe and Tony organised their workforce. Rising before first light, we would sit on the ridge, wrapped in our sleeping bags, and watch the sun filter through the orange mists that drifted along the Jimi Valley from the direction of Mount Wilhelm. At this most memorable part of the day, the birds and insects came to life. We would then have breakfast and Joe would ask if we had felt last night's earth tremors. No, we'd reply, feeling cheated. After breakfast we'd check out the neighbours: beautiful butterflies; a praying mantis that hung about the guesthouse doorway; a golden orb-weaver that had spun its web at the back of the house; and the columns of ants marching across the ridge. We would then take the camera and a few pieces of fruit and head up among the ridges or down into the valleys, returning to Karap in time to watch the sun go down.

On the third morning, guilt caught up with me. I joined the mission workforce. Joe and a group of village men were going off in the four-wheel-drive to dig sand from one of the riverbeds.

'I never thought I'd see the day when *you'd* be building a church,' Cora howled as we bobbed off down the track. 'You'll never live this one down.'

At the river I joined the men and started to shovel sand into bags. The sight of a white man digging caused consternation. I was *'olsem kanaka'* (same as a native) I was told in amazement. Why did I work like this?

I was doing fine, attracting plenty of approval, until my third attempt to cross a log bridge that spanned a gully between the river and the track. Bag of sand on shoulder, I made my dash and ended up on the flat of my back, six feet down in the undergrowth. The stunned response of my co-workers who quickly rescued me suggested that white men falling into gullies was even more improbable than white men doing heavy work. For the remainder of our stay at Karap I was pursued around the village by the good-natured jibes of those who had seen, or heard of, the famous flop.

'Fancy a walk to Koinambi?' Tony asked that night. 'It's about twenty miles further into the Jimi. There's a young Cork woman there running a bush hospital, a nurse called Catherine Sutton. Don't suppose you know her?'

'No,' Cora said, 'but visiting her sounds like a great idea.'

'That's at least five hours' hard walking,' I said. 'What's the track like?'

'Well,' Tony said, 'if we're lucky we might catch a coffee pickup going as far as Tabibuge. That's about twelve miles away. But we'd need to be away early.'

At first light on the Friday morning we were on the track, climbing the hill behind Karap. The morning was crisp and dry, our packs were light, and the walking was relatively easy once we had covered the initial climb. Gradually, as the forest filled with birdsong, we found ourselves high on a ridge, looking down on a valley brimming with morning cloud out of which the mountains grew like islands. A half hour later the cloud began to lift, great silvery streamers creeping up the slopes until the valleys and rivers were in sharp relief. We drank from a bamboo spout, shed a layer of clothing and steamed ahead. Three hours after setting out from Karap, we were waltzing down the track to Tabibuge, not a care in the world, having walked the whole way.

'Now for the booze,' Tony said. We had planned to buy a bottle of whiskey at Tabibuge and bring it with us to Koinambi, which we had marked as a potentially dry spot. Tony had a friend in Tabibuge, a hospitable, middle-aged Australian coffee-plantation owner named Ted Kennedy who ran a small trade store. Ted was surprised to see us on foot at nine in the morning.

'A bottle of whiskey!' he exclaimed. 'At this hour of the bloody day?'

We went to the store but Ted was out of drink. He would not, however, see us leave empty-handed and insisted, as he treated us to our second breakfast of the day, that we take eight bottles of beer from his own fridge. He then cracked open four more beers and we sat with Ted and his beers until noon.

'You could try the other store on your way through,' he advised as we left. 'They might have a few bottles left.'

But again there was no whiskey, only beer. And only sold in packs of twenty-four. It was a big decision: we bought a pack. Adding Ted's eight bottles, we stuffed the lot into a yellow PVC bag and left for Koinambi, eight miles of rough mountain track, one 3,000-foot descent, and one 1,500-foot ascent away. The Relief of Koinambi, Tony called it. But setting off with such a cumbersome load at noon, some six degrees south of the Equator, was altogether a bad idea. As we marched along the exposed mountain tracks, the sun and the beers at Ted's place began to take their toll. The sack got heavier and heavier as Tony and I took turns to carry it.

'If we drank a bottle each,' I suggested, 'it would lighten the load a little.'

We sat under a tree at the edge of a precipice and cracked open three bottles. Ten minutes Tony had a thought.

'Let's crack open three more.'

By the time we got up to go we had drunk nine bottles (on top of the beers we had with Ted), were quite tipsy, and the sack had *gained* in weight. So we opened three more bottles for the road. An hour later we were tottering along the track and singing loudly, with half the beer gone. An hour later we were dehydrated wrecks and two thirds of the beer was gone. At four o'clock in the afternoon, burnt, exhausted and legless, we arrived at the village of Kuibin. Across the valley, half way up the mountain, lay a sloping bush airstrip, a clearing of gardens and the village of Koinambi. Looking across, it was immediately clear why Koinambi's airstrip was so notorious: it was too short. Landing wasn't such a problem as the uphill drag was enough to stop the bush planes. Taking off, however, involved a downhill rush and a freefall into the valley - the only way to pick up momentum for takeoff.

To get to Koinambi we now faced the 3,000-foot drop to the Jimi River and a 1,500-foot vertical climb up the far side. After a 20-mile walk over mountains and an afternoon binge.

'Wish we'd never drunk that beer,' Cora said.

'Wish we'd never bought that beer,' Tony said.

Over the next hour, we skidded and bum-slid into the Jimi Gorge. The foot track first curved downhill along an exposed slope of kunai grass. It then plummeted through dense rainforest to the river. Startled green parrots rose in front of us. A Raggiana Bird of Paradise, with its orange feathers, green chin and yellow crown, dropped from a tree to glide towards the bottom of the gorge.

By the time we reached the shelter of the trees our legs were buckling, our throats were rasping-dry and we were soaked in sweat which attracted clusters of small black sweat bees. With the loss of altitude the climate had changed: it was now hotter and more humid as we slipped on the rough track, grabbing at overhanging creepers and cursing colourfully. About 150 yards above the river we stopped and ate some corned beef and dried fruit, our first food since Ted Kennedy's place. We then stumbled on towards the river. Ten minutes later Tony and I heard Cora shouting from below.

'Have you found the water?' I called.

'I'm in it,' she yelled.

Another brief surge and Tony and I could see the river. A brown turgid flow, it cut between walls of black rock connected by a bridge of bamboo and vines. Cora was further downriver, lying full-length in a stream. In seconds Tony and I were in beside her, having left a trail of clothes, boots and packs on the rocks.

Cold water never felt so good nor tasted so sweet.

At 5.30 p.m. we crossed the freely waltzing bridge - a single line of bamboo for the feet, two vine rails for the hands. The river surging below. Refreshed from the stream, we started uphill with a burst. It was short-lived. In minutes we were flattened by exhaustion, heat and the gradient.

'We could always stay here by the river for the night,' Tony suggested.

'We could light a fire and sleep by it,' I agreed. 'It shouldn't get too cold down here in the valley.'

'We'd freeze our arses off,' Cora said and away she went.

Half an hour later, as night dropped into the Jimi Gorge, we caught sight of Koinambi. We had about 600 feet to climb. Swallowed up by the darkness we plodded on until we heard voices. 'Aie-e-e-e!' came the cries of a group of grass-skirted women sitting at a fire. We entered the village. The air smelled of frangipani. At Catherine Sutton's hut, we dropped our sack with the few surviving offerings.

'We brought you some drink from Tabibuge...' Tony started.

Catherine, a dark-haired woman of about twenty-five from Currabinny in County Cork effectively ran a small informal hospital on her own. She was stunned by our arrival. She and an English VSO volunteer named Phillipa were seated at a table. In front of them were two glasses. Far from being pauperised in the matter of drink, there was enough wine in the hut to fill the cellars of Beaujolais.

CHAPTER 18

Rats, Sorcery And A Dodgy Night

Kurumul was famous for its tea: we remember it for its rats.

During our stay at Banz we had met Peter and Nick. They ran a VSO community school among the tea fields of Kurumul and invited us to drop in. Peter, a fair-haired, bespectacled Belfastman in his early twenties, was feeding ducks when we arrived.

'Welcome to our castle,' he said. 'Nick should be back any minute. He's trying to amuse three Australian teachers who are being shown around by a lay missionary who lives nearby.'

Nick, a tall, relaxed Englishman with dark collar-length hair, was heard before seen.

'Ah, the Irish have landed,' came the welcome. 'Let me show you around the survival conditions of Kurumul Community School.'

The tour began at the school kitchen, a hut with two gigantic copper pots used for cooking the evening meal.

'Rice and tinned fish. Every night. And here [indicating two cane-grass huts] are the dorms for the boarders. One for males and one for females. The beds are spaces on the floor. We get our water from the tank at the *haus kiap* [a house set aside in more accessible villages for visiting officials] and the bathroom is the river.' A collection of long huts provided the classrooms. 'See,' Nick said. 'Desks.'

He and Peter then led us to their own place, a rough cane and thatch hut at the edge of the village. We dropped our packs in the 'guestroom', really a store for the rice and tinned fish with enough free space for two sleeping bags. An alcove in which we prepared dinner on a primus stove was the kitchen.

'You mean to say that you cook on this all the time?' Cora said as she beat off the cockroaches, beetles and flies. 'Surely VSO can do better than that?'

But one primus it was. And oil lamps and a pit-toilet. And everything in jars to keep it from the cockroaches, beetles and flies. Or so Cora and I thought - until bedtime.

'Peter,' Nick said, 'do you think we should do something about the rats?'

'We've got a slight problem,' Peter explained. 'Because we have windows and don't have a fire to keep the thatch vermin-free, we get lots of bugs. And rats.'

'Don't worry,' I said. 'We're used to them. We had a rat eat a hole in my rucksack while we slept in Banz. One or two rats won't bother us at all.'

'One or two rats, this ain't,' Nick said. 'Not by a long shot. Follow me and you'll see what I mean.'

Picking up the oil lamp he led the way to the guestroom and flung open the door. In the dark, dozens of black monsters bolted from the sacks of rice, scattering into holes in the floor and up into the thatch. This was the rice that the students ate!

'Right,' Nick said. 'I suppose it's about time we did something about this.'

For the next hour, we charged around the house with sticks and a spade. We chased rats across the floors. We attacked them up in the roof beams. We followed them around the outer walls. We ripped down internal studs to get at nests of juniors. It was a gruesome hour, but pretty fruitless. In all, we killed four and the villagers, attracted by the wild commotion from our hut, killed a fifth. Peter used the occasion to explain to his stupid cat that rats were the enemy.

'We've probably done as much as we can,' Nick said. 'Hopefully, we scared them off for the night.'

Oh yeah?

No sooner had Cora and I put our heads down than they were back. We were stretched out in the blackness of the room, when the first one snuck in through a hole in the raised floor close to my right ear and scurried past the back of our heads to the sacks of rice. Immediately on its heels came a second. And a third. Simultaneously we could hear the others up in the thatch and moving down the woven cane of the walls. In no time at all, the room was full of squealing fighting rats and the sound of crunching rice. We did our best to ignore them until we couldn't stand the loathsome din any more.

'BASTARDS!' I roared and scared the wits out of Cora.

We spent the rest of that night, and all of the next night, periodically flashing our pocket lamp on scrambling tangles of fur, teeth and tails, and hurling boots and other missiles to clear the room. This would give a few minutes peace in which we might doze in and out of fitful nightmares of vengeful rats that swapped the rice for our faces. Why, people would later ask, did you stay that second night?

Two days after our arrival at Kurumul, Peter showed us around the local tea factory and some of the surrounding plantations where groups of women were picking the leaves from rows of squat bushes.

'They spray from the air,' he told us, 'never warning the villagers or taking any precautions that might protect them. Lots of the chemicals used in places like New Guinea are banned in the countries that produce them. Yet, people here get landed with direct hits, often while they're still working in the fields. And when they come down with strange crippling diseases there's nobody around to tell them why...'

The following day 200 pigs were slaughtered in Kurumul in one of the biggest pig kills of the season. While the carcasses were placed in pit-ovens, Cora and I bade farewell to Peter and Nick and left for Nondugl to spend a few days with Mike Wallace. From there we would travel to Goroka where the annual gathering of the clans - a mighty spectacle by all accounts - was due to take place towards the end of September.

We would also, we hoped, be going to a place called Marawaka.

* * *

Mike Wallace was having a bit of a problem with the sorcerers of Nondugl.

'A woman died on her way to church,' he explained. 'I'm being held responsible, accused of possible sorcery, and there's a rumbling demand for payback.' He was philosophical about it, but also respectful of the power of the sorcerers among the local population. 'Two hundred years from now things will still be the same with the sorcerers. I don't suppose we'll see any great miracles in my lifetime. Sometimes I even wonder what we're doing here at all.'

We spent a weekend at Nondugl Catholic mission with Mike, playing chess in the evenings and drinking whiskey, or sitting outside in the moonlight, listening to crickets and watching fireflies. Twice during our stay, large war parties passed through on their way to wreak havoc elsewhere. On both occasions Mike stiffened at their approach.

On the Sunday of our stay, his *sang froid* was put to the test. An elderly man collapsed at mass. It had been yet another odd religious happening, with Mike in priestly robes and Teddy-Boy hairstyle, and the usual collection of painted warriors and women among the segregated congregation. There were mothers breast-feeding their children, and everyone in uproar when Cora and I walked in, and an irate woman pacing the lines of men looking, it seemed, for her husband. The mass was conducted by Mike in Pidgin, with an interpreter translating into *tok ples* - the local language. Five minutes into the ceremony the old man, who was wearing a pair of underpants on his head and an old jacket over his bark apron and arse-grass, went down directly in front of myself and Cora, crashing against a wooden bench on the way. Pandemonium erupted. Men on all sides jumped back. The bench in front cleared completely. Sorcery!

A wide circle gaped at the figure on the ground. The men shouted at one another. The women followed suit. The men began to shout at the women. The women shouted at the men. Mike, above at the altar, attempted to maintain the decorum of the occasion. More and more seats were vacated as panic rippled through the congregation. Finally Mike came to investigate. Considering the precariousness of his existing position around Nondugl, he was infinitely calm in the face of another possible calamity.

'Don't touch him,' Cora warned as I leaned towards the fallen figure. 'Unless you want to get blamed and end up like a bloody hedgehog.'

Then lo! A hush settled over the church. The old man was opening his eyes. He sat up and groggily pulled himself to his feet. Bewildered, he realised he had wet himself.

The crowd roared and he was ejected from the church with waves of indignation. After a few more minutes of confusion, Mike restored order and the mass went on. Until the next incident - the rout of a barking dog. Followed by the headwoman chasing another woman whose baby was crying.

'An eye for an eye and a tooth for a tooth,' Mike was telling the flock in Pidgin, 'was the law for before. It was not a good way. Killing in revenge was also the law for before. But now we must love everybody, not just those of our own line; because to God, there is only one line and all men and women belong to that line.' I couldn't help wondering if Mike was trying to build a space of refuge for himself.

I watched the faces of the men in my vicinity. Some weren't listening at all. Others looked puzzled. One chap was vehemently shaking his head. The day before I had seen him down in the marketplace. His daughter, a girl of about ten, was one of several young women and girls dressed in all their finery. They were for sale as potential brides to the highest bidders.

Later, over another game of chess, Mike expressed his profound relief that the man in the church hadn't died. Otherwise, his sorcery credentials would have been complete. And maybe his life. However, although he had escaped this time, he still faced the threat of revenge for the woman's death. And the sorcerers weren't letting it go. As we left on the Monday morning, we wondered how it would all work for him in the end.

* * *

Thomas Pelika, the 23-year-old Papuan cop introduced to us in Sydney by Small Eddie, had given Kundiawa police station as his address. If we could find him, we planned to stop a day or two before going on to Goroka. We were lucky: we arrived just as Thomas, a sub-inspector of the Chimbu province's police force, was about to leave for the 24-mile drive to Chuave where he was now stationed.

At first we hardly recognised him. In his peak cap, light blue shirt, dark blue shorts, knee-length woollen socks and gleaming black shoes, he looked older than the guy we had met in Sydney. But as soon as he saw us coming, a big boyish grin lit up his face, and it was Thomas from Sydney again.

'You have arrived just as you said,' he beamed. 'Come inside. You must meet my colleagues. Then you can come and stay at my house.'

After we had been introduced to everyone in Kundiawa police station, Thomas announced that we were leaving for the bumpy, headlong charge to Chuave.

'You in here with me,' he said to myself and Cora as he consigned a burly sergeant, three decrepit typewriters and our two packs to the back of his Land Cruiser. Across the way a sign in Pidgin reminded us that shitting in the street wasn't on.

On the outskirts of Chuave, a small bush settlement, we were flagged down by a group of people milling about a stationary PMV. A young woman, badly battered and soaked in blood, lay in the back on a makeshift stretcher. Several people explained that she had been bludgeoned by her husband and seemed to be dead. Thomas directed the group to the bush clinic.

'I will look into this matter later,' he told us. 'This man killing his wife is very bad.'

We drove on to his house, a simple, one-roomed, wooden building, lit by a kerosene lamp and raised on stilts.

'You can sleep here,' Thomas said. 'Next to my bed. And how are all my friends in Australia?'

We reminisced over dinner about Sydney and Small Eddie; and Thomas explained the mixed bag of duties of a Chimbu sub-inspector of police. They included watching his back with the sorcerers and running for his life if he crossed the payback line. He then presented us with a wooden bow, strung in traditional fashion with a strip of bamboo.

'This has been confiscated by my men during one of the Chimbu wars.' he told us. 'You bring it to Ireland with you to remember me.'

The next day Thomas finished work early and drove us on a sight-seeing tour of the mountains. He stopped twice and let it be known that he wanted to buy some arrows. On the way back, our path was lined with eager warriors displaying beautifully decorated ceremonial arrows. Thomas bought a bunch and handed them to Cora

'For your bow,' he said, 'and to remember the Chimbu.'

On our second night at Thomas' house, a row broke out in the local 'tavern'. Thomas' burly sergeant, who wanted nothing to do with it himself, came hammering at the door. Thomas listened for a short while, then grabbed his pistol.

'You must not open this door for anyone else,' he warned as he left. 'You must only open for me.'

After half an hour he came back looking worried.

'A very bad fight,' he said. 'Big trouble. We must be careful this night. Chimbu men might come. Not so long ago, a man was brought in to Chuave with twenty-seven arrows in his body.'

'Was he dead,' I asked. Thomas craned his neck and gave me an odd look.

It transpired that Thomas had been over-zealous in his intervention down in the 'tavern' and had pistol-whipped one of the protagonists before dragging him off to the lock up. He was now deeply worried about the man's condition and the clan response. Cora and I were deeply worried about guilt by association. Lying in the dark for the rest of the night, none of us slept too well as the village echoed with prolonged bouts of shouting and Thomas periodically stirred to check the location of his gun.

At one point a dog barked furiously outside and he was up like a shot, peering out the window, pistol in hand, as Cora and I lay flat on the floor close to the wall, waiting for a shower of arrows. In the movies, Thomas would now have armed myself and Cora with Winchesters. In the real world, we were all crapping ourselves.

The shouting was still going on as we slipped out of arrow-range well before daylight the next morning. The early start allowed Thomas to drive us to the top of the Daulo Pass before the sun rose so he himself could be back in time for work which now included the very real threat of a revenge attack by the Chimbus of Chuave.

'Wish me good luck,' he said as he turned his Land Cruiser, leaving us looking down from 8,000 feet on a vast ocean of cloud on which mountains floated in a circle.

'Good luck,' we both yelled after him.

Far from being killed by the Chimbus, Thomas Pelika went on to have an illustrious career, reaching the rank of Chief Superintendent of police. In 1992, he entered politics and in July 1997 became Minister for Internal Affairs for Papua New Guinea. On his third term in parliament, he suffered a stroke, and died on October 30th 2019 at the age of sixty-four, leaving behind a wife and four children.

We still have his bow and arrows.

CHAPTER 19

Line Bilong Marawaka

At the Air Niugini office in Goroka, the only place in town with information about travel into the interior, we asked how we might get to Marawaka. The woman behind the desk, an Australian of about thirty, looked at us for a few seconds.

'Marawaka?' she said. 'You want to go to Marawaka? Do you know who lives in Marawaka?'

'Who?' I asked.

'The Kukukukus,' she said. 'The Kukukukus live in Marawaka.'

'Besides the Kukukukus?' I asked.

'Besides the Kukukukus!' she howled. 'Besides the Kukukukus? Just a minute. I have to make a call.'

She picked up the receiver and dialled. *Happy days,* I thought. *We've landed.*

'Jim,' she hooted. 'Wait till you hear this. I've got two people here who want to go to Marawaka.'

More hoots from the other end of the line. She made two more calls, covering the mouthpiece each time to tell us that whoever was on the other end 'thinks you're completely bananas.'

'No,' she said in the end. 'None of them have any idea how you can get to Marawaka; but, tell you what, if you do get there or better still, if you get back, come in and tell us all about it.'

We called to a government office, a wooden building where we were met by a painfully thin man of about forty with a bushy moustache and narrow eyes.

'Excuse me,' I said. 'Can you tell us how to get to Marawaka?' He looked slowly from me to Cora and back again.

'Do you know,' he replied, 'that the Kukukukus live in Marawaka?'

'Yes,' I said and he considered the discussion closed.

Several more fruitless attempts caused us to check in despondently to Goroka's Lutheran mission guesthouse. It was a fortuitous choice.

On our second evening, one of the women who had been at dinner the previous evening didn't show up.

'She is in bed,' the manager explained. 'She is in terrible pain from a kidney stone.'

Funny how the world works. Not long before leaving Sydney, I was struck by a severe pain in my side that had come and gone erratically since childhood. Doctors couldn't make head nor tail of it. As Cora and I prepared to go into the bush, it knocked me for six in Sydney's railway station. This time, however, it didn't go away. It became so excruciating that I ended up in hospital. After a dose of morphine, I passed a kidney stone the size of a match-head. Afraid that this might happen again somewhere in the interior of New Guinea, I had the Sydney doctors prescribe me pethidine.

'I'm no doctor,' I said to the manager, a stout German woman in her fifties, 'but one of these might help.'

Twenty minutes later, the woman with the kidney stone came downstairs.

'God sent you,' she said. 'Now, where's that you want to go? Marawaka?'

'We Lutherans have a mission there,' the manager said. 'There are no missionaries at the moment; but a small plane flies in every Thursday. That is tomorrow. If you go over to the airfield now, you might be able to persuade the pilot to bring you in. But, be careful in Marawaka. The Kukukukus are a fierce people. They have the reputation of being the most warlike tribe in the Highlands.'

We hightailed it over to the airfield and found the pilot, a tall, fit-looking, clean-shaven Australian in his late thirties. When he heard that the guesthouse had sent us, he agreed to take us to Marawaka.

'But you'll need to come early in the morning,' he said, 'so that you and your packs can be weighed. I have to be sure that I don't overload the plane.'

'What kind of plane can be overloaded by two people and their bloody rucksacks?' Cora wanted to know as we left the airfield.

Thursday morning, we arrived two hours before the flight. The pilot, looking spruce and smart in khaki shirt and shorts, long woollen socks and sturdy boots, was waiting.

'What brings you to Marawaka anyway,' he asked as the weigh-in proceeded.

'Him,' Cora said.

'We read a little about the Kukukuku culture,' I explained, 'and thought it might be an interesting place to visit.'

'That,' he said, 'could be the understatement of the year. But you've picked a good time. Independence celebrations are happening this weekend, so there should be a big *sing-sing*.'

'Oh God!' Cora exclaimed. 'Don't tell me *that's* the plane?' I turned to see two men pushing a five-seater Cessna out of a hangar.

'That's her,' the pilot grinned. 'The real flying sensation.'

Cora, who hates flying, saw a Transit van with wings.

At 10.30 a.m. we were taxiing down a minor runway, me seated in front beside the pilot, Cora behind, and the remaining space piled high with mission supplies and our two packs. The pilot ticked off a checklist as he carried out the various steps that would get us off the ground. Then, at surprisingly low speed, we were airborne and rising shakily over Goroka.

For the next forty minutes we flew across the mountains in an exhilarating and sometimes terrifying ride. Instead of the smooth, almost stationary experience of an airliner, the little Cessna bounced around like a cork in wind. It shook. It swayed from side to side. It rose and dropped and jerked. And every now and then it seemed simply to stop, as the land beneath moved along ever so slowly. Everything below was visible: every village, every hut, every gathering of people. We sailed over green kunai slopes crisscrossed by brown foot tracks. We skimmed across the tops of mountains furrowed by sparkling rivers, and over great tracts of wild jungle. We then began to climb steadily towards a distant gap in the highest of the ranges ahead.

'Marawaka,' the pilot said, 'is on the far side of the pass. You know, the first time they had Independence Day celebrations in there, there were an awful lot of very disappointed people who had walked over the mountains for days to see Bikpela Mr. Independence.'

He then re-checked his instruments and didn't look at all happy as we hauled up along a deep gully, the plane audibly labouring and the tree tops coming closer. Soon, they were directly below and on both sides and there were birds, and a magnificent waterfall. A few minutes more and we had topped the pass and were turning, the plane dropping its right wing in a petrifying manoeuvre. Rigidly gripping the seat, I found myself staring sickly downwards at the swimming forest.

Cora hyperventilated in the back.

'There she is,' the pilot said.

The plane began to drop into a narrow, elongated valley girdled by tall mountains, one an extinct volcano. We aimed for a grassy bush airstrip that terminated close to a collection of circular thatched huts.

We sailed down the valley, arced into another sickening turn at the base of the old volcano, and lined up for the landing which came in a series of skids and bumps and a loud gasp of relief from Cora. As we slewed to a halt at the village end of the airstrip, the pilot let us in on a secret.

'You probably saw me checking the load as we came over the top. Well, we were overloaded by four hundredweight. That's why she was so sluggish in the climb and why the landing was so rough. Someone back there has thrown on some extra bags of rice when I wasn't looking. When I get hold of him I'll wring his bloody neck. He could've got us killed.'

As Cora and I wriggled from the plane, some fifty people lining the top of the runway stood motionless and stared. They looked very different from anyone we had seen so far. The women and children wore grass skirts and what looked like hessian sacks but were actually cloaks of beaten bark. Beads, shells, and strings of yellow cane-grass segments acted as jewellery. The men also wore bark capes and grass skirts, but their skirts were hugely bulbous. Made of as many as 250 layers, they were worn smooth along the line of the legs as if cut by a scythe. The men were armed with machetes, axes and bows and arrows. The degree of welcome or not was hard to gauge.

Quicker than we had expected, the pilot and two other men had dumped the plane's cargo on the airstrip and the pilot was waving cheerio. Next minute he was in the air and circling back towards the mountains. We were standing on the airstrip staring at the crowd that was staring at us. Nobody spoke. Nobody made a move.

'I wonder what we do now?' Cora said.

'I suppose we should talk to someone,' I said. 'But who?'

Just then a warrior in his late twenties strode out of one of the huts. He was wearing the Kukukuku skirt and a red headband and was weaving an armlet from fine yellow grass, using the bone of a bat as a needle. Pushing his way through the crowd he walked over and extended his right hand.

'Hello,' he said. 'My name is Jons. Welcome to my village.' He shook our hands and bowled us over with the next comment. 'The tourist board in Port Morseby did not tell me you were coming.'

'I'm hearing things,' Cora said.

I flashed back to the reaction generated around Goroka by the mention of the Kukukukus and couldn't quite marry it to the tourist board in Port Moresby.[21] All the same, we were glad that the ice had been broken. Other men were now coming forward to shake our hands and question us through Jons. Once they heard that we had come to visit their village and stay for a few days, they offered us the *haus kiap* close to the vacant Lutheran mission as our sleeping quarters.

'You come,' Jons said. 'I will bring you to the house.' He called out to the people standing around. Seconds later, Cora and I were being escorted by some fifty Kukukukus towards the river at the far end of the village.

'You will live here,' Jons said, bringing us into an empty rectangular hut. 'You will make fire here,' he pointed to a stone fireplace in the centre of the floor. 'And here you will sleep,' he waved towards the cane-grass floor. 'Now,' he concluded, 'you must eat.'

We were overwhelmed by Jons' efficiency and foresight. All possible requests were pre-empted. Firewood arrived via two young boys. Sweetcorn, tomatoes and onions were placed beside us by a young woman. Sweet potato was added by a *bikpela man* who had come to greet us. We sat in the middle of it all as if we had been hit over the head with a mallet. Were these not the fiercest of the fierce, the notorious warlike Kukukukus we had been so warned against?

'I will come in one hour,' Jons said, 'and show you my village.' Other than a few small children, everybody politely departed and we were left to our own devices.

'If my mother could see me now,' Cora said, 'she'd say "Girl, what did I rear for a daughter?"'

As promised, Jons was back within the hour to lead us around the village - several clusters of closely-packed mushroom-shaped huts shaded by trees. Everywhere, the villagers were preparing for Saturday's Independence Day celebrations.

'That is why everybody is working,' Jons explained. 'Making the bands for the arms and the head, getting the firewood, preparing the food, the small boys practicing with the bows and arrows, the children gathering the flowers...'

While he worked on his armlet with the bat bone, two women in grass skirts and bark cloaks passed: one carried a 20th-century, steel spade, the other a Stone Age digging stick.

Jons introduced us to six Lutheran 'evangelists' from Morobe who

---

21.   Jons had heard of this entity at the mission where he had also learned his English.

were busily carving hourglass-shaped kundu drums from freshly-cut tree trunks. The drums would be the only instruments at the festivities. The Marawaka people had no instruments of their own.

'Are the Kukukukus planning to send any warriors to the Highland Show in Goroka?' I asked.

This gathering of the clans, organised initially by the Australians as a means of breaking down inter-tribal suspicion and hostility and curbing warfare, was now an annual event. It was where Cora and I planned to end our stay in New Guinea. As soon as I had asked the question, I knew I had transgressed. Jons stopped dead, bat bone frozen above the next weave, a dark scowl spreading across his face.

'I have seen this before,' he said. 'In a *National Geographic* at the mission. This "Kukukuku". My people are not "Kukukukus". This means "thief" in our language. My people are the Marawaka people - the *Line bilong Marawaka*. I must write to the government about this. I think this name came from the white people. They used to steal from our gardens, so when we saw them coming my people would say, "Here come the *kukukukus*". Then the white people thought this was the name for my people. Yes, I must write to have this changed.'[22]

Hopefully, this misunderstanding has been cleared up.

On Friday, as the *sing-sing* preparations continued and Cora and I lazed about by the river, Jons joined us again. By now we were beginning to wonder how we were going to get from Marawaka to some point where we could pick up a truck or PMV going towards Goroka.

'Yes,' Jons said when Cora asked for directions. 'You must go this way.' He pointed to the far end of the valley and up into the mountains. 'But,' he warned, 'it takes a long time. Maybe four days. Maybe two weeks. Maybe you cannot go if you are not strong.'

'How far is it?' I asked.

'*Longwe,*' Jons said.

'How many miles?' I asked, 'How many kilometres?'

'One moment,' Jons said. He reached down into the folds of his grass skirt - and pulled out, of all things, a pocket calculator! 'Thirty-five miles to Wonenara,' he said after a few seconds of furious banging on the keys.

'Thirty-five miles?' I queried.

---

22. An alternative narrative claims that the name was coined by their neighbours who feared their murderous surprise raids on their villages.

'Yes,' he confirmed. 'Wonenara is the first big village. Then you must walk from there.'

'How far from there?' I asked. Once more he banged away at the calculator.

'Maybe one week,' he said.

We gave up. We would take it in stages. First to Wonenara and then to wherever was next.

* * *

Friday, September 15th: the eve of Independence Day in Marawaka.

We sat towards one end of the bush airstrip, looking up the valley as daylight was replaced by a full moon. Once night had settled, a row of fires sparked into life along the airstrip's perimeter. And out of the night, the clans of the *Line bilong Marawaka* came in all their primordial splendour to celebrate the third anniversary of Papua New Guinea's independence.

Bouts of yodelling would echo from the dark mountains. In the distance at first, then drifting closer. Sometimes, two or three groups closing in on Marawaka from different directions at the same time. Then silence - until the warriors and women burst from the forest in an undulating wave, yelling, waving weapons and sweeping across the moonlit airstrip to the fires and a further roll of welcoming ululation.

As the night progressed, the build-up of warriors and women created circles of painted ghosts around the fires. The men wore the bulbous grass skirts, along with small crown-like headdresses with salmon-coloured feathers, armlets of woven grass, and heavy bandoliers of shells and yellow cane-grass segments, wound many times across their chests. With their pig tusks and paint they looked fierce enough to warrant their reputation. The women wore skirts of grass, brand-new bark capes, and enormous quantities of shell jewellery, complemented by strings of the yellow cane-grass segments. Spears and bows and arrows were much in display. Several slender lengths of brightly decorated bamboo rose like totem poles

Relatives and old acquaintants greeted one another. *Bikpela men* made speeches. Women and children brought food to the fires. Along the airstrip, circles of people shuffled, danced, ululated and chanted. Although we were close enough to one of the fires to feel the heat, we resisted the temptation to join its circle, preferring not to taint the night with an incongruous presence.

Instead, we moved back a little and sat on the ground without a word, shivering in the mountain air and catching the drift of wood smoke. Occasionally, a warrior would walk by in the moonlight and greet us or stare at us, until eventually we were alone, witness to something so moving in its antiquity that it brought silent tears.

Returning to our hut, we left the door open to the moon and the night breezes, and lay on the cane-grass floor in our sleeping bags. Out in the ululating night, the pounding of the kundu drums reverberated along the valley. Bats flew in and out of the hut. From the river came the croaking of frogs; from the rainforest the din of insects.

There would never again be a night like this.

* * *

At sunrise, we washed at the river as the warriors and women gathered in the centre of the village: Everyone was painted in streaks of red, yellow and blue ochre. This was the day of the *sing-sing*.

'Good morning,' somebody said. We turned to find a fierce-looking warrior in full regalia, his face and body heavily painted. It was Jons. 'Everybody is very tired,' he said. 'But we must go. The *bikpela men* will talk now.'

The great orators did their best, giving forth with passion and exuberance, but the speeches fell on clay. Exhausted from the night's festivities, the gathered clans sat cross-legged in a blazing circle of colour, and dozed off in the morning sun. An exasperated roar might momentarily bring a twitch of life but it would be short-lived. A bit like midnight mass after closing-time on Christmas Eve.

The conclusion of the speeches, however, triggered a miracle. The shattered audience rose in a single wave, fragmenting into several circles, and the dancing began. In a sort of semi-trot, men and women went round and round, the men chewing betel nut and twanging the bamboo strings of their bows, the women munching on sticks of sugarcane. Chanting and ululating in unison, they danced for hours while Cora and I were pretty much ignored. Not so, however, the Morobe men.

Biding their time until the whole of Marawaka was in a self-induced trance, the six forgotten evangelists came leaping from one of the huts in a pounding of kundu drums that brought the whole place to a standstill. Dressed in flowing grass skirts and anklets, with strings of shells across their chests and woven armlets festooned with green leaves, they cut a mighty dash. But it was their headdresses that made the greatest impact. Looking a little like the paper boats of children, they were made of bark on cane frames, with gunwales of white feathers and a banana-leaf keel from which protruded a foot-high, diamond-shaped structure of cane and feathers.

Beating a loud, urgent rhythm from the drums, they formed a circle to which flocked the women and children from the dancing circles, to the dismay of the Marawaka warriors. From the looks on the women's faces and the embarrassed giggles, it was clear that the evangelists were considered to be totally off the wall.

'Ah, there you are.' Jons was beside us, accompanied by a gangly boy in his mid-teens. 'This boy will go with you in the morning. He will show you the beginning of the track to Wonenara. Come with me now. We will see the men being picked to go to Goroka.'

'Will Marawaka be sending any women?' Cora asked, noticing their absence in the line-up.

'No,' Jons frowned. 'Last year we sent some women and they fought very much. They must not bring a bad name to Marawaka.' Jons had evidently missed the stories doing the rounds about the *men* of Marawaka.

The warriors were chosen, two hundred of the finest clansmen of the *Line bilong Marawaka*. In a few days they would begin the long march to Goroka; and if Jons wasn't exaggerating, Cora and I would find them sailing past as we flopped up the faces of mountains.

As night fell, the cooking fires were kindled and the people gathered in circles to hear the orators of their tribe bring the day's activities to a close. Cora and I retired to our hut with a selection of arrows purchased from some of the visitors. Serenaded by the river, the frogs, owls and insects, we lit our own fire and tossed in some taro and sweet potato.

I remembered an eight-year-old boy who had one or two funny ideas about himself and wanted to travel the world to see what its hidden ends had in store. He would have been well pleased.

As sleep took hold, the words of African-American poet, Langston Hughes (1902-1967), filtered through the polyphony of the night:

> *'Hold fast to dreams*
> *For if dreams die*
> *Life is a broken-winged bird*
> *That cannot fly'*

* * *

Our guide was waiting for us at the upper end of the village just after sunrise. He escorted us through the rainforest as far as the *smellwarra* (smelly water), sulphur springs about half an hour along the Wonenara track. He left us in a belt of tall Pandanus palms where the track began to climb. By the time the first fire-smoke seeped from the huts of Marawaka, we were well above the valley. It was a beautiful morning, cool at first, then gradually warming to a pleasant, dry heat. There were birds and butterflies and dewy spiders' webs; and as Jons had predicted, the going was tough.

An hour out of the valley the first of the home-going Wonenara men caught up with us. A stocky muscular man of about forty, he was wearing the full traditional dress, complete with cloak. He had a bow and arrows over his shoulder, a machete in his right hand - and a red biro through his nasal septum. He sat with us for a while and we exchanged some sign language. He smelled of wood smoke, as we ourselves did, and was impressed by the weight of our packs and our bundle of arrows. He walked with us for some time, always staying behind and stopping whenever we stopped. When the climb steepened, he tired of us and went on ahead. He would see us, he indicated, in Goroka. Later, we heard him yodelling from further up the mountain, the sound carrying through the forest and being answered from behind. More people coming from Marawaka.

We forded a stream and climbed again, up along the exposed spine of a narrow ridge, the track following a line of rock, gouged into footholds by bare feet over thousands of years. It was hot in the open, and the steps were just too far apart for an easy stretch. Soaked in sweat and completely whacked, we stopped and were joined by the oncoming Wonenara people. Two men and three women were beating their way up the mountain at an astonishing speed. One of the men carried an axe, the other a machete. Light loads. The women were weighed down by *billums* of sweet potato slung on their backs and supported by forehead straps. Food for the journey home. One of the women carried a baby in a second *billum*.

'*Yumi go* [Let's go.],' the man with the axe said, urging us to get up and walk.

'Knackered,' I explained. 'Tired. Exhausted. Shagged out. Need to rest for a while.'

The two men had a smoke and waited, saying nothing. The women laughed at the state of us and darted off up the mountain. The men finished their cigarettes. Without another word, each picked up one of our packs.

'*Yumi go,*' the axe man said again. And as Cora and I struggled towards the 10,000-foot pass, the men carrying our packs casually smoked. Neither rested nor stopped again - nor would they return the packs - until we reached the village of Yhani that evening.

At the top of the ridge the view back towards Marawaka was spectacular: great peaks rising out of the jungle and pink serpents of cloud weaving through the trees. Further up, we entered the cloud forest - cool, damp and silent except for the squelching of mud. And a heavy shower that soaked us in minutes. At a kunai hut alongside the track, we collected a third man and two more women, one of whom was grey-haired and elderly. In the latter part of the morning the cloud lifted and we found ourselves emerging from the bush onto a razorback ridge with magnificent views of the jungle-covered valleys far below.

This was as good as it gets.

The afternoon was met by a massive thunderstorm and rain that sliced in by the thimbleful. Within minutes, we were cold, wet and miserable. Meanwhile, the descent down the mountain had turned into a runnel of mud and water through which Cora and I tripped and skidded. Our unshod companions smiled sympathetically and pranced along without a bother. Emerging briefly from the forest, we slid down a wet kunai slope where the older woman finally cracked. Grabbing Cora's hand, she guided her down the most difficult section, choosing the more treacherous route for herself and leading Cora to the safer footholds.

At the Kukukuku village of Yhani, eight hours from Marawaka, we were passed over to the villagers who showed us to the *haus kiap*. One man immediately lit a fire to dry our clothes. People then began to arrive from all corners, bringing food and water. In no time at all, we were among a circle of some twenty men and initiated boys who were sitting around the fire and watching our every move and every item we pulled from our bags. A tin can with a lid! A plastic cup! A pocket flashlight! A group of women and children crowded the doorway but weren't allowed in. The three oldest men in the group were introduced as *bikpela men,* one being the village headman.

We made tea in the biggest pot in the village. Poured into bamboo sections with powdered milk and saccharin sweeteners, it was a major hit. The village men, having now chased the women, turned the event into a big ceremony in which the *bikpela men* got first take. Sometime later, when the crowd had thinned a bit, we made a second pot of tea, whereupon the headman produced a small packet of 'cuptea' biscuits.

Unknown to us, he had earlier bought them at the village trade store to mark the occasion. Only to return and find that the first round of tea had all been drunk. But he had said nothing. Even when we offered to make more tea he showed no great interest. But, once the second pot had been made, he immediately produced the little packet. By now, the group had shrunk to ourselves, the headman, two younger warriors and three boys, but there were only four biscuits. He offered Cora one, then me, but we assured him that one would do. The other men got one to share and the boys got the third. He then sat up with his own biscuit and showed us what 'cuptea' biscuits were for - dunking of course.

In an ongoing conversation that relied heavily on signs and drawing pictures, he went on to tell us that we would have to walk another two days at least before we'd be able to pick up a vehicle for Goroka. The heavy clay on the dirt track was impassable for vehicles after rain and it rained every day on the high passes. Only one vehicle, a government tractor, had ever made it as far as Wonenara. When it arrived, women from the surrounding valleys flooded in with bags of sweet potato to feed it. And by the way, he said, be careful in the Lamari Valley: they're all cannibals.

In return for our tea, he offered us a seat at an initiation that was taking place that night in one of the huts; but once we entered we would have to stay until morning and we were just too tired for that. Instead we sat outside in the frangipani-scented night with a small gathering of bark-cloaked warriors and women, listening to the chanting and singing, and watching another full moon climb from the mountains to throw silver light on trees, pig fences and the thatch of the village huts. Back in our own hut, the headman was looking after our gear.

In the morning we set off along a dirt track through well-populated countryside and arrived around noon at Wonenara where we met a Goroka man who was slowly going out of his mind trying to introduce modern farming and new crops to the villagers. We then wound along a narrow valley past numerous hilltop villages before climbing again into the cloud forest. Shortly before dusk, as we looked in vain for a clear space for our tent, it began to rain. We were at the top of a pass, afraid that darkness would catch us without a spot for the night, when there in the middle of nowhere, sat a small thatched shelter. It had been built for people like us. We lit a fire, used an anorak, billycan and plates to trap rainwater spilling from the roof, and cooked a meal. Fed, watered, secure, and dry for the night.

In the morning, we climbed for several hours before working our way down into the Lamari Valley to an unexpected welcome. Outside the first village we ran into a man who explained with great excitement that there was a four-wheel-drive in the valley. A few more bends in the track and we saw a group of warriors and women surrounding a parked Toyota Land Cruiser, in which there were six deliriously happy Papuan evangelists from the Asaro Valley. A minute later, the fascination switched from the evangelists to us and we were set upon in a loud chorus of exclamations. A group of small, curious men armed with bows and arrows, mobbed us. Some rubbed our skin, then looked to see if the colour had come off. Others pulled through my shirt at the hair on my chest and pointed to their own bare chests. Clearly I was a freak. The women then joined in the fun. As Cora had her hair tied back and we were both dressed in shirts, hats, boots and jeans and looking a mite dishevelled and muddy, they must have assumed at first that we were both men; but one of them quickly sussed the situation and grabbed at Cora's breasts for confirmation. 'Aye-e-e-e!' she called and they all joined in, men tugging chest hair, women pulling breasts.

'Ciarán,' Cora pleaded half seriously. 'He-e-e-elp...'

That we had come from Marawaka across the mountains amazed them all: back there, they said, they were all cannibals. The evangelists told us they were going to the Highlands Highway in the morning. They would pick us up if they saw us.

From then on it was a pleasant walk to To'okena, except for a twisted knee that began to give me trouble towards late afternoon and was made worse by the weight of my pack. Food for the day had consisted of one green tomato and a passion fruit, both of which were found by Cora along the track, until we reached a village at four o'clock and were able to pick up some sugarcane and a pineapple.

* * *

We landed in at To'okena's Swiss mission to find a young, fair-haired nurse tending a man with an axe wound to his head. Heidi was the only person in residence. Astonished to see us, she explained that things were a bit rough at the moment, that whispers were threatening the mission.

'A kid from a neighbouring village died on his way to the mission school and the father blamed his death on the 'poisoning' sorcery of the To'okena people. So, no more children from that village were allowed to attend our school. Then a second child died here in To'okena and the father of the first child claimed that this was his own 'poisoning' revenge. Now there is a lot of trouble between the two villages.'

Tribal wars had brought other previous woes, Heidi told us. Like the time the mission had unwittingly played host to visitors from an enemy clan and had subsequently been attacked by the warriors of To'okena. And now the mission was again in a state of siege.

'Down the valley, in the village where you were given the sugarcane and pineapple, one of our staff rolled her Land Cruiser over the edge on the mountain track and a 16-year-old boy in the vehicle broke his jaw. The villagers grabbed the sister and held her for a time against the boy's life and she has since had to flee the valley as the mission was attacked by warriors and the issue is still simmering.'

There were powerful sorcerers in To'okena, Heidi explained, who were in competition with others of neighbouring clans to see who could sing most people to death. The mission was now high on their target list. This had implications for me and Cora. We were *wantoks* who could easily figure in revenge calculations, a charming thought for what would be our final night in the bush.

It was Friday morning and we were woken at sunrise by the ululation of many voices. Thinking at first that our hour had come in some unfortunate error of local judgement, we bounced out of bed and dressed in a big hurry. But, no worries. The voices belonged to a band of people on their way to Goroka for the gathering of the clans. There were about fifty of them, men and women trotting along the track and singing, then stopping to dance and wave their weapons before trotting on for another few hundred yards. Heidi told us that Highlanders could cover up to forty miles a day in this manner.

After breakfast we sat outside the mission and watched the warriors and women of the mountains pass by. Many of the men had hair woven into thin plaits that finished in pigskin. Their eyes were watchful, their weapons ready, as they passed through this village of the stranger. The women carried *billums* of sweet potato. They had come from Marawaka and Wonenara, and the villages further down the Lamari Valley, dancing out of a land that time forgot into the 20th century and the final resting place of an old civilisation. The people of To'okena watched in uneasy silence as the strangers passed.

In the afternoon the deliriously happy evangelists careered into To'okena and Cora and I had our ticket out. They were going as far as Kainantu on the Highlands Highway and they were exhausted, they told us. Up all night with village fleas. At the village of Obura, large numbers of people were gathering, coming in from all directions and waiting for the PMVs that would take them to Goroka. By midnight we ourselves were back in Goroka where we stayed with a local family as the Lutheran guesthouse was booked for the night. All through the dark hours the town echoed with ululating voices as the mountain people flocked in for the Highland Show.

On Saturday morning, a few hundred yards from the showgrounds, Cora and I stood on a Goroka street and watched the long formation of warriors and meris making their way to the annual gathering. Seventy-four Highland tribes, in full ceremonial dress, had come to town. Shuffling a few steps at a time, the huge procession sang in what was more a drone than a chant, with the men twanging the bamboo strings of their bows. We tagged along to the showgrounds where we joined a handful of non-Papuans, and thousands of Papuans, for one of the last great tribal spectacles on Earth.

All morning, the clans arrived at the showgrounds, each new group charging through the gates in a pounding of drums and a display of weapons and feathers, until the entire showground was an ocean of colour and sound. They came from every quarter: the flute-players of the Chimbu; the mudmen of the Asaro Valley with their mud helmets and bodies covered in blue ochre; the penis-gourd wearers of the Sepik; the Hagen clans with their bodies glistening in sump oil; the Huli Wigmen of Tari; the two hundred hard-muscled men from the *Line bilong Marawaka* and countless others. Thousands upon thousands of warriors and women, dancing, singing, ululating and waving weapons. Walking about among them, we ran into Peter from the VSO community school at Kurumul, and the poor exasperated agricultural man from Wonenara, and an Anglican priest we had met in Koinambi when we visited Catherine Sutton from Currabinny.

For the next two days the great swaying mass of warriors and women would sing and dance and raise huge clouds of dust and stare at, or laugh at, one another's attire, and occasionally fight. It was one of the most moving events we would ever witness.

On the final afternoon, we were close to the action when our friends from Marawaka went by, chanting and waving their weapons, bulbous skirts and headdresses bobbing in the sunlight, paint and pig tusks giving their best aura of ferocity. Last year, somebody said, they had brought with them some strawberries, pineapples and tomatoes from the Lutheran mission garden, then bought a quantity of each vegetable available at Goroka market, and displayed the lot as the agricultural produce of Marawaka. They won first prize as gardeners.

Somebody else said that the other tribes would only participate in the gathering on condition that the *Line bilong Marawaka* were held under lock and key at night.

These were the feared and terrible warriors whose warlike disposition earned them awe and adulation. They looked every bit of it. As they trotted past, several of them recognised us and waved. People spun around to see who the hell could possibly be waving back. That remains my final memory of the great gathering of the Highland clans of Papua New Guinea.

A couple of days later, we flew back to Cairns. As hand luggage, I carried three bows and thirty arrows. Cora carried a machete strapped to our tent.

Those were the days.

CHAPTER 20

Rub-a-dub-dub

Greg McManus, a social worker with the Australian air force, liked the Shoalhaven idea so much that he reckoned he and his partner, Averil, would follow in our path later in the year. Tall, curly-headed, bearded, and in his mid-twenties, Greg had once hitchhiked to Western Australia for an eclipse of the sun, stayed twenty minutes, then hitchhiked home again. Averil, a thoughtful woman with darting eyes and shoulder-length, blonde hair, was a keen bush person who wanted nothing more than to retreat into the forested folds of New South Wales and walk with her feet on the earth.

On Sunday, October 22nd 1978, a few weeks after returning from New Guinea, we set off from Nowra as planned in Alan and Chris' Land Rover. After forty-five miles of dirt track, we reached Nerriga - a few houses and a pub - where we stopped for a drink.

'She's treacherous,' the old boy at the bar said of the river. 'Feller drowned there not too far back. Tried to take a kayak down.'

'What about rubber rafts?' Alan asked.

'It don't make no difference,' he said. 'River's rough. You don't want to go down there. No sir. Not at all.'

'That was a bit off-putting,' Greg said as we climbed back into the Land Rover.

'People are always telling you not to do things,' I said. 'If you listened you'd never get out of bed.' Needless to say, that quelled all doubts.

At the ford it was obvious that the warning was without merit. The river couldn't have been more benign. Running through a rocky basin of eucalypts and wildflowers, with butterflies flitting across its surface, it sparkled and gently danced. Even more reassuring, there were two kayakers already at the river.

'People sometimes come here on Sundays,' one of them said, 'to do a one-mile run downriver to where there's an exit spot.'

'Greg and I might go with you for that bit,' Averil suggested.

Good idea, we all agreed.

When we unloaded the Land Rover, Greg's eyebrows began to rise at the mountain of gear spilling onto the riverbank. Two tents, two cameras, two rucksacks, my guitar, five onion bags of fresh vegetables, two cardboard boxes of tinned food including desserts, and the bunch of books to be read as we bobbed downstream to the strains of the guitar, took up an awful lot of space. The rubber rafts came next, one orange, one yellow. The orange one, which belonged to myself and Cora, was the one we had used in Cape York Peninsula, the one that warned: 'Use only under adult supervision'. This would be its final trip. Alan and Chris' raft, brand new, said nothing about adults but maybe it should have.

Curiously enough, when the rafts were spread out, they occupied less space than the gear. When they were inflated they occupied even less again.

'That ain't gonna fit,' Greg said, but we managed to confound him.

'Maybe Greg and I should just stay here and kind of wave you guys off,' Averil said.

'Not at all,' I said, 'there's plenty of room.'

'Ciarán,' she said, 'where?'

Right enough, the boats looked pretty full. Nevertheless, logic won. Greg scrambled onto the yellow raft with Alan and Chris. Averil hopped aboard ours and we pushed off for Nowra, three pairs of feet dangling in the water.

'I had almost forgotten how this thing has a mind of its own,' Cora said as we were taken by the current. Seconds later we suffered our first misfortune. Averil lost a paddle, leaned out to grab it, toppled overboard, and almost brought Cora with her. Once she was back on board, we set off again, only to be whisked away with some force through a narrow channel that ran between a small island and the riverbank.

Spinning out of control, we were swept onwards into a chop of white water towards a tree that leaned unreasonably into the river. Luckily, the current swung us clear. We sailed around a bend into a long deep stretch of quiet water and were able to regain control.

'Very pretty forest,' the slightly eccentric Averil said. 'But we'll never see the fairies again until we get back to nature.'

On both sides, the bush rose along rocky slopes to sixty feet. We could see large lizards. And a crimson rosella in a bottlebrush tree. We then noticed the lack of a second raft. We stopped paddling and drifted.

'Smell the gum trees,' Averil said.

'Listen to the birds and the water,' Cora said.

After a short vexed lull we spotted something floating downstream.

A plastic paddle. And hot on its heels came a second. Something was wrong upstream.

We pulled to shore, retrieved the floating paddles, tied up the raft and went back upriver. On the far side of the bend we found the second raft, beached and full of water. Chris, wet and shaken, was standing beside it. A drenched Greg was unloading the contents.

'We steered a bit more to the left than you guys,' Chris said. 'But when we hit the rapids we lost complete control. We were caught by the current and swept up against that overhanging tree. The river flooded in over the back of the raft and pushed it right under the tree. Greg and I managed to hang on but we lost the paddles. Alan is back there, dangling on the tree. Once we'd got clear of the rough patch, Greg swam ashore and dragged the raft in on its rope. This is a bit worrying. We're only five minutes out and we've sunk a bloody rubber raft.'

Minutes later a wide-eyed Alan appeared.

'Those two kayaks,' he said. 'They've capsized on the bend. Maybe we should think a bit more about this before we go any further.'

'I've thought about it,' Averil laughed. 'I'm getting off right now.'

'Me too,' Greg said. 'Enough excitement for today.'

Some people would consider this a time to cut their losses, but not the sons and daughters of *Róisín Dubh*.

'I'm going on,' I said. 'I can't come all this way to turn back.'

'I'll go on too,' Cora said. 'Maybe if we have something to eat we'll all feel good again.' Cora would in later life put this down to 'lemming influence'.

Being from that other island, Alan and Chris were undoubtedly impressed by this Celtic Boadicean resolve. Or maybe they carried it themselves. After baling out, dumping the sodden cardboard boxes, drying the wet clothes and having a sandwich, they were heart and soul ready to go again. None the less, Cora and Chris skirted the next rapids on foot while Alan and I, splayed flat along the gear, shot the rapids on our own. Greg and Averil gave a final wave as we passed out of sight.

And so began the great 1978 expedition into the Shoalhaven Gorge.

* * *

Clear of the rapids, the river mellowed and Cora and Chris climbed back into the dinghies. For the next hour we drifted downstream at a steady pace in the kind of trip we had dreamed of. As it was our first night we pulled off the river early, making camp beside a still black hole. Peace was absolute. Nothing but the sound of birds and insects, and a light breeze sifting through the trees. We built a fire of driftwood, using dried eucalyptus leaves as tinder. And as termites and beetles fled the crackling timber, and sweet-smelling smoke wafted over the camp, I took out the guitar. A bottle of whiskey was cracked open and before we knew it, we were alone in the darkness with our fire and the company of bats, moths, crickets and frogs.

'Man,' Alan laughed as we drained the whiskey, 'I very nearly turned back after we'd hit that tree. We had absolutely no control of the dinghy and that was one hell of a shock.'

'Let's just hope that it's all like this bit,' Chris added. 'But why do I have an awful feeling it might not be.'

It's as well none of us was clairvoyant.

* * *

That first morning on the Shoalhaven was pure silence, accentuated by the ripple of the river and intermittent bird calls. We had breakfast on sand crisscrossed by the drag marks left by lizards during the night. We soaked alfalfa seeds in water (Alan's idea) so we'd have fresh sprouts in a couple of days. We then broke camp and ambled down a sandbank to where the boats were tethered. A startled wallaby took off in a series of dull thumps. We loaded the boats and pushed off. We were the new-deal us.

'See you in Nowra!' Chris yelled as the yellow raft took the lead.

Almost immediately we were in a rough current; but after some initial caution, we managed somehow to keep our noses with the flow. Until a roar downriver prompted us to pull over. White water was waiting. Alan and I went to investigate and decided to again lie flat across the gear on each raft, tuck in the paddles, hang onto the rowlocks, and splash through the rapids.

The weighted dinghies proved remarkably stable and we cleared the run without a hitch. Cora and Chris got back in the boats and we paddled on. Armed now with a strategy, we cleared several more sets of rapids without a problem.

By midday, rapids were being slotted into three categories. There were 'clear runs' when the four of us stayed on board and coasted through, relatively sure of a safe passage, important in the absence of helmets or life jackets. The next grade were the 'limpets' when Alan and I did our thing splayed across the gear. Finally there were the 'walk-throughs'.

These were pretty lethal stuff, where conditions were so violent that it took all four of us, barefoot and stripped to shorts, to run the boats through on ropes, sometimes with all the gear removed to avoid it being lost to the river. Hopping from wet rock to wet rock, often across churning water, we'd follow as fast as we could, playing out the rafts on their thirty feet of rope, tossing the rope ends to one another, and manoeuvring through situations where one slip would have cut the music. Sometimes the pressure was so great on the ropes that we were in danger of either having the boats ripped from our grasp, or being pulled in after them.

'No reading or guitar-playing today,' Cora would say.

Early in the afternoon, shortly after we had seen a platypus in the river, we discovered a fourth condition: a waterfall that stretched from one riverbank to the other. There was no option but to unload and carry everything around, including the dinghies which would simply have tipped over if we had run them through.

'Wouldn't you say that there was something incongruous about that guitar,' Chris laughed. 'If I didn't know better, I'd say the owner was a complete and utter lunatic.'

It was now becoming clear that we were in for an unquantifiable ride. Although we had good maps they didn't show river conditions. We had no idea what lay downstream. But, as the day drew to a close, after some more waterfalls and climbs down rock faces, one thing became evident: the longer we followed the flow, the more the prospect of going back upriver seeped off the menu. It was also clear that the nineteen feet a mile calculation back in May was a bit of a clanger: the river looked set to drop the first 1,500 feet (the drop in elevation to Badgery's Lookout) in one go.

On the third day we descended into the gorge in deadly earnest. We were now alternating between the good, the bad and the worse. In the deeper pools we could glide along. In rougher water we were holding the boats to a course and crashing through some moments of adrenalin-pumping glory. But, more often than not, we were in various kinds of trouble as waterfalls or runs of rock-strewn rapids were negotiated by our riverside ballet where a misplaced foot could have dire consequences. Even at its most genial the Shoalhaven was capable of nasty turns. During one of the more gentle runs in deep water Alan and Chris were caught in a sudden swirling eddy and jammed against a rock face, in danger of being swamped again. That night, Chris had a suggestion.

'We're carrying too much weight. Maybe we should stop a day and eat some of those fresh vegetables and tins of pudding. We could probably do with the rest as well.'

We sat around the next day, playing music, stuffing ourselves with as much of the 'luxury' food as could be eaten in sixteen hours, and discussing the existence or not of Don Juan Matus. Don Juan was the Yaqui shaman from Sonora who was central to Carlos Castaneda's *The Teachings of Don Juan: A Yaqui Way of Knowledge*, a popular book of the counter-culture of the day which was first published by Castaneda through the University of California Press in 1968 as his master's thesis in anthropology.

On Don Juan, Alan was a believer. I was a sceptic.

'But Ciarán,' Cora said, 'you haven't read the book.'

'I know,' I said.

Holding the high ground from such a controversial position is what's known as a quare trick.

'The river is locking us in,' Alan said at some point during the day. 'The walls of the gorge are getting higher and the river is getting worse. Those long runs of white water, and those waterfalls and rock faces, would probably make any attempt to go back upriver on foot impossible. Every night feels a bit like hauling down your rope after abseiling from the point of no return.'

'How far would we have gone?' Cora asked.

We figured we had covered no more than ten miles.

'Today was beautiful,' Chris said. 'Yet, this is probably the scariest place I've ever been in my life.'

Moments were given to the pondering of that sentiment.

* * *

On the fifth morning, we maintained our descent with conditions worsening by the hour. By midday, despite our best efforts, we had lost the rafts four times when the ropes were torn from our hands as we danced along the rocks. On three occasions it was clear that we'd be able to retrieve them once they had cleared the rough water. On the fourth we were set to lose the orange raft and its contents so I went in after it. Seconds later I was being churned along, sometimes below the water, sometimes above. During one of the latter moments I heard Cora and Chris yell 'Rocks!' just before I hit them. The resultant underwater tumble was a reminder that white water is full of bubbles. But I did manage to grab the side of the raft and travel with it until I could drag myself to the riverbank.

'You've got to agree,' Cora said, very annoyed, 'that was pretty bloody stupid.'

The morning of day six saw myself and Cora bobbing through a rocky defile on a fast-running current, a bit of a gamble as there was no way of getting off the river and no way of knowing where it led. However, the flow eased after a quarter of a mile and deposited us on some rocks on the lip of the next waterfall. There, in bright sunshine, we waited for Alan and Chris. Ten minutes passed. They didn't come. Nothing for it but to leave Cora with our raft and go back and see if they were okay.

'And how will you manage that?' Cora wanted to know. 'There's no riverbank.'

'Climb along the rocks.'

'Above the river? What if you fall in?'

'I won't,' I said although there was no historical evidence to back this up.

'Oh sweet Jesus…,' I heard in a mutter, 'please give him a dig for me.'

It took some time but upriver, exactly where we had left them, I found our expedition's other half waiting for a puncture repair to dry.

'As soon as we got on the water,' Alan said, 'the boat snagged on a submerged log.'

'Half the dinghy went flat,' Chris said in her rippling laugh. 'We'd have gone down like a stone if we'd been out on the river.'

With hindsight I suppose we should have given that some consideration but we didn't. And when we arrived back to where Cora was waiting we found her perched motionless on a rock. She was calmly watching a five-foot red-bellied black snake make its way up towards her. Although not an immediate threat, red-bellied black snakes, with their neurotoxins and myotoxins, were also worth some consideration. I don't think we did consideration too well back then.

For the next three days we wound our way downriver until we were deep in the belly of the gorge. At times, we'd skim across the currents to avoid the worst of the river. (With shallow draughts, we could often beat our way across the precipice of a waterfall before being whipped over.) Other times, we'd have to inch our way along walls of rock to carry the rafts and all the rest of the gear over some insurmountable barrier. Finding a chunk of fibreglass wedged among the rocks was a reminder of how lethal the gorge could be. It had probably belonged to the kayaker who had drowned. 'The footprint of a ghost,' Chris called it.

At the end of each day we'd find us a flat sandy spot, cook a meal, roll a joint and talk about the river. How one of us had slipped. How we had to drag one of the boats off a tree stump. How a particular set of rapids, or a waterfall, had almost done for us. How the whole thing was becoming a bit of a duel. The past, the present and the future were all river. And as we lay down to sleep, consumed by images of surging water, the Shoalhaven scurried past, a living, scheming demon with a whole night to plot the next day's shenanigans.

It had become one of those situations where you start to wonder how you ever got from there to here?

On the afternoon of the eighth day the balance of power shifted decisively towards the river when we almost had a casualty. At the end of a deep pool we came to a cleft in the gorge, a definite 'walk-through' of white water. Two channels, separated by a large rock, surged into the cleft. We decided to take one raft through at a time, the orange one first. Cora, Alan and Chris positioned themselves downriver so they could feed the rope from one to the other as the boat raced through. I paddled out to the dividing rock and climbed up on it. (Not the best idea when you think about it.) I then let the dinghy run.

Feeding out the rope, I made ready to throw it towards Alan. But there was a tangle and the whole thing was ripped from my hands. As it tumbled into the rapids, spilling its contents right, left and centre, Cora, Alan and Chris ran downstream over the rocks to grab what they could. Among the items saved was my guitar, which coursed through several hundred feet of white water but was kept afloat and dry by its PVC case. Among the items lost were a pair of my jeans which had in the right-hand pocket my Swiss army knife. We also lost the raft, but found it shortly afterwards in an eddy downriver. Meanwhile, as spilled contents were being retrieved, I was in trouble back at the rock.

On losing the raft, I had, without thinking, jumped into the river to swim for shore. Caught immediately by the current, I was swept forward. Grabbing for the rock, I managed to find a hold with my left hand while the right one found a submerged rock. Nothing short of an agnostic miracle. And thus was I left, yelling *Help!*, arms straining and legs stretched in front. But, no matter how I yelled, nobody else could hear a thing.

Realising that I would soon be missing if I didn't do something, I took the only course available. I let go with my right hand, somehow reasoning that, if I could hold on with the left, I'd be swept in against the rock where the force wouldn't be as great as in mid-stream. It worked. I managed to climb out; but the scare threw a lengthening shadow on the gorge. A watery version of summit fever could get you killed. As those who seek the summits say, there are old mountaineers and bold mountaineers but there are no old, bold mountaineers.

Earlier in the day, Chris had taken a fall and had injured her left leg, causing us all concern. Down in the gorge, incommunicado, that could also have been big trouble. That evening, boxed in by the walls of the gorge, we encountered a series of waterfalls that required high-risk manoeuvres, including racing across an obstacle course intent on whisking us to a bad end. By the end of the day, everyone was cut, bruised and exhausted. It was becoming clear that, if we continued on downriver, someone was going to be injured. How on earth would we then get out of the gorge? As we made camp I put forward a terrible proposal.

'Maybe we should throw in the towel and try and get out of here before one of us is killed.'

'Man' Alan smiled, 'that's the best idea we've had all day.'

Cora and Chris added great big nods of the head.

Decision made? Just like that? I was stunned. 'Are we all sure?'

'Take a wild guess,' Cora said.

'But keep us posted,' Chris laughed. 'Any other little trips you have up your sleeve.'

Drawn by some primal urge, there was a collective sigh. Neither relief nor sorrow was ever pinned to it.

'It was worth a try,' Cora concluded. 'But this place is beginning to give me the creeps. As well as that, it feels like it's going to rain.'

This was a new wrinkle.

Clouds had been massing all afternoon. A breeze had whipped up and there had been a dramatic drop in temperature. Our search for a suitable camping spot had yielded nothing until it was almost dark. It wasn't the best - a sandy slope that ran a short distance uphill to the wall of the gorge - but we couldn't risk going on. The tents now stood pitched among some stunted trees back from the river, while we wondered what a flood might do. Australia was renowned for flash floods and we had little space in which to retreat. Just upriver was the last waterfall we had negotiated. A hundred feet downriver lay another significant drop. A storm here could be high up the risk profile and we knew it.

Shortly after nightfall, we had the first flashes of lightning as the weather took a turn for the worse. Then the rain came. First a few large lazy blobs spitting on our tents and pots. Then the absolute opening of the skies. In a last act as we abandoned the campfire and made a run for the tents, Alan stuck a stick into the sand at water level.

'We'll keep an eye on this during the night,' he said, 'so we can see what's happening down here.'

The Shoalhaven River is 203 miles long and has a catchment area of some 2,700 square miles. The headwaters rise on the eastern slopes of the Great Dividing Range at an elevation of 4,500 feet. When it rains in the catchment, an awful lot of water can pack into the gorge and it can pack in fast. Before leaving Nowra, Greg had warned us not to camp too close to the river.

'If it rains a hundred miles up some tributary, you could be suddenly hit by a wall of water that comes ripping down the gorge.'

As the rain hammered down on our tent, I reminded Cora of this. Anxiety-charged fits of sleep followed. During the night's black hours I got up three times with a mix of adrenalin and dread to check how our stick was doing. On the third occasion, I found Alan down by the river.

'The stick is gone,' he said. 'We need to get the hell out of this place.'

By morning the Shoalhaven was churning dirty foam and bits of trees through a wet, grey world that promised more of the same. The water level had risen more than three feet and was still rising. Hungry and damp, we could do nothing but huddle in our tents and ponder the pickle. Early in the afternoon, the rain stopped for an hour and we managed to get a fire going to cook a meal. We then moved the tents as far up the slope as possible and stuck another stick in the sand before the skies opened again. On one front we now had a rising river: on the other, a sandstone wall. By late afternoon the second stick was half-immersed in surging brown water.

Tomorrow, we decided, no matter what, we would have to get out of the gorge.

Curled up in one of the tents, we checked our maps. Good news of sorts: a bush track curved to within a half-mile of the river. Bad news of sorts: to reach it, we would have to cross the flood and negotiate our way up the gorge wall.

'You know,' Chris chuckled, 'I couldn't imagine this happening with any of the other people we know. Could you Allie..?'

But a decision was made. Down here was danger; up there was escape. There was only one thing for it. Alan and I would attempt a crossing in the morning. If we found that we were likely to be swept over the lower waterfall, we'd turn back. The low draught of the rafts would be in our favour, but...

'Why,' Alan laughed, 'do I feel like I'm holding the parcel when the music stops?'

* * *

It was late into the morning before a lull in the rain allowed us to light a fire and have breakfast. Alan and I then brought one of the rafts as close as was safe to the upper waterfall. Cora and Chris took the 30-foot rope that was tied to its nose. They would feed it out as we crossed. If it looked like we were being swept away, they would haul us back.

'If this was a bookie's,' Chris said, 'the money would be on the current.'

'Remind me again,' Cora added, 'about that gentle cruise downriver...'

'That,' Chris grinned, 'is what the Aboriginals call the Dreamtime.'

We launched the raft and struck out, paddles hitting the water like rotor blades. As we'd hoped, the low draught prevented the river from taking a good hold, but it would still be a race to reach the far side before we were taken by the lower waterfall.

'A piece of a tree!' Cora yelled. 'Coming over the waterfall!'

Apart from the danger of it hitting the dinghy, an entanglement with the rope could have pulled us downstream. There was a fiercer burst of paddles while Cora and Chris moved to higher ground and raised the rope. The threat sailed past. We paddled on and made it across.

'There,' Alan said with the kind of laugh you might expect from someone who had just been shot at. 'That was easy.'

On the far side, our luck held. We found a route up through the trees to the rim of the gorge. It would be a slow climb with our equipment, but it was possible. Then came a niggling doubt. Maybe we were being impulsive? Maybe the rain would stop? Maybe the gorge wasn't really that bad? Maybe the worst was behind us? Maybe we could go on? What! In defence, I would offer the words of 19th-century philosopher, Henry M. Taber:

> *'Doubt is the herald of progress; the genius of reason; the pathway to truth; the advance guard in the contest with intellectual darkness.'*

We walked to where we had a commanding view downriver to see if things got any better. They didn't, affirming and vindicating our decision to get out. We had won the contest with intellectual darkness.

By the time we got back to camp, it was raining again and too late to pack up and flee the gorge. Darkness would have caught us on the climb. We had no choice but to chance another night on the sandbank. We would get everything ready for the morning so that all we had to do was pack tent and sleeping gear, eat and go. As the rain danced around us, we sat in Alan and Chris' tent, swaddled in sleeping bags in the light of a flashlight, and I got out the guitar.

'Nero,' Alan said, 'eat your heart out.'

Much time has since passed. It's been long decades since we last met and we have all probably ploughed most of our furrows. Yet I have no doubt that, were we four to somehow connect again tomorrow, the conversation would spin on a single bunch of crazy days.

* * *

The rain lasted until morning, by which time the river had risen again. Then the sun appeared. Down in Hyman's Beach, however, Greg and Averil were having seizures. Two days after dropping us off at Oallen Ford, Greg had gone to Nowra's kayaking club with a question that had begun to bother him.

'What's the status of the Shoalhaven River? Downriver from Oallen Ford.'

'Un-navigable,' he was told.

'Oops,' Greg said and went on home to tell Averil.

A week later the rain came and they watched the river rise at Nowra until it burst its banks. Finally, Greg's nerve cracked. The result was impressive.

As we sat on the sand cooking breakfast, we heard an odd sound. At first we thought it was the river, but could then clearly make out the percussive clatter of a helicopter. Gradually, it came into sight, flying up the gorge. Now, it was hovering forty feet overhead and blasting sand all over our instant scrambled eggs. As we stared up in disbelief, a side door opened and a figure in an orange jump suit and helmet began to drop down on a wire. Greg!

'I thought I'd find you all dead,' he said as he landed in our midst. 'I couldn't take the suspense any more. So I asked one of the guys at the Navy base [where Greg was a social worker] who needed to put in some flying time if he'd run me up the gorge. The river is really bad all the way down and if the rain comes on again you'll be in deep shit. We can lift you out, but you'll have to leave the gear 'cos we can't hang about up there while you pack up.'

Although the offer of a lift by chopper to Nowra was tempting, we turned it down and arranged instead that we'd chance another night by the river and that Greg would come with the Land Rover to the track on the far side at noon the following day.

Thus the great Shoalhaven run of 1978 drew to a close.

Eleven days after leaving Oallen Ford we emerged from the bush onto the track, having made three runs across the river - still in deadly spate - early in the morning. We had then relayed our gear in stages from the bottom of the gorge and through the forest. We were bruised, bedraggled and dreaming of a bed. But it was a beautiful calm day, the bush with its insects, birds and butterflies bursting in freshness and colour.

'Listen,' Chris said.

'What?' Cora asked. 'I can't hear a thing.'

'Exactly,' Chris smiled. 'Silence. For the first time in eleven days I'm not listening to the bloody Shoalhaven River trying to kill me.' Then, in perfect timing, we heard the sound of the Land Rover.

'Never again with you guys,' Chris said.

'And if there's a god up there,' Alan added, 'let this be known.'

But it was all good-natured. Over the coming years, we would meet again in Ireland and Australia.

A few days later, Alan and Chris handed me a present. I unwrapped it to find a replacement of the Swiss army knife that I had lost in the gorge. Engraved on one side were the words, *'Rub-a-dub-dub.'*

NEW ZEALAND

Aukland

Hamilton

Rotarua

EAST CAPE

Mt. Egmont

Ngauruhoe

Palmerston North

Picton

Wellington

Aathur's Pass

Franz Josef

Fox Glacier

Mt. Cook

Christchurch

Twizel

Routeburn Track

Queenstown

Invercargill

Stewart Island

CHAPTER 21

Two Months In New Zealand

When we left for New Zealand on the night of November 20th 1978, Alan and Chris drove us to the airport. Tom Wilson and Glenys were also there to see us off.

As we all hugged and said goodbye, there was a deep sadness about the occasion - we were leaving good friends behind - but there was also the lure of New Zealand and the rush of continuing on the journey that would prove to us that the world really was round.

Landing in Christchurch after midnight, we took a taxi into town and booked into a B&B in the city centre. We woke up in the morning to a beautiful city of old buildings and parks set on the meandering Avon River.

Our first priority was to locate Viv Holmes. During a trip around Europe in the early 1970s, Viv and a friend had stopped off in Belfast where they became teachers in a secondary school on the Falls Road. We had met her through Jean Campbell, a mutual friend, in 1972 and had remained close friends until Viv left Belfast. We then lost contact. However, as far as we knew, she was living in Christchurch.

In a café close to the old Victoria Clock Tower we made a plan. Viv was a teacher. If she was in Christchurch, we would most likely find her in some school. We took a taxi to the headquarters of the Department of Education.

The official we met was sympathetic and looked up the records.

'She's not with us,' he said. 'But, if she works in a private [Catholic] school, she wouldn't be on our records. So, here's a list of all the private schools in Christchurch.'

We returned to the B&B and Cora went out to the nearest phone box where local calls were free. On her second attempt, she reached a school secretary who knew Viv.

'She doesn't work here,' the secretary said. 'But I know where she does.'

Cora rang the school.

'She not here,' the secretary said. 'But I'll hang a note on the staff notice board to say where you are.' Two hours later the B&B owner knocked on our door.

'There's a friend of yours down in the hall,' he said, looking puzzled.

Viv, was waiting at the bottom of the stairs, her large eyes agog under her fringe.

'Where in the name of Jesus have you two come from?' she said.

Half an hour later we were drinking wine on the living room floor of Viv's flat while Viv played audio tapes of children she had taught in Belfast.

'I must go back soon,' she said. 'I'm feeling all nostalgic.' [She would go back, but not for another twenty-eight years.] 'But now, that you two have dropped out of the blue, where will we begin the adventure? Maybe the mountains?'

On our second afternoon Viv had us out in the Southern Alps, sitting on a mountainside of pine and lupin above the spectacular Erewhon Valley. A valley so immense that it took a while to appreciate its scale. Viv, an aorta of knowledge on all things New Zealand, explained the origins of the vast fan of gravel that formed the valley flats.

'The gravel was dumped by the river over the last two million years. In times of glaciation, huge amounts of debris would have been brought down by the glaciers. Over time it spread across the valley to form the flats which are hundreds of feet thick.'

We then reminisced again on her time in Belfast while a mix of sunlight and cloud wove its magic across saw-toothed snow peaks, enormous glaciers, braided river channels and magnificent, multi-hued lupin displays.

'Yes,' Viv said of the lupins. 'They look lovely with all the colours. But they're a curse. An invasive species. Like all the other crap introduced to New Zealand, they're impossible to control. Take for example the deer. In the late 1800s and early 1900s, 250 red deer were introduced for so-called sport. With no natural predators their numbers exploded. Now they're wreaking havoc on the process of tree regeneration across the mountains. Then you've got the gorse, the feral cats and the possums...'

As we delved into invasive species (a pet hate of mine), Cora lay back in a sunlit clearing of tussock grass.

'Ignore me,' she said. 'I'm having a snooze.'

'Looks like a good idea,' Viv said. 'I might follow the fine example.'

I must have dozed off too because I woke up again.

'I'll be in Palmerston North with my family over Christmas,' Viv said on the way back to her flat. 'But I've arranged for you to spend

Christmas in Christchurch with my boyfriend, Robert. You'll meet him tomorrow.'

'We wouldn't want to impose...' I said.

'Robert and I wouldn't hear of any other arrangement,' Viv said. 'We'd be very offended if you chose to spend Christmas on some mountaintop.'

'Thank you very much then,' I said and went on to outline our own plans of spending the rest of November and most of December in the South Island before going on to the North Island after Christmas.

Even more perfect,' Viv said. 'Robert and I are planning to go on a camping trip around the East Cape of the North Island after Christmas, so we can all go together. It's all Māori land up there. I think you'll enjoy it.'

Sound as a pound, we said and stayed two more days.

* * *

Leaving Viv and Christchurch behind, we took our first big step into New Zealand's extraordinary landscape by heading south-west across the Canterbury Plain towards the Mount Cook region. The plain, a broad patchwork of braided rivers and pastoral perfection separating the Southern Alps from the Pacific, was New Zealand's food basket, producing eighty percent of the country's grains, crops and seeds.

Turning north-west from Timaru, we journeyed on to Lake Tekapo and a village of the same name that faced onto the drama of the Southern Alps. Lake Tekapo, we read, derived its intense milky-turquoise colour from fine rock flour, ground by glaciers and suspended in the water.

Forty miles south-west of Lake Tekapo, we stopped at the settlement of Twizel to stock up with food. Built as the base for the Upper Waitaki hydro-project that began construction in 1968, Twizel was a new town: streets spreading out in a radial pattern from the centre and walkways to provide safe havens for pedestrians. Shelterbelts and windbreaks had been added as part of a project that was transforming the formerly treeless landscape of the Mackenzie Basin into a haven for wildlife.

From Twizel, we walked two days to the entrance of Mount Cook National Park, wild-camping overnight on the shores of Lake Pukaki where we enjoyed stunning views of Mount Cook. As with Lake Tekapo, the sun striking the surface of the water of Lake Pukaki bounced off its rock-flour particles in brilliant blue.

At the Mount Cook visitors' centre, we put some coins in telescopes to scan the glaciers and slopes of New Zealand's highest mountains.

'Don't even think about it,' Cora said.

'I'm not,' I said.

'You are,' she said. 'I can always tell.' To be honest, I wasn't.

We bought an ice cream, donned the rucksacks and took off across broad treeless flats to the base of Mount Sefton where we pitched our tent, intent on hanging out for a couple of days.

The Mount Cook area, declared a national park in 1953, consists of 70,696 harsh hectares of ice and rock, with glaciers covering forty percent of its area and the lot dominated by the peaks of the Southern Alps, nineteen of which rise to almost 10,000 feet. To the Ngāi Tahu people, the mountains are seen as ancestors, with 12,220-foot Aoraki (Mount Cook) the most sacred of all. The European habit of climbing its slopes meets with deep disapproval.

Although the whole area was virtually devoid of forest, this was more than compensated for by meadows of wildflowers, sunsets that glowed on the snow-packed face of Mount Cook and nights that were lit by fantastic skies where every star was a glittering diamond. Although it also had its edge.

You'd be lying in your sleeping bag in the silence, with the base of Mount Sefton not too far away, and there would come a roll of thunder. Except that it wasn't thunder: it was an avalanche up on the heights, tumbling down from massive snow shelves to crush anything in its path. Even though we figured we were a safe enough distance away, in the darkness there was always room for doubt.

During our stay, we did a couple of walks, nothing too strenuous, just enough to take in the enormity of the peaks and be able to say that we didn't just sit around. Hitching up with Ken Mahren from California, we walked to the Mueller Glacier, scrambled down a boulder slope into the desolate Hooker Valley, then went back to our tent for another night of tumbling avalanches.

On our way out the following day we stopped for a final look through the telescopes. An old man at the next telescope was staring up at the summit of Mount Cook.

'My son is up there,' he said. 'He left us one day to go for a climb and never came home. An avalanche took him. I come here every year on his birthday.'

His eyes brimmed and he put another coin in the telescope.

That's why Cora and I never climb that kind of mountain.

* * *

'Gold,' the owner of the old café said. He was a heavily-built, balding man with a huge moustache and a voice like rolling gravel. 'That's what made this town. There would be nothin' here if it wasn't for gold. Back in 1862 a couple of sheep shearers hit pay dirt at the Shotover River. That triggered the gold rush and this town grew out of it. It was called Queenstown because it was deemed "fit for Queen Victoria".'

We took his word for it, finished our coffees, re-stocked on supplies, and walked down through tree-lined streets to the shores of Lake Wakatipu, with its moored boats and views of the surrounding mountains. We then continued along the lakeshore for a couple of hours before camping beside a shingle beach and catching a large rainbow trout that we immediately lost when it hopped back into the lake. In the morning, we hitchhiked north to Glenorchy, a village perched against the aqua blue of the lake, some twenty-eight miles from Queenstown.

Originally a base of scheelite miners, Glenorchy was the springboard for one of the most outstanding mountain traverses in the world - the 20-mile Routeburn Track that links Mount Aspiring and Fiordland National Parks through vistas of mountains, lakes, forest, rivers and waterfalls that are picture-perfect. We both love walking in mountains. As well as providing spectacular views, they also tend to preserve the cultures of the people who make them their home. Although no communities lived along the Routeburn Track, we had chosen it on Viv's advice as our one big walk in New Zealand.

Another fifteen miles of unsealed forest road, overshadowed by the mighty Forbes Mountains, and we were at the trailhead. We then entered the forest at the Route Burn (river) and began to climb.

It was a steep two-hour haul through dense beech forest, across suspension bridges and past the beautiful Bridal Veil Falls to the rim of the Route Burn Gorge and on to the open grassland of Routeburn Flats. As we would be climbing again, we stopped at the Flats for a swig of whiskey from a bottle we had bought in Queenstown. To the north, snow-capped Mount Somnus rose 7,522 feet into a clear blue sky.

Back towards the trees we could see some of the introduced red deer that Viv had railed against back in the Erewhon Valley.

Another sharp climb brought us to the bunkhouse at Routeburn Falls on the edge of the tree line. We dropped our packs, went back outside, and sat on the ground to enjoy the views of the heavily forested Route Burn Valley and the Humboldt Mountains. To the sound of the adjacent waterfall, we drained the last of the daylight and the rest of the whiskey.

At the bunkhouse, a basic affair, nobody was in charge. Whoever turned up managed their own affairs, cleaned up in the morning and left the place in decent order for the next arrivals. We had six companions that evening: Marion and Kim from Wellington, Steve and Lucy from Melbourne, Andy from Kansas and Carol from Munich. Doing their utmost to add to the numbers were several endearing and mischievous mountain parrots known as keas.

Considered one of the most intelligent birds on the planet, the keas snooped around outside and inside the hut and grabbed at anything left unguarded until they decided it was time for bed, see you in the morning. Said to have developed their skills during the last Ice Age, they had a head start on us. In the morning they woke us up by sliding down the tin roof of the hut. When we went outside, we discovered that one of them had eaten a chunk of leather from one of Andy's boots. The culprit was on the ground choking.

'It's a diversion,' Marion from Wellington shouted from inside the hut. 'While we've been outside commiserating, his mates have been in here clearing out the grub.'

Ten out of ten to the keas.

Leaving Routeburn Falls, we climbed through wetlands and tussock flats into the Serpentine Range before sidling along the bluffs above Lake Harris, a lake so clear that we could see deep into its vegetation-free depths. Staying above the tree line, we crossed the Harris Saddle, then trekked along the exposed heights of the Hollyford Face to magnificent vistas of the valley below and the snow peaks of the Darran Mountains. After three hours of blistering sunshine, we re-entered the forest and dropped down in a series of sharp twists to the bunkhouse at Lake Mackenzie.

Within sight of the hut, we were met by a tragic reminder of just how fickle and treacherous New Zealand's mountains could be. A plaque screwed to a rock had been left *'In memory of Heather Anne McElligot, aged 13 years, and Bryan William Lamb, aged 13 years, who perished in a storm near this spot on December 19th 1963'*. Part of a school group, they had become separated from the others in a mid-summer blizzard.

We shared the bunkhouse at Lake Mackenzie with Tom and Mick, two sorry-looking, long-haired Australians who were the only people we had seen all day. The cause of their misery was outlined by Tom.

'We're confined to barracks. It's the blackflies. Swarms of the bastards attack as soon as you stop moving.'

An attempted walk along the lakeshore by the four of us ended in flight, confirming Tom's analysis.

'But the real problem,' I pointed out, 'is that the blackflies are also in the hut. They're coming in through the mosquito mesh of the windows that are open.'

'We'll be eaten alive,' Cora said.

'I know,' Tom said. 'But if we close the windows, we cook.'

We tried to suffer the bites, but the situation became intolerable.

'This is a bit like the midges at home,' I said in the end. 'The only way to sort it is to close the windows, kill all the flies inside, and suffer the heat until the sun goes down or the flies bugger off.'

Unpalatable as it was, there was four-way agreement.

'There's a Māori legend,' Mick said, 'that says that Fiordland was so beautiful that the gods decided that humans should never live here so they sent in the blackflies to do the dirty work.'

'Cunning as fuck,' Tom said.

In the evening, a cool breeze brought some respite and we were able to go outside to enjoy a flawless reflection of several snow-capped peaks in the surface of the lake as the bats swooped in to tackle a new wave of bugs.

Despite the blackflies, Cora and I stayed an extra day at Lake Mackenzie where we were joined by seven other people coming from both directions. The windows remained shut again as us old hands recounted the Māori legend to each newcomer in turn.

On our fourth day we walked three hours to Lake Howden, climbing again above the tree line before gradually descending past the 570-foot Earland Falls to the lake. We could have gone on to the Milford road, but there was great excitement at the Lake Howden bunkhouse. A Scottish woman was delivering news of sorts to five other trekkers.

'Some guy who was on magic mushrooms claims that he ran into a moa somewhere on the Milford Track. He said it was ten feet tall.' [The moa, a giant flightless bird, was considered by science to be long extinct.] 'Someday, somewhere' she prophesied, 'someone's gonna find a dinosaur.'

A big bearded guy from Christchurch offered a possible explanation.

'He might have seen a takahe. That's another big flightless bird. They used to think it was extinct but it was rediscovered in 1948 in the Murchison Mountains. It grows to maybe two feet and looks nothing like a moa. But the mushrooms could have filled in the gaps.'

The following afternoon Cora and I were back on the bitumen, hitchhiking south towards Stewart Island to trek its coast and bushland, checking out blue penguins, abalone fishermen, basking sharks and shoals of sharp-toothed barracuda.

At one of the bush huts, a few hours' walk from the tiny settlement of Halfmoon Bay, we did such a good job at welcoming new arrivals that we were mistaken for hut wardens!

* * *

During our passage back up north, we met Harry. This was significant. At this stage in our travels Cora had taken to calling every guy we met Harry. Hello, the guy would say, I'm Joe or Denis or Klaus or Abdul. Hello Harry, Cora would say, first chance she got. Then the real Harry came along, a tall curly-headed Dutchman travelling in a pickup with his long-haired Australian friend, Neil, who had the very Irish surname of Murphy.

'Jump in the back,' Harry invited. 'We'll take you as far as Franz Josef.'

'Now,' I said to Cora, 'this is the real McCoy. *Harry* has arrived.'

Frank, she called him, first chance she got.

With Harry and Neil, we crossed the Southern Alps through the Haast Pass and the gorge known as the Gates of Haast. Between Haast and Makarora villages, a distance of almost seventy miles there wasn't a single settlement.

Diverting from the main road, we stopped at the renowned Fox glacier which had dropped 8,500 feet during its eight-mile journey from the snowfields.

'It's over 900 feet deep,' the real Harry said. 'But it's receding. You can see how far it's gone back in the last few years.' He pointed towards the moraine we had passed on our way to the face of the glacier.

Arriving at Franz Josef town late in the evening, we booked into an actual campsite. After a much-needed shower, I was on my way back to the tent when I heard my name being called.

'Ciarán, is that you?' Followed by a loud 'It *is* you!'

In the semi-dark I had walked right past Kay Trulove, last seen during our three-day farewell party in the Sydney home she shared with Mark Ierace.

'Kay!' I said as we flung our arms around one another. 'A tent party is in order. Barring our friend, Viv Holmes, who lives in Christchurch, you're probably the only other person we could possibly know in the whole of New Zealand.'

'Last time I saw you two,' Kay said, 'you were heading for New Guinea. You know, a lot of people thought you'd never be back.'

'Give our love to everyone in Sydney,' was the last thing we said to a groggy Kay as we left in the morning after a wine session that had rolled into the early hours. Although we returned in the coming years to Australia, she and Mark had gone their separate ways. We never saw her again.

The next day we trekked out to the Franz Josef glacier which had a character all of its own. Moving under its colossal weight and emitting audible groans, the frozen mass had fragmented at its base into enormous upright columns. Coruscating figures of ice marching on the valley. We sat for a while, drank from the meltwater escaping from the ice, then turned north-east for Arthur's Pass, arriving to plummeting temperatures and a roaring blizzard. At the Arthur's Pass backpackers' hostel, we were the only visitors.

By morning the blizzard had passed and towering Mount Rollerston looked splendidly white in the sunshine. But we had to wait for the roads to be cleared of snow before we could set off again. Tomorrow would be Christmas Eve and we were on our way back to Christchurch. Travelling at speed in the back of a pickup, we were approaching the city on a dual carriageway when a car drew level.

'Look at those guys,' I said to Cora. 'They're smoking a bloody joint!'

Cora wagged a censuring finger - whereupon the passenger rolled down his window and passed across the joint.

'Happy Santa Claus,' he shouted and they sped on with a seasonal wave. As Christine Hakkers said back at Lake Toba, it was hard to escape the old ganja.

* * *

As planned, we spent Christmas day in Christchurch with Robert Loughran, his parents and his brother and were treated to their absolute generosity. While we ate dinner, Robert, a thin guy of about thirty-five, with brown curly hair and excessively good manners, sat in pressed shorts and pressed shirt and told us how he was once in India and offered to make a 'traditional New Zealand dinner' for his host family.

'I roasted a chicken, boiled some potatoes and carrots, added gravy and, hey presto! But the family, used to the spicy standards of Indian cuisine, wasn't that impressed.'

This resurrected tales of Lord of the Moon and our stay in Delhi which horrified Robert's mother.

'I've decided to change the pronunciation of my surname,' Robert said later in the afternoon, 'from "Lockran" [the only way I have ever heard this County Armagh surname pronounced] to "Lofran".'

The less said, the better, I warned myself. I didn't really need to have an opinion about that.

On Boxing Day we moved on, planning to meet Viv at her parents' place in Palmerston North. Robert would join us in a few days for the trip around the Māori lands of the East Cape.

It being the day that it was, the hitchhiking was slow. At the Clarence River Bridge, north of Kaikoura, about 140 miles from Christchurch, we gave up and slept under a tree. Next day, however, we quickly covered the remaining seventy miles to Picton, former whaling station and gateway to the islands and inlets of the Marlborough Sounds. We had time to look around before leaving on the evening ferry to Wellington.

Fur seals and flocks of sea birds colonised the rocky coast as we left the forests of Picton harbour and sailed for Cook Strait.

Forty miles to the north, Stephens Island was the site of a tragic milestone in the environmental catastrophes of New Zealand. In 1894, they built a lighthouse there. When lighthouse keeper, David Lyall, arrived, he came with cat in tow. Soon, he noticed that the cat was bringing him little identical birds that it had killed. When curiosity got the better of him, he sent specimens to Wellington museum where one of the curators identified the dead birds as a relic species of flightless wren - the only flightless perching bird remaining anywhere on Earth. The ecstatic curator set off immediately for the island, only to find on arrival that Lyall's cat, Tibbles, had become the only non-human animal in recorded history to have wiped out an entire species. Ironically, the wren was posthumously named Xenicus Lyalli - after the architect of its destruction.

* * *

Two days after crossing to Wellington, we left Palmerston North with Viv and Robert in a pretty loaded car. Heading north east, our destination was the Raukumara Range in the East Cape of the North Island, lands primarily owned by the Māori. Although some of these peaks reached to well over 4,500 feet, they were pimples compared to those of the South Island. But the region had plenty of forest, a fantastic coastline and clear sparkling rivers. And an introduction to sea eggs.

We spent the first night camped on a beach and the second and third in the middle of a large vineyard, courtesy of a Māori family. On the fourth afternoon we found ourselves a secluded riverside clearing where we decided to spend a couple of days. We tried to get permission from the Māori families who lived in the vicinity; but finding nobody at home, we pitched our two tents, lit a fire and caught some trout for dinner.

On our second day by the river, a car came trundling down the track and a young Māori couple got out.

'Good afternoon,' the man said with a big smile, 'I'm Hohepa and this is Amiria. We are the owners of this land.'

'We called to all the houses around,' Viv began to explain, 'to ask permission to camp but we found nobody at home.'

'Nothing to worry about,' Hohepa said. 'Everyone was away for the New Year's party. Traditionally, we put up a big marquee and anyone can come back to the tribal land and stay. There were lots of people there and we killed a sheep and cooked it in the *hangi* [pit oven].'

Amiria then went to the car and returned with a plate of wild boar and venison.

'For you,' she said, presenting it to Viv and Cora. They both then sat with us and shared some beers and small talk as we ate.

'Are you still hungry,' Amiria asked.

'No-o-o-oh,' we all chorused. But it didn't stop her. She went back to the car and left us with the biggest Pavlova in the world.

'Join us at the house tonight for drinks,' Hohepa invited. He gave us directions and he and Amiria drove off.

When we drove up that night to their home in the forest, Hohepa and Amiria were waiting with more food and drinks. A question from Cora about the origins of the Māori people led to a long discussion about culture and mythology.

'Māori and Irish mythologies bear remarkable resemblances to one another,' Hohepa said in the end.

We agreed that if we went back far enough, we probably all came from Hawaii or Connemara.

'Would you like to try some sea eggs?' Hohepa asked at that juncture.

Not having a clue what a sea egg was, we all said yes. Amiria went to the kitchen and came back with four sea urchins, each with a hole punched in the top.

'You just suck out the contents,' she said.

Up went the four arms and down the hatch went the contents. *I'm gonna throw up,* I thought as a thick sludge not unlike a mixture of snot, seawater and blood slithered down my throat.

'How was it?' Hohepa asked.

'Very nice,' I said, polite behaviour prevailing.

'Please have another,' Hohepa said and rushed off to the kitchen.

Cora and Viv looked stunned as I sat there, still full of polite smiles.

'Who's a big eejit,' Cora mouthed.

At the night's end we all promised to meet up again down the road but that was never likely to happen.

The following day we went to visit Rosie Davies, a friend of Viv's who lived near Te Puke in the Bay of Plenty where she shared a farm with her sister and brother-in-law.

'We have a Māori burial chamber on the land,' Rosie told us. She led us off across the fields to see it. In a shelf hollowed out of a small rise a skull and a collection of bones lay where they had been left by the people who once owned the land that was the Davies' farm.

'Although we don't know anything about who the person was,' Rosie said, 'we try and respect the site in the same way the Māori might have.'

We wondered how Hohepa and Amiria would have felt about it.

It was a short run from Te Puke to Rotarua where Viv's brother and sister-in-law, and their two young children, Jo and Steve, lived and where we and Viv stayed while Robert left for Christchurch.

* * *

Our first impression of Rotarua was that it smelled like the smellwarra of Marawaka. Viv provided the second.

'There are bubbling steam vents, boiling pools, mud-pots, geysers and sulphur deposits. In Māori homes, the women use hot water bubbling up in their back gardens to wash clothes while the kids enjoy the natural Jacuzzis. The thermal heat is also part of the town's heating system. The excess spews out of gratings along the streets.'

You'd think people couldn't get out of there fast enough.

'Poisonous gases too,' Viv added. 'They find cats dead in the streets.'

'How can anyone sleep soundly?' Cora asked. 'Live cats are bad enough.'

Cora hates cats.

We baled out after the three days; but before we fled, we called with Viv to the Māori Pa at Ohinemutu, where we visited St. Faith's Anglican Church. The attraction was a depiction of Christ etched into a huge plate-glass window. When you sat in the pews and looked out the window, you got the impression that the figure was walking on the surface of Lake Rotarua. Christ was a Māori chief, draped in a flowing, feathered Māori cloak. None of that blue eyed, fair-haired nonsense.

After arranging to meet Viv again in Auckland, we hitchhiked south to Lake Taupo - the flooded caldera of an ancient volcano - and camped a few days by a small river that carried the occasional floating white boulder to the lake. Cora took a photograph of a smiling me holding in my arms what looked like five ton of rock. We then continued to Tongariro National Park, a vast area of lakes, forest, desert-like flats and active volcanoes.

Tongariro, Ruapehu and Ngauruhoe form the southern frontier of the Taupo volcanic zone that contains two outstanding features: Ruapehu's crater-lake, one of only two in the world where glacial meltwater and boiling magma periodically combine in cataclysmic eruptions; and Ngauruhoe, one of the world's most active volcanoes which erupted forty-five times during the 20th century.

To the Ngati Tuwharetoa, the early inhabitants of the area, this was a place of great cultural and religious significance. Their ancestor, Ngatoroirangi the great navigator, had arrived here at the dawn of time. After exploring the region, the old man, frail and close to death, called to his sisters in his homeland in Hawaiki, the ancestral home of the Māori, to send him fire. When it came, it tore a trail of volcanic vents across the land, from Tongatapu through White Island, Rotarua and Tokaanu before reaching the feet of the dying navigator on the slopes of Tongariro. Ever since, the area had been at the heart of existence for the Ngati Tuwharetoa. It was therefore an act of monumental resignation when in 1887, Te Heuheu Tukino IV, supreme chief of the tribe, passed on the sacred lands of his people to the new nation of New Zealand.

We hadn't planned to climb Ngauruhoe until we were smack at the base of its cone.

Volcanic Activity, a sign warned. *During eruptive periods keep off slopes of Mount Ngauruhoe as gas, ash or rocks may be a danger.*

'What it doesn't tell you,' I noted, 'is what kind of advanced warning you can expect. The last time it blew, two years ago, there was none. It just shot rocks and burning ash four miles into the air.'

'Running down the slopes, being chased by something like that, would be a bummer,' Cora said.

However, having deduced that we could climb straight up the 7,516-foot cone, we dumped one of our packs in a park hut (void of wardens or other hikers), put a few items of food into the other pack, and set off. It was some time in the afternoon.

It began relatively benignly, with a long walk across the flats, then a gradual climb on the lower reaches to the base of the mountain proper. We then began to scramble, hand over foot, on steep slopes of scree. But this was no ordinary scree. This was a havoc of loose pumice that slipped and slid away beneath our feet. It was like climbing along the top of a giant slag-heap of coke, some of the pieces the size of a fridge, and all of it ready to give way underfoot. If that wasn't enough, the slopes had an additional surprise: here and there, perched atop the pumice, were massive boulders of heavy rock.

As the scree slipped beneath our feet, it loosened the layers above and occasionally dislodged the rocks. And down they came, sweeping away sections of the scree slope and threatening to subtract us from the mountain. Alternatively, we ourselves would dislodge one of the heavy rocks and send a landslide downhill with us surfing the wave. To avoid either of us swatting the other, we climbed a distance apart.

At the top, wrecked and soaked in sweat, we were met by a howling gale and the juxtaposition of three of the world's great wonders.

One was the caldera of Ngauruhoe, a demonic place of hissing fumaroles that fell down to a smoking vent, and a rising stench of rotten eggs from the yellow sulphur that caked its walls. Down in the depths there wasn't a great deal of activity, other than the occasional belching of thick smoke, but there was a terrible sense of threat.

The second was the snowy rim of Mount Ruapehu and the Tama crater lakes.

The third was the sunset. Away to the west, some 100 miles across the plains, sat solitary Mount Egmont (known today by its Māori name, Taranaki), beyond which the sun was sinking into the Tasman Sea in a blaze of orange.

'Do you know what?' it suddenly dawned on me. 'We're seven and a half thousand feet up and the sun is setting. That means that it has already set at sea level. Which means that it's going to be dark up here in no time.'

Sliding, rolling and dislodging half the mountain, we took off in a headlong dash, keeping ahead of a barrage of runaway pumice and boulders.

We did pretty well and made it safely to the bottom; but had it not been for a full moon and a clear night, it might have been a different story. And, believe me, there is no worse sound at night, as you tumble down a jumble of pumice and rock, than the rumblings of an overhead landslide.

In the park hut that night, sleep was engulfed by pyroclastic flows.

* * *

A vanload of stoned hippies brought us from Hamilton to Auckland. They put us up for the night in their commune and dropped us off the next day to where Viv was staying with two friends, Mim and Margaret. We were greeted at the door by Mim, a tall smiling woman who worked as a nurse in the city.

'So, *you're* the ones,' she said.

'What could that mean?' Cora wondered.

Inside, we were reunited with Viv in a great round of hugs and kisses.

On January 19th, our last day in New Zealand, we all went down to the harbour to protest against a visiting American nuclear submarine.

'What's that?' Cora asked as Viv produced some home-made wonder.

'Bacon and egg pie,' Viv said. The proper term, we later found, was Quiche Lorraine.

In the middle of our lunch, the big sleek sub arrived, being buzzed by a flotilla of small boats and a few wind surfers who rammed it. We threw some stones but were too far away to worry the Yanks.

Coincidentally, the next stage of our journey would bring us across the Pacific to the United States. We then hoped to complete a loop through Mexico, Central America and South America before returning to the States.

CHAPTER 22

Meeting The Family

We officially entered the United States at Honolulu on January 20th 1979. At customs we were pulled from the crowd by a bald, suspicious-looking official in plainclothes who evidently didn't like the cut of us.

'Are you carrying any U.S. currency?' he grunted.

'No,' I said, feeling the familiar border guilt crowding in.

'Where are you from?' he grunted.

'Ireland.' I said. The transformation was astounding. His eyes lit up like sunbeams.

'I'm Irish myself,' he gushed, shaking hands with both of us. 'Second generation, from County Offaly.'

'We're from Cork,' Cora said.

'Welcome to America,' he said. 'On you go.'

A few hours later we landed in Los Angeles and were met outside the airport terminal by my uncle Killian. Prior to that moment, he and I had never met. Killian, who at thirty-nine, was eleven years older than me, had left Ireland along with most of my mother's family before I was born. But I recognised the likeness to my grandfather who had been back to Ireland a few times. Neatly dressed in a brown suit and open-necked shirt, with a trim brown beard and bald crown, he threw his arms around us.

'Welcome to California,' he said. Jet-lagged and exhausted, we got into his car and hit the freeway.

'This,' Killian said, pulling a joint from the glove compartment of the car, 'is standard Californian grass.' Half an hour later, he reached into the glove compartment again. 'This,' he said, 'is *prima* Californian grass. Soon you guys will be meeting all the family, and that must be so fucking weird.'

On December 4th 1947 my mother's father, Gerry Anderson, left Cork to start a new life for his family on the other side of the Atlantic. Gerry had been a cabinet-maker in Cork where he and a partner had opened a factory and developed a thriving business until World War II came along. When the export of timber was prohibited, the business collapsed in 1945 and Gerry was forced to go off to England to look for work, a terrible ignominy for a man who had fought with the IRA against the British during the Irish War of Independence. Seeing no future there for his family, he began to seriously discuss with his wife, Lily, the idea of emigrating to the United States rather than watch his family go off one by one, a pattern common in Ireland at the time. Finally the decision was made and Gerry left for the U.S. Ten months later, he was joined by 22-year-old Kevin, the oldest son. And, on December 30th 1948, Lily followed with seven more of the children, leaving behind my mother, who had met my father and had chosen to stay in Ireland, and Brendan, who had an acute learning disability.

With the seven children in tow Lily travelled first to Dublin by train - in those days not the slick journey it is today. From Dublin they went by boat to Holyhead, and from there by train to Southampton where they all boarded the Queen Mary. Over the coming weeks she dragged the family more than 6,000 miles, first across the Atlantic to New York, then on to Los Angeles. A series of chaotic misadventures included the Queen Mary running aground on January 1st 1949 off Cherbourg in France, a port call it made before turning for America.

At the train station in Los Angeles, overwhelmed by relief and exhaustion, she was finally reunited with Gerry after thirteen months of separation.

'I can't wait to get home and fall into bed,' she told him, collapsing into his arms.

'Hang on a minute,' Gerry said. 'We haven't got a home yet...'

In the thirty years that had since passed, America had remained the home of my mother's family. Apart from visits home by Gerry and Lily, and one each by my aunts Eithne (with daughter Sandra), Maeve (with son James) and Fionnuala, all other aunts, uncles and cousins lay entombed on distant shores. Ours was the first visit from the oul' sod. Killian, as family ambassador, had been sent to meet us off the plane.

Killian, who harboured a genuine love for humanity in all its forms, was an artist and a poet. When we later went to stay with him, he showed us photographs of his paintings, many of them hugely surrealistic, with fried eggs for the sun and so on; based, he said, on that prima Californian grass.

'Where are the originals,' Cora asked.

'The paintings are just an expression of emotion, of feeling,' he explained. 'When I'm finished, I'm done with them. I pass them on to other people.'

One of his friends, a laid-back, searching soul named Dave, who grew grass for a living and had a mop of dark hair that complemented an impish grin, was so impressed by one of Killian's gifts that he knocked away an interior wall of his home as he felt the painting needed 'distance' to be fully understood. Dave's wife, clearly not in the same critical league, came home from the shops, failed to concur, threw Dave and painting out, and filed for divorce.

'But that's life,' Dave said as he drove myself and Cora down to Santa Monica beach in a January wind to build giant sand castles with army shovels.

'What's that at the bottom of your paintings?' Cora asked after a couple of days in Killian's flat. It looked like the lines of a polygraph test.

'That's my signature,' Killian said. 'Happened during the last big earthquake.'

Killian worked as a driver in an old people's home where he was so revered by the residents that when we went to visit, Cora and I were treated regally for being related. *How does he stay so young?* they asked us. When we drove with Dave, the art connoisseur, to San Diego to visit other friends of Killian's, we discovered one of the routes to eternal youth when Killian took advantage of the anti-aging apparatus the friends had rigged up in the garden shed. It consisted of a pair of ski boots attached to a plank attached to a rope attached to an overhead beam. I have a photo of Killian, in smart grey trousers and white shirt, arms folded, and suspended upside down from this odd contraption.

Killian's poetry came in a large volume, bound together by Aidan, another of my uncles. Entitled *Stuck Together Like A Trucker,* it was a brilliant compilation of poetry, drawings and humorous scribblings, among which were some irreverent masterpieces. Take for example the poem called 'MacArthur Parked' which opens up with:

Pigeonshit was on the genril
On his knee anon his face
(I was stoned myself, but the way he
Held his place) made it hard
For me to see how he was ever
Quick
He had pigeonshit for epaulets
Half an inch thick

On the day he picked us up at the airport, Killian first drove us to the youngest of my aunts, 31-year-old Maeve who had left Ireland as a baby, to return in 1973 as an auburn-headed woman of twenty-five who turned a few heads around Cork. (During a visit to the seaside village of Crosshaven, young guys in bars wanted to know if there were any more aunts like that left in America.) A woman of fun and energy with a terrific sense of humour, Maeve lived with her partner and her son, James. As a collector of beautiful things, she had turned her home into a museum of miniatures. Her collection of unusual keys alone ran into hundreds. Our stay with Maeve would be an artistic highlight on par with our stay with Killian.

On that first day, Killian followed the visit to Maeve by dropping us off with my grandmother, Lily, in whose Pasadena apartment we were to spend a couple of days. This would be the beginning of an odyssey that would bring us around all the Californian relatives. Lily was now a feisty 72-year-old whose 85-year-old boyfriend had recently rolled his car on the freeway.

'I'm safe enough,' she confided. 'He hurt his back a few years ago and can't do anything.' A cup of tea later, Killian left. 'Oh,' Lily said, 'would you look at that. Every time Killian comes around he does that.'

She reached up and started to uncouple all the porcelain dogs, cats and pigs that lined the mantle piece in varying permutations of public fornication.

* * *

The next three weeks were a swirl of events and cameos as we stayed with a steam of relatives all over L.A. who couldn't do enough for us, and met with others who came from further away. Shades of my own brothers and sisters, of my mother, of my grand-aunts who were sisters of Lily, were all to be found in the looks, mannerisms and idiosyncrasies of this pool of strangely-familiar strangers.

Kevin, silver-haired and silver-bearded, with a bald crown like Killian's, had become the patron of the family since Gerry's death in 1974. A lover of animals, he had a pair of semi-tame skunks in the garden. Kevin's wife, Bridget, who came from Turner's Cross in Cork, told us that we'd have to visit their son, Niall, up in the Sierra Nevada when we got back from Central and South America. Their daughter, Maureen, thought our slides of Papua New Guinea were outrageous. My cousin, Sandy, a speedy woman, was partying on the fringes of Hollywood. She was partying when we arrived with Killian. She was partying when we left. She couldn't remember that we ever called.

My aunt Fionnuala threw a Sunday bash that was my undoing (drank far too much, asked Maeve for a glass of water, poured it over my head and flopped onto the floor). Not the best impression. Consequently, Fionnuala's 13-year-old daughter, Angela, invited her school chums home the following day to meet the visiting relatives. And there was Angela's brother, Tommy, practising to be a singer. And my uncle Aidan, and Martha, his Mexican wife who showed us photos of my half-Mexican cousins.

I looked like Brian, they all said. He lived in Oregon and would be down in a few days.

In varying combinations of relatives, we were treated to everything L.A. could offer.

We went to the Planetarium for a light-and-sound show. We visited Chinatown and Universal Studios, and traipsed along the Avenue of Stars. We went to Forest Lawn cemetery where old IRA man, Gerry, was buried. We spent a day in Disneyland. We went with Maeve to the Watts neighbourhood, scene of the Watts Rebellion of 1965, to see the Towers of Simon Rodia, a collection of spiralling steel towers and mosaics built within the artist's own property and decorated with shards of pottery, glass, ceramics, seashells, figurines, mirrors and a miscellanea of other 'found objects'. We returned to Santa Monica Beach with Maeve and her son, James, for a spot of roller-skating and a viewing of the performing clowns of Muscle Beach. And we went up into the hills behind the city with Killian to listen to the dulcet sounds of Californian gunfire. Finally, we spent two days with Kevin's oldest daughter, Fiona, who lived in Orange City. We then left my guitar with the relatives, took a train from Santa Ana station to San Diego, and crossed the border by bus into Mexico. On the U.S. side nobody cared that we had met the relatives or that we were leaving: neither passports nor visas were checked.

MÉXICO, BELIZE AND GUATEMALA

U.S.A.

San Diego
Tijuana
Guaymas
Mazatlán
Sierra Madre Occidental
San Blas
Tepic
Ruíz
Guadalajara
Pátzcuaro
Petatlán
México City
GULF OF MEXICO
Campeche
Mérida
Palenque
San Cristóbal de Las Casas
Flores
Tikal
Chichén Itzá
Cancún
Isla Mujeres
Tulum
Belize City
Honduras
El Salvador
Guatemala City
Antigua
Lake Atitlán
Huetzaltenango

CHAPTER 23

Takers For What?

We were a long way south of Mexicali, and late into the night, before anyone bothered to find out who we were. The check, when it happened, was at a small roadside hut. Two friendly immigration officials - thin men with moustaches, military uniforms, pistols and peaked caps - shook our hands and stamped our passports.

'*Irlanda?*' one of them said. '*Bueno.*' We were off to a good start.

'Long may it last,' Cora said.

The border town of Tijuana had been a dusty hustle of ramshackle buildings, small businesses, loud music, horse-carts, burros,[23] crumbling trucks, young hopefuls aiming for the border, and American day-trippers wandering the craft shops of the narrow streets. Deciding to move on, we made our way to the booking office of *Tres Estrelles de Sonora* and bought tickets for the four o'clock bus to Guaymas, a port town more than 600 miles to the south. It would be a 16-hour bus ride, crossing the granite folds of northern Baja California before turning south from Mexicali into the Sonora Desert.

On board, men and women in straw hats dozed, smoked, shushed their chickens and threw up in plastic bags as we swung along on narrow pitted roads at speeds that gave far too much credit to road conditions. During daylight hours, single-lane bridges had a simple code: whoever flashed their lights first had the right of way. After dark the driver added a new angle, regularly switching off his lights to see if anything was coming the other way.

'We can only hope,' Cora said, 'that anything coming against us hasn't switched off theirs as well.'

It was a long sleepless night but the desert and its cactus forests, glowing under a full moon, made it a night of compulsive viewing. Casting moon-shadows on a blue-white world were giant Saguaro,

---

23.   Mexican donkeys.

multi-stemmed Organ Pipes, the strange Jumping Chollas (tree-like cacti with spider-leg arms), desert Ironwoods with wood dense enough to sink in water, and countless others of the plant species that made the Sonora Desert the most bio-diverse desert in the world.

By the time we saw the sun again, we were deep into Mexico. In villages of adobe, the people were rising: men in jeans and shirts, with straw hats of all shapes and sizes that stuck hard to their heads, even on motorbikes; women whirling by in dazzling dresses and shawls. Indian and Latin, then Latin-Indian, Latin-African and Indian-African. Men rode on mules like beings from a Sergio Leone movie. Not long after eight in the morning, we reached the outskirts of Guaymas, passing a long line of burros carrying vegetables into town. Here, the coastal fringe of the Sonora Desert met with the Sea of Cortez.

Alighting from the bus, we were joined by Merilyn - Australian and a traveller like ourselves - who had boarded with us in Tijuana. Exhausted, the three of us wandered the town looking for a cheap hotel (although Australia had stacked our coffers well, old habits die hard), but we kept being turned away by people who either didn't like rucksacks or thought we were a threesome up to no good.

Eventually, for $5 each (outrageous!), we got into the Ruby Hotel on the harbour, a rectangular, two-storey, flat-roofed building wrapped around a tiled courtyard. We had rooms on the first floor, with blue walls, doors that opened onto a walkway, and a westward view of the towering red monolith that overlooked the town. We slept for most of the day. The hotel owners were fascinated: their siesta only lasted the afternoon. When the markets opened, post siesta, we strolled among the kerosene lamps, goats and chickens, and bought some food to cook back in the rooms.

In the morning Merilyn decided to take a train from Los Mochis through the Copper Canyon to Chihuahua. Cora and I booked our room for an extra night, then headed off eastwards through a shanty town built of rubbish until we were back in the cactus forests of the desert. We stayed among the red hills until evening, returning to the seafront to watch the antics of the Magnificent Frigate Birds, black pterodactyl-like creatures that soared on the evening breeze with hardly a flap, using their deeply forked tails to steer. These master aerialists, with their bulbous red throat displays, were the pirates of the sky, swooping from on high to rob in midair the hard-earned catch of other sea birds. A display of aerobatics in sharp contrast to the clumsy grey pelicans that crash-landed below on the water.

Once the sun had gone down, people came to shop and shoot the breeze. As we moved about, we discovered the kindness of people. If we asked for directions, nobody said I don't have a clue. They said go down that way and turn right and go up this way and that way and you're there. Even if they hadn't a clue.

'This is a happy place,' Cora said. 'I like Mexico.'

'*GRINGO!*' came an angry roar. All of a sudden we were being accosted by a stubbly old boy in jeans, sandals, oil-stained shirt and battered straw hat. '*AMERICANO!*' he went on in a breath humming of drink. He spat in every direction and put up a fist. *Time*, I thought to myself, *has been cruel to this boy.*

'Hang on a minute,' I said. '*No Americano. Irlanda.*'

'*Irlanda..?*' he said in apparent bafflement. He lowered his fist and shooed a fly from his face. '*Bueno. Bueno.*'

Despite us having no more than a few words of Spanish, he invited us to a bar.

'*Americano* no good,' he said as if we had agreed on something. 'Rat-tat-tat-tat-tat!'

He raised both hands and sprayed the bar. We could only wonder what the *Americanos* had done to Mexico, apart from stealing half their country in the mid-19th century.

From that point on, every time we had *Gringo* thrown at us, we responded with *Irlanda* and it mostly worked. We had *amigos* all over Mexico.

From Guaymas we took a 12-hour bus ride to the coastal city of Mazatlán, immediately below the Tropic of Cancer. As we travelled south, with the peaks of the Sierra Madre Occidental to the east, the landscape morphed from the baked desert of Sonora to heavy scrub and, finally, to farmland, forest, coconut palms and houses raised on stilts that allowed hammocks to be hung underneath for the siesta.

Arriving in Mazatlán at half eleven at night, we had a hard time hunting down the cheapies, but eventually got booked into a dingy dive where a rat ran across my foot as we signed the register. The room didn't disappoint: it was a filthy mess, with stained sheets, a broken sink and a fungal effluvium seeping from the walls. A window, caged in wrought iron, opened out to a noisy street. We left first thing in the morning.

'Excuse me,' an American voice called from behind as we reached the street corner. 'Do you know how to get to Isla de Las Piedras?'

Doug and Jean, packs on their backs, had come down from California.

'Sorry,' I said. 'Never hear of it. What is it?'

'A cool place to be,' Doug said.

If Cora and I had a plan it was there and then dumped and we were all on our way to the Island of Stones.

A skiff ferried us across the harbour to a narrow peninsula that ran parallel to the coast. We then followed a sandy path that led from the boat-landing to the far side of the peninsula and a quiet settlement of flat-topped, concrete buildings, interspersed with huts of palm trunks and thatch. Simple restaurants among the coconut palms of the adjoining beach provided fried fish, rice, omelettes, refried beans and *huevos rancheros* (scrambled egg with tomatoes and onions), rustled up on adobe stoves by grandmothers, mothers and daughters.

We asked two passing horsemen about accommodation. They pointed to one of the restaurants, behind which were half a dozen thatched huts and an elongated concrete structure with a tiled roof, divided into several rooms. Each hut and room had two plank beds and a healthy population of large scorpions. (At night, when everybody was stoned on Oaxaca Gold, the scorpions delighted in crawling up and down the walls of the huts and the supporting poles of our restaurant.)

The old patriarchal owner, who was amazed to find that you could travel from California in two days, explained that the only available space was in one of the thatched huts. Cora and I insisted that Doug and Jean should have it. We would get the next free room. In the meantime, we could camp beside the restaurant.

'Camping is free,' Maria, the big homely woman who ran the restaurant, said. 'But you must eat two times every day in the restaurant.'

It sounded a reasonable deal, but the meals turned out to be a bit shoddy. I complained when I was served a section of bone left behind after a large fish had been filleted. Even the woman who had fried it up for me, and sprinkled it liberally with lemon, had to concede that I perchance had a point.

While I was lodging my complaint, Doug had his sleeping bag stolen from the hut.

In the afternoon Merilyn turned up - the train through Copper Canyon wasn't running.

'No more rooms,' Maria explained. 'But you can sleep here, on the restaurant tables, when the restaurant is finished for the night.'

Same deal: she had to eat twice a day at the restaurant.

Josh and Rolf were the more permanent of the ten transient residents of our home at Isla de Las Piedras. They were to be found in two of the concrete rooms. Josh, from the U.S., was about thirty, squat with a bushy beard and a big hairy stomach. He wore blue jeans and a red beach hat that covered his bald patch. Rolf was German, tall and skinny and in his late twenties, with the bleached, sun-scrunched look of a castaway. In ragged black waistcoat, jeans and baseball hat, he spent much of his day leaning against anything sturdy enough to take his weight.

'Come on in,' Josh invited shortly after we had arrived. 'What do you think of this place? I got scorpions in the roof, gigantic spiders all over the walls, a boa constrictor up in the rafters and iguanas in the roof tiles. I reckon the boa must eat the iguanas at night, 'cos he sure as hell don't do very much during the day. He just lies up there, havin' a snooze, then pops his head down now and again for a smoke. I get a great buzz outta that guy.'

A few days later, he confided in us that he was a half-baked cocaine mule.

'I came down here a coupla months back to do a coke run to the States so's I could get the money to come back down here again. But I can't straighten out long enough to get it together.'

Josh had spent so long thinking about it that the marijuana seeds he had tossed out the door when he first arrived were now healthy plants twelve inches tall.

Our first night at Isla de Las Piedras was a hectic one. Antonio and Sebastian, two brothers who lived in one of the neighbouring *palapas* and were of a similar age to the guests, joined us for the craic. With the moon rising, Antonio played his guitar and he and Sebastian sang while joints the size of bullhorns did the rounds. I was sitting on the ground facing the beach when I saw flames rising among the coconut palms.

'There's a house on fire,' I said.

'No, no,' Antonio said. 'It is somebody cooking.'

'If that's somebody cooking,' I said, 'it's the biggest cooking fire in Mexico.'

'He's bloody right!' Doug yelled. 'There *is* a house on fire.'

We dropped everything and raced down the beach to find a family battling a spreading blaze in the thatch of their wooden home. They were filling a bucket from an outside tap and tossing shovelfuls of sand onto the roof, but it was a losing battle.

'Right,' I said to Rolf (more organized than I should have been). 'The bucket is useless. Grab that tub.'

While Rolf and I ran to the sea and staggered back with a tubful of water, the others weighed in with shovels and hands to toss sand on the blaze. Taking turns to fill the tub we kept the water coming and managed over the next half hour to douse the fire, keeping it pretty much controlled most of that time. It was hard graft but we saved two thirds of the roof and most of the house. The middle-aged man whose home it was, was in tears. He shook our hands as we left and to each in turn said a huge 'Mucho thank you.'

Blackened and smelling of smoke, but with a collective sense of usefulness, we went back to the bullhorns, the moonlight and Antonio's guitar. Then, sometime around midnight, we all retired.

As Cora and I settled down, we could hear Merilyn sorting out her bed on the table closest to our tent. Twenty minutes later I heard a twig snap. Out through the fly screen, I spotted a dark figure creeping up on the restaurant. As quietly as I could, I undid the zip of the fly screen. When the would-be robber reached the sleeping Merilyn and her gear, he was within touching distance of our tent. I pounced and he near shat himself.

'What the hell!' Merilyn shouted. She woke up as the prowler bounced off her bed. A little worse for wear, he took off and the whole camp was up.

'That was brilliant,' Merilyn said. 'You must be related to Batman.' I accepted the accolade graciously while Merilyn accepted Cora's offer of the extra space in our three-person tent.

'You should have held the bastard,' Doug said. 'He probably has my sleeping bag.'

Antonio wanted a description: there would be a body on the beach, he said, if he found out who it was.

We stayed five days at Isla de Las Piedras, spending our time on the beach, or watching the iguanas on the rocks behind the village, or sitting in the restaurant and looking out to sea at the birds and the sunsets. Sometimes, during the day, Mexican tourists would turn up in the local 'taxi' - a cart with a straw canopy pulled by a mule. They would stay a few hours, then head back to the boat for Mazatlán, leaving us the deserted beach and its burning skyline. On the third day, Doug and Jean left and Cora and I moved into their thatched hut.

Later in the day we returned from the beach to find Josh at home with two tough-looking guys in their late twenties, one Mexican, the other American. We joined them for some Oaxaca Gold, then realized too late that Josh had a hang-dog look in his eyes that said: *I don't trust these guys at all, at all, at all.* The feeling percolated across the hut and gained heaps of ground when the Mexican started describing nasty Mexican jails. Then, abruptly, the two got up and left.

'Man,' Josh said, 'that was the fuckin' DEA [U.S. Drug Enforcement Administration]. They just turned up here, got me stoned on *my* dope, then started asking all kinds of questions. That's how they operate, man: a Mexican and an American working together. We're gonna get busted.'

Out the door I shot and into our hut, grabbing our little cache. Josh followed close behind with his. Off down the beach we raced to dig a hole and bury the lot, with a rock to mark the spot. For the rest of the day Cora and I kept our distance from Josh's hut. But nothing happened.

Next morning, we were mulling over the event.

'We were paranoid,' I said.

'Yeah,' Josh agreed. 'That was really stupid. I mean to say, they were stoned as well.'

'But there was still something weird,' I said. 'The way they went on about Mexican jails and then buggered off without a word.'

'Tell you what,' Josh said. 'Why don't we have another joint and see how we feel?'

So, off down the beach with us to dig up the stash, then back to Josh's hut for the social experiment.

'Shit,' Josh blurted, half way through the joint. 'That *was* the fuckin' DEA.'

Scooping up the plastic bags, we raced off down the beach again to dig another hole. For the rest of the day nobody would go within a donkey's screech of that spot. (How things change! Nowadays in many parts of the U.S. itself this recreational preference is no longer the bugaboo that it was in the 1970s.)

In the afternoon a horseman rode in - the municipal DDT man. Over the next hour he sprayed all the huts, prompting howls of protest from the guests as groggy scorpions, spiders and crickets spilled from the roofs and walls.

'Now the fuckin' things are gonna fall down and sting us to death in our sleep,' Josh predicted. 'And what about my poor buddy, the boa?' But the boa was fine.

'He's happy,' Josh said in the morning. 'He's just been down for a smoke.'

On our last night in Isla de Las Piedras, two 19-year-old German women turned up at the beach. We had previously met them in Guaymas and again at some bus station on the way south. Angélica and Marisa, in T-shirts and red dungarees, were pleasant examples of the fighting-fit after months of delivering the post around Berlin. When they spoke of their travels, it was with an eloquent sense of wonder that hadn't yet been displaced by familiarity with the absurd. Fresh of face and fair of hair, they drew men like wasps to strawberry jam.

'Maybe we will see you again,' Marisa said as we left the next morning for Tepic, six hours to the south.

I don't suppose any of us expected it to happen, but Angélica and Marisa would become a significant part of this story.

* * *

Tepic was an important centre of Indian art, particularly that of the Huichol and Cora (yes!) Indians of the Sierra Madre Occidental, many of whom could be seen about town in their colourful embroidered costumes. In the town's museum of ethnology, we found displays of the life and art of the Indians along with a rough map of their isolated lands in the mountains to the north and west. I stared at the map for a long time, then wrote down the name of a village: Jesus Maria.

'Imagine that,' I said to Cora. '*Cora* Indians.'

'If you're thinking what I think you're thinking,' Cora said, 'forget it.' But I knew she would come around.

We stayed a day in Tepic. We then backtracked forty-five miles to San Blas. A drowsy fishing village of narrow cobbled streets, blue wooden doors and terracotta roofs, it sat amidst the tropical estuaries, mangrove swamps and lagoons of Matanchén Bay. Stilted thatched huts in the swamps were reached by boat. In a reminder of its former glory as the earliest port on the west coast of America, the ruins of a Spanish fort overlooked the ocean from San Basilio Hill.

San Blas was also touted as the centre of a wildlife haven that hosted over 250 bird species, including thirty endemic to Mexico. With luck you could spot such treasures as the Northern Potoo and the Blue-footed Booby. Signs around the village, however, warned people to be careful in the estuaries as these were also home to the American crocodile. (At the turnoff from the main Tepic road, Cora and I, while on the bus, had an unexpected sighting of one of these. It shot out of what looked like a waterlogged dip in a field, grabbed a grazing duck, swallowed it, and retreated backwards into the water.)

In San Blas we checked into *El Dorado*[24], a campsite down by the beach where sunsets came through a skyline of coconut palms. Our neighbours were a fine bunch of people: Lars from Norway, Karl from Switzerland, Mike and Ron from the States, a French Canadian and

---

24.   No connection to the title of this book.

a couple from southern France. Once the sun went down, we shared food, bottles of mezcal, and coco-locos served in green coconuts.

'Watch the maggot,' Mike said as I swigged in the dark on a bottle of mezcal. I thought he was joking until it hit the back of my throat. Later we all went into the village and sat under an old church that dominated the square. Night vendors sold cooked food, drinks and cakes, along with stuffed turtles, stuffed iguanas and stuffed raccoons. So much for the wildlife reserve.

The days in San Blas took on a routine that soon became familiar. At seven in the morning the sandflies drove us from the tent. At half seven, reveille would sound from the tiny naval base, followed by a single shot. Every morning we hoped it was the bugler. After breakfast we all went to the beach to swim, body-surf, watch the dolphins and eat smoked fish in the shade of Marcos' Restaurant. An occasional Indian, or Marcos himself, might then try to sell us carvings or hammocks or opals or necklaces. Or a mariachi band might come to entertain. Or passers-by might stop to say hello or offer us slices of melon. In the sea breeze that managed to temper the day's rising heat, Cora found Marcos' shaded hammock very much to her liking and spent an inordinate amount of time snoozing in it.

In the village harbour there were big turtles, and crayfish that could be caught by hand. It was a matter of getting behind them and chasing them in on a wave. When the wave retreated, they were left stranded on the sand. The day I discovered this, I was in the water to my waist when Cora screamed, 'Shark!' (You'll remember that I hate that word.) I turned to see a black dorsal fin slicing my way. On panicked legs I lunged forward but there was no way of beating the fin to shore. I almost collapsed when, at the anticipated moment of impact, a dolphin popped to the surface.

I later used one of the crayfish as bait and caught a catfish and some other fish of unknown species. After checking with Marcos that both were edible, we added them to our haul of crayfish and all at the campsite ate like kings.

Every night, the *El Dorado* denizens would go into the town square to listen to local musicians and entertain the local kids. The cops, with forty-five automatics stuck in their belts, would walk by and throw us dirty shapes but we ignored them. We would then have a beer, grab a few bottles of rum or mezcal and head back to the campfire. One night we were joined by a reclusive banjo-player from the Appalachian Mountains who played and sang until sunup. Then Carnaval came to San Blas, and Angélica and Marisa showed up in the square. Great to see you again, we all said as we swapped stories, and I began to wonder. Would they fancy a walk into the Sierra Madre? To Jesus Maria.

In a village version of the Mardi Gras, festivities were opened by a fireworks display that ran dangerously out of control as Catherine wheels, rockets, and other pyrotechnic traceries whizzed through the crowd in the square while kids shrieked and adults ran for cover. Mariachi bands led a parade of local people dressed in all their finery. Some Navy guy followed, twirling a high-velocity rifle around his finger. And finally the kids came, chucking flour bombs and cracking eggs full of confetti over people's heads.

Carnaval ran the full weekend, culminating in a surfing competition that was a bit of a washout due to the absence of surf, but nobody cared. Further down the beach, the residents of *El Dorado* engaged half a dozen of the local senoritas in an hour of frisbee-throwing.

Wandering alone back along the beach, I again ran into Angélica and Marisa who had swapped their red dungarees for red bikinis. This time I mentioned the idea of visiting the Huichol and Cora Indians in their tribal lands.

'That is an amazing coincidence,' Angélica said. 'When we were in San Francisco, we went to see an exhibition of Huichol art and had thought of doing exactly that until we realized how inaccessible the area is. How would you plan to go there?'

'By public transport as far as possible, then on foot from there, aiming for a village called Jesus Maria.'

'We speak some Spanish,' Marisa said. 'That would be a help in the mountains.'

'Cora,' I said when I got back to the tent, 'we have two takers.'

'Takers for what?' Cora asked.

CHAPTER 24

Dondé Esta El Camino
A Jesus Maria?

On Tuesday, February 27th 1979 we left San Blas, rucksacks loaded with food for a trek of unknown duration. The plan was to catch the Guadalajara bus from San Blas to the main road, then take another bus to Ruiz, a small town at the foot of the mountains. Then see what happens.

At Ruiz we found a man who spoke English.

'There is a dirt road into the mountains,' he told us. 'You can take a truck from here to the village of Venado and another from there to San Pedro d'Ixcatan. That is a village of the Cora people. After that, it is walking country only.'

'What about walking to Jesus Maria?' I asked.

'I know nothing about that,' he said. 'You can ask at San Pedro.'

We also got some conflicting reports of jaguars in the mountains.

'This woman,' Marisa translated at one point, 'thinks we will be eaten in the night. She thinks it's very funny.'

The truck-transport to Venado, a long open vehicle with a slatted wooden canopy, soon had us bouncing at crazy speeds towards the mountains. At Venado, a conglomeration of low houses with overhanging roofs in the foothills of the mountains, we had a two-hour wait for the truck to San Pedro.

When we arrived, the cobbled main street was deserted. However, as soon as we moved into the shade, planting ourselves on the ground between two pillars that supported the roof of the village shop, the woman who ran the shop appeared with four chairs. We bought some drinks and had lunch of eggs and tortillas, after which the shopkeeper again appeared. Please have some pastries, Angélica translated, her aunt had baked them. Then, little by little, villagers gathered. Angélica again translated.

'They are amazed at the blonde hair, blue eyes and green eyes

[Cora's]. They are also saying something about a girl in the village.'

One of the women hurried off. Five minutes later she was back with a young girl in tow. The girl had blue eyes.

'She is a village celebrity,' Angélica said. 'In a few years, they are saying, every man in the mountains will love those eyes.' Much inspecting of eyes followed. Finally, the San Pedro truck arrived and the whole village saw us off.

From Venado we climbed through lush forest until we were high above the beautiful valley of the Rio San Pedro. Along the way, we passed small groups of Indians, some on foot, others riding burros or horses. The men, with long hair cut in a fringe, were dressed in flat sombreros, white cotton shirts and trousers, and sandals made from leather and old car tyres. The women wore three-layered skirts and blouses layered in frills. A style apparently copied from the early Spanish invaders. Their hair was either tied back or woven into pigtails.

As the truck topped the first pass, it became clear that we were not heading for high desert as we had been told back in San Blas, but to heavily forested mountain country of pink cliffs and wild canyons. At San Pedro d'Ixcatan, the dirt track veered off to San Miguel, and a wall of mountains rose to the east. Jesus Maria, we were told, was somewhere over those mountains.

It was late afternoon in San Pedro and there was music outside the *cantina* in the small square. We got off the truck, waded through a melee of pigs and chickens, and literally stopped the music. The entire village came to a standstill, then slowly gathered around us, shy and curious. Marisa and Angélica spoke to a few men who appeared to be elders.

'They are telling us that we can sleep in the schoolhouse,' Marisa said. 'The bus driver and his two helpers will also be sleeping there. They are providing the morning transport back to Venado.'

'*Gracias,*' we all said.

In the failing light, the music resumed and we began to ask about jaguars and how to get to Jesus Maria. On the jaguars, we again got conflicting reports. Of the five people we asked two said we wouldn't have a problem: three said we could run into jaguars or mountain lions or wolves. We chose to believe the two.

As for getting directions, it appeared that the walk to Jesus Maria could take anything from two days to a week. That it might not be possible but that people did it all the time. That you first had to go to San Miguel, but if you went to San Miguel, you couldn't walk from there to Jesus Maria. If there was accuracy in there, it was hard to pick.

In the single room of the schoolhouse we cooked a meal of rice and tinned fish and shared it with the crew of the transport truck as the children of San Pedro piled in through the door. We managed to win the confidence of half the kids. The other half bolted every time we moved. When Marisa took a flash photo of a group of them, one of the truck driver's helpers caused a screaming panic by telling them that they would all now disappear before morning. To calm the situation, we had one of the children take a flash picture of all of us.

Before bedding down on the schoolhouse floor I loudly sang *Happy birthday to me* to celebrate twenty-eight years on Planet Earth.

I have never heard such a racket as went down that night. Every so often, dozens of village burros would bray in unison, a signal for the dogs, pigs and roosters to follow suit. Only to be joined in the middle of the night by a bunch of yahoos out in the square who started up with trumpets, guitars, bass and fiddles.

'Bastards,' I growled. 'The only thing that can be robbed from you without any hope of getting it back is a night's sleep.' I was for going out with a cricket bat but the nearest one was in England.

In the morning a surprisingly cheerful Cora, unfazed by sleep loss, was making breakfast when an almighty hammering shook the schoolhouse door. The truck driver, a happy man with a fuzz of black hair, long sideburns and a curling moustache, stuck his hat on his head and opened up. Outside, his truck was full of seated San Pedro Indians, including the musical mob of the night. Nonplussed, he came back inside and he and the other two had breakfast at leisure. They then bade us *adios* and were away on the quite late, eight o'clock truck to Venado.

A little later, as the children turned up for school, the four of us, itching to be on our way, left the village. We had decided to take a chance and follow a mule track that led due east from San Pedro. As we had no maps of the region, we would now need to get our directions from the people we met along the way.

Moving up the narrowing valley of the Rio San Pedro, we passed through patches of cultivated land that gradually gave way to deep forest full of butterflies and hummingbirds, where the trail deteriorated to boulder slopes that somewhat blunted the skip of our stride. Over the next couple of hours we encountered small communities of Cora Indians, and occasionally strayed into villages where, among scatterings of pigs and chickens, our arrival would cause consternation. Women and children would run into the forest, while the men stayed hidden in the adobe huts.

'Hola, we would call. *'Dondé esta el camino a Jesus Maria?* [Where is the path to Jesus Maria?]' This would be the only complete Spanish phrase Cora and I would ever learn.

We would then have to sit tight among the huts and the raised grain stores until one or two of the men plucked up the courage to appear and point us in the right direction. If there were various suggestions, we would follow the majority view.

It soon became apparent that this was a part of the world that saw few, if any, outsiders. With a simple existence, relying on corn, eggs, bananas, forest plants and fruits, and occasional pork and chicken, the Indians had little cause to leave the mountains, and even less cause to have anyone in. The appearance of white strangers who had no apparent reason for being there would, we were to learn, fuel all kinds of wild speculation. In addition, only the men spoke Spanish, for use mainly when trading in the markets of the nearest towns. Other than that, people spoke their own native language.

Eventually, after another wait in a village until a single frightened man appeared, we were directed to a big mountain at the end of the valley, and a track that curved up to the right, leading to a pass. *'Allá,'* he pointed; that was the way to Jesus Maria.

It was a steep climb, but the forest gave reasonable protection from the sun and provided endless wildlife distractions. Of the countless bird species that darted among the trees, the most striking were the iridescent hummingbirds that floated in a blur of wings as they sucked nectar from the flowers, and the long-tailed, crested, magpie jays with their magnificent blue feathers. On the ground, lizards darted off at our approach and there were all sorts of fungi and insects. But the beauty of the forest lay in its profusion of wildflowers, some large, some tiny, some covering entire trees, with petals of every colour under the sun arranged in every conceivable manner.

We climbed all morning, delaying an eating stop until we reached what seemed to be the top of a pass. At times it was difficult to find the way, as tracks would run off in several directions; but this was resolved when an Indian man arrived on our heels and told us that he too was going to Jesus Maria. This was a double bonus. We had confirmation that walking to Jesus Maria was possible. And, for a while at least, we could follow the distinctive zigzag prints of the car-tyre soles of his sandals.

After sharing lunch, the Indian left with an uphill sprint. We stayed put, choosing to see out the hottest part of the day under a tree. Mid-afternoon, we set off refreshed only to find that it was still a long uphill drag to the pass. This time, however, we were climbing out of the forest to spectacular views that lessened the pain. Red bluffs and buttresses. Vast mountain folds with forests climbing their slopes. Villages tucked away on parcels of farmland down in the valleys. On the western horizon, the sheen of the sea. And all the colours deepening with the westering sun. At the top of the pass, we turned into the high mountains as the sun set.

We were on a sparsely wooded ridge, still following the Indian's tracks and looking for a camping spot, me out front, enjoying the birdsong and the fact that we had come so far without a hitch.

'Why did you stop dead?' Cora asked. 'And why are you staring at the ground?'

I pointed a finger. A big paw-print blotted out part of one of the Indian's footprints. As it was now nearing dusk - when big cats went hunting - we figured that whatever it was, jaguar or mountain lion, it was probably not too far away. And that was a load of claws and teeth that could jump a lot faster than we could run.

'What now?' Cora said as we stared at the nearby thickets.

'Everyone grab a rock,' was my advice on that. 'Anything jumps out, be ready to bash it over the head.'

Maybe not the best plan in the world, but better than none.

With the scrutiny we lavished on the bush, we strayed to the wrong track. Soon it was pitch black but we had to keep moving until we found a spot flat enough to take our tent. Once the tent was pitched, we sat outside wrapped in sweaters on a night of shooting stars. Perfect were it not for the fact that we hadn't come across water for several hours and were unable to cook or drink.

On a faraway mountain two fires flared and then slowly died, signalling the presence of others. Like ourselves, they were travelling through. We wondered who they were. We knew that they could see our fire, and must have felt the same affinity that we were feeling. Then the fires went black and we were alone in the night.

An hour later, we were drifting off to sleep when we heard voices. Through the fly screen we could see two Indian men coming towards us with an oil lamp. They screamed when I sprang out to ask if there was any *agua* nearby. Without answering, they skirted wildly around the tent and raced on down the track as if they'd just had a run-in with the Headless Coachman. We went to sleep parched and hungry.

* * *

In the morning we dropped about 1,000 feet and arrived in a village where the snorting, squawking and howling of pigs, chickens and dogs brought a middle-aged woman to her doorway. Wearing a loose white dress and huge earrings, with her hair in a ponytail, she stood stock-still and gaped.

'*Dondé esta el camino a Jesus Maria?*' Cora asked, doing well now with the Spanish.

The woman jabbed a finger in a northerly direction.

'*Agua?*' I asked. She again jabbed north and hurried back inside the hut. Nobody else wanted to see us.

Beyond the village the track wound down through dense forest to a boulder-strewn riverbed and there it was. Crystal-clear water.

Angélica and Marisa had a shower. Cora washed socks. I lit a fire and boiled water. We had tea. We filled our water bottles. We luxuriated for an hour in the river. We had breakfast of porridge, tortillas and eggs. Heaven, we said, was in little things.

Climbing again, we came to a plateau and a second collection of huts.

'*Dondé esta el camino a Jesus Maria?*' Marisa asked an old Indian who was sitting on a hillock. The man spoke several sentences.

'He says we are going the wrong way. The woman in the last village has not understood us or she has wanted us to keep moving. We should go back down and cross the river again.'

The Indian pointed to a towering rock face away in the distance. That was our direction.

It was a long arduous walk through the forest to the base of the rock face, followed by a tough climb, often on exposed ledges, through the hottest part of the day. We again ran out of water, but sometime in the afternoon we broke through a cleft in the rock, found a spring and emerged into forest that afforded shelter from the sun.

Throughout the remainder of the day we came across several bands of Indians - Coras and the colourful Huichols with their red-tasseled shirts and sombreros. Some ran off into the forest. Others gingerly greeted us as they went by and confirmed our directions, essential given the number of tracks.

Eventually, every Indian in the Sierra would know we were heading for Jesus Maria. As for how long it would take? It still varied from a day and a half to a week.

Shortly before dark, we came to a village that was divided in two by a narrow ridge. We camped on the ridge, close to where the track crossed a path that connected both sides of the village. Cora and Marisa walked down to the nearest hut, in the smaller part of the village, to ask for water. But the woman who met them simply fled to the rear of the hut and only peeked out once to point downhill at nothing. On the other side of the village, Angélica and I had even less luck, only making contact with pigs, chickens and barking dogs. When we reconvened at the tent without water, Cora and Marisa agreed to try again. Angélica and I would get the fire going.

When the woman saw Cora and Marisa coming again, she left her barking dog behind, grabbed her little boy and ran into the forest. As we had to have water, there was no choice but to sit and wait until she returned.

Eventually, after Marisa had spent fifteen minutes using her Spanish in efforts to coax the woman back from the forest, she slowly inched her way forward and agreed to show them to the water.

'We managed to win her trust in the end,' Cora said. 'It just took time.'

But as night closed in, the whole population of that side of the village fled with bag and baggage for the safety of the far side.

'Well,' Cora said. 'It looks like we didn't win that much trust after all.'

After eating, we sat by the fire in hazy moonlight and pulled out the Oaxaca Gold.

'How could you describe this to anyone?' Marisa said. 'Even with the best photographs, it would not be possible. When we were leaving San Blas, I could not imagine how beautiful and amazing this would be - the birds, the butterflies, the people, the mountains, the forest, the flowers - so how could anybody else imagine it if they had not been here?'

'And we were thinking,' Angélica said, 'that maybe we would find some hostility from the Indians, but *they* are afraid of *us*.'

'Imagine what they're talking about down in the village,' Cora said. 'God only knows who or what they think we are.'

And while we were able to crawl into our tent and drift dreamily away from the world, the village entered a night of angst unlike any in its history. What we couldn't have known at that point was that rumours were spreading across the mountains that 'the CIA' was coming.

The third day began in a series of misty illusions as we climbed a rough, rocky trail through forest wreathed in cloud. A distant village would show in a brief opening in the fog, the luminous smoke of cooking fires drifting among the huts. A man on a burro would appear, and disappear as quickly. We'd hear voices, amplified by the stillness, but see no people.

As we gained height the hardwoods gave way to pine forest. We crossed a high pass on a trail of broken rock before dropping into heavy bush where the going would have slaughtered us had the sun been shining. Along the way columns of leaf-cutter ants carried their loot back to the nest. The leaves would serve as the nutritional base for the fungal gardens from which these farmers of the insect world would feed their larvae.

As the morning progressed, the track climbed along tiers of dripping cliffs and we began to again meet small groups of Indians. Jesus Maria, they told us, was now no more than two or three days away. At midday, we stopped at a water hole in the forest, joining a 14-strong band of Coras. They were friendly in a mocking way until one of the older men went to throw my pack on his shoulder and discovered that he could barely lift it.

'A-a-a-aw...' he said and let it drop to the ground. Immediately the attitude changed.

'*Bueno,*' the old boy said of the pack. He then squatted in front of us and began to draw in the dirt with a stick. Speaking in Spanish he explained that we would have to clear another high pass, a very high one. Then wind our way around the ridges and canyons to La Mesa which was the biggest village of the Coras. From there, it was downhill all the way to Jesus Maria. And be careful, he said, of the jaguars. And the snakes. When he had finished, he shook all our hands and wished us luck. Then everybody smiled, said *Adios,* and followed the older man into the forest.

By late afternoon we had reached the top of the high pass and were looking down on a spectacular network of canyons. We then dropped some 800 feet into a ravine, crossed a stream and made camp on a flat outcrop above the water. After dinner, when darkness had seen off the last glimmer of light, we sat around the fire, elated.

'Well,' Cora said, 'we're on the downhill run. The high passes are behind us, and not a broken bone between us.'

Out came the Oaxaca Gold for another bout of star-gazing.

The fire was warm and sparking. The crickets were chirruping. Stars were shooting across the sky. I was sitting beside Marisa. I was recounting tales of the Shoalhaven Gorge when something crawled up under the leg of her dungarees.

'Hold it a minute,' I said. 'Don't move.' I pulled the leg of the dungarees outwards and flicked the thing to the ground where it wriggled in the shadows.

'What is it?' Marisa asked.

'A mole cricket,' I said. I reached down to lift it. I then thought better of it and scooped it up in a dessert spoon.

'Shit!' I yelped as the tail arced upwards. 'A scorpion! It must have come from the firewood.' Instant paranoia. 'Check your legs! Check your backs! Check everything!'

We leapt up, tucked our trousers inside our socks, put on our boots, grabbed the food, and beat a retreat to the tent. Inside, I had a thought.

'They're probably under the tent too! And in our sleeping bags!'

We whipped off our boots and crawled around, smashing our sleeping bags and the tent floor with the boots in a five-minute, scorpion-killing frenzy.

'Phew,' Angélica said. 'Now we must throw out the bodies.'

Flashlights were engaged and sleeping bags trawled for the bodies but they were nowhere to be found.

'We must have scared them off,' Cora laughed. 'Some day, we'll all get sense.'

In the morning a family rode past. The parents and three children were driving half a dozen cattle to San Pedro. La Mesa, they assured us, was just around the corner. We packed up and wound our way another 1,000 feet downhill until we reached the floor of one of the larger canyons we had seen from the pass. Here, a river had to be forded. As we hit the water, a group of Indian children who were coming against us on the far side moved downstream, bolted across to our side, and stayed put until we were out of sight. We climbed to the canyon rim, passing through several villages, and slogged on until the canyon floor was far below. The land was now much drier, with more cacti and grass that was burnt to yellow.

'Look,' Cora said, pointing ahead. 'Like something from the Wild West.'

On a grassy hillside, a lone Indian on horseback sat silhouetted against the skyline. As we approached, he dropped slowly out of sight, a scout bringing news of the strangers to La Mesa. He had been watching for us. Immediately past the hill, we found ourselves on a broad plateau, backed by rocky hills of scrub. It was late afternoon and we had reached La Mesa.

* * *

Walking into La Mesa felt like walking into Geronimo's camp. Across the plateau some 200 dwellings of stone, adobe and thatch lay scattered at random, with the village centre dominated by a massive stone church and stone water-tank. There was the odd tree, some covered in pink blossom that glowed in the slanting light. And there was absolute silence.

As we made our way towards the heart of the village, the only movement came from children who broke and ran. Other than that nobody budged. Those at doorways stood and stared. Those inside stayed inside. Two Indians on horseback sat still as statues as we approached. They returned our greeting but eyed us with deep suspicion.

'It would be nice to stop here,' Cora said. 'But it doesn't look like anyone's rushing out to offer us a cup of tea.'

'Well, at least nobody is firing arrows,' Angélica joked.

Marisa asked the horsemen where we could get food as we were down to the last of our beans and rice. They pointed towards the village shop, whose meagre supplies were erratically flown in by bush plane from Tepic. At the shop, run by an old Indian man, we re-stocked with coffee, sugar, biscuits, eggs, fresh vegetables and tinned fish. The old man wanted to know where we came from, but had never heard of *Irlanda* or *Allemania*. Not much conversation left in that. Then we were saved.

'*Hola! Hola!*' a female voice called. A smiling young woman with a mass of black hair was running barefoot from the direction of the church. She was dressed in a blue skirt, white blouse, massive silver earrings and a red headband. She was Yaqui, she told us, and she worked with the village's Catholic mission. We should go with her once we had bought our food. The *padre* was away, she explained, but one of the sisters and one of the lay volunteers spoke English.

The welcome at the mission compound was overwhelming. We could stay the night. We could sleep in one of the school classrooms. We could hear the children sing. But first our stay had to be approved by the village headmen, so one of the mission sisters was sent forth. Half an hour later she came back and told us that six of the most dignified-looking men we could ever hope to encounter were waiting for us in the village square.

'But,' she warned, 'they think you might be the CIA. There are rumours.'

We were speechless. It was worse than being called child-eating goblins.

The headmen were probably in their late fifties or early sixties, wrapped in dark brown homespun blankets and carrying woven shoulder-bags, each with long greying hair and the poise of a statesman. The first thing they wanted to know was whether or not the rumours were true. Were we the CIA? They weren't sure who the CIA were but they knew they were bad news. Once we had convinced them that we had no truck with any bunch of thugs anywhere, they offered us the communal house. We then had a diplomatic quandary on our hands and had to tread carefully to make sure nobody was offended. With the sister translating, we thanked the elders profusely for their generosity but explained that we had already been offered a place at the mission and that we would like to stay there so we could hear the children sing and play music; and that we would also like to be able to speak to the people at the mission so we could learn about the culture and history of La Mesa. When the elders realised that we and some of the mission people spoke the same language, they agreed that the mission was indeed the best place for us. They then strode off into the gathering dusk. Men from the time of Columbus.

Back at the mission, the English-speaking sister, a motherly woman with bright eyes and hair tied back in a scarf, told us that this was a very old Cora settlement that had seen much history.

'These people were here when the Aztecs came through, and we believe that the strange-looking symmetrical hill on the far side of the canyon could well be an Aztec pyramid, but we are keeping that quiet. The Spaniards also came and they built the church and the stone water-tower, and brought Catholicism to the Indians, and the Indians built this into their own peyote religion and traditional system of beliefs and this is very much the kind of Catholicism they have today.

'The people of the Sierra are a conservative people who do not want to see their race absorbed into the bigger Mexico. They wish to keep their own customs, dress and languages. When the mission brings in clothes, the women take them apart and remake them in the traditional way. The government put in electricity but the people refuse to turn it on. They also resisted the coming of the present padre in case other whites would follow, and maybe even bring a road. So, you are honoured that they offered you the communal house.'

She then went on to the history of the old stone church and the mission itself.

'The church was built by the Spanish but the last priest was killed 380 years ago. He had managed to convert the Cora king who then decided to cease warring with the neighbours. This greatly displeased some of the other Cora elders of the time, so they kidnapped the priest and threw him in the canyon. According to the story, his body was never found, probably taken by mountain lions or jaguars. The church then fell into ruin, and the people took all the religious artefacts and hid them in caves up in the mountains. And there they were preserved until recent years. Many of them are now in the church and the little museum we have at the mission, but others - including a large chest of vestments - are still up in the mountains. The people also preserved many of the Christian rituals. When the present *padre* came ten years ago, there were people at La Mesa who could read Latin.'

But, ten years ago, she told us, we wouldn't have been able to stay at the mission. At that time, when the present *padre* came, the Indians first boycotted him in an effort to drive him away. He was left to his own devices and had to fend for himself as best he could. When this failed to get rid of him, they opted for poisoned cheese.

'The next day some of the Indians came back to see if he had eaten the cheese and they were amazed when he showed them the small remaining piece. They took it from him and threw it to one of the village dogs. In a quarter of an hour the dog was dead. This they took to be a sign from God and accepted the *padre*. Since then he has won the confidence of the people and persuaded them to rebuild the church, with individuals donating one beam or one flagstone. And now we have a strong mission here, with many children at school.'

Interestingly, the mission garden was the greenest patch of land at La Mesa. In the ten years of his ministry, the *padre* had signally failed to attract a single convert away from the Coras' traditional forms of agriculture.

Once word got around that we weren't the CIA, the villagers came in trickles to view the strangers, scrutinizing our equipment, our clothes and our hair. Wrapped in homespun blankets, they would stay a while and watch every move, then drift off and make way for the next group. The children living at the mission had nowhere else to go, so they sat and watched as we cooked and ate our food. Most of them were poorly dressed, but they seemed healthy and happy. They were also dying to play and sing for us and this they did as we ate. Later, in the light of candles and oil lanterns, a guitar appeared and the entire mission and many of the villagers sang and danced around the mission courtyard to celebrate our stay. Cora led the young Yaqui woman in an impromptu Irish Céilí swing with a vigour that was astonishing.

'What is your name?' one of the men asked through the Yaqui woman when the swing had finished.

'Cora,' Cora said, causing a sensation.

'You might be a Cora,' the man said. 'But you're not one of us.'

Beyond the mission perimeters, the light of a crescent moon brushed the plateau and village fires flickered as they had since long before the Spanish priest went hurtling into the canyon.

Later on, when La Mesa had quietened to a whisper, Angélica, Marisa, Cora and I spread our sleeping bags on our classroom floor.

'I was thinking earlier,' Angélica said, 'that nobody in the world knows where we are at this moment except the people of this village. If my parents could see me now, they would not be able to understand how I could ever be in such a place as this. And if they had known that I was planning something like this, they would have died with worry. Yet, it is so gentle.'

'As long as nothing goes wrong,' Marisa said, 'I do not want to think what would have happened if that scorpion last night had stung me...'

'That's why it's best this way,' Cora said. 'Dead or alive, it's all over before anyone knows, so nobody worries.'

In the morning we were given a tour of the village by the mission staff. Outside one house a woman was weaving on a loom attached to a tree while the rest of the family - who looked to me like your stereotypical Apaches - had breakfast. Across the way another woman was making cornmeal tortillas, grinding the corn into a paste, using a round stone on a stone slab. Other women were washing clothes in a stream while four young boys used a long pole to pluck pea-like fruits from some of the trees. People were friendly but reticent. The mission staff then boiled our eggs for us and we set off for Jesus Maria, stopping briefly in the old church to view wooden chests full of priceless vestments and plaster statues left by the Spanish 380 years before. In the outside walls, holes acted as open burial chambers for dead babies. Adults who had been baptised were buried in the church grounds without headstones or other markers.

'Be careful in the canyon, along the river,' the sister warned as we left. 'Two years ago there was a jaguar there and it killed two people.'

The sun was high and the heat oppressive as we made our way down the tortuous track that led to the canyon floor. Keeping an eye out for jaguars, we tagged along the riverbank for another half hour, still exposed to the sun. We passed through small villages. We walked through carpets of flowers. We waded through clouds of butterflies. Eventually we found what we were looking for: a secluded spot by the river, hidden by trees and invisible from the track, with plenty of shade, sandy banks and a deep pool for swimming. And there we settled, washing off several days' grime, swimming in the river, and enjoying the absolute peace of the Sierra and the sounds of the river. Extra stimulus was provided by birds, lizards, butterflies, ants, beetles and flowers that we studied in great detail. Finally, as the day waned and our resident kingfishers made their final sorties into the water, we lit a fire and set off to collect additional firewood.

'Watch out for scorpions,' Cora warned as we picked up pieces of driftwood lodged in the branches of trees.

'Oh shit,' Marisa said as she threw down a log she was carrying. A large brown scorpion crawled from a crevice in the dead wood. 'Bastard,' Marisa said politely as she splatted the monster with her boot.

'Throw it in the fire,' Angélica said, 'so we don't stand on the sting when it is dark.'

'Another one here,' Cora called. More scorpion paranoia. We put on our boots and tucked our jeans inside the socks. We then sat by the fire and ate as the sun went down behind the line of the mountains. A short distance away, a tree with peeling red bark, stood against the skyline, its branches seemingly coated in purple flames.

Next morning when the sun hit the tent I got up, went to put on jeans that I had washed the previous evening, then thought I had better check. When I turned them inside out a scorpion, clutching a half-eaten cricket, toppled onto the sand.

Our second day by the river was as lazy as the first. Sometime in the afternoon, an Indian on horseback, attracted by our fire smoke, came to check us out, said hello and rode off again. Then another burning sunset and bats coming out of the east.

'In the morning, whoever wakes up first is the alarm clock,' Cora said as we crawled into the tent sometime around ten. We wanted to get an early start so as to get a few hours' walking done before the sun was too high.

We were away by half seven, tramping downstream to a second canyon and a river that had to be forded. A group of Indians assured us that we were almost in Jesus Maria, but we weren't. However, three hours after breaking camp, I crested a hill and there it was, sitting below in a narrow gorge. A cluster of stone and adobe houses surrounded a massive church with twin bell towers flanking a curved gable with a big wooden door. With bells tolling and two horsemen riding across the dirt square in front of the church, it could have been straight out of *High Noon*. To one side, a group of Indians sat on the ground in the shade of a building while a woman drew water from a well. Pigs, dogs and chickens poked about for scraps. The river that ran behind the village sparkled in the sunlight.

I walked on and waited by the church, immediately attracting a fascinated crowd. When the others turned up, the crowd grew exponentially and, with Angélica's and Marisa's Spanish, we engaged in conversation. Basic but satisfying. And leading us to one of those experiences you'd rather forget.

'There is a possibility of a flight from here to Tepic by bush plane,' Angélica said after an exchange with an older man. 'Or we can travel in the back of a small truck on a dirt track over the mountains.'

The flight idea took root. There was one a day, we were told, but the airstrip was two hours' walk away. However, a truck went at 5.00 a.m. You needed reservations for the plane, but don't worry: tomorrow there's plenty of room. The plane would take seven people and cost 250 pesos each. It was a half hour to Tepic. This was all good news. We could relax.

We stayed a couple of hours in the square before going out of the village to pitch our tent. Sitting by the fire, we watched life go by: Indian groups arriving from the hills or leaving for their villages; families fording the river on burros, the women with babies strapped to their backs; birds flitting through the bush; raptors harnessing the thermals; everything rimmed by the imposing mountains.

At dusk, we swam in the river while small fish plopped around us. On the surrounding hillsides, cooking fires appeared. Voices carried along the river. The church bells tolled and lights went on in the village. Electricity! What a weird sensation.

As we made dinner, a fresh breeze blew up. By the time we had finished eating, we had a gale whipping up dust and sending showers of sparks into the night. Before going to bed, we had to secure our guylines to rocks and place a few more inside the tent to hold it in place.

At four o'clock in the morning we were up and packing so as to be ready for our 5.00 a.m. ride to the airstrip. We arrived at the truck driver's house amidst a chorus of roosters, dogs and burros, only to find it in full darkness. He didn't appear until half five.

'What time does the plane leave?' Marisa asked.

'Seven, eight or nine,' she was told.

The old Dodge pickup forded the river with the four of us in the back and three Indians in the cab. We rattled up the mountain track with gears grinding and the oil light glowing a constant red. Gradually a cold pink and green sky faded before the rising sun as heat was punched into the day. It would have taken a lot more than two hours to walk to the airstrip.

At the airstrip there was confusion. The cheerful people in the hut would only take four passenger names, including two of ours.

'But there are four of us,' Marisa insisted in Spanish.

'The woman with the list is telling us not to worry,' she translated. 'That we will all get on the plane.'

'So, why do you not take the names?' Marisa persisted. The woman extended both hands in a calm-down gesture.

When the plane - a five-seater Cessna - came bouncing down the dirt runway two hours after our arrival, we were confused all over again. This was not the seven-seater we had been told about yesterday. And there were now nine passengers waiting for four seats. But the number of seats had nothing much to do with anything: all nine of us were told we could board the plane. It was just that, officially, we couldn't. Officially, five of us weren't there at all.

'Do you remember when we took one of these in New Guinea?' Cora said. 'The pilot weighed us and our gear so he could spread the weight and not overload the plane. Surely they're not going to try and put ten people on this thing?'

'They are,' Angélica said.

The pilot organised the loading. He was a droopy-eyed Indian of about thirty-five with long hair, a sizeable paunch and a casual approach to aeroplane loading.

Two Indian women sat in the back two seats with their two kids on their laps. All the gear was stacked haphazardly to the roof behind them. Cora sat in the middle seat. An old Indian man and I occupied a small space on the floor. Angélica sat on Marisa's lap in the front passenger seat, her arms around Marisa's neck. Plane loaded, the pilot hopped in and slammed the door. I will never forget the pleading look on Angélica's face as the engine spluttered to life and we started down the runway.

'Do you think we are insured?' she asked. 'Or will it make any difference?'

'*Senor,*' the older Indian on the floor said as we taxied through the potholes, '*Muchos personas?*' The pilot turned and nodded.

'*Si,*' he said. Then without any of the checklisting of New Guinea, we were in the air, juddering over the canyons as the pilot fidgeted distressingly under Angélica's legs. He then leaned over and found what he was looking for: the mail. So he could read the envelopes as we flew along.

The country below was a maze of canyons, valleys and bluffs but we were all too terrified to take much notice.

'I have heard that these can flip if they are overloaded,' Angélica said.

At this, Cora succumbed to tears. On the floor, I accepted that death was coming. The old Indian beside me shrugged and threw his eyes to Heaven, probably expecting to be there soon.

But, despite a rocky flight, we landed safely on a siding at Tepic airport half an hour after leaving Jesus Maria. We then returned to San Blas. Cora and I checked back in at *El Dorado*. Angélica and Marisa booked into a cheap hotel. Two days later Cora and I left for Guadalajara.

We never saw our Sierra companions again.

CHAPTER 25

Earthquake

Guadalajara, capital of Jalisco state, home of mariachi music and a city of mestizos (a mix of Spanish and Indian), my diary dismissed as *'a dirty, noisy, air-polluted hole'*. Despite its stately architecture, lively markets, parks, tree-lined boulevards and plazas, we were unimpressed. We left after a day, taking the Morelia-bound bus to the town of Quiróga where we would change for Pátzcuaro, home of the Tarascan Indians.

Our journey took us through fertile valleys bordered by mountains, where peasants in wide sombreros worked the fields like figures from medieval paintings. Wooden ploughs and bullocks broke the sod. Along the road, horses and burros hauled impossible loads. At every stop you could lean out the window and buy blankets, lottery tickets, tacos, chewing gum, ice cream or lacquer-work.

At Zamora a blind man in rags boarded the bus and begged his way down the aisle, mercury eyes rolling in his head, his hands lightly touching the people in the aisle seats. I passed him a few coins and he issued a loud *'Gracias! Gracias! Gracias!'* When the engine kicked into life he exited by the side door.

On reaching Quiróga, the cobbled streets and tiled houses were so atmospheric that we decided to stay the night. We booked into the Hotel San Diego, a two-storey building wrapped around an open courtyard where a young Mexican picked out soft melodies on a classical guitar. We spent the afternoon wandering the sprawling market: a pleasant experience had it not been for the jaguar skins, stuffed raccoons and stuffed iguanas that were again for sale.

The following day we took the noon bus to Pátzcuaro, an old colonial town set at 7,000 feet among the volcanoes and pine-clad hills of Michoacán. On arrival, we booked in at the Hotel San Augustin and were allocated a room overlooking the craft and food market of Plaza Gertrudis Bocanegra. Down in the shaded square, mules plodded past the statue of María Gertrudis Teodora Bocanegra Mendoza, the 'Heroine of Pátzcuaro', who was shot by firing squad in 1817 for her support of the Mexican independence movement.

In the town's market, most of the stalls were run by Tarascan women, distinctive in their long pleated skirts, finished off with frilled, embroidered aprons, short-sleeved blouses and navy-blue striped shawls slung across the shoulders when not is use as a baby sling or shopping basket. Their hair hung in long pigtails, finished in woollen strings which were then tied loosely behind. They and their menfolk were what remained of one of the most powerful branches of Mexico's indigenous people.

Although little is known of their origins, the Tarascans flourished in the area that is now the state of Michoacán from 1100 to 1530 when they were decimated by the Spaniards. Primarily a rural people, the centre of their empire was Lake Pátzcuaro and their capital, dominated by five temple pyramids, was at Tzintzuntzan (place of the hummingbirds), now an archaeological ruin.

Situated on the western borders of the Aztec empire, the Tarascans rivalled and repeatedly repulsed the Aztecs who tried to colonise their lands. During the reign of Tarascan king, Tzitzic Pandacuare, the Aztecs launched their most determined offensive, which developed into a bloody war that lasted from 1469 to 1478. In a final offensive in 1478, the ruling Aztec lord, Tlatoani Axayácatl, marched on Michoacán with an army of 32,000 warriors, only to find himself confronted by more than 50,000 Tarascans. The ensuing Battle of Taximaroa (today's city of Hidalgo) ended after a daylong bloodbath during which more than 20,000 of Axayácatl's warriors fell to the arrows, stones, spears, and swords of the Tarascans, who had the advantage of copper in the manufacture of weapons and shields. Later remarks of Spanish soldiers and missionaries in the early 16th century gave the impression that the then Tarascan king was considered to be second in power, if not equal to, the Aztec ruler Moctezuma.

Ironically, both the Aztec and Tarascan empires were destroyed by the same *conquistadores*, led by Hernándo Cortés, who landed on the east coast of Mexico in April 1519. Aware that the Spaniards were on their way to the Aztec capital of Tenochtitlán, the Aztecs asked the Tarascans for military assistance; but instead of helping, the Tarascans sacrificed the Aztec emissaries, one of whom had brought smallpox which killed the Tarascan king. Tenochtitlán subsequently fell to Cortéz in 1520 after a long and bloody siege. Two years later, it was the Tarascans' turn when Tangoxoán II, the last Tarascan king, surrendered to Spain. In the years that followed the Spanish conquest, more than ninety percent of the Tarascans were wiped out in a holocaust of slaughter, disease, and slavery.

The worst period followed the 1528 appointment of Spanish lawyer, Nuño Guzmán de Beltran, as head of the Spanish government's First *Audiencia*, designed to replace the rule of Cortés in Mexico. Guzmán engaged in an orgy of ruthless savagery across Mexico, selling Indians into slavery, ransacking temples in search of treasure, killing those who opposed him, exacting heavy taxes from villages, and kidnapping women.

When the Spanish state eventually confronted him at the end of 1529, Guzmán set off for Michoacán with an army of 350 Spanish soldiers, and some 10,000 Indian warriors. When he reached Tzintzuntzan, he demanded that Tangoxoán turn over all his gold. Unable to deliver any gold, the king was tortured, dragged behind a horse and burned to death. Guzmán's forces then plundered the once-grand and powerful Tarascan nation, destroying temples, houses and fields while forcing the terrorised population to flee into the mountains of Michoacán.

Eventually Guzmán was arrested and shipped to Spain for trial and in 1531 the Spanish crown appointed 60-year-old Bishop, Don Vasco de Quiróga, to replace him in Michoacán. A Spanish aristocratic lawyer and humanitarian, de Quiróga managed to bring the Tarascan people back from the brink of extinction. In time he would become known by the Tarascans as Tata (Daddy) Vasco, and would establish a system of village specialisation in woodwork, weaving, pottery, embroidery and lacquer work that gave a new economic base to the plundered villages. The man who gave Pátzcuaro its distinctive flavour died in the town in March 1565.

When Cora and I arrived in Pátzcuaro on Tuesday, March 13th 1979, the majority of the 90,000 remaining Tarascans were living around the lake, on its islands and in impoverished mountain communities where subsistence agriculture supplemented the craft specialisations established by Vasco de Quiróga. Out on Pátzcuaro Lake, fishermen in canoes still tossed their trademark butterfly nets in pursuit of the whitefish that were a local delicacy.

* * *

It was a night like any other. Crickets shrieked; moths played around the street lights; bats swooped low over the tarpaulins of the market. When it was time to close, everything was packed into boxes for the night, the tarpaulins came down and the stalls were dismantled. The whole shebang was then wheeled away on trolleys while the permanent stalls withdrew their displays, took the light bulbs out of their sockets and closed their shutters. Only the food stalls remained, along with a band of musicians out in the square. Then eventually, even they went home and Cora and I went back to our room on the first floor of the Hotel San Augustin.

Shortly after five o'clock on the morning of March 14th, I was shaken out of my sleep by a great rattling and banging. The bed was shaking violently and bouncing on the floor. Outside, the street lights were blinking and the electricity wires were swinging like skipping ropes. The wood and tin of the marketplace creaked and groaned and splintered as the shuddering increased. The shutters of the Hotel San Augustin beat off the walls and windows, and plaster fell from the ceiling.

My first reaction was to wake Cora so she wouldn't miss out, as we'd both slept through minor tremors in Papua New Guinea's Jimi Valley. Cora, however, was managing just fine to wake up all by herself.

'Shi-i-it!' she was saying. 'Shi-i-it! What the hell...'

'An earthquake,' I was saying. 'We're in the middle of an earthquake.'

For the next minute we sat transfixed, hanging on to the bed, saying more Shi-i-t, as we rocked in a circular motion and the whole of southern Mexico shook to an earthquake of 7.6 magnitude, centred off the southern coast near the town of Petatlán, 140 miles south of Pátzcuaro

Strangely enough, once we got used to the idea, and the roof wasn't coming in, it was more mesmerising than frightening. After a minute, the shaking and banging subsided and there was a moment of deathly silence, broken only by the swinging of the electricity wires. Then the whole town erupted onto the streets and we all stayed there, well away from the buildings, until we were sure the danger had passed. The fright came then, when you realised what could have been. But, despite the length of the quake, Pátzcuaro suffered no major damage although other places were badly hit. Overall, however, there were very few deaths, and seismologists praised Mexico for its ability to absorb such a big quake that lasted more than a minute and could have caused a catastrophe elsewhere. Six years later Mexico wasn't so lucky.

On Thursday, September 19th 1985 at 7:19 a.m. local time, Mexico City was hit by an earthquake of magnitude 8.1, one of the most devastating to have ever struck the Americas. It left at least 9,000 people dead, 30,000 injured and 100,000 homeless. We were lucky, it seems, in March of 1979.

CHAPTER 26

A First-class Train Ride

We travelled on through Morelia to Mexico City, crossing a plateau where dry-stone walls carved the landscape, and stone and adobe gave way to concrete. Late in the afternoon of March 14th we hit the city's outskirts and a blinding cloud of dust that turned the sun into a pale-yellow moon.

We took a bus from Terminal Central del Norte to the city centre, driving through streets of shattered windows, buckled pavements and buildings split down the middle as if by a giant axe. We checked into the Hotel Rey, a short walk from the junction of Reforma and Insurgentes, two of the city's main thoroughfares. On Thursday morning, the day after the quake, we called at the Guatamalan Consulate to pick up visas, and found everybody working as normal in a building that looked as if it had been smashed up by sledgehammers.

'Are you worried that the place might fall down?' I asked the Consul.

'Maybe if we have another earthquake,' he said. 'Maybe then we must find another place.' Behind him a chunk of plaster the size of four dinner plates hung on the wall by a thread.

'What about that?' Cora asked. He got up and thumped the wall, and the plaster crashed to the floor.

'Yes,' he said. 'Now no problem.'

That afternoon, we took a bus to Teotihuacán, some thirty miles northeast of Mexico City and were surprised to find the sprawling ruins virtually empty, given the site's archaeological significance. In sheer scale alone Teotihuacán, once the capital of Mexico's first great highland culture, was mind-blowing, considering that only a fraction of the total site had been excavated. From its southern extreme close to the space once occupied by the Temple of Quetzalcoatl, the Plumed Serpent,[25] the

---

25   Known as Kukulcán by the Maya of Yucatán.

complex stretched one and a half miles along the Avenue of the Dead to the Pyramid of the Moon. On both sides were the remains of the temples and palaces, sculptures and frescoes that once made up the centre of the fabled city.

Dominated by the Pyramid of the Moon and the more imposing Pyramid of the Sun - the third largest pyramid in the world - the Avenue of the Dead spoke volumes of the people who once walked that broad boulevard.

Just as the ancient Olmec civilization - the parent culture in Mesoamerica - was weakening in around 400 BC, a new civilization rose in the Valley of Mexico. With its centre at Teotihuacán, it would remain dominant for a millennium, stamping its cultural and religious influences throughout Central America. At its zenith between 150 and 450 AD, when it wielded power and influence comparable to its contemporary civilisation in ancient Rome, the city covered over eleven square miles and held a population of more than 150,000 inhabitants, making it America's largest ancient city and the sixth city in the world at that time.

Sometime around 650 AD, for reasons that can only be guessed, Teotihuacán began to decline sharply and had been completely abandoned by 750 AD.

Archaeological evidence points to a great fire that destroyed much of the city in 700 AD. Some argue that the fire was caused by invaders, possibly the Toltecs. Others argue that the burning was restricted to the buildings of the elite and indicates an internal uprising. Others argue drought and famine. The mystery remains.

As we left Teotihuacán, lightning tore the landscape, thunder crackled and the rain came in torrents. The resultant flooding was so heavy in towns and villages that it sometimes felt like our bus was shooting rapids between banks of flooded houses.

After two more days exploring Mexico City, including a half day spent at the Museum of Anthropology, we left for Campeche in the Yucatán on the night train of Saturday, March 17th – St. Patrick's Day. It was a 32-hour journey; so for the only time in our lives we decided to treat ourselves to our own first-class compartment. What a mistake that proved to be!

At eight o'clock at night we pulled out of the station and enjoyed the first few hours immensely. But, when we tried to sleep, the flaws appeared. Theoretically, the tiny cabin was air-conditioned: in fact, the air conditioning was broken, the fan only worked on 'low' and the windows didn't open. However, we were still in the mountains and it was cool enough. But there was another barrier to sleep - the bouncing of the train.

Not just pitching and rolling which went on apace, but bouncing as if the track was corrugated steel. We had seen trains mount the rails back at Mexico City but never imagined it as an integral feature of Mexican rail travel. But so it was. It never let up all night, nor the following day, nor the following night. After the first night of fitful dozing and loud swearing, I was fit to be tied and ready to get off but Cora reminded me that we had paid $50 for our passage to Campeche.

'We should count ourselves lucky,' she said. 'There's a whole load of people out there who've paid for first-class seats but there's no first-class carriage on the train. They've been standing in the corridors all night.'

But the first night proved a breeze compared to the next twenty-four hours (the journey took thirty-four hours in all). By morning, we were out of the mountains in a tropical setting and as the sun rose, so did the heat and humidity. All of us passengers in the first class compartments now took turns to stand at the open windows of the carriage doors to catch the only air in circulation. As the hours ticked by, the situation worsened. Our hair was drenched in sweat; our clothes stuck to our bodies; the food we were carrying spoiled in the heat; and the bouncing was so bad at times that we couldn't even read. Slowly the day dragged on as we passed through vast swamps teeming with bird life, through lush rainforest festooned with creepers, and through village pastures of grazing cattle.

'Fuck it!' I kept yelling but no bastard cared.

'Don't hold back on my account,' Cora said.

Night brought no respite. Though it cooled down outside to a tolerable level, nothing changed inside except that we of the first-class compartments grew more listless and got more of the shits. When it came my turn at the door, ecstasy reigned for a while: there was an exhilarating breeze; a three-quarter moon brightened the landscape; the flashing beacons of fireflies were everywhere; and the lights of hopeful homes periodically dotted the countryside. Then I was back again in the furnace. Somehow we managed to steal two hours' sleep between half nine and half eleven; then at Palenque more people boarded the first-class compartments and added to the pressure at the air-duct. By one in the morning I was pulling out hair.

'Not to mention the waste of *money*,' I shrieked. 'When $16 would've got us seats in second class, with windows and *fuckin'* AIR!'

'People are looking,' Cora said.

At six in the morning, after two more brief flirtations with sleep, we dragged ourselves onto the railway platform at the hot and very humid port of Campeche on the Gulf of Mexico. We crawled to the nearest cheapie and slept until the middle of the afternoon. We then went out, bought some food, and came back to make a meal in our big, bare windowless room, into whose bowels streamed no natural light, on whose walls grew a menacing black fungus, on whose wood-beamed ceiling rested dozens of fat mosquitoes, on whose grotty floor stood a narrow bed of rough planks, and on whose buckled, metal, fold-up table stood a medicinal bottle of rum. And as Cora crashed out a second time, I sat in the dim light of a naked, 10-watt bulb hanging from some very dodgy-looking wires, and wrote down the account of our one-and-only ever, first-class train journey. I then lit a mosquito coil, stuck it under the bed and lay down beside Cora in a bog of sweat.

Welcome, I said to myself, *to blessed Yucatán, land of the blessed Maya.*

Although I'll grant you this: that wording may not be precise.

CHAPTER 27

A Yucatán Loop

Mayan women walked the streets of Campeche in knee-length *huipiles*, just as they had when the Spanish arrived. A single piece of brightly-embroidered, white cloth with holes for the arms and a square opening for the head, was draped over a lighter lace-fringed petticoat, a style that hadn't changed in Yucatán for 2,000 years. The men wore white cottons, similar to the dress of the Coras, or Western clothes given a Mayan flavour by the choice of colours.

The Maya are the largest homogenous group of native American people north of Peru. Belonging to a culture that can be traced back to 2,000 BC, they inhabit a vast area, encompassing the Yucatán Peninsula and parts of Tabasco and Chiapas states in Mexico, along with Guatemala, Belize and parts of Honduras and El Salvador.

Often establishing their settlements close to *cenotes* - natural water holes gouged out of the limestone of their homeland - they became over time extremely successful farmers, highly accomplished in art and craftwork, who built immense cities with tall pyramids and stone temples adorned with fantastic sculptures, murals and motifs. These they connected with a network of raised causeways, and recorded the details of their accomplishments in a complex form of hieroglyphic writing. They navigated the coasts of the Caribbean in massive dugout canoes, engaged in extensive manufacture and trade, and left behind much evidence of an extraordinary knowledge of mathematics and astronomy, including a unique calendar more precise than the one in use today.

To appease a pantheon of gods - who included the ubiquitous plumed serpent, Kukulcán (Quetzalcoatl of Teotihuacán), and the rain god, Chac - they observed an annual round of festivals and human sacrifice, accompanied by an intoxicating honey mead called *balche*. Then, like the people of Teotihuacán, and for reasons similarly unknown, they abandoned their cities and returned to the forests.

With no sign of war or natural disaster, city states that took centuries to build melted away. By the time the *conquistadores* arrived in

Yucatán, the great temple cities were long deserted - some for as much as 500 years - and the lofty pyramids and stately palaces had been swallowed by jungle. When they were rediscovered - in great part by chicleros, chicle-tree scouts who roamed the forests in search of the tall sapodillas that provided the raw material of chewing gum - the grandiose architecture was at first thought to be Roman or Phoenician, or maybe even the work of one of the lost tribes of Israel.

Like the Aztecs and the Incas, the Maya were to suffer appallingly at the hands of the conquistadores, their ascendancy finally coming to an end in an orgy of slaughter in March 1697 when the Spaniards overran their last living city on the peninsula of Tayasal on Lake Petén Itzá in Guatemala.

Nevertheless, they survived as a people and still inhabited huge areas of their former lands, albeit no longer as rulers of those lands. For myself and Cora, the Gulf port of Campeche was our point of entry. We would spend the next two months among the descendants of the remarkable people who built the great ancient cities of Mexico and Central America.

It took a full day to recover from the train journey before we began to appreciate the friendly warmth and historical significance of Campeche, with its colourful markets, ancient city walls, fortified ramparts, colonnaded buildings, pastel-painted houses and 500-year-old cathedral. And the impromptu fish stalls thrown up each evening by sea-scoured men returning from the Gulf with the day's catch.

Founded by the Spanish in 1540, Campeche sat on the ruins of the earlier Mayan town of Ah-Kin-Pech, unknown to the outside world until March 1517, when a small Spanish force under Francisco Hernández de Córdova landed to replenish its water supply. Surrounded by Maya warriors, the Spaniards panicked and fled. A few days later they ran into a storm, and pulled in again, this time at Champoton, forty miles to the south. Here, their luck ran out when a Maya force, led by Moch Couoh, decimated their ranks, mortally wounding de Córdova.

Ten years later, Commander Francisco de Montejo the Elder made the first serious attempt to conquer the Campechanos but was repulsed. For the next thirteen years the Maya fought the invaders. Suffering terrible losses through warfare and imported diseases, they eventually succumbed to the forces of Francisco de Montejo the Younger (son of the Elder) in December 1540, after which the first Spanish settlement was established at Campeche. A year later, at the bloody Battle of T'ho, Francisco de Montejo the Younger broke the power of the Maya and founded the new capital, Mérida, on the ruins of T'ho. From there the slaughter of the Yucatán Maya continued until the final conquest in 1546, after which tens of thousands were sold into slavery.

Over the coming centuries Campeche was to become one of the most important ports in Mexico and a regular target of English, Dutch and Portuguese pirates who sacked the town whenever their rum ran dry.

We spent three days exploring the city's past, and three nights under the 10-watt bulb of our windowless room, planning a loose Yucatán loop. The first stop would be the Mayan ruins of Uxmal, 105 miles to the north-east.

* * *

The noon bus to Uxmal arrived at Campeche bus station at 1.15 p.m. to loud clapping from the waiting passengers. Grateful that it had at least arrived, we stepped out into the oppressive midday heat and went to board, only to be confronted by a now-familiar hiccup. Whereas we and many of the passengers had bought tickets in the station and had been allocated specific seats, others paid at the door and were allowed to board first; then many of those with station tickets found their seats taken, which led to rage-control issues and further delays. And when we finally pulled out of the station - an hour and a half late - some floppy-legged loser come careering out of nowhere, yelling nobody told me.

Eventually, we cleared the bus station and the city, and chugged and roared eastwards towards Hopelchén before turning north through the hottest hours of the day when most people were snoozing off the siesta in homes lifted from ancient Mayan art. Oval in shape, they were raised from stone or withes covered in adobe, with high-pitched roofs of black thatch, no windows, and open doorways beyond which hung the gloating hammocks.

We had regular stops to pick up more passengers, many of the men in white cottons and carrying long machetes in scabbards that were slung over their shoulders to dangle at their waists.

Eighty-seven miles from Campeche, we passed through the Mayan ruins of Kabah which straddled the road. Half an hour later we arrived in Uxmal.

'We'll not be staying here,' Cora announced after checking the cost of the only hotel. Exhausted from recent days, we grabbed a quick peek at the ruins and took a lift to Mérida from a French couple. Not exactly an archaeological triumph, but a good move as it turned out.

'This is more like it,' Cora said as we booked into the Hotel Francia where $3.50 got us a double with a fan. 'I hate rip-offs.' [a.k.a. the cost of a large hotel. We never really did get over the economising mindset of a decade of penniless travel.]

Mérida at night was a city of restaurants, young travellers, 'straight tourists' (considered degenerate and best avoided), and a beautiful, brightly-lit Plaza Grande of trees, green grass and S-shaped benches designed for conversation. It was also hot and humid. After an hour of dipping in and out of the Indian food stalls, we'd had enough and retreated to the hotel with two ears of boiled corn smeared in chilli sauce and lemon juice. The room next door was now occupied by Rod from England and two young French women, Marie and Francoise, the latter on crutches after losing a leg to gangrene. Rod, dark-haired, with the kind of muscle definition that comes from travel emaciation, was an artist.

'I'm putting together an exhibition,' he told us, 'based on my travels and liberal infusions of magic fungi. To add to my material, I'm going to Chichén Itzá tomorrow. It's the spring equinox and the Mayas are having a bit if an event. Something to do with the Pyramid of Kukulcán, or *El Castillo* as they also call it around here. You guys might be interested...'

Our Yucatán loop went in the bin.

CHAPTER 28

The Descent Of Kulkulcán

Our bus left Mérida at noon and pounded off, packed to capacity, for Chichén Itzá, one of the greatest of the ancient Mayan cities. Cora, Marie and Francoise got seats. Rod and I had to stand as we hammered into the bush through the hottest, most humid, hours of the day, crushed from all sides by Mayan pilgrims.

'This is gonna be one long journey,' Rod said, 'unless we have a little something to pass the time.' He rummaged down into his artistic satchel and pulled from it a jar of mushrooms preserved in honey. 'Watch out for the maggots,' he warned as he popped a bunch into his mouth and handed me the jar. Pleasantly, we reached Chichén Itzá.

'A few people got here before us,' Cora noted.

Parked vehicles lined the road. Buoyant crowds were on the move. And we were still a couple of miles from the site. By the time we were dropped at the gates the huge site and adjoining village had the atmosphere of a rock festival with stalls selling food, drinks and handicrafts as 10,000 Maya gathered for the Descent of the Plumed Serpent, Kukulcán.

In the middle of the ancient ball court in front of *El Castillo* (the Temple of Kukulcán), Mayan dancers were putting on a display. On the Altar of Sacrifices the mother and sister of Mexico's president waited with their entourage for the moment when Kukulcán would do his thing.

El Castillo, the large pyramid dominating Chichén Itzá is so positioned that, on the afternoon of the spring equinox, shadows cast by one of its stepped corners strike the outside of the northern staircase in the shape of an undulating serpent, each hump touching the edge of the balustrade, and all connecting to the serpent's head at the foot of the stairs. As the afternoon progresses, the serpent loses its humps, one at a time from the top down - the slow and magical Descent of Kukulcán. This effect could only have been obtained by the most precise architectural, mathematical and astronomical skills. You only got one chance.

'In ancient times,' the announcer crackled in Spanish into the archaic sound system, (translated by Francoise) 'people came from all over

Mexico and Central America to see this great spectacle. A long way on foot in those days before roads and railways.'

Cora, Rod and I climbed onto the walls of the ball court where we had a commanding view of the unfolding drama. As the sun moved into position, the curvatures of light began to find their position on the balustrade. At that precise moment Rod's mushrooms kicked in with a thought.

'I know what I could do. I could go and explore the ruins on the other side of the road while there's nobody there.'

'You'll miss what we've come for,' Cora warned.

'Naw, I won't.'

'Bad idea,' Cora said.

On the far side of the road, all was as expected: nothing but birds and iguanas as I wandered the temples, the bare stone rooms with their secret pasts, and the observatory. I became one of the astronomers of long ago, perched on their very seat, calculating the exact dimensions that would give *El Castillo* its descending serpent. (A bit to the left there, boys.) In the background, the announcer's voice crackled on. 'In the year 1200,' he had earlier told us, 'there were many people still living in this city state but by the year 1204, not one remained.' Why and where had they gone? I sat and worked it all out, providing the answers where archaeology had failed. But they elude me now.

Back at *El Castillo,* the serpent was undulating closer to the finale. On the level below Cora and Rod, thousands were sitting on the ground so that everyone could get a clear view of the entire pyramid. But as the climax approached, three women up front refused point blank to sit down. Eventually the crowd was yelling. Something to the effect of *Sit fucking down!* But, they stood their ground, braving the growing torrent of abuse and a barrage of missiles. Glaring at the yelling thousands, they ignored the pleas of the announcer until they finally decided to teach the crowd a lesson. They swept up their bags and stormed off.

By the time I found Rod and Cora, Kukulcán had gone to bed. I had missed the show.

'What did I tell you?' Cora said.

'Don't worry,' Rod, the mushroom villain, said. 'You can come back tomorrow and see it all again.'

Within an hour, the crowd had dwindled, leaving the ruins to our little group and a few of the villagers gathered at the sacred cenote where human sacrifices were once tossed into the water. Away to the west, the sun went down in a blaze of orange while Francoise astonished us by scooting up and down the steps of *El Castillo* like spiderwoman on crutches.

In the evening all five of us attended an outdoor concert a few blocks from Mérida's Plaza Grande. We then went to eat in an open-fronted restaurant. In mid meal, a great commotion rose from the kitchen. This was followed by the cook charging into the restaurant whacking away with a brush at a fleeing rat. Around and between the tables went the chase with the brush bashing right, left and centre. Then the rat somehow jumped up on an empty table and splat! As diners held forkfuls of food in mid-air, the brush came down with tectonic force. Blood and guts sprayed across several tables. The cook picked up the remains and tossed them into the street.

'*Bon appetite,*' Francoise said and we all raised glasses to that.

On the day after the equinox, Cora and I went back to Chichén Itzá for an exclusive rehash of Kukulcán's descent. When it was over, we climbed the steps of *El Castillo* to the temple at the top and came face to face with the Red Jaguar - believed to have once been a throne. Although it wasn't the exact experience of the day before, the consolation prize was that there wasn't another soul in sight.

* * *

Being an artist, Rod didn't travel light. His gear weighed in excess of 100 pounds and was broken down in four parts: an easel strapped to a rucksack frame which he carried on his back; two large cases, and a bulky string bag full of sharp, dangerous protrusions.

'These are my sketch-pads, paper, paints, brushes, inks, pencils and general artistic shit,' he explained. 'A bit over the top, I suppose.'

'Not at all,' I assured him. 'In Guadalajara we saw a French guy staggering through the street with a hand-painted porcelain sink.'

Rod, Cora and I had arrived in Puerto Juarez on the Caribbean coast at half-eight on the night of Saturday, March 24th. Destination: Isla Mujeres, eight miles off the coast.

One look at the hotels was enough. Unaffordable. We took a two-mile bus ride into the centre of Cancun in an effort to find cheaper accommodation. Only to find that it was even more expensive.

'And full of *tourists,*' Rod said in disgust.

As Isla Mujeres was only an hour by boat from Cancun, we began to worry.

'It could be full of the same weirdos,' Rod said.

'We could go on to Tulum,' Cora suggested, 'and give Isla Mujeres a miss.'

We agreed and lugged all the gear around to Cancun bus station. However, the next bus to Tulum didn't leave until 3.15 a.m. so we had a few beers.

'What about we flip a coin?' I suggested. 'Heads, Tulum. Tails, Isla Mujeres.'

Tails it was. We took a taxi back to the wharf at Puerto Juarez to become the only passengers on a small open ferry as it made an unscheduled night run to Isla Mujeres.

Arriving at 11 p.m. we had a quick snack of *tortas* with chicken and salad, then walked around to Coco Beach Hostel, a sheltered tent site and a collection of rickety huts where guests hung their hammocks. As we pitched the tent, the mosquitoes came on with a vengeance. The rain followed and we were grounded for the night.

We stayed two days on the island, some four miles long and 700 yards wide, and it confirmed our fears. My notes of the time describe: '*an ugly centre full of shops and restaurants, a whole community committed to exploiting foreigners... characterless, colourless... selling hamburgers, neutral food and overpriced trinkets. The beach a narrow strip of sand and already one concrete obscenity [hotel] casting its shadow across it... Dozens of bored-looking foreigners wandering about during the day and eating and drinking at night...*'

The proprietors of the Coco Beach Hostel included an elderly man who appeared to be senile and regularly turned off the gas supply, and a younger guy who wanted to massage all the women.

Rod, Cora and I returned to the mainland on the Tuesday and took a bus to Tulum where we booked into the local campsite.

Tulum was a gem. The old Mayan ruins, built as a defence against invading Caribs, stood on cliffs overlooking a turquoise sea. Just offshore, the surf broke over a coral reef. Palms lined a beach of white sand, cooled by the trade winds. Rod, who stayed with us for the next two days, called the exhaustion of doing nothing 'compensation'.

Once Rod had left, we moved from the campsite and pitched our tent among the palms close to where a couple of French hippies had built themselves a shelter. In that secluded place, we listened to Roberta from 'New Awlins' play the flute and stared out to sea in case a whale passed. Or a dragon.

CHAPTER 29

'Wop Him Mon!'

'Oh mon,' the Creole Immigration Officer said, 'why only stay two weeks?' He was a large man with a touch of Rasta about his hair, and a peaked cap that almost covered his eyes. 'Belize is the country of God.'

He gleefully stamped two-week visas into our passports and signed them.

'Have a nice stay,' he said. 'You are the first Irish people I have met.' (The old refrain.)

We were in English-speaking Belize, which was then moving from the colonial status of British Honduras to full independence.

Half an hour after arriving at the frontier we were moving south along a badly corrugated dirt road through dense rainforest - a continuation of the jungles and swamps of Quintana Roo on the Mexican side of the frontier. This was the land of the great trees - mahogany, cedar and chicozapote - and home to jaguars, ocelots, howler monkeys, boas and hundreds of bird species. Further east, the jungle melted into swamps, mangroves and lagoons that provided a refuge for crocodiles, turtles, iguanas and manatees.

In the Maya and Mestizo villages, poverty was far more evident than in Yucatán. Children in rags begged for food. Pigs and chickens rummaged in muddy clearings between stilted wooden huts. But, north of the town of Orange Walk, the land opened out into neat farms, and the houses reflected a more prosperous environment.

As we commented on the sudden change, a fair-skinned couple came towards us in a horse and buggy. The man was dressed in denim overalls and a straw hat. The blonde-haired woman wore a long, old-fashioned dress and bonnet.

'Who on Earth are they?' was my question as another similar man came out of a field on horseback.

'Mennonites,' a voice answered from behind. The voice belonged to Tim, a former stockbroker, now a long-haired peacenik from Virginia, who had boarded the bus in Corozal on the Belize side of the border. 'About 3,000 of them came down here in 1958 from the States, Canada and Mexico. They're Anabaptists, originally from Holland, who still speak an old dialect that's a mix of Dutch and German. They're pacifists and they don't believe in using modern technology. They grew out of the Radical Reformation of the 16th century in Europe, and then had to get out due to persecution because of their beliefs, especially the beliefs that stop them paying land taxes or joining the military. They mostly live along the River Hondo and around Orange Walk, and they run their own form of local government and their own banks and schools. Pretty cool, eh?'

In Orange Walk Tim joined us for fish stew and bread. Like ourselves, he was heading for Belize City.

'It's a really laid-back place,' he said. 'Full of cool music and them funky Creoles.'

In the mix of Creole, Mestizo, Carib, Spanish, Maya, Mennonite, Chinese and South Asian that made up the small population of Belize - 143,000 in 1979 - forty percent were Creole, the offspring of European adventurers and slaves brought over from West Africa to work the country's logging camps. In time, all had adopted the Creole culture and the Creole dialect, peppered with American hip jargon. Most of the 40,000 people of Belize City were Creole.

Occupying a peninsula that jutted out into the Caribbean, Belize City was more of a town, much of it built of wood and tin on dirt streets. It was divided, north from south, by Haulover Creeek, so called because cattlemen of the past had to haul their cattle across with ropes. A hand-cranked swing bridge, installed in 1923, now connected both sides. Along the waterfront, an old world character prevailed. The bars were rough.

Overall, the atmosphere was relaxed. Much of the traffic consisted of horses and carts and bicycles, while many of the townsfolk spent long hours watching the world from the verandas or wooden staircases of their homes. Along Haulover Creek, we noted that some of the houses were leaning at crazy angles as if they had fallen sideways and nobody bothered to straighten them up. The small harbour, with its dugouts and sailed fishing boats was tranquillity itself at dusk: the sky and buildings blue, and the first lights quivering in the black water.

'Hello mon. What's the trip? What's happening?' We had barely stepped from the bus. The cool guy accosting us was dressed in lemon shorts, a red and blue flowery shirt, earrings, reflective sunglasses and a wool hat. 'Hey mon,' he went on, 'what you doin'? If you just cruisin', Belize is a real nice place for cruisin'. But you gotta feel good mon, you gotta feel real good; like you gotta catch a slice o' the action; an' that's why I'm here. Got some real nice smoke here in my hat. Hey mon, how would you like to freak out?'

'We're just looking for a place to stay,' Tim said. 'A cheap hotel.'

Our man led us across town to a place that had no vacancies. Tim dropped off but Cora and I decided to follow him once more and ended up in a friendly family-run guesthouse. It sat at the top of a wooden staircase, close to the Swing Bridge. Below this vantage point, Creoles in sunglasses and straw hats would saunter down the street until they heard some music from someone's house or a bar, whereupon they would immediately break into dance, and dance on until the music faded. They would then fall back into the saunter until the next musical interlude. Even the cops did this. One afternoon, a cop stopped myself and Cora for cutting diagonally across a junction.

'No mon,' he said. 'You don't go that way. You cross one street, then you cross the other. Oka-a-ay?' He then clicked the fingers of both hands and jigged off down the street, with the benefit of no music at all.

The travellers' focal point in town was Mom's Café. Mom, a large robust woman from the United States had arrived in Belize around 1970 and set up an American-style diner in a warehouse adjacent to the Swing Bridge. This quickly became the meeting point for expats, backpackers and adventurers, virtually anyone passing through the city. If you wanted information in Belize, the only way to get it was to talk directly to someone who was in the know and that person would be found at Mom's Café.

On our first visit, we made the acquaintance of Hartmud from Germany and Valerie from the States who were travelling together. Hartmud, in jeans, psychedelic shirt, white socks (what!) and sandals, was a slim speedy guy with thick wiry hair parted in the middle and hanging to his shoulders. Valerie, thin with a finely-etched face, brown collar-length curls and a long loose dress with a tiny floral pattern, was a demure soul with a streak of mischief in her eyes. Like so many of the travellers we had met, they were both in their early twenties.

'We were thinking of checking out the local music scene,' Cora said.

'We'd also like to find some music,' Valerie said.

'I did not know that,' Hartmud laughed. 'But it sounds like a nice idea.'

The conversation then drifted animatedly to other topics and the music idea seemed to fade.

However, once night had fallen, it surged back: we would go and catch some reggae music. But no luck. When our search of the town proved unsuccessful, we returned to Mom's to see if we could enlist the help of a local. That was how we met Danny Young, hustler and gentleman pugilist, a tall, muscular, 23-year-old Creole with slightly bloodshot eyes, a huge smile, long sideburns, a thin curling moustache and two tufts of hair that stuck out each side of a yellow and blue baseball hat where he kept his 'bullets' of dope. In faded blue jeans, green singlet and flip-flops, he came striding through the door and was immediately sympathetic to our cause.

'You wanna hear some good music, some good reggae music, find the high spots an' get mellow?' he said. 'I'll take you to a real cool place, sure mon, you'll hear some good music, the best. The place I'll take you is the liveliest spot in Belize City. Let's go.'

And off we went, across town to the dark waterfront.

'This is the place,' he said stopping outside a rough-looking, wooden tumbledown called Blood Isle. He barged through the saloon-doors and led us into a dark dungeon where the only lighting was provided by low-voltage, fluorescent strips that gave a lavender glow to everything white. Danny ordered a bottle of some kind of anise rotgut between the five of us.

'You can take the bottle to any other bar,' he explained.

A group of drunken Creole men at the bar argued loudly about some woman. In a corner, two young women sat drinking. Small groups of men and women milled about the front and back doors. The smell of hash pervaded all.

'I don't find this place very relaxing,' Hartmud said.

We had our first drink as another row brewed over at the bar and Danny rolled a joint.

'We go outside to smoke,' he said and we all trooped out.

In the weak light thrown by the bar, men and women went by in twos and threes, appearing suddenly from the shadows, then disappearing into them again. When Danny reached out for a passing woman, a husky male voice, whose owner never showed, spoke from the darkness.

'Hey mon,' it growled, 'don't touch the forbidden fruit.'

Another man went by, slowly clicking his fingers in our faces. Hartmud and Valerie fled, leaving myself and Cora with Danny's undivided company.

We did a full crawl of the waterfront bars, carrying a second bottle of anise from one to the other until the night meshed into a single, elongated blur of blaring rock, fluorescent lights, brightly daubed walls, glowing joints and wild dancing. In one bar, a thin guy in a wrinkled crimson suit ran a card school. Behind him a naked woman astride an enormous green key smiled from the wall. 'Put something nice between your legs,' the poster said. A sign above the jukebox urged all to 'freak out with me'. Each place reeked of dope and was full of very rough-looking, mellow guys rolling very long cigarettes.

'What about taking photos in the town?' Cora asked Danny.

'Momma,' Danny said, 'people just *want* you to slap them a photo.'

'What about the reggae music?' I asked.

'Mon,' he said, 'that machine there eats quarters. You gimme a quarter an' you'll get all the nice music.' However, no sooner had he fed the machine than the plan changed. 'We should go shoot some pool.' Danny said and he ushered us out the door. 'Mon,' he said when I protested, 'they got the same kinda music up the other place.'

At the pool hall, a steamy back-room full of stoned men and women, we had to 'go catch some breeze.' As we stood outside the back door, letting the trade wind cool the sweat that trickled down our necks, a young woman in a white dress, flushed out by the pool-hall music, came gyrating to the doorway of her home.

'What happened all those lopsided houses down by Haulover Creek?' I asked Danny.

'Big breeze came in one day mon,' he said. 'Knocked 'em all down like flies.'

The big breeze turned out to have been Hurricane Hattie that swept in from the Caribbean on Halloween of 1961, eighteen years before!

Next morning we turned up at Mom's for a late breakfast, much to the surprise of Hartmud and Valerie who had assumed that we had been murdered down some back alley. It was Sunday, sleepy Sunday, when few of the town's 40,000 residents were about. Nevertheless, music filled the air from pubs and homes alike. At the old Belize Club, people hung out the windows while the town's serious drinkers were already bringing custom to the downtown pubs. The swing doors of one pub warned in a scrawl: *'No bums; No bad men; No loafers'*. A sign over another pub proclaimed that Francisco Castaneda was *'licensed to sell fermented and spirituous liquors'*. The four of us went in and had a few to escape the afternoon swelter. Across the street a sign on a gate said: *'For those who can read and understand, no parking outside this gate.'*

In the evening Danny turned up at Mom's for a second round of the waterfront bars. Hartmud and Valerie, inspired by our accounts of the previous night, decided to take a chance.

'It's all happening at Johnnie's Bar tonight, momma,' Danny said to Cora. 'They got a live band playin' live music. It's from the guys who won the soccer match today.' [Whoever they were.]

354

Off we went through the darkened streets to Johnnie's Bar where the only light was a red glow. The music would have blown the head off an octopus and the dancing was in full swing. The kind of dancing in which every part of the body seems to move independently of every other part, the kind you could watch all night but never equal. I went to the bar, ordered a shared bottle of cheap Jamaican rum and five glasses, and we settled in.

'You don't dance to no technique mon,' Danny said of my prancing efforts. 'You gotta move to the vibe o' the music. So why don't you get speeded up mon an' shake a leg.'

'Danny,' I said, 'you're talking to the wrong guy. My favourite dancing position is sitting at a table with a glass in my hand.'

As joss sticks burned and people in the semi-darkness shoved joints in our mouths and got 'speeded up', Cora and Valerie were pinched in the ass and some unseen bastard grabbed Cora between the legs.

'Rough place,' Hartmud said. 'I am not too sure that it is really safe.'

Then the floor began to clear to give space to a young couple who appeared to be in some kind of frenzied delirium.

'The marimba,' Danny said. 'They are going to dance the marimba.'

I have never since seen the likes of what happened next. Moving with a speed and stamina that was prodigious - the guy in jeans and singlet, the woman in almost nothing - the couple went up in a blue flame, furiously shaking, wriggling and spooning one another until they were coated in sweat that looked metallic in the red light. The band, taking the cue, ratcheted up the tempo, and the woman swung her curves at the crowd. For fifteen minutes, they never let up. While the crowd hooted and cheered, they danced into one another. They rubbed groin to groin. They each pushed a thigh into the other's crotch and somehow spiralled down to the floor, each riding the other's thigh like it was Shergar. Then up again, the woman shoving her breasts in the guy's face, slapping him with one and then the other as the crowd roared, swilled their rum and passed the joints. And on it went. If the band hadn't stopped for a break, I reckon the two would have keeled over dead.

'Okay,' the lead singer bellowed over the mike. 'Give the dudes a drink.'

They were whisked off shoulder-high and dumped on the bar where rum and smoke were poured down their throats.

That was the marimba. Well at least that's what they called it in Johnnie's Bar.

'Break-time mon,' Danny said. 'Let's go shoot the breeze, take a walk up the street, see what's goin' down at the Bismark. You go now. I follow you in one minute.'

Outside the Bismark, a similar establishment to Johnnie's, we encountered a true-life Caribbean pirate. Dressed in a loose shirt, and baggy trousers, with a handkerchief tied to his head and a dead snake wrapped around his wrist, he was about forty, lean and wiry, with a wispy beard and slits for eyes. Part of a gang, we later learned, that robbed small boats along the Belizean coast. Against our better judgement, he managed to hustle the four of us inside the Bismark where he began to throw so much at us that it was hard to keep up. He did a dance, tried to sell us bracelets, coral and grass, offered to marry Valerie, and loudly farted four times. He was in the process of producing more goods from his satchel when Danny arrived. There was a moment of sharp tension when the pirate helped himself to a large glass of rum from our bottle. Danny snapped at him; but the show went on and Danny sat down.

Rum in hand, Wispybeard the Pirate stood in front of us, stretched out his right leg, and lowered himself to the floor with the leg rigid in front of him. But he slipped and almost fell over.

'Ha!' Danny said, rising from his seat. 'He can't even do that.'

Danny repeated the trick without falling. He even went one better by crossing the outstretched leg over the bent one.

'Can you do *that*, eh?' he asked the pirate.

The pirate ignored him, reaching up instead to an overhead beam and slowly hauling himself up on one arm until his face was level with the beam, which he kissed before slowly lowering himself back down. He repeated this three times, challenging Danny to follow. Danny refused.

'My weight is more than you,' he said.

'Fuck you,' the pirate said. 'Your mother was a whore.'

'Your mother was a pig's whore,' Danny said. Upping the ante, the pirate grabbed Danny's glass, threw the remainder of the rum on the floor and smashed the glass on our table.

'Fuck you mon,' Danny said. 'That was good rum.'

At that, several burly customers helped the barman toss the pirate into the street. Our company bought another bottle of rum and went back to Johnnie's Bar. But the pirate followed.

'This smells like trouble,' I said to Cora. 'If it blows, be ready to get the hell out. There could be alliances here that we know nothing about and the whole place could go apeshit.'

Hartmud and Valerie took a powder. We didn't see them again.

For a while everything was okay. The music raged. We tossed back rum. And the pirate eyeballed us from the bar. When he made his move, it was against Cora.

'Momma,' he said. 'Why you take my fuckin' cigarettes?'

'You fuck off now,' Danny advised. The pirate turned and slapped Danny's glass from his hand.

'Leave it,' I suggested. 'He's not worth it.' But Danny was past advice.

'Mon,' he hissed, 'that was my last rum.'

'Fuck your rum and your mother,' the pirate said.

Danny swung a punch. They both rolled onto the table and the lot tumbled over.

'Go!' I shouted to Cora. We made for the door as the bar erupted.

Out into the street the fight spilled, with men shouting and trying to break it up. In a sudden move, the pirate had a knife in his hand. Yelling and lunging, he hit Danny in the neck. Danny wiped a hand across the wound and looked at the blood. Murder in his eyes, he grabbed a heavy lump of wood from a broken fence and creased the pirate over the head.

'Wop him mon! Wop him good!' some guy shouted as blood soaked the pirate's shirt.

Danny hit him another three almighty whacks over the head. This should have done it. But, like the Dolt of Flanders back in 1917 (a.k.a. Field Marshal Douglas Haig), the pirate didn't know when to stop. He came on again with the knife. Then, realising that the length of wood gave Danny a distance advantage, he too grabbed a lump of fence. More head-whacking followed, but it was all done by Danny. The pirate slumped to the ground and lay still in a spreading pool of blood.

'Danny,' I said, 'we're outta here. Before somebody ends up dead.'

'You see that, mon?' Danny grimaced. 'He juked for me with that blade and I had to wop him five, ten, times to cool him down.'

The following evening we met Danny again outside Mom's Café. He had been 'groovin' around at Johnnie's Bar'. As far as he could fathom, nobody had died the night before. As we talked, a thin Creole with a beard staggered over from a knot of drunk men who were using one another to stay upright.

'Nice day mon,' he said. 'Nice rocks. Nice bush. The cleanest water in all Belize. Lots of tigers in all them caves.'

* * *

We were in Mom's Café again, having breakfast, when we met Erich, a slim, bearded German who had driven from California in a clapped-out International that looked like a cross between a standard car and a four-wheel-drive. He and two companions were poring over a map of Guatemala.

'You want to travel to Tikal?' he called from the next table. 'We are looking for two more passengers to help with the petrol as the car will only go fifteen miles to the gallon.' For effect, he pushed wire-rimmed glasses further up the bridge of his nose.

'Sounds like a plan,' I said and we moved tables.

'This is Reinhard and Danielle from Switzerland,' Erich said, introducing the other two. 'We met yesterday.'

Reinhard looked the part, with his collar-length hair, jeans and a loose shirt. Danielle, with short hair cut in a shiny fringe, and a blue knee-length dress, looked like the lost model of Mom's Café.

'When do we leave?' I asked.

'After breakfast.'

'Sounds like a plan,' Cora said. 'Before we have a chance to visit any more bars.'

* * *

It was stinking hot as we drove along the dirt track that ran west through the jungle from Belize City to Belmopan and onwards to the Guatemalan frontier. There was very little traffic and not too much evidence of people; but plenty of snakes, iguanas, parrots and macaws. As we bounced through the potholes, the old International wasn't doing too well, with several stops needed to fill the radiator. However, after about two hours, we reached Belmopan, a collection of ugly concrete buildings that had been the new capital of Belize since 1970, a move prompted by the devastation of Hurricane Hattie that had exposed the risks of a low-lying coastal capital. In this 'city' of a mere 4,000 residents we stopped for a coffee. With the car chugging and backfiring, we then travelled on to the small settlement of San Ignacio where we stocked up with food. A few miles further on, Cora and I thought we were hallucinating when we passed a mobile patrol of British soldiers in two armoured cars.

'What are *they* doing here?' I squeaked. (Belfast traumas kicking in.)

'They are still here,' Danielle said, 'because Guatemala wants to take Belize. They say it is the eastern province of Guatemala.'

'Keep going,' I urged Erich, 'before I throw up.'

From San Ignacio, we drove to the Mayan ruins at Xunantunich overlooking the ford of the Rio Mopan. As we came within sight of the ruins, the car overheated and cut out.

'Not good,' Erich said, throwing a dumfounded look at the rest of us. 'We need to get out for a minute.'

To fix the problem, Erich tossed petrol over the carburettor. To check that the pump was running properly, he said. But as soon as he hit the ignition the lot burst into flames. This was followed by Erich throwing water over the flames, then dousing them with a cushion as the rest of us dived for cover.

'Shit man,' Reinhard said. 'Where did you learn this trick?'

'Very old trick,' Erich replied. 'Called now you see us, now you don't. Boom!'

After a second incendiary display of Erich's mechanical skills at the ford of the Rio Mopan, outside Benque Viejo, Cora had a suggestion.

'It's a lovely evening. Why don't we just camp here beside the river, let the engine cool down, and go on to Guatemala in the morning.'

'I think it is the best,' Erich agreed.

We pulled off the road, threw up two tents and built a fire. Visitors included an enormous toad, two kingfishers, a very large spider and several herons. After dinner we swam in the river, where small fish did their best to eat us. After furious attempts to nibble us to death, they turned their attention to anything we threw them: banana skins, bread, tomatoes; it didn't matter. Then, as night gathered and the birds went frantic in the trees, Cora spotted flames rising in the forest.

'Not another bloody house fire,' she said.

'Maybe we should go and investigate,' Reinhard suggested and both of them went off into the bush.

The fire proved to be the harmless burning of rubbish. But on the way back Cora strayed off to one side when she heard strange incantations coming from a small cabin. Emerging from the bush, she came on a group of people who were attempting to cure a sick woman through a voodoo-style ritual.

'Come,' an older man invited. She went in and sat with the family while the priest figure did his utmost to exorcise the 'demons' causing the woman's condition.

'It was sort of amazing,' she said when she came back to the campfire. 'Like something out of a film. A pity you all missed it.'

'So, you were alone in the jungle with the voodoo,' Erich said. 'Very good.'

We sat up late, gazed at the stars and the fireflies, listened to the night chorus, finished the last of gentleman Danny Young's 'bullets' and reverted to type with tales of derring-do shared in a halo of soporific euphoria. We then settled down for the night in our tents, lulled to sweet dreams by the soft gurgling of the Rio Mopan.

CHAPTER 30

El Petén And Tikal

Sure enough, at the Guatemalan border all maps showed the country stretching right to the coast where Belize should have been. The border guards were in absolute denial, checking passports and baggage on a border that didn't, according to the map behind them, actually exist.

Border formalities were pleasant enough, with the relaxed officials much taken by the Irish passports and the fact that the IRA was at war with Britain. It was obvious that they resented the British presence that forced them to patrol a non-existent border.

The road from the border twisted through the hot, steamy jungle of Petén - a tangle of creepers, bamboo, palms and trees, rich in mahogany, tropical cedar, rubber, and the chicle-bearing sapodillas. By noon, however, we hadn't gone very far, delayed by frequent drink stops, swim stops, overheated-engine stops, and a road that was even worse than the day before. But nobody was much bothered as we shaded under trees and soaked in the immense variety of wildlife. Iguanas and lizards. Hummingbirds, parrots and Scarlet Macaws. Praying mantises, termites, spiders, butterflies and bizarre caterpillars with huge tufts of stinging hairs. On the ground there were orchids and fungi in striking shapes and colours while many of the larger trees were festooned in bromeliads. These floral aristocrats of the rainforest, capable of taking nutrition from the air, presented themselves in an endless array of form, size and chromatic display.

When we arrived in the afternoon at El Cruce where the Tikal road swung north and the road to Flores, the tiny 'capital' of El Petén, went southwest, the old gas-guzzling International needed a fill-up. But, problems. A hundred and fifty miles southeast of Flores, the bridge at the Rio Dulce was down and few supplies were getting through. Erich, who was planning to drive to Tikal, then on to Guatemala City, could only get twenty-five litres for the car.

'This is a big problem,' he said as we started again for Tikal. 'If that bridge stays down, it is not possible to get the petrol I need to drive to the south. I do not think I can drive to Tikal. I must think about this.'

It was well after dark when we threw up the idea of finding some place to stay. We could then maybe take the bus to Tikal. Surely, there had to be buses.

'*El Gringo Perdido*,' Cora said as we passed the sign. 'A campsite by Lake Petén Itzá. Just the ticket.'

'I would prefer to go on to Tikal,' Reinhard said.

'You are in a minority,' Danielle said. 'The lake sounds too romantic.'

El Gringo Perdido (The Lost American) was two miles north of El Remate on a rough road that circled the lake. With shaded gardens and a small thatched restaurant, the camping area was surrounded by forest and palms, and perpetually visited by parrots, hummingbirds, macaws and deer. There was so much bush on site that the whole place merged into the blanket of rainforest that crept into the hills behind. The lake itself was crystal clear with good swimming and a small wharf that jutted into the water. A thatched roof at the end of the wharf provided much appreciated shade and a daytime roost for sleeping bats. There was also a dugout for general use. No electricity or phones meant that the forest subsumed the place once darkness had fallen.

By the time we pulled in, the three young women who ran the restaurant were about to end their shift. However, they opened up again and served us fruit pie and drinks with charm and smiling faces. When six others arrived in our wake, the women smiled again. Finally the eleven of us were done and it was time to leave a tip.

'Don't overdo it,' an Austrian guy said. He put in the equivalent of five US cents. And, sure enough, nobody overdid it. Fifteen cents were left on the table by eight people to be shared between the three women. Until Cora, Erich and I topped it up to an amount that wasn't an insult. After that, we grew a little distant from Reinhard and Danielle. A reminder that not all on the road was love and peace.

During our stay, there were never any more than twenty people at a time at *El Gringo Perdido*. You could walk down to the lake and have it to yourself. If you took out the dugout, you were alone for as long as you chose. Cora and I spent quite a bit of time in that dugout, enjoying the birdlife and the occasional snake that took to the water.

However, there was an ugly side. In the little restaurant, a jaguar skin hung on one of the walls and there were dead butterflies in a display frame, the same butterflies that could be seen alive all around the campsite. There was also a Scarlet Macaw with clipped wings, and an ocelot, a sleek jaguar-like creature, stuck in a cage. Disturbed by this treatment of wildlife, I had a thought as we stood at the ocelot's cage.

'I wonder if we could free this guy? The padlock looks like it might give with a bit of effort.'

I had no sooner spoken than the animal sprang from the far corner of the cage, hit the ground once, and was on the wire in our faces in a flash.

'I'll tell you what,' Cora said. 'If you're planning to let that thing out of the cage, give me ten minutes and I'll be in the dugout on the lake.'

On our second night at *El Gringo Perdido*, under a moon two thirds full and not a nudge of wind, we paddled the dugout out onto the lake and drifted silently for over an hour.

On the third night we sat by the water in a soft breeze and watched sheets of lightning gash the clouds away to the south. Overhead the sky was clear and bright, and the lake glowed in chevrons of moon-silver. Toads hopped about our feet. Bats zoomed around the thatch of the wooden wharf. The trees were full of fireflies.

'Shhh...' Cora whispered. We held our breath as a deer came to drink at the water's edge, almost close enough to touch.

* * *

After three days at the lake, we went north in a cloud of dust. Erich had changed his mind about driving to Tikal. However, he was soon regretting his decision. 'Oh my poor car,' he repeated as we slammed over an atrocious road, sections of which were being repaired by men who hid from the sun under mobile shelters of branches and palm fronds. Ten miles before we reached the ruins, we entered Tikal National Park and continued on through lush jungle to the visitors' centre.

'Holy shit,' Erich said as we got out of the car. 'We have arrived in New York.'

He was exaggerating but he had a point. The remoteness of the Petén jungle was blasted to bits by small planes landing on a dusty airstrip and by the frenetic construction of hotels.

If you asked for it in those days, you could get a special permit that allowed you to stay at Tikal for the setting of the sun. After booking in at the campsite, we armed ourselves with those permits, walked to the ruins, more than a mile away, and stepped into a world beyond belief.

Standing among the palms and yuccas of the Great Plaza, we were surrounded by enormous pyramids topped by comb-roofed temples. Beyond the plaza the site stretched for miles into the jungle. Once the largest of the old Mayan cities and one of the oldest, Tikal at its zenith 1,500 years ago, is estimated to have had a population of 100,000 people.

Cora and I spent the morning in the ruins which were protected by guards carrying pistols, shotguns, and belts of ammunition. Nobody was going to run off with a Tikal pyramid. We visited the stelae, the sculpted altars, the residential and administrative palaces and the ball court. We then wandered into the forest for much of the afternoon. On a poorly defined animal track, we entered a labyrinth of palms, buttress roots, drooping lianas, smothering aerial-root systems of strangler figs, and tree trunks that were protected by six-inch thorns. Back at *El Gringo Perdido* I had stood on thorns like these and they had shot through my flip-flops like harpoons.

'According to the information I have here,' I said, 'there are 410 different species of bird in this jungle.'

'According to the information I have,' Cora said, 'there are pumas, ocelots and jaguars. And if we're not careful we could end up lost and walking around in circles until we die.'

On our way back to the Great Plaza, we were followed by a troupe of spider monkeys, many of the females carrying young on their backs. Shrieking through the canopy, they came to rest on the fringe of the plaza before disappearing back into the forest to re-emerge at sunset.

By 5.30 p.m. the small tour groups that had flown in for the day had gone, and the guards cleared the site of all but those who had evening permits. The guards then disappeared. One by one, the seventeen people remaining at Tikal gripped the safety chain on the Pyramid of The Great Jaguar and climbed the ninety-six worn limestone steps to the temple at the top. Two hundred and thirty feet above the ground, we sat on the stone floor and looked westwards towards the roof combs of three more of Tikal's temple-pyramids, two of which rose from the jungle canopy beyond the Great Plaza. Across the forest, the howler monkeys were at full throttle while the surrounding trees echoed with the raucous chorus of spider monkeys, parrots, toucans, macaws and countless smaller birds. Down in the empty plaza, ocellated turkeys, with blue faces and iridescent feathers of green and bronze, toddled about. There was nothing left now but to sit in silence and watch the sun go down over the most magnificent of the old cities of the Maya. And to imagine how it must have been, fifteen hundred years before, when the Great Plaza was loud with the voices of men, women and children, and the land beyond twinkled with the flames of thousands of cooking fires.

In a sudden flapping of wings, a stream of bats left the temple entrance, flew over our heads and vanished into the dusk.

By the time we left the Great Plaza at 7.00 p.m. the ruins were washed in moonlight. Among the fireflies, crickets and frogs, Cora discovered a centipede with a luminous head.

* * *

At first light we were back in the ruins, the first to arrive. Though shrouded in eerie mist, the place was teeming with monkeys and birds. After wandering about for an hour we returned to *El Gringo Perdido* for a fourth night. During the afternoon, Erich decided three times that he would most certainly drive to Guatemala City, and three times that he most certainly would not. In the evening he made a startling announcement.

'I am going to sell the car in Flores.'

Next morning, however, he was for driving again; so he left with myself, Cora, and two others, a Frenchman and an English woman. On the 16-mile journey to Flores, he thought first that he had enough petrol, then that he didn't, then that he definitely did. With the bridge at the Rio Dulce still down, supplies weren't getting through by road, but he hoped to be able to top up as he got further south. At Flores, a small town with cobblestone streets and a cathedral built on a hill, he made the first fruitless attempt; it then took three quarters of an hour to find the one road back out. At one junction we drove in the four possible directions and doubled back on each, with everyone we asked absolutely sure it was the other way. The car then started to cough.

'I have had enough,' Erich said. He stopped, took out some paper and a black crayon, wrote *'Se Vende* [For sale]', stuck it on the dashboard and we walked back to town. The other two passengers took the night bus; Cora and I booked into a small hotel that had a pair of crested guan (turkey-like birds with blackish plumage and bright red throat wattles) in the garden; Erich walked off the face of the Earth.

Next day Cora and I flew to Guatemala City in a small plane that made unsettling clunking noises on takeoff. Arriving in the city so suddenly after our time in El Petén, and having to deal with the crowded streets, the chaotic public transport and the high levels of pollution came as a shock. None the less, we could appreciate its 4,900-foot elevation and the cooler climate of the Guatemalan Highlands.

We booked into a cheap hotel in Zona 4, which turned out to be the seedier side of town. But it was also close to the bus station and the Indian market where the Highland Maya came to trade in an incredible variety of richly embroidered tribal costumes that were a stark contrast to the simple *huipiles* of Yucatán.

They, and the people who wore them, would become the enduring memory of the Guatemalan Highlands.

CHAPTER 31

Lake Atitlán

We left the city on Good Friday morning in a minibus full of Indians. We were heading to Antigua, former capital of Guatemala until it suffered massive earthquake damage in 1773. During the past three days we had been told again and again that no place in Latin America celebrated *Semana Santa*[26] like Antigua. We were caught in a sort of religious fervour.

However, during the hour's drive this was somewhat dented by the swearing that could be heard from the seat beside me. It was triggered by the driver's brinkmanship and several near misses on mountain bends.

'Look,' I would say in religious tones while pointing south-west towards the volcanoes that had been old Antigua's undoing. 'That's Acatenango, the one belching the thick black smoke.'

'Jesus, Mary and St. Joseph,' Cora would say. 'I wish this bastard would slow down.'

On such parallel conversations doth religious fervour perish.

As soon as we arrived in Antigua we joined the crowds already assembled and wandered the streets of the Old Town to marvel at how, 200 long years after the earthquakes and volcanic explosions that had wrecked the 1773 feast of Santa Marta, much of the destruction was still preserved in the remains of churches and monasteries, and most strikingly in the semi-ruined Catedral de Santiago.

Remarkable no doubt. But equally remarkable were Antigua's famous rectangular *alfombras* (street carpets) that lined the route to be taken by that day's Passion of Christ procession. To create these masterpieces, sand was spread over the cobblestones to level them. Next, dyed sawdust in shades of black, red, yellow, purple, blue and green was pressed through intricately designed stencils. Flowers, seeds,

---

26.   Easter Week.

plants, and pine needles added the final touches to designs containing images from Christianity, Mayan traditions and nature.

The *alfombras* grew from a time when local carpenters spread sawdust to cushion the path of the penitents of the parade. They were also said to represent the transient nature of life: after all the work that went into their creation, the procession marchers and their floats would trample the beautiful *alfombras* into oblivion.

'Well, well, if it isn't my saviour!' We turned to find Merilyn from Australia making her way towards us. 'So what have you guys been doing since Isla de Las Piedras?'

'It's a long story,' I said, delighted to see our old friend again. 'What have you been up to?'

But the procession stole the future. The crowd surge that broke from the Plaza Mayor to greet its arrival whisked Merilyn away. Over the eight hours that it would take the parade to pass we didn't see her again.

Roman soldiers led the event. Behind them came thousands of purple-robed men carrying pikes. Then came the first of the incense-burners who led the polished hardwood floats, their censers churning out a ghostly fog. Then it was the turn of the floats, carrying enormous statues of Mary, numerous saints and Christ on the Via Dolorosa. Weighing thousands of pounds and carried by up to eighty bearers, the floats swayed from side to side, creating an illusion that the statues were actually walking. (Could have lessons for the no-longer-moving statues of Ireland.) Funeral bands followed, announcing themselves with slow drumbeats, clapping cymbals and deep-throated tubas that sat well with the heat of the afternoon.

Self-flagellating penitents were followed by Pontius Pilate and legions of 'Arabs' and 'Jews'. The 'two thieves' were roped to poles slung across their shoulders. They in turn were tailed by streams of Catholic clergy and officials.

The climax was a gigantic, red-robed sculpture of Christ-with-crucifix that swayed through the streets to an atmosphere of near hysteria. People prayed, chanted, cried and blessed themselves. The rear of the procession was taken up by the ordinary punters, pursued by ice cream vendors, candyfloss sellers and balloon men.

By four o'clock, the passing marchers were wearing black. Christ was dead.

* * *

At noon on Easter Saturday, April 14th 1979, almost three years after leaving Ireland, we departed Guatemala City by bus for a second time. We were on our way to Panajachel on the shores of Lake Atitlán, a town also known as Gringotenango. Lake Atitlán, we had long been assured, was the jewel of Guatemala and we were looking forward to basking a few days on its shores.

The bus was two thirds full of Atitlán Indians. They included two men in the embroidered shirts and trousers, and distinctive black-and-white check *rodilleras* (wool wrap-arounds worn like skirts) of Panajachel. Just before the bus left, the older of the two, a small squat man in a tatty straw hat, decided to go and get a refill of tequila, having already quaffed one small bottle. Off he trotted through the stalls of the market, his kaleidoscopic pant legs bobbing up and down under the knee-length *rodillera* until he had disappeared. When the bus engine coughed to life and he hadn't yet returned, his young companion began scanning the market for his friend, but to no avail. He was still looking when we left the station. Ten minutes later, we were approaching a bus stop when, trotting towards us on the pavement, one arm waving, the other cradling a big bottle of tequila, came the old man. He jumped aboard and cracked open the bottle, and he and his young friend partied their way to Panajachel.

Our journey took us through heavily populated countryside, mountains that were sadly stripped of most of their trees, and villages in which tribal costumes were an ever-expanding riot of colour. Men and women who rode by on burros and horses, or worked the fields with hoes and machetes, became fashion statements of Highland Guatemala. Anticipation bubbled up in our hearts.

At Los Ecuentos we turned for Panajachel. At Solola, we dropped from the plateau towards Lake Atitlán, five miles away. The final approach was a downhill sweep through heavy forest to a lakeshore headland and a small town that jutted into the serene waters. A backdrop of craggy mountains ran in a sweep around the lake. Aldous Huxley had written of this place: *'Lake Como, it seems to me, touches on the limit of the permissibly picturesque, but Atitlán is Como with additional embellishments...'*

At 1,120 feet deep, Lake Atitlán is the deepest lake in Central America. It fills a huge collapsed caldera left behind by an eruption 85,000 years ago. In a reminder of its violent origins, the encircling walls of the old caldera contain three dormant volcanoes - Atitlán, Tolimán and San Pedro. They provide the southern backdrop that defines one of the world's most beautiful lakes. It has (or at least it had) the additional attraction of surrounding forests that are/were home to the national bird, the Resplendent Quetzal. Stuff the idea of basking lazily on these shores. A couple of days in Panajachel, we immediately agreed, and we'd see if we could walk around the lake.

Easter week had brought large crowds to Panajachel. The town was teeming with holidaying Guatemalans, foreign visitors and Indians who had come to sell their wares. Prices everywhere were jacked up to make the best of the seasonal boom. Inspired by rampant commerce and exploding firecrackers, an eight-year-old businesswomen with the most exquisite face looked us straight in the eye and told us without a flicker that the blanket she was selling was worth three times its real value.

All this life and bustle, charming as it was, meant that there wasn't a room to be had anywhere. We had to pitch our tent at the camping site.

No sooner had we done so than we ran into Hartmud and Valerie, last seen fleeing Johnnie's Bar in Belize. They had some grim news.

'We met some people,' Valerie said, 'who were up in a mountain village when a group of guerrillas came in. They shot the mayor and then rounded up the whole village to give them a lecture, denouncing the injustices of the Guatemalan junta, and the evils of the United States and capitalism.'

'Where did it happen?' I wanted to know, preferring to give an area like that a big miss.

Valerie couldn't remember.

'We have been here for a week now,' Hartmud added. 'We are leaving in a couple of days for El Salvador. But Valerie has the trots.'

'You have a fever too,' Cora said after putting a palm to Valerie's forehead like Doctor Google. 'But we might have a cure.' She handed Valerie an assortment of pills. We then boiled her up some rice on our stove. 'You'll be right as rain in the morning,' Cora prophesied. And Valerie was.

On Easter Sunday we moved into one of the rooms at the campsite, a wooden box with bamboo slats for windows. Our next door neighbours were Don and Michael Stein, two brothers who were driving back to the States from El Salvador. Pinched, wiry Don, with biker moustache and collar-length hair matted in sweat, didn't look the best. Yellow, hooded eyes and yellow skin suggested hepatitis. But he was none the less holding up well to the demands of a large bag of Oaxaca Gold.

'Smoke like this,' he advised, 'keeps you from getting hep.' Don was in denial.

Dedicated brother, Michael, big, blond and mellow, was keeping the joints coming. I was wondering if hepatitis could hop from a joint.

'Have you heard about this?' Michael said, handing me a copy of *Time Magazine*. 'It's about this Jim Jones guy and his followers. In November, 900 of them, *nine fucking hundred,* did a big suicide thing down in the jungles of Guyana. Or maybe it was mass murder.'

The article was accompanied by disturbing photos of the dead who included 280 children. It was a measure of how in touch we had all kept with world events that none of us had heard. In fact, we hardly knew what month it was.

'That's what we're goin' back to, man,' Don said. 'A fucked-up place that produces fucked-up people who go off to other fucked-up places to fuck themselves up even more.'

'That,' I said to Don, 'is a remarkably enlightened observation.'

'America isn't all bad,' Michael countered. 'The Great Plains are the bread basket of half the world.'

'We're going back to Ireland,' Cora said, 'where it rains all the time.'

And so the conversation drifted until it made no more sense.

* * *

By now our desire to walk around the lake had become a plan. But good food, and the great company of Don and Michael, put paid to the plans two days running. Finally, on Wednesday morning we dumped half our gear at the campsite, stuck everything we needed into one of the packs and a cactus-fibre shoulder bag, skipped breakfast and made a bolt for Solola at the top of the mountain road.

It took nearly two hours to walk to Solola, but we hopped along, high as kites on the scenery. Ravenous by the time we arrived, we had breakfast in a small café and produced a variation of our one and only Spanish sentence.

'*Dondé este el camino a Lago Atitlán?*' I asked the woman who had served us breakfast. She pointed towards a dirt track that led out of the village. Half an hour along that track, we should turn left along a mule trail. That would bring us back to the lakeshore. She then explained that we could only walk as far as the village of San Pedro La Laguna. We would have to travel by boat from there to Santiago Atitlán.

'*Muchos gracias,*' we both said and headed off.

'Our Spanish is incredible,' Cora said.

* * *

It would take three days to walk to San Pedro. In echoes of the Sierra Madre, our arrival in the first village was greeted by children scattering in terror. On a ridge on the far side, however, we were joined by three young women.

'Hola,' we said, using more of our amazing Spanish.

They sat in front of us. They stared. They made occasional comments to one another. They wanted to know if we had any home to go to. *Irlanda* meant nothing so I pulled out maps and added some drawings to explain how far away Ireland was.

'A-a-a-ah,' one of them said. I was delighted with my efforts. Only to discover that the woman had spotted Cora's rings.

I had to sit through a four-pronged jewellery debate.

The next village was Santa Cruz la Laguna which sat on a rise above the lake. As Cora led the way in among the adobe huts, adults greeted us warily and children again scattered. Suddenly we were hit by a torrential downpour, causing us to run for shelter in the square. A group of women who were filling water urns at a large tank in the middle of the square, dropped everything and bolted.

Late in the afternoon the rain cleared. We left Santa Cruz and dropped down through gardens of onions, tomatoes and corn to the lake where a row of *cayucos* - stubby, flat-bottomed fishing canoes - lined a narrow beach. A little further away we found a more secluded beach out of view of the village, and called it a day.

As we set up camp two men in a *cayuco* came paddling furiously out of the lake. Gliding through a belt of reeds, they beached the canoe and made straight for us, shaking hands and checking every aspect of our gear. They then showed us the day's catch: a single fish and a basket of small freshwater crabs. The older man smiled and presented us with two of the crabs.

'Muchos gracias,' we both said, putting the crabs in a billy of water.

'Buenos noches,' the fishermen said and off they went towards Santa Cruz.

As soon as they were out of sight, we released the crabs. They scuttled off to the water, each with a claw raised in diminutive defiance. With nobody but ourselves, we then sat on the shore and watched a great blue serenity settle over the lake. A canoe of standing fishermen, no more than a gliding silhouette, passed offshore. Then it was dark and there was only us and the sparks of our fire, and the smell of smoke and cooking food, and the fireglow on the tent, and the stars, and the lights of faraway lakeside villages, and the crickets and frogs. But the night wasn't done yet.

It began with a lightning storm at the southern end of the lake, behind the sleeping cones of Tolimán and San Pedro. Blue pulses followed by dull, muted thunder. Then a closer flash that would light up the whole lake.

And all of a sudden the world was full of fireflies. More than you could ever imagine. In the lakeside reeds. In the trees and bushes. In the cornfields. Up along the surrounding hillsides. All around us in the air. A million twinkling, iridescent-green Tinkerbells.

To get the best view of the entire light show, we swam out into the dark water.

* * *

The path from Santa Cruz to San Pedro La Laguna meandered along the line of the shore, sometimes rising on precipitous slopes, sometimes crossing the fertile flats. In places we were puffing up the sides of exposed hills under the full glare of the sun, genuinely worried about overheating. In others we were surrounded by lush forest full of cicadas, grasshoppers and birds. Magical views would appear: an early-morning village coming to life; a canoe out on the lake; the line of the three volcanoes; fire-smoke rising from thatched huts; women weaving on hand looms or embroidering cloth; men slashing and burning for the next season's crops, or carrying enormous sacks of onions, strapped around their foreheads.

The stillness between villages would be broken by the distant clang of a machete striking stone, or the screech of a disturbed bird, or the shrill of cicadas, after which the silence of the lake would appear even more profound and enchanting.

Around noon of the second day we set up our flysheet in a hidden cove, cooked some food and swam in the lake. When the smell of rain filled the breeze we packed up, chased away some gathered vultures and marched on to San Marcos, arriving just in time to shelter from another downpour in the village church.

At the village of San Pablo, where they were weaving cactus fibre into rope, a threatening storm put paid to all plans of continuing. Beyond the village we camped by the lake, secured the tent guylines with rocks, and braced ourselves as the storm broke.

'Listen,' Cora said as we lay in our sleeping bags. 'There's a motorbike coming this way.'

That was very odd. What would a motorbike be doing down here? There was no real track. But closer and closer it came. Then the sound stopped in a dull thud on the front of the tent.

'What on earth is *that*?' Cora said as the nylon fabric was dragged in on itself. 'You look,' she said as the drag moved upwards.

I undid the zippers on the fly screen and door and carefully poked my head out into the pouring rain to find a massive beetle crawling up the tent.

On Friday morning we arrived in San Juan as the village children were making their way to school.

'Oh look,' Cora said. 'It's assembly time. Boys to one side, girls to the other. And there's the teacher parading up and down like a witch.'

Six of the boys failed the clean test and were sent across the street to one of the village taps. They rubbed their hands and faces clean, inspected one another and followed the others into school with all the indignation of clean little boys.

'Would you listen to that,' Cora said. 'Sounds just like Miss Russel long ago in Ballyphehane: same voice, same parrot-fashion repeating by all the terrorised children.'

Having got that off our chests, we continued on to San Pedro La Laguna. From here, we would have to take a boat to Santiago Atitlán. There was no track around the sheer base of the San Pedro volcano.

We got ourselves a room down by the lake, then went into the village and bought some bread from Francisco the baker, a friendly man who was also a Protestant pastor. He was the father of six children, he told us, and he had heard of Ireland. In the small talk that sign language and single words of Spanish and English allowed, we enjoyed Francisco's company and were sorry when customers insisted he sell them bread.

Visit again, he told us.

We will, we said but we never got around to it.

After a much-needed shower we ate at *Michel's*, a ramshackle lakeshore restaurant run by two French couples. *Michel's* served the best food in the world in 'boats' of bamboo.

'If you're interested,' one of two Canadian guys at the next table said, 'you're looking out at a species heading for extinction.' He pointed to a pair of large, dark-brown water birds down at the shore. 'That's the Atitlán grebe. It's endemic to the lake. Exists nowhere else in the world. But it's the victim of an environmental catastrophe in the making.'

'Oh gawd,' I said. 'Not here as well.'

'I'm afraid so. In an attempt to develop tourism and draw fishermen to this area, Pan Am got the government to introduce black bass to the lake back in 1958. The black bass is a big fish and it did what big fish do, only better. The lake is losing all the crabs, snails and native fish that used to feed the grebes. As well as that, the bass eat the grebe chicks. Those birds would have been wiped out by now if it wasn't for a rescue project set up in 1966 by an American woman called Anne La Bastille. But, even with that, there are no more than a hundred left.'[27]

'When will people learn?' Cora asked but we knew the answer to that.

At 7.30 a.m. the next day Cora and I joined eight Indians and the two Canadians at San Pedro's long rickety pier of sticks and planks to catch the 'ferry' to Santiago Atitlán.

Out at the boat, barely big enough to take the eight of us, an older 'shark of a man' according to my diary, who owned the service and wasn't travelling, charged myself, Cora and the Canadians a quetzal (worth one U.S. dollar) each as we boarded.

'I didn't notice the locals paying,' I said. 'I'm suspicious.'

The boatman started the outboard motor and we cruised off in the direction of Tolimán volcano. When we disembarked in Santiago Atitlán twenty minutes later my suspicions were vindicated. All the Indians paid 50 centavos each. An outrage.

'I don't mind paying for a service,' I railed. 'But I hate the dirty rotten tricks of ROBBERS!'

* * *

Rising up between the lake and the mountains, Santiago Atitlán's streets were lined with stone and adobe houses. But the main attraction was in the costumes of its Tzutujil Mayas. Wildly embroidered, purple-and-white-striped, calf-length shorts for the machete-carrying men. Beautiful *huipiles* and head cloths for the women, the latter comprising 30-foot strips two inches wide and wound repeatedly around the head to form a kind of embroidered halo.

A thriving market, several craft-shops and a bunch of hustlers catered for the boat visitors who arrived daily from Panajachel.

And, of course, there was Maximón.

We were introduced to this bizarre personage by three young girls. They ran out in front of us, stuck tin cans on their heads and posed.

---

27.   The Atitlán grebe was declared extinct in 1990. But the catastrophe didn't end there. Once the bass had wiped out most of the life that controlled bacteria in the lake, bacteria thrived and fish numbers declined even further. The resultant pollution and stench coming from the lake meant that the once burgeoning tourism industry suffered the same fate as the airline that hoped to profit from it.

'Tek pitcha,' the tallest one said. 'Gif money.' When that brought no juice, she had a second idea. 'Come,' she said. 'See Maximón. With cigar.'

'Who is Maximón?' Cora asked.

'Come,' the girl said. 'Maximón with cigar, with hat.'

'Why not?' Cora said. 'It might be the local chief.'

Again, as Donald Trump would say, bigly wrong.

We were led to a dimly-lit room in a private house some distance from the village centre. There, guarded by two seated young men, stood blank-faced Maximón.

Maximón was a wooden effigy and a bit of a freak. Both 'saint' and cosmic intermediary, his origins were all but unknown. He was apparently a vague mix of an ancient Mayan god called Mam, bits of Catholicism, and pieces of a legend relating to Pedro de Alvarado, *conquistador* of Guatemala. Considered a touch of the bully-boy, he was most likely to be of use if you were hoping for someone's untimely end. The Catholic Church had a bit of a problem with 'Saint' Maximón and refused to have him in the local church. He therefore lived in the homes of members of the Brotherhood of the Holy Cross, the principal indigenous authority of Santiago Atitlán, and grandiosely moved house each year during *Semana Santa*. When his clothes got their monthly wash on two special boulders down by the lake, the rinsing water, we were told, was a great antidote to fear, sadness and sorcery.

Clad in leather shoes, a long red-and-blue shirt and a Stetson, with a polka-dot tie and numerous scarves and handkerchiefs hanging from his neck, he was, just as the girls had promised, smoking a big fat cigar. The floor around him, and a table behind, were littered with burning candles, pooled wax, and a clutter of offerings, including rum, flowers, money, bananas, two tins of Coca-Cola and various photos and religious pictures. On the floor in front knelt a beer-swilling, smoking shaman who was chanting in Tzutujil, and placing cigarette offerings at Maximón's feet.

Feeling a little stupid, I went up before the 'saint' and mumbled what I hoped would sound like a Tzutujil prayer into his inscrutable mug. I then dropped a couple of quetzals in a bowl at his feet. Cora did likewise. Our three guides rubbed their hands at the sight of such promising extravagance.

'That was ridiculous,' I pointed out. 'We just paid to see a pagan.'

At the lakeshore, Santiago Atitlán's women were washing clothes on some boulders when along came a boatful of gringos. It swung in close so the cameras could get a better angle, the wash of the boat sweeping the drying clothes into the water and sending the women scurrying for higher ground.

Sometimes it's embarrassing to be white.

In the evening we were joined for dinner in the best eating place in town by two other travellers: a greying Swiss guy in his late thirties named Paul, and a Dutch guy named Denis who was studying tropical agriculture.

'Things are not looking good for the future of Guatemala,' Paul said.

'What do you mean?' I asked.

'The civil war is getting worse in the north and the west.'

'What civil war?'

Cora and I had managed to travel around Guatemala without coming across any sign of a civil war that had been going on since 1960! Leftist guerrillas were attempting to overthrow the military regime put in place in 1954 by a CIA-organised coup that had overthrown the democratically elected, leftist President, Jacobo Arbenz Guzmán. Apart from Valerie's report of the killing of the village mayor somewhere in the mountains, we, and the other travellers we had met to date, had no awareness that anything major was amiss.

'You must have heard about the Panzós massacre last May,' Paul said.

'No,' I said. 'We were living in Sydney at the time. But we could have been in the bush. What happened?'

'On the 29th of May the military fired at 800 Kekchí Indians in Panzós' square. The Indians were protesting because the military junta was taking their lands and homes and giving them to the International Nickel Company in mining concessions. Thirty-five people were murdered and forty others were wounded. Another eighteen drowned trying to escape in boats on the Polochic River.'

'How did we not hear about that since we arrived in Guatemala?'

'Panzós is remote from here,' Paul said. 'And there's no sign of any guerrilla activity around Lake Atitlán. But it will come, as long as the junta keeps stealing the land from the Indians.'

Paul was tragically correct. By the time the civil war ended in 1996 the government of Guatemala and its death-squad allies, supported by the United States, would be responsible for the killing of 200,000 mainly-Indian citizens, the disappearance of 40,000 more and the torture of untold numbers, with the worst years just around the corner.

That night's sleep was tortured by the horrors of U.S. imperialism, and by visitations of Maximón.

On the morning of Sunday, April 22nd 1979, as we left by boat for Panajachel, the tranquillity of Santiago Atitlán was terribly deceiving. In a few short years, the town would have had 300 of its people 'disappeared' and would have become synonymous with two of the defining moments of the Guatemalan civil war: the July 1981 murder in his church of Fr. Stan Rother from Oklahoma, gunned down by soldiers; and the December 1990 massacre of thirteen unarmed civilians following a protest march to the military base after an attempted kidnapping by soldiers earlier in the day.

In San Pedro La Laguna, Francisco the baker, whose bread we had eaten a couple of days before, would be among the disappeared.

* * *

Long before I ever heard the term, Don Stein was road rage incarnate. Not alone did his personality change behind the wheel, but his physical shape did as well.

When we got back to Panajachel, we booked into Mario's Rooms, Spartan by any standards. We then went off to the camping ground to seek out Don and Michael who were still in their wooden hut.

Things were bad for the brothers: they were both now down with hepatitis. Yellow-eyed and miserable, they were also running out of time on their visas.

'We've only got two days left,' Michael said. 'So we're driving to Guatemala City tomorrow in Don's Beetle to get them renewed. Like to come?'

'Yes,' I foolishly said. 'I'd love to. I need to go back to the *post restante* to check for mail.'

At half five the next morning, I got into the back seat of the Beetle. Michael sat in front and Don sat in behind the wheel, whereupon he was instantly transformed. His jaw went square and his whole frame jerked upright as if somebody had stuck a needle in a voodoo doll. He turned the key in the ignition, snorted like a horse and did a wheelie out of the campsite. By the time we reached Solola, I knew that I should get out now and walk back down the hill. There was a quality to Guatemalan driving that bordered on the homicidal; there was a quality to Don's that said I want to die. Horribly. Now.

Excluding one short straight stretch, the road from Panajachel to Guatemala City was a high mountain ribbon of twists, turns and terrifying abysses. At first, Don was simply speeding along, cutting corners, swerving on patches of gravel and overtaking everything in front. On one bend, however, he spooked a burro being led on a rope by an Indian who was mounted on a second burro, resulting in both animals bolting across our path. We missed them by a finger. This appeared to invigorate Don. He now took to overtaking on crests and blind corners. Micheal, sitting beside him, said *whoa!* Don snarled something about 'stupid fuckers', and roared on. But the traffic was still light and our luck held. We then came to a 10-mile stretch of road that was dug up on one side like a ploughed field. Just as we arrived, with six vehicles ahead of us, a barrier was drawn across our side of the road. Theoretically, it was single-lane traffic only across the 10-mile stretch. And we had just missed our slot. We would now have to wait until they had cleared the ploughed section, and it would then be the turn of the oncoming traffc.

'I don't *believe* it,' Don howled. 'Now they're tryin' to do my fuckin' *head* in.'

You just knew things weren't going to improve.

We waited for over an hour while bright-eyed Indian children sold us food and drinks and a great tailback built up. Little by little, the more impatient drivers filtered up on our left until, to Don's burgeoning chagrin, there were two lines of traffic waiting at the barrier. Eventually, the oncoming traffic came swinging by and all engines on our side were gunned. Once the last oncoming vehicle had passed, a third line formed to the far left and we were all ready to go. Away went the barrier, and the race was on.

A blue pickup led the way with a cop car in second place. A jumble of buses, trucks, cars and motorbikes, leap-frogging like maniacs, sped along the mountain road, haring around bends two abreast on what should have been one lane. But the most manic feature of all was our little Beetle zooming in and out of the lines, until we beat all the other loonies to third place. The mad motorcade then careered over dirt and gravel and stupendous potholes, with the mob behind still battling it out and Don zig-zagging wildly to prevent any sneaky overtakes. Michael and I hung onto our seats, petrified.

Once we were clear of the road works, the remainder of the journey saw us overtake everything in sight, the overtaking invariably happening on blind bends, most often against oncoming traffic.

In the city, Don and Michael sorted out their visas. I had a couple of stiff drinks to regain my equilibrium, and I checked out the *post restante*. The death run from Panajachel had been for nothing: all that was waiting was a telegram from Australia from Tom Wilson, Ian and Arthur. 'Mail strike in Sydney,' it proclaimed.

At 4.30 p.m. we were back in the car, white-knuckling it through the city's rush-hour traffic at speeds that defied logic. I don't know how we survived the bedlam; but we were out of the city before most Guatemalans had jumped their first red light. And heading straight for our first problem.

We were on our way uphill on a blind right-hand curve with Don overtaking a long line of traffic when the inevitable happened: a similar long line came pounding downhill, straight at us, with a big truck leading the way and nobody giving quarter.

'Jesus Christ, Don...' I blurted.

'PULL FUCKING IN!' Michael screamed. But it was too late.

Don tried to cut back into our lane but the bus beside us was having none of it. He put down the boot and we bounced off the side of the bus, right back into the path of awful, oncoming perdition. Then Don had a great idea, plucked from the foundry of madness: he charged the oncoming traffic with the intention of forcing them - all of them - onto the dirt verge. Now, as anyone can tell you, a Guatemalan in a big truck is the last person in the world to be forced off the road by a Volkswagen Beetle. At the last mili-second, we swerved onto the dirt verge on the wrong side of the road as the truck and everything behind it came barrelling past.

'Jesus Christ!' Michael yelled. 'You nearly fucking killed us!'

But Don's blood was up. We careered onwards, still swerving and skidding on the dirt verge on the wrong side of the road, myself and Michael rigid in our seats and Don determined to hog that verge until he had passed all the Panajachel-bound traffic. He then shot out between two oncoming trucks to return to his own side of the road. For good measure, he stuck his hand out through the open window to give all of Guatemala the fingers.

When we came again to the ploughed section of road, Don drove on the wrong side up alongside the waiting traffic, right to the barrier; and when it was time to go, he tried to cut out in front of everyone else. But he hadn't seen the cops, who pulled us over and made us wait until every last vehicle had gone. This put Don's head away again and the rest of the journey to Panajachel was spent trying to snatch back on lost time. Then Don stepped out of the Beetle, readjusted his jaw, shrank back to his normal size, and became a gentleman again.

'You look a bit grey,' Cora said when I flopped into Mario's Rooms. 'Was everything okay?'

* * *

On Wednesday April 25th, we took a bus to Chichicastenango, a small town of stucco-white buildings which had been a major trading centre for the western Highlands since pre-Hispanic times. When we arrived, preparations were under way for what was reputed to be the most colourful indigenous market in all of the Americas. We spent Thursday in the market along with thousands of Indians in an array of costumes that was bewildering. Musicians played at various points, cooking fires flamed on pavements and homemade rockets burst randomly into the sky. At one of the food stalls, we met four other foreigners who were as surprised to see us as we were to see them.

On the steps leading to the 400-year-old church of Santo Tomás, a chanting shaman and kneeling worshippers were gathered around a fire, all swinging burning incense in makeshift censers made of tin cans and bits of wire. On the venerated steps that once belonged to a pre-Columbian Mayan temple, they sacrificed a chicken to their own gods. Inside the church, small candles burned on wooden slabs and people talked aloud to statues - and to the Stetson-topped figure of Maximón who had somehow wheedled his way past the guardians of Santo Tomás.

The next morning, while out buying bread, we came across six members of a local Mayan religious brotherhood dressed in black capes, black knee-length breeches, head-coverings of embroidered red cloth, and clogs. They too had sacrificed a chicken and were burning incense on the steps of the church.

After breakfast, we took a bus to Quetzaltenango. And ran smack bang into ourselves.

* * *

During a catastrophic eruption in 1902, the Santa María volcano killed more than 5,000 people. It spewed a column of ash and rock seventeen miles into the air, dumped two and a half cubic miles of debris over south west Guatemala, destroyed the region's crops and blew a .2-cubic-mile hole in the side of the mountain. The eruption began at 5.00 p.m. An hour later, ash and rock began to fall on Quetzaltenango which sits at the base of the volcano. Santa Maria has been active ever since.

We spent a weekend at the Pension Altense, a small friendly place in a back street close to the centre of this precarious city. In the cool of the evening we would sit in the soft seats of the courtyard veranda and cogitate. What were we going to do?

When we left Australia the grand plan had included travelling the length of Central and South America. But by the time we reached Papua New Guinea, we had begun to waver. We were missing the connectivity we had with Ireland. There was also a feeling that we needed a break. We needed to internalise all that we had experienced. However, by the time we left California for Mexico this had mostly been forgotten.

But now, in Quetzaltenango, seven months after leaving New Guinea, we suddenly reached the point of return.

It would take another year to do justice to Central and South America. We needed big energy for that. So what about this for a plan? We could make our way back to the U.S., go home for the summer and come back to El Salvador in the autumn to head south again.

A brilliant plan; but deep down I think we both knew that the final part was already dead in the water.

While wandering the back streets close to the Pension Altense on Saturday afternoon, still ruminating on the future, we were drawn to what my travel notes described as *'unworldly music coming from an old building further down the street'*. Pushing open a studded door we peered inside to find two men in a large, semi-derelict room. The only light came from a slanting dusty shaft that poured in through a small window. The men were striking the keys of a large xylophone-type instrument with soft mallets. The older of the two beckoned us in.

Pausing the music, he showed us how the instrument's rich tones were achieved by the use of metal resonators hanging below each key to amplify the tone. We were then invited to stay for a private concert of what my notes described as *'extremely moving melodies'*.

'What is the instrument?' I asked in my best sign language.

'Marimba,' the older man said.

'I thought that was a dance in Johnnie's Bar in Belize,' I said but it was lost in translation.

CHAPTER 32

Chiapas

Our final day in Guatemala was spent crossing the Highlands on our way back to Mexico. Picturesque villages. Mountains carpeted in forest. Spectacular gorges. Men on horseback with machetes and rifles. A bus that had plunged into a ravine.

At the Mexican border hostile guards with guns in waistbands were waiting.

'*Gringos,*' they spat. They didn't give two shites about *Irlanda*.

Once we had cleared immigration, we waited in the awful heat for a bus that would take us to San Cristobal de Las Casas, an Indian city in the highlands of Chiapas, a region of dense jungles, towering mountains and fantastic gorges. When the bus pulled in, we heard our names being called. Hanging out one of the windows were Hartmud and Valerie, back from El Salvador! Hartmud and Valerie to whom we had said a last goodbye at Panajachel.

At 7.30 p.m. we reached the city, just in time to join a torch-lit procession that was the prelude to the following day's Labour Day celebrations and was led by a green pickup on which sat a choir of two women and a man, backed by an organist, two guitarists, a bass player and a trumpet man.

Once we reached the centre, the four of us booked into a small hotel with pink rooms and dim lights. After settling in, we went to the roof terrace to look at the stars and listen to the celebrations. Then boom, boom, boom! Seconds later, showers of colour cascaded from the sky.

For the remainder of the night, the fireworks wreaked a semi-pleasant havoc, peaking at the crack of dawn in a barrage that sounded like a bad day in Flanders. They continued throughout the day. By the third morning, the pleasant bit had dimmed. Shattered nerves and bloodshot eyes prompted a day-long retreat to the village of Amatenango where the Indians turned grey clay into exquisite pots and jugs.

Eventually, Hartmud and Valerie couldn't take it anymore.

'We are going to Oaxaca,' Hartmud said. 'Before we have a nervous breakdown.'

'I wonder where we'll meet again,' Valerie said. But that was the last goodbye.

Cora and I stayed another day to take some photographs. Though not as colourful as their Guatemalan relatives, the Maya of Chiapas were equally famous for their costumes. In later times they would also become the backbone of pipe-smoking Subcomandante Marcos' Zapatista rebellion against the Mexican state.

* * *

Leaving San Cristobal behind, we travelled on through the mountains to Villahermosa, and from there to Palenque, a town surrounded by rainforest, sitting four miles from the Mayan ruins of the same name. Having spent the recent past in the mountains, our submersion into the steamy nebulosity of this 200-foot elevation in the run-up to the wet season was a shock.

We checked into a small guesthouse with nothing more than a fan to combat the temperature. We then went outside to buy food and bumped into two English women we had already met in San Cristobal. Lyn and Penny invited us for coffee in their place which proved to be even further down the accommodation ladder than ours - no fan. We should visit the ruins together tomorrow, we all agreed. We then decided to do some field-watering in the hope on encouraging Palenque's magic mushrooms from the soil but abandoned that plan in favour of a walk to the central square.

In the morning we set off on foot, but were delivered to the ruins by a busload of Mexican tourists on their way to San Cristobal.

Despite having visited Chichén Itzá, Tikal and Tulum, the Palenque complex was a sensory ambush. Located at the base of the Tumbalá Mountains, its palace and temples sat on a ridge surrounded by dense jungle, a humid envelope that dictated the atmosphere of the ruins. Although smaller in area than the other three cities, the excavated buildings of Palenque contained some of the finest architecture, sculptures, roof combs and carvings of the Mayan world. Unusual features included a four-storey 'observation tower' attached to the palace, an aqueduct that carried water from the Otulum River to the city, and the A-shaped corbel arches that were to be found throughout the complex.

Although the ruins are believed to date back to 226 BC, glyphic texts discovered at the site dated the Palenque known to modernity to the reign of three rulers: Pakal the Great (603-683), his son, K'inich Kan

Bahlam (635-702), and his grandson, K'inich Akul Mo' Naab (678-736). The records suggested that the site was attacked by the opposing kingdom of Calakmul in 599 and again in 611. In 615, following the second attack, Pakal at the age of twelve, became ruler, setting in motion a vast rebuilding programme that lasted until 683, and was continued by his son and grandson. In 711, Palenque was sacked by the kingdom of Toniná, after which further rebuilding took place, still under the direction of Pakal's grandson. Then, for reasons unknown, the construction of elite buildings ceased sometime around 800 AD and a gradual population decline ensued. By the time the Spanish got to Chiapas in the 16th century, the Maya had long abandoned the city.

We shared Palenque's ruins with howler monkeys, parrots and two Mexican tourists. Wandering through the empty complex, often separated to a point where each of us was alone with the birdsong and the secret passageways, it was easy to imagine how it must have felt to those European explorers who rediscovered the lost city in the 18th century. As we had no water and none was available at the site, the heat got to us, causing headaches and muscle cramps; but other than that the morning was beyond words, with no better finale than the Temple of the Inscriptions. A rudimentary map directed us to the southern edge of the plaza, and the 68-foot-high temple. With its eight stepped terraces, this building housed a remarkable secret, discovered in 1948 by Mexican archaeologist, Alberto Ruz Lhuillier.

While investigating four odd-looking stone plugs in the temple floor, Ruz Lhuillier discovered a secret stairway. When fully excavated in 1952, it descended seventy-five feet under the floor to a triangular slab door. Behind the door, the archaeologist found a stone chamber that forever changed the world's perception of Mayan pyramids: it contained an elaborately carved sarcophagus - the largest ever found - covered in perfectly preserved relief carvings that were the most detailed and elegant exposition ever found of the Mayan concepts of death and the afterlife. Under the seven-ton lid, lay the remains of Pacal the Great, Holy *Bacab* of the Jaguar Dynasty and 11th ruler of Palenque.

Ruz Lhuillier later described how: *'Out of the dim shadows emerged a vision from a fairy tale, a fantastic, ethereal sight from another world. It seemed a huge magic grotto carved out of ice, the walls sparkling and glistening like snow crystals. Delicate festoons of stalactites hung like tassels of a curtain, and the stalagmites on the floor looked like drippings from a great candle. The impression, in fact, was that of an abandoned chapel. Across the walls marched stucco figures in low relief. Then my eyes sought the floor. This was almost entirely filled with a great carved stone slab, in perfect condition.'*

Pakal's sarcophagus, built for a very tall man, held the greatest treasure in grave offerings ever found in Mesoamerica and the richest collection of jade seen in a Mayan tomb. A jade mask covered Pakal's face and a suit of jade plaques adorned his body, each piece hand-carved and held together by gold wire.

The rubble that Ruz Lhuillier had to clear from the stairwell had been dumped there by the Maya to protect the tomb and its treasures before the city was abandoned.

Forty-seven years after Ruz Lhuillier's discovery, the 1,300-year-old sarcophagus was no less awe-inspiring. It was so immense that the only way it could have been placed in the chamber was to have the pyramid built around it.

* * *

Leaving Palenque behind, we hitchhiked to Campeche, stayed the night, and took the 6.30 a.m. bus to Mérida where we collected some gear that we had left behind on our last visit. On Friday, May 11th, we boarded the flight that would take us back to the United States.

After a delay of an hour, we found ourselves crossing back over the vast forests of Yucatán to Cancun, where we had a further delay of an hour and a half while we picked up more passengers. At 6.30 p.m. we came in low over Lake Pontchartrain and the five-mile concrete bridge that linked New Orleans to Slidell in Louisiana.

'Lake Pontchartrain Causeway,' the captain announced. 'Longest bridge in the world.' We were back in the land of the biggest.

We had a story when we were kids. A Texan came to Ireland and ran into a farmer who owned a few acres in West Cork.

'At home,' he told the farmer, 'it takes me two days to drive around my land.'

'I had a car like that once,' the farmer said, 'but I sold it.'

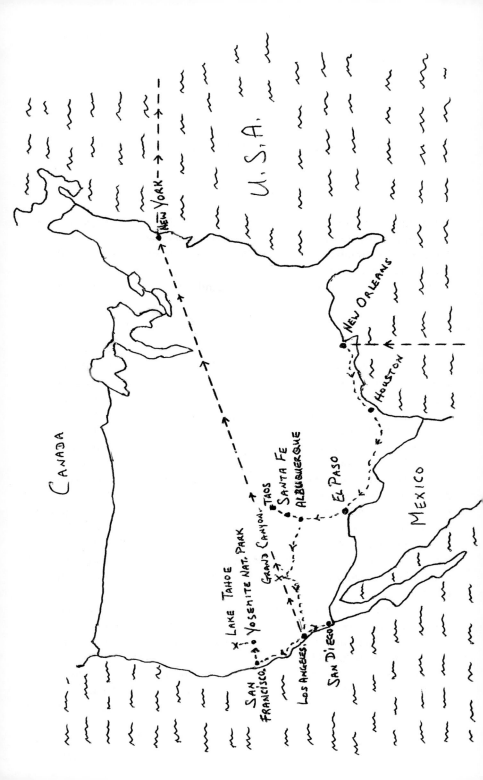

CHAPTER 33

Hitchhike Across America

It was the last hurrah. The hitchhike from New Orleans to California.

It began with another brush with American officialdom. Just as had happened in Honolulu, we were pulled to one side by a chubby-faced man in his early forties.

'Can I see your passports?' he asked. And just as had happened in Honolulu...

'Ireland?' he beamed. 'I'm from Ballynahinch myself...'

We were waved on with a big handshake. Never, ever has the Irish passport been a liability.

But no sooner had we entered the terminal than another issue loomed. It was almost 7.00 p.m. on a Friday evening and the airport bank was closed. As the city banks wouldn't open until Monday morning, we now had no access to money. (No cash machines in those days.) Even our travellers' cheques would be useless. They were in Swiss Francs, considered a stable and strong currency at the time, but damn-all use on the streets of New Orleans. With nine U.S. dollars in our pockets, we spent the next three hours at the airport trying every angle we could think of to get sorted. We even spent two of our dollars on a phone call to the number of a woman we had met in Yucatán. But all we got was her incoherently drunk mother who kept telling us: 'I's three hours f' New Awlins - gotta go to Ba'on Rouge.'

'All we can do,' I concluded, 'is take the bus into the city and hope we can find some cheap place that will let us sit it out until the banks open on Monday.'

Despondent, we went outside and were waiting for the bus when a car pulled up. Three guys got out, one with a rucksack, the other two wishing him well on his travels. All were of the long hair variety. One had exceptionally long blond hair and a beard.

'They look like our kind of people,' I said to Cora. 'And they look like they might be heading back into the city. Away over and ask them if they know of any cheap hotels in town, or where we might change a traveller's cheque, and see what happens.'

Cora, with her effervescent personality, was always very good at this kind of thing, a quality I have often, to my shame, exploited. Off she went as the guy with the rucksack disappeared into the terminal.

Two minutes later, I was summoned. The guy with the beard and the long blond hair, which fell in a sweep over his shoulders, was writing something on a piece of paper.

'This is Eric,' Cora said. Eric reached out his hand. 'And,' Cora said, turning to his dark-haired companion, 'this is Mark.'

'Well,' Eric said, 'Cora here has been telling us of your troubles with the bank. Unfortunately, we can't bring you into town as we're picking up some people here, but we live in the city and this is the address, and you're welcome to stay.' He handed Cora the piece of paper. 'Here's ten bucks,' he said. 'That will get you there. Two bus rides and a ride on the street-car will take you to Dufossat Street junction. From there, it's two blocks to Prytania Street. We'll see you there shortly.'

We stayed ten days with Eric and Mark, partly because of the company and partly because of New Orleans.

Eric, a newly qualified doctor who seemed to have heaps of spare time (and even larger heaps of female friends) introduced us to the iron-lace balconies, French and Spanish architecture, jazz and bluegrass, and Cajun cuisine of the French Quarter. We sat with the street musicians of Bourbon Street. We watched the Mississippi paddle boats from the levees that protected the city. We drank in the bars. We wandered the streets for their own sake. We shot the breeze in a park where Eric climbed a tree while exploring altered states of consciousness. We visited a 'city of the dead', a cemetery lined with raised stone and marble tombs laid out in 'streets'.

'You'll notice that these graves are above ground,' Eric said. 'The reason for this is that much of New Orleans is below sea level. If you dig a grave you can get water. One time, they used to have to push floating coffins down into graves with poles. Then they decided to drill holes in them so they'd sink by themselves. But the sight of a drowning coffin and the noise it made as the air bubbled to the surface was a bit much for the relatives; so now they don't dig graves anymore in many of the cemeteries..'

'Where I grew up,' I said, 'we had a Quaker graveyard in the next street where the Quakers were said to be buried standing up. A kind of 'save space' idea: keep the land for the living.'

'What a good idea,' Eric said. (Nowadays I wouldn't be standing over that story.)

In a long chain of memorable times, those ten days were up there with the best, thanks to the fun-loving generosity of spirit of Doctor Eric Ehlenberger.

As I put the finishing touches to this book, I thought I might check the Internet to see if there was any sign of Eric and discovered that he ran a clinic in New Orleans that specialised in the treatment of chronic pain and addiction. We spoke for the first time in forty-one years and time pancaked.

What joy to have known you Eric, if only for a little while.

* * *

On a Monday morning, we set off to hitchhike to California. One of Eric's friends, a pretty and witty woman called Nancy, drove us two thirds of the way to Baton Rouge. From there, we got another lift that dropped us off on the western side of that city. We were then picked up by an inordinately stupid Texan trucker named Hank. Hank was about forty, a thick-faced guy with greying hair and a big belly that bulged out of a beer-stained T-shirt. As we raced at seventy miles an hour along Interstate 10 across the Atchafalaya Swamp, Hank and two fellow truckers, coordinating through CB radios, found amusement in terrifying a young woman by hemming her car in between the three speeding trucks while Hank swilled beer from a peanut can.

'This is Cajun Country,' he drawled. 'Used to belong to the Choctaw Indians, but mostly the swamps and bayous are Cajun now. In days gone by, the rivers and bayous were the only roads the Indians and Cajuns and fur trappers could use. At the same time you had guys like Jim Bowie and Leather Britches Smith crossing these swamps on horseback. It's also where Cajun and Zydeco music comes from.'

I had to ask: 'Who the hell was Leather Britches Smith?'

'He was an outlaw. Some folks believe he was wanted for murder in Texas. He used to ride about with two six-shooters and a Winchester rifle and pounce out of the woods to rob people. They say he used to ride into Merryville over by the Texas border, put on a shooting display, then sit about heavily armed, daring anyone to arrest him. He was killed by a posse in an ambush in 1912...'

'All through these bayous,' Hank said as we drove across the middle of Lake Bigeux, 'you got beaver, otters, deer, mink, squirrels, turtles and alligators. I've seen a black panther crossing the road one night.'

In the maze of rivers, streams, lakes and swamps, the occasional Cajun shack or houseboat could be seen from the road. These were the descendants of people who had migrated to Nova Scotia from Brittany and Normandy in the early 17th century. When the British took Nova Scotia in 1755, the 'Cajuns' as they were then known, were driven out. Some 3,000 made their way to Louisiana to establish a homeland in its swamps and prairies. In time they would become the most significant portion of south Louisiana's population, exerting an enormous impact on its culture, music and cuisine.

Although beautiful to behold, the bayous looked decidedly uninviting, with the inevitable mosquito and snake hordes, and the gaunt stumps of dead trees that poked up from the water like broken headstones.

At the Jennings exit, Hank swerved all over the road and we made an excuse to get out. Walking into the small town, we spread our sleeping bags on a grassy patch beside a petrol station and slept until morning.

We left Jennings at 9.00 a.m. on the Tuesday morning and were in El Paso, 930 miles away, at 7.00 a.m. on the Wednesday. It was the fastest 930 miles we had ever hitchhiked, and we wouldn't want to do it again.

A truck brought us from Jennings to Houston and dropped us on one of the highways that cut the city. A series of short lifts brought us through the city traffic and deposited us twenty miles to the west of town. A Mexican called Adrian, with twenty-two tons of steel girders on his truck, brought us from there to El Paso.

'You're in luck,' he told us when he picked us up. 'I'm goin' all the way. In fact I've driven all last night *from* El Paso to Houston, where I dropped one load, picked up this one and should be back in El Paso by early morning.'

'You look wrecked,' I commiserated.

'Ah'm fine,' he said. 'I take these pills to stay awake, and I keep talkin' to the other truckers over the CB radio. We're all in the same boat. If you don't put in the hours, you can't make a livin' at this game.'

'You still look exhausted,' Cora said.

As we crossed the flat forest country of eastern Texas, deer appeared among the trees, and big-hatted rednecks drove by in pickups with racks of rifles.

'You gotta be careful hitchhiking in these parts,' Adrian said. 'Last week some of the locals grabbed a guy who was hitchhiking through. They stripped him, beat the crap outta him, shaved his head and dumped him in sheep dip.'

He reached into the glove compartment and pulled out a revolver.

'You gotta have one of these,' he said, 'to keep safe.'

Personally, I hate guns. And people who show them to me.

Day became night and night became late. Traffic was reduced to the occasional truck and Adrian began to fade. Simultaneously the CB kept us up to speed on trucks that had rolled off the highway, presumably driven by snoozing drivers. We saw several, gone off the edge with not a skid-mark in sight. In a roadside truck stop, we shared a coffee with half a dozen other haggard pill poppers, racing like Adrian to make a suicidal buck. At about 2.00 a.m. as we droned on through the night, Cora went to sleep in the cab's bunk. Adrian looked ready for sleep, so I figured that someone had better stay awake. Despite my best efforts to keep him alert, I had to shout twice as he dozed off.

'Would you not like to grab an hour's sleep?' I suggested. 'It's becoming a bit nerve-wracking.'

'Naw,' Adrian said. 'Ah'm fine.'

Shortly after 4.00 a.m. we came to a left-hand curve in the road, and Adrian wasn't turning.

I looked at him. His eyes were open, so I assumed we were moving into the slow lane. Until we were on the hard shoulder and heading for the embankment with our twenty-two tons of steel bearing down from behind.

'ADRIAN!' I shouted as Cora shot out of her sleep. Nothing. 'ADRIAN!' Nothing again. He was unconscious. I grabbed the wheel and shouted again. Adrian snapped out of it as we swung back onto the road.

'Look,' I said as calmly as I could. 'You're going to kill us all if you keep this up. Either you pull over for a while or we get out here.'

Reluctantly, he stopped at the next lay-by, and instantly collapsed onto the wheel. Cora and I got out to stretch our legs.

'Jesus, it's cold,' Cora said. 'But there's no way I'm getting back in, in case we wake him up and he wants to go on again.'

Two hours later, Adrian shot upright in a rage. 'Shit!' he said. 'I'm late! I'm late! It'll take me a *week* to make up for this.'

With the arrival of daylight, and the couple of hours' sleep, Adrian's driving became less horrifying, but it was a great relief to get off outside El Paso.

* * *

The flat green forests of eastern Texas had become hot, brown desert as we faced north into New Mexico. Albuquerque lay ahead, then a westward turn towards the Grand Canyon in Arizona. Fifty miles later, we were on the side of the road outside Las Cruces, with the Organ

Mountains to the east and buzzards overhead, when a battered red pickup approached.

'Don't bother trying this one,' Cora said. 'It's a wreck.' But it stopped anyway.

A small, bearded, middle-aged man with a grey ponytail pushed open the passenger door.

'Northern express,' he smiled. 'Hop on board.'

With much hand-shaking he introduced himself as Gill Webb. In his blue overalls, he looked like a farmer out for a run.

'I don't know how caught for time you folks are,' he said, 'but I'm on my way to Taos up at the base of the Sangre de Cristo mountains, and you're welcome to come and spend a few days.'

Without hesitation our plans changed; and as we drove north through drifts of sand and tumbleweed, Gill unveiled his more recent history.

'I used to be a lecturer in Austin University until Charles Whitman shot all those people from the bell tower back in August '66. I was there, watching people being gunned down and trying to drag the wounded to safety, and that was the turning point for me. Whitman, who was a precision sniper, had killed his mother and wife the day before; and he picked off another sixteen people that day and wounded thirty-one on the campus and the streets around the university. I thought there had to be something more to life, so my wife and I moved to the San Cristobal Valley outside Taos ten years ago and I grew the hair and beard. Since then I've settled into a meditative, spiritual life under the guidance of an old yogi. Many of the other people living in the valley are fellow yoga brothers, or yogins as we call ourselves.'

He had recently moved back to Las Cruces to live; but his son, Count, and Count's wife, Alice, still lived at his earlier home.

'Sadly,' he added, 'my youngest son is also there. He took his own life a few years back and is buried close to the house.'

As we climbed into high desert, passing through Santa Fe and winding our way along the gorge of the Rio Grande, he told how he was accepted as 'a fellow shaman-type figure' in the peyote huts of the Pueblo Indians who lived outside Taos, and he spoke of the racial tensions that percolated throughout the area.

'It's mostly trouble between the Anglos and the Chicanos. New Mexico was settled by the Spanish long before the whites came. It was part of Mexico until 1846 when it was annexed during the early part of the Mexican-American War. Even after that, there was a revolt in this area against U.S. control that ended with a two-day battle at the San Jeronimo Church in Taos. Resentment lingers.'

In general, Gill's was a tolerance that was otherwise hard to locate in that part of the world. However, he had his limits: the Hispanic love of 'low riders'. These were flash cars dropped low on their suspensions as part of a local fad.

'My god, man,' he said. 'They ruin good American cars.'

On arid wastes once tackled by wagon trains, the red cliffs and buttes caught the last of the day's sun.

'Taos,' Gill said, nodding towards the approaching lights of a small town. 'Home to artists, crafts people, adobe buildings and sixty art galleries. And 3,000 people trying to create a different kind of society.'

* * *

The house Gill had built was fifteen miles out of town and so big that parts of it had been turned into apartments. It sat on thirty acres, surrounded by national forest and backed by the snow peaks of the Sangre de Cristo Mountains. When we arrived, Alice was weaving, preparing for an exhibition of her works in one of the town's galleries. Count was running the farm, ten acres of which Gill had given him so he and Alice could build their own home.

'But,' Gill said, 'you've arrived in the middle of a kind of range war. Count needs access to the land and some of the neighbours, who are yoga brothers, are denying him this. One in particular promised to sell him some land for an access road, but now he's backed off on the deal. That's why I've come up here right now, to see if we can find an alternative.'

Cora and I hoped aloud that all of that would work out well. Gill then showed us to a spacious room with a view to the mountains.

On May 26th, two nights after our arrival, a storm brought Taos its worst flooding in thirty years. Bridges were down in the mountains and none but the older Indians of the Pueblo could remember the Rio Pueblo de Taos ever being so high. The following morning Cora and I went down to Santa Fe to change some money and found sandbagged homesteads sweating it out the length of the Rio Grande Gorge.

Santa Fe sits in the Sangre de Cristo foothills. Founded as a Spanish colony in 1610, it was now renowned for its adobe architecture, crooked streets and traditional plaza where Navajo and Hopi vendors sold sand-paintings and silver-and-turquoise jewellery. In the old days the plaza was the junction of *El Camino Real*, the 1,500-mile trail that ran all the way to Mexico City, and the Santa Fe Trail that ran east to Missouri.

On the advice of Steve, a friend of Gill's who had driven us from Taos to Santa Fe, we called at Our Lady of Loretto Chapel. The chapel had been completed in 1878 for the Sisters of Loretto who had been brought from Kentucky by Bishop Jean Baptiste Lamy to open a school for girls. Standing at the end of the old Santa Fe Trail, the tall Gothic church was made of granite hauled on wagons from a quarry some fourteen miles to the north. Its stained-glass windows and reed organ came from France. But the detail we came to see was the 22-foot, spiral staircase, built, the story went, by a mysterious man who arrived one day in 1880 with a donkey and toolbox, looking for work. Months later, with the elegant staircase complete, the man disappeared without pay or thanks.

Confounding architects and engineers alike, the thirty-three steps of the staircase complete two 360-degree turns, resting solely on the staircase base and against the choir loft - with no central support. The builder of the 'miraculous staircase' who, without glue or nails, constructed his masterpiece from a species of spruce not found in that part of the world, still remained unknown; but legend, never lost for a plausible explanation, had it that he was Joseph the Carpenter.

* * *

On Saturday morning, Cora and I went with Gill to visit Taos Pueblo but it had been flooded by the rains. Nevertheless, the multi-storied complex of reddish-brown adobe, with wooden ladders connecting the different levels, reeked of history. Set against the mountains and divided in two by the Rio Pueblo, Taos Pueblo is the oldest, continuously inhabited village in the U.S. Its past includes a prominent role in the Pueblo Revolt of 1860 against the Spanish, and a siege by U.S. forces in 1847; and it was the beneficiary of an uncharacteristic act in 1970 when Tricky Dicky Nixon returned to the Pueblo people 48,000 acres of mountain land stolen earlier by Theodore Roosevelt and designated the Carson National Forest. The sacred Blue Lake, believed by the Taos people to be the source of their origins, was included in the handover, an event considered by the Indians to be the most important in their history.

In the afternoon, the San Cristobal Valley range war was hotting up.

To resolve the road issue, there was a gathering of the yoga brothers, at which Gill and Count managed to harness the agreement of most of the valley people. It was accepted that a joint access road would benefit all, and Gill was offering to do the work with his own machinery. One couple, however, were holding out and would not be giving their position until noon on Sunday.

Noon Sunday came with no word from down the valley. Gill went off to get his response and came back angry. The word was no.

'I'm a peace-loving man,' Gill said, pacing the floor like a bear in a cage, 'But this is really testing my limits.'

As Gill pondered the next move, Steve drove myself and Cora around 'The Enchanted Way', a circular route through the cottonwoods and pine forests of the Sangre de Cristo Mountains. We ate at a café where we discovered that an American 'sandwich' was enough to feed a family and its livestock.

In the evening, as Alice was providing weaving lessons to Cora, Gill arrived in with the errant neighbour. The dispute was resolved. The road was assured. Everyone was on the best of terms again. Cora and I felt that we could now be on our way with honour.

On Monday morning, Steve drove us into Taos. We then got a lift from outside town to Santa Fe from a crazy guy who had survived a jailbreak in Mexico.

'I was on holiday and they arrested me and charged me with organising a breakout of fifteen smugglers. I didn't know what the fuck they were talking about. But they put me in jail for thirteen months and tortured me over and over, trying to get me to admit to the crap about the smugglers. In the end I couldn't take it anymore, so I got this girl I knew to smuggle me in a small handgun. Then I pretended to be very ill and they sent me to hospital in Juarez and on the way I managed to break away from the guard. He pulled his gun and I pulled the one I had and we both stood looking at one another. I never thought this could happen for real, but I swore to the cop that we'd both die so he agreed to let me make a run for the Rio Grande. Maybe he just didn't want to shoot anybody that day. Anyway, I got to the river and then got involved in a running shootout with other cops who spotted me. I had to swim the Rio Grande with my wrists handcuffed, and bullets flying everywhere...'

Our next lift came from a prosecutor dispensing decisions over a two-way radio.

From Albuquerque we travelled west into Arizona, stopping off to visit the Petrified Forest and Painted Desert National Parks, before going on to Flagstaff where we spent the night in a motel, the only accommodation paid for during our time in the U.S.

The following morning we hitchhiked through the forests of the Colorado Plateau to the Grand Canyon and were dropped off just short of the rim. At first, the canyon wasn't visible because of the trees. But a short walk and there it was. Carved out by the Colorado River through two billion years of Earth's history, the 220-mile canyon, ten miles wide in places and a mile deep, looked fit to swallow the world.

We stayed four days, sleeping on the rim in our tent and spending the daylight hours watching the bluffs of sandstone, limestone and shale change colour until they were at their most dramatic in the late afternoon. We gave a full day to the Bright Angel trail, a steep descent through 100 switchbacks and a climate and temperature change that transported us from pine forest to cactus. At the little oasis of Indian Gardens, having dropped 3,060 feet, we rested under some trees before the final push across harsh open desert to Plateau Point. Barring the mule-deer, lizards and rock squirrels, we had the unimpeded use of the trail until we reached the overlook of the Colorado River where we were joined by a Swedish guy.

'Would you mind taking a photo for us?' I asked. 'With the river and the canyon walls in the background.'

'Sure,' he said. 'Maybe for your children one day?'

Twenty-two years later, I took another photo at the exact same spot - of our daughters, Tríona and Áine standing beside a desert bush that had grown there in the meantime.

Leaving the Grand Canyon, we hitchhiked across the Mojave Desert to Los Angeles and the relatives, staying again with Fionnuala, Maeve and Killian. We then took a Greyhound bus north to Ventura where a bunch of Hells Angels wished us the best. Hitchhiking again, we hugged the rocky Californian coast with its poppies, sea otters, quails and turkey buzzards. At Morro Bay we spent two nights with friends of Killian's. We stopped again at Point Lobos State Park and spent a night in a campsite with the RV that had given us a lift. Then on through Monterey, and other places made famous by John Steinbeck, to Felton where we visited some very big redwoods and camped for a day by a river in the company of deer, jays and squirrels. Outside Santa Cruz, a young barmaid gave us a lift, then loaded us with beer in the bar in which she worked. Then on to San Francisco where we were delivered to Chinatown by a wild-eyed chap in a white van with a hookah and pistol on board.

'Would you like to come to the beach,' he asked after getting us fully zonked and paranoid.

'No thanks!' we both squawked like an echo.

In the steep hills of that beautiful city we called to John Vogel and Kathy Rooney on the recommendation of a guy called Bill that we had met back in Quetzaltenango.

'John and Kathy are great people,' he said when he gave us the address. 'Just tell them you met Bill down in Guatemala and you'll get a warm welcome.'

Really...?

Well, John and Kathy proved indeed to be the great people Bill had promised.

Our last port of call before turning again for Los Angeles, was with my cousin Niall and his wife, who lived up in the Sierra Nevada. We spent a couple of days, visited more redwoods, and drove to Lake Tahoe and Yosemite. Away up on Half Dome, some lunatics were pitching hanging tents for the night.

On the way back to Los Angeles, the final lift into the city came from 'Tex' from Texas who lived in the city and was married to Maureen from Ireland.

'You'll have to come and stay the night before going on to your relatives,' Tex insisted. 'My wife will never forgive me if you don't.' So we drove past one of my relative's homes and stayed with Tex and Maureen.

Our last memory of California was of my uncle Kilian driving us to the airport and us arriving to find massive queues clambering for non-available tickets. Freddie Laker's DC-10 'Skytrain' airbuses and all U.S. DC-10s had been grounded on June 6th after a DC-10 had crashed on takeoff in Chicago on May 25th with 271 fatalities. The grounding had left passengers stranded across America.

'This don't look too g-o-o-od,' Kilian said, but fifteen minutes later we were somehow running through the airport, past all the forlorn stranded passengers, with rucksacks on our backs and tickets for a plane that left for New York in fifteen minutes.

In New York, we weren't so lucky. We bought two standby tickets for a flight to Shannon. However, as sometimes happened with standby, there were no last minute seats. We didn't get away. But our baggage did. Stranded, we resigned ourselves to at least a 24-hour wait, without as much as a toothbrush. But luck took a turn. Cora met a middle-aged Lithuanian airport cleaner who invited us to stay the night with herself and her daughter. We spent the next day in Manhattan and managed to get on a plane that night, arriving in Shannon to find all our gear in the terminal, stacked against a wall, waiting for us.

'You've been around a bit,' the guy at immigration said when he flipped through our passports. 'Welcome home.' For some reason the bus driver who then brought us from Limerick to Cork reminded us of Mexico.

The highlight of our day in Manhattan had been a visit to the World Trade Centre where we took a high-speed lift to the roof of one of the Twin Towers. A young woman on top of the gently swaying building was giving a guided tour.

'The towers,' she explained, 'have been built to withstand the impact of a Boeing 707...'

In Saudi Arabia, Osama Bin Laden, the only son of his father's tenth wife, was twenty-two years old.

Chapter 34

An Epitaph For Tarzan

'There's a race of men that don't fit in,
A race that can't stay still;
So they break the hearts of kith and kin,
And they roam the world at will...'

Robert Service (1874-1958)

On March 11th 1959 the parents of 29-year-old Michael 'Tarzan' Fomenko received word that their missing son had been found living a hermit's existence in the North Queensland jungle. He had been rescued by native fishermen, having made a return journey in a home-made dugout canoe from Cooktown to what was then Dutch New Guinea. Among the titles that would follow him for the remainder of his life would be 'the guy who paddled a log to New Guinea'.

Michael Fomenko was born in 1930 in Georgia, then part of the Soviet Union, to the former Princess Elizabeth Machabelli, a member of the pre-revolution aristocracy. His father was one-time champion athlete and university lecturer, Daniel Fomenko.

After the family had fled, first to Japan, then to Sydney, the culturally-alienated Michael began to see himself as a character from Homer's Odyssey, the Greek epic of endurance and alienation. Strong and handsome, he won state medals as a decathlete and was tipped for a place in the Australian team at the 1956 Melbourne Olympics. But by then, to his mother's dismay, he had left the family home for the jungles of Queensland.

After leaving school, he had taken a job cutting sugarcane near Cairns, whereupon he fell in love with the rainforest. And there, by and large, he stayed. On one of his few return trips to Sydney, he summoned an early girlfriend from her home with blasts on a conch.

He then quit the city permanently and lost himself in the wilds of Cape York Peninsula to worship what he called 'the nature god'.

In 1960, Elizabeth Fomenko - convinced that her son needed help - set about having him committed. In 1964, 'the wild man of Cape York' was chased into a swamp by a mounted cop and arrested for vagrancy and indecent behaviour, namely wearing only the front section of a home-made lap-lap. Declared insane, he was locked up in a series of psychiatric institutions where he was sedated and subjected to electric shock therapy.

After he was freed in 1969, Michael took off again for the forests of the north. He returned to Sydney twice, the last time in 1988 for his mother's funeral.

Sometime around 1990 he shifted his base to an area south of Cairns, where locals grew used to seeing him loping along the highway between Babinda and Cairns on supply runs, trademark sugar bag over his shoulder. Then in late 2012 he vanished off the face of the Earth, only to resurface shortly afterwards - at the age of eighty-two - in Gympie's Cooinda Aged Care facility.

During his lifetime, the adventures of Michael 'Tarzan' Fomenko became legend. He had lived among Aborigines, killed crocodiles and wild boar with a machete, built his dugout canoes, fought against convention, almost succumbed to starvation during his epic voyage to New Guinea, and had been dubbed 'Tarzan' during that voyage by children he had befriended in the Torres Strait.

He died in August 2018, at the age of eighty-eight, forty years after we had met him in Cedar Bay.

Was Michael Fomenko crazy?

To whomsoever thinks he was, let us say this: he never burned a forest, poisoned a river, nor dropped a bomb on children.

Perhaps we could reflect on the words of the 'Cellist of Sarajevo'. During the Siege of Sarajevo that was part of the Bosnian War of 1992-95, Vedran Smailović could be found playing his cello as artillery pulverized the city's ruins.

'Are you crazy?' somebody asked one day. 'Playing the cello while they're shelling Sarajevo.'

'Ask them,' he replied, 'if they are crazy. Shelling Sarajevo while I am playing the cello.'